OXFORD WORLD'S CLASSICS

AN ENQUIRY CONCERNING HUMAN UNDERSTANDING

DAVID HUME (1711–76) was born and educated in Edinburgh. In 1739–40 he published *A Treatise of Human Nature*, a great work but poorly received, and Hume came to regret the style and haste in which he had written it. Far more successful were his *Essays, Moral, Political, and Literary*, published from 1741, which proved highly influential in political theory, aesthetics, and especially economics.

In 1748 Hume revised the abstruse epistemology of the *Treatise* in essay form, as the *Enquiry concerning Human Understanding*, the definitive statement of his mature theoretical philosophy. Combining elegance with devastating insight, it presents the views for which he is now most famous, including his scepticism about induction and causation, his compatibilist account of free will, his rejection of religious miracles, and his advocacy of 'mitigated scepticism'.

In the course of a colourful life which included episodes in the military, diplomatic, and civil services, Hume went on to write major works in ethics, philosophy of religion, and history. But the arguments expressed in the *Enquiry* are those on which his revolutionary importance, as one of the greatest philosophers of all time, mainly rests. This is the first modern edition to reproduce faithfully the text of the *Enquiry* in its final form.

PETER MILLICAN, Fellow and Tutor in Philosophy at Hertford College, Oxford, studied at Oxford University and has also taught at Glasgow and Leeds. His philosophical interests and publications cover a wide range but with a particular focus on Hume and related topics, especially the *Enquiry*, on which he also edited the collection *Reading Hume on Human Understanding* (OUP, 2002). He runs the website *davidhume.org*, and is co-editor of the journal *Hume Studies*.

OXFORD WORLD'S CLASSICS

*For over 100 years Oxford World's Classics have brought
readers closer to the world's great literature. Now with over 700
titles—from the 4,000-year-old myths of Mesopotamia to the
twentieth century's greatest novels—the series makes available
lesser-known as well as celebrated writing.*

*The pocket-sized hardbacks of the early years contained
introductions by Virginia Woolf, T. S. Eliot, Graham Greene,
and other literary figures which enriched the experience of reading.
Today the series is recognized for its fine scholarship and
reliability in texts that span world literature, drama and poetry,
religion, philosophy and politics. Each edition includes perceptive
commentary and essential background information to meet the
changing needs of readers.*

OXFORD WORLD'S CLASSICS

DAVID HUME

An Enquiry concerning Human Understanding

Edited with an Introduction and Notes by
PETER MILLICAN

OXFORD
UNIVERSITY PRESS

OXFORD
UNIVERSITY PRESS

Great Clarendon Street, Oxford OX2 6DP

Oxford University Press is a department of the University of Oxford.
It furthers the University's objective of excellence in research, scholarship,
and education by publishing worldwide in

Oxford New York

Auckland Cape Town Dar es Salaam Hong Kong Karachi
Kuala Lumpur Madrid Melbourne Mexico City Nairobi
New Delhi Shanghai Taipei Toronto

With offices in

Argentina Austria Brazil Chile Czech Republic France Greece
Guatemala Hungary Italy Japan Poland Portugal Singapore
South Korea Switzerland Thailand Turkey Ukraine Vietnam

Oxford is a registered trade mark of Oxford University Press
in the UK and in certain other countries

Published in the United States
by Oxford University Press Inc., New York

Editorial material © Peter Millican 2007

The moral rights of the author have been asserted
Database right Oxford University Press (maker)

First published as an Oxford World's Classics paperback 2007
Reissued 2008

British Library Cataloguing in Publication Data

Data available

Library of Congress Cataloging in Publication Data

Hume, David, 1711–1776
[Philosophical essays concerning human understanding]
An enquiry concerning human understanding / David Hume; edited with
an introduction and notes by Peter Millican.
p. cm.—(Oxford world's classics)
Includes bibliographical references and index.
ISBN–13: 978–0–19–921158–6 (alk. paper)
1. Knowledge, Theory of. I. Millican, P. J. R. (Peter J. R.) II. Title.
B1481.M55 2007
121—dc22
2006102409

ISBN 978-0-19-954990-0

17

Typeset by Cepha Imaging Private Ltd., Bangalore, India
Printed in Great Britain by
on acid-free paper by
Clays Ltd, Elcograf S.p.A.

CONTENTS

Abbreviations   vii

Introduction   ix

1. From Ancient to Modern Cosmology   xi
2. From Aristotelian to Cartesian Intelligibility   xiii
3. Corpuscularianism, Locke, and Newton   xvi
4. Free Will, and the Dangers of Infidelity   xx
5. God's Design, and Human Reason   xxiii
6. Inertness, Malebranche, and Berkeley   xxv
7. The Humean Revolution   xxix
8. Section I: The Aims of the *Enquiry*   xxx
9. Sections II and III: The Origin and Association of Ideas   xxxii
10. Section IV: Hume's Fork   xxxv
11. Sections IV and V: The Basis of Factual Reasoning   xxxvii
12. Section VI: 'Of Probability'   xl
13. Section VII: 'Of the Idea of Necessary Connexion'   xlii
14. Section VIII: 'Of Liberty and Necessity'   xlvi
15. Section IX: 'Of the Reason of Animals'   xlviii
16. Section X: 'Of Miracles'   xlix
17. Section XI: 'Of a Particular Providence, and of
       a Future State'   lii
18. Section XII: 'Of the Academical or Sceptical Philosophy'   liii

Note on the Text   lvii

Select Bibliography   lxi

A Chronology of David Hume   lxiii

AN ENQUIRY CONCERNING
HUMAN UNDERSTANDING

   Advertisement   2

1.   Of the different Species of Philosophy   3
11. Of the Origin of Ideas   12
111. Of the Association of Ideas   16

IV. Sceptical Doubts concerning the Operations
of the Understanding   18

V. Sceptical Solution of these Doubts   30

VI. Of Probability   41

VII. Of the Idea of necessary Connexion   44

VIII. Of Liberty and Necessity   58

IX. Of the Reason of Animals   76

X. Of Miracles   79

XI. Of a particular Providence and of a future State   96

XII. Of the academical or sceptical Philosophy   109

Hume's Endnotes   121

Appendix I: Abstract of *A Treatise of Human Nature* (1740)   133

Appendix II: 'Of the Immortality of the Soul' (printed 1755)   146

Appendix III: Excerpts from Parts I and II of the *Dialogues
concerning Natural Religion* (1779)   152

Appendix IV: Excerpts from Hume's Letters   161

Appendix V: 'My Own Life'   169

Textual Variants   177

Explanatory Notes   185

Glossary   212

*Glossarial Index of Major Philosophers and Philosophical
Movements*   220

Hume's Index   229

Index of Major Themes, Concepts, and Examples   231

Index of Names Mentioned in the Enquiry   233

Index of References to Hume's Works   235

ABBREVIATIONS

References to Hume's works are to the following editions and, except for the *Enquiry* and the *Treatise*, indicate page numbers.

D   *Dialogues concerning Natural Religion*, ed. Norman Kemp Smith (Edinburgh: Nelson, 2nd edn. 1947)

E   *Enquiry concerning Human Understanding* (this volume). References to the *Enquiry* are given using section and paragraph numbers. In the endmatter (such as the Explanatory Notes), the initial *E* is usually omitted: thus the first paragraph on p. 26 of this volume can be referred to as either '*E* 4.19' or simply '4.19'. For detail concerning marginal numbers and footnote references within the *Enquiry*, see the Note on the Text, below, pp. lvii–lx.

Essays   *Essays, Moral, Political, and Literary*, ed. Eugene F. Miller (Indianapolis: Liberty Classics, 2nd edn., 1987)

History   *The History of England*, ed. William Todd, 6 vols. (Indianapolis: Liberty Classics, 1983)

HL   *The Letters of David Hume*, ed. J. Y. T. Greig, 2 vols. (Oxford: Clarendon Press, 1932)

NHL   *New Letters of David Hume*, ed. R. Klibansky and E. C. Mossner (Oxford: Clarendon Press, 1954)

L   *A Letter from a Gentleman to his Friend in Edinburgh*, ed. Ernest C. Mossner and John V. Price (Edinburgh: Edinburgh University Press, 1967, containing a facsimile of the original 1745 edn.)

T   *A Treatise of Human Nature*, ed. David Fate Norton and Mary J. Norton (Oxford: Oxford University Press, 2000). References to the *Treatise* are given using book, part, section, and paragraph numbers. Thus, for example, '*T* 1.3.6.10' indicates paragraph 10 of Book 1, Part 3, Section 6.

INTRODUCTION

DAVID HUME (1711–76) was one of the great philosophers (arguably the greatest) of that prodigiously fruitful era known as the early modern period. During the seventeenth and eighteenth centuries, scholastic Aristotelianism, a world-view which had dominated thought for many hundreds of years, finally began to be overshadowed by a recognizably modern scientific perspective. René Descartes (1596–1650), building on the discoveries of Galileo Galilei and others, was the first philosopher seriously to threaten Aristotle's dominance. Then in the next generation, John Locke (1632–1704) developed a rival account of the world, incorporating scientific developments from England associated particularly with Robert Boyle and Isaac Newton. By the end of the seventeenth century, scholasticism was in terminal decline, but intense debate continued as philosophers sought to make sense of the world and man's place in it, accommodating the new discoveries. Some of the points in dispute were essentially scientific, but many others concerned what we would now call *epistemology* (i.e. theory of knowledge) or *philosophy of science*, and many of the most intractable also had a theological dimension. Both Descartes and Locke found ways of tying these threads together, and they were followed by others, such as respectively Nicolas Malebranche (1638–1715) and George Berkeley (1685–1753), who later developed their theories in novel ways.

Despite this variety of speculation, these thinkers all shared some important assumptions, notably a view of the world as created by divine reason, and—relatedly—as potentially 'intelligible' to human reason. Hume's special significance is as the first great philosopher to question both of these pervasive assumptions, and to build an epistemology and philosophy of science that in no way depend on either of them. Over a century before Charles Darwin's *Origin of Species* of 1859, Hume argued powerfully that human reason is fundamentally similar to that of the other animals, founded on instinct rather than quasi-divine insight into things. Hence science must proceed by experiment and systematization of observations, rather than by metaphysical theorizing or a priori speculation. This outlook, revolutionary in its time, was to be powerfully vindicated during the twentieth century as the successes of relativity theory and quantum mechanics forced scientists—often very reluctantly—to accept that intuitive 'unintelligibility' to human reason is no impediment to empirical truth. Hume's once scandalous message has thus become almost scientific 'common sense'. Outside the laboratory, however, we still inhabit a world infused with ancient assumptions, and largely blind to the need for, or the consequences of, their abandonment. So Hume's attempt to forge an empirically based, naturalistic world-view retains a unique contemporary relevance.

Hume's first publication, *A Treatise of Human Nature* (1739–40), began as 'an attempt to introduce the experimental method of reasoning into moral subjects'. But in both advocating and pursuing the empirical study of the human world, the juvenile Hume 'was carry'd away by the Heat of Youth & Invention' (see p. 163), producing a long work in which his strokes of critical genius were confusingly mingled with unrealistically ambitious psychological generalizations and—at least in Book I—unresolved sceptical paradoxes. Hume quickly regretted this, as his letters testify, and even before the final Book III of the *Treatise* was delivered from the press, he was already reformulating his approach in the short 1740 *Abstract* (included in this volume as Appendix I). By 1748 he had produced a second major work, the *Enquiry concerning Human Understanding*,[1] following the pattern of the *Abstract* in focusing on his central philosophical message, expanding and clarifying the key arguments that support it (for example in Sections IV, VII, and VIII), and limiting his psychological speculations to modest hints of 'explications and analogies' (*E* 5.9). The sceptical paradoxes are also limited or 'mitigated', but this, perhaps surprisingly, gives the *Enquiry* more rather than less critical bite. Anyone who reads the *Treatise*—with its radical suggestions that even our trust in logic is ill-founded, and that even our basic beliefs in external objects and the self are incoherent—may be puzzled but is unlikely to be convinced. If *everything* is equally doubtful, then most people will hang on to what is comfortable, and though radical scepticism may do something to jolt the complacent dogmatist, it is unlikely to yield any settled change of mind. The *Enquiry* is more potent, because more discriminating. It reveals the relatively humble basis of

---

[1] Called 'the first *Enquiry*' to distinguish it from the 1751 *Enquiry concerning the Principles of Morals.*

human reason, in much the same way as Book I of the *Treatise*, but instead of going on to advocate ever more radical forms of scepticism, it then takes human reason seriously for what it is, and builds on it a persuasive structure that can vindicate disciplined modern science while condemning traditional metaphysics and irrational superstition.

The magnitude of Hume's achievement is best appreciated by surveying the depth of the tradition he undermined, stretching back to the beginnings of philosophy in ancient Greece. Although, as we shall see, the early modern world into which he was born had already rejected much of its medieval dogmatic legacy, that legacy was replaced with a new dogmatism which was less obvious because so pervasive. Having identified the common threads that linked the ancient, medieval, and early modern worlds, we shall then be in a position to turn with more appreciation to the pages of the *Enquiry concerning Human Understanding*, one of the very finest works of philosophy and the authoritative statement of David Hume's mature epistemology.

1. *From Ancient to Modern Cosmology*

Aristotle was supremely honoured in the medieval period because his philosophical outlook could be comfortably combined with Christianity, a synthesis impressively refined by Thomas Aquinas (1225–74). The Christianization of the Roman Empire had long since brought about the suppression of all the pagan schools of philosophy that had thrived in ancient Greece (such as the Academic and Pyrrhonian sceptics, the Epicureans, and the Stoics).[2] These rival traditions were then largely forgotten until the Renaissance, when pagan manuscripts that had been preserved in the Greek or Muslim worlds were brought west by scholars fleeing the Ottoman Turks. Suddenly a range of new intellectual horizons opened up, combining with other events to prompt a general questioning of traditional authority. Population growth, technological innovation (notably gunpowder), and the discovery of new lands, cultures, and religions unknown to the ancients,

---

[2] The Roman emperor Theodosius I ordered the destruction of pagan temples (including great libraries such as that in Alexandria) in 391; the emperor Justinian then suppressed all the remaining pagan schools in 529. For a brief review of the various philosophical traditions mentioned here, see the Glossarial Index of Major Philosophers and Philosophical Movements, below. Likewise the Glossary can be consulted for unfamiliar technical terms or antiquated meanings.

all provoked political, economic, and doctrinal instability. Finally the Reformation, starting with Martin Luther's rebellion against the Church of Rome in 1517, led to widespread religious wars founded on philosophical differences: one side took Church authority and tradition as the criterion of truth, the other appealed instead to the Spirit of God acting within the individual believer. Suddenly traditional authority looked open to doubt, and the questions of the rediscovered ancient sceptics became highly relevant, inspiring natural philosophers (i.e. scientists) to examine the world with a more critical eye.

Aristotelian physics and cosmology was based on the idea that material things have *natural* movements according to their elemental composition. The four terrestrial elements, earth, water, air, and fire, of which everything below the Moon is composed, *strive* to reach their natural place in the cosmos: earth at the centre, water in a sphere around the earth, then air and fire. Stones thus naturally fall towards the centre of the universe because they mainly consist of earth, while fire rises. Heavenly bodies such as the stars, however, are seen to move perpetually in circles around the Earth, implying that they are made of a fifth element, a celestial 'ether', which Aristotle took to be some kind of crystalline solid. Again these movements are driven by a *teleological* (i.e. purposive) striving: heavenly bodies eternally move in circles because this is the nearest they can approach to the pure actuality of God, the unmoved mover. Around the Earth at the centre of the universe, the Moon, planets, Sun, and stars are arranged in a series of concentric crystalline shells, forming a heavenly clockwork driven by the steady rotation of the outermost sphere, repeating its circuits eternally with perfect accuracy, while generating the dance of the planets as seen in the sky. However, the visible motion of the planets is in fact very far from being a steady circular movement around the sky: sometimes a planet will 'regress' for a time, moving backwards from day to day before turning again to continue in its usual direction. Accounting for this observed complexity requires much more than a simple pattern of circular orbits, and over the years the Aristotelian model was progressively refined, most notably with the addition of *epicycles*, or orbits around orbits. It eventually achieved definitive form through the work of Ptolemy around AD 150, and was then destined to dominate European astronomy for almost 1,500 years.

In 1543 Nicolaus Copernicus famously advanced the theory that the Earth is a planet orbiting the Sun, but it was not until the early seventeenth century that observational evidence became available to mount a decisive challenge to Ptolemaic astronomy. In 1609–10 Galileo Galilei made his own telescope (a device invented only in 1608) and viewed the heavens in unprecedented detail, immediately publishing what he saw in *The Starry Messenger*.[3] Amongst his discoveries were craters, mountains, and valleys on the moon, whose dimensions could even be gauged from the observed shadows, and whose existence suggested a world much like our own, of rugged rocky irregularity rather than smooth etherial perfection. Likewise the four Galilean moons orbiting around Jupiter undermined the idea that all celestial motion must centre on the Earth, while the sequence of the phases of Venus in shapes from crescent to almost circular—invisible to the naked eye but very obvious through a telescope—gave decisive evidence against the Aristotelian-Ptolemaic model of the planetary orbits. Less decisive, but imaginatively suggestive of the need for a new world-view, Galileo saw innumerable new stars of varying brightness, seeming to stretch out well beyond the crystalline sphere that was supposed to hold the known visible stars.

2. *From Aristotelian to Cartesian Intelligibility*

If the Earth is not at the centre of the universe, then not only Aristotle's cosmology, but also his account of terrestrial motion must be seriously in error. Moreover when tested critically, specific predictions derived from his theories were found to be quite wrong, even applied to such everyday things as the flight of a cannon ball, a sledge sliding over an icy pond, the dripping of water from a gutter, or the fall of stones of different sizes. Galileo is reputed to have demonstrated this publicly, by dropping a heavy and a light ball simultaneously from the Tower of Pisa, both falling with similar speed.[4] He went on to develop

---

[3] Galileo's weren't the only relevant observations. In 1572 Tycho Brahe had observed a supernova, and in 1604 Johannes Kepler observed another (also seen by Galileo). Meanwhile in 1577, a major comet appeared, which Brahe—by triangulation against observations of astronomers elsewhere in Europe—proved to be more distant than the Moon. All these indicated that the heavens beyond the Moon were far from the eternally incorruptible domain envisaged by Aristotle (who had dismissed comets and meteors as atmospheric phenomena, hence the word 'meteorology'). See p. 160 below for Hume's comment on the significance of this undermining of the distinction between the heavenly and earthly domains.

[4] Aristotle claimed that heavy objects fall faster than light ones in proportion to their weight, whereas in fact they usually fall faster only very marginally, the difference being

an alternative theory of motion, based on the concepts of *inertia* and *forces*. This was taken further by René Descartes (or 'Des Cartes')—widely considered the first great early modern philosopher—and it was his 'Cartesian' mechanics that was to dominate the thought of much of the seventeenth century.

Galileo and Descartes between them established a new way of understanding the physical world, replacing purposive strivings (what Aristotle had called 'final' causes) by mathematically formulated laws framed exclusively in terms of mechanical, 'efficient' causation. The new science took bodies to be essentially passive, their movement changing according to the action of external forces. Left to themselves, bodies will simply maintain their state of rest or uniform linear motion, this so-called *inertia* applying equally whether the body is stationary or moving in any direction (so the concept of *natural* place or direction is completely abandoned). A body's motion changes only when it is acted upon by a force, though the precise magnitude of the force associated with changes of movement remained a matter of controversy.[5]

Descartes's vision of mechanics had an elegant simplicity, and also a reassuring air of *intelligibility*. In place of Aristotle's five elements with their somewhat arbitrary 'natural' tendencies, Descartes substituted a single type of matter, whose *essence* (i.e. central defining quality) he identified as simple spatial *extension* (i.e. geometrical size). All the fundamental properties of matter then supposedly follow logically from this essence, in a way intelligible to our rational (and immaterial) minds; for example, extension implies no power of initiating change, so matter's passivity and inertia are fully explained.[6] This approach also provided an ingenious solution to the resulting problem of accounting for the motion of the planets as well as cannon balls. If the essence of matter is extension, then empty space—that is, extension

due to air resistance. In 1971, David Scott of Apollo 15 performed Galileo's experiment on the Moon, showing that a hammer and a feather indeed fall at the same rate in the absence of air.

  [5] The so-called *vis viva* controversy is alluded to by Hume in the *Enquiry*, at *E* 7.29 endnote [E].

  [6] This is of course only a brief caricature of Descartes's position. He was far less rationalist about the practical conduct of scientific enquiry, viewing experiment as the means of discovering which mechanisms are actually operative in nature. Note also that he sees mind as a substance quite distinct from matter, whose essence is *thought* rather than extension. For a typically forthright Humean dismissal of such 'substance dualism', see the beginning of his essay 'Of the Immortality of the Soul' (Appendix II, below).

without matter—becomes an impossibility, so the entire universe must be filled with matter (i.e. the universe is a *plenum*). But in such a plenum, movement of one piece of matter can happen only if another piece 'moves out of the way', and as soon as it itself moves, its place must be taken by yet another piece of matter. Hence all motion through space must involve matter moving in circuits, and Descartes concluded that the universe must be structured by 'vortices', or whirlpools of circulating matter. This provides a very elegant explanation of how the planets can be retained in circular motion around the Sun despite their inertial tendency to move in straight lines. The Sun is thus the centre of a giant vortex, with smaller vortices within it ranging from that which carries the Moon around the Earth, down to the minuscule vortices in our own bodies that constitute the mechanisms of these intricate machines.

Aristotelian physics had likewise aspired to make the operations of nature intelligible, by explaining the behaviour of things in purposive terms, but such explanations now came to seem vacuous compared with those of the new science. This is the point of Molière's clever parody in Act III of his play *Le Malade imaginaire* (1673):

'I would like to ask you the cause and reason why opium makes one sleep.'

'The reason is that in opium resides a *dormitive virtue*, of which it is the nature to stupefy the senses.'

Here the appeal to 'dormitive virtue' is clearly no more than giving a fancy name to an unknown cause of the observed phenomenon. Any appearance of explanation is entirely bogus, and most natural philosophers understandably became anxious to distance themselves from such *occult qualities*. They accordingly aimed to confine their explanations to *efficient* rather than *final* causation (i.e. processes that bring things about rather than purposes), and to appeal only to causal mechanisms that depend on the types of qualities manifested in experience and whose mode of operation seems intuitively comprehensible, such as size, shape, and motion. All this helps to account for the great influence of Cartesian physics, which operated exclusively by means of *mechanical* causation: interaction between contiguous parts of matter by pressure and impact. Such causation has a reassuring familiarity (since its action can be observed amongst everyday things such as water and billiard balls) and also an apparent *intelligibility* (in that it operates through physical touching which requires only familiar geometrical properties). Hence the appeal of this sort of 'mechanical philosophy' was not confined to the followers of Descartes.

3. *Corpuscularianism, Locke, and Newton*

A less rationalistic form of mechanism was inspired by the atomism of the ancient Epicurean school, and championed initially by the Frenchman Pierre Gassendi. However, it flourished better in Britain, whose natural philosophers tended to be suspicious of the Cartesian attempt to derive scientific principles from pure reason, and followed Francis Bacon in emphasizing the role of experimentation. Robert Boyle, one of the most influential scientists of the seventeenth century,[7] advocated what he called 'corpuscularianism', a name that avoided the atheistic associations of Epicurean atomism. Boyle's interest in chemistry led him to speculate that material substances are composed of imperceptible 'corpuscles' whose physical interactions on the atomic scale are responsible for the large-scale perceived properties. All corpuscles are formed from the same 'universal matter', and the various properties of different substances arise from the way in which these minute corpuscles are organized: their individual size, shape, and motion, and the resulting texture. It is only these so-called 'primary' qualities that feature in the physical theory, and they are to be distinguished from 'secondary' qualities such as an object's colour, taste, or smell, which represent the effects of the object on the human senses rather than anything genuinely intrinsic to it. Because the primary qualities are essentially geometrical (and hence mathematically describable), this theory—like that of Descartes—held out the promise of explaining objects' behaviour in terms of straightforward mechanical interactions whose results could potentially be calculated. But unlike Descartes, Boyle took matter's fundamental properties to include impenetrability as independent of extension. This opened the possibility of penetrable extension (i.e. extension without matter), thus enabling a distinction to be drawn between atoms and empty space, and avoiding the Cartesian plenum.

Boyle's corpuscularianism became philosophical orthodoxy in Britain through the work of his friend John Locke, a philosopher destined to

---

[7] It seems that Boyle was a major focus of natural philosophy teaching in Edinburgh when Hume studied there in 1724–5.

eclipse Descartes, and whose epistemology and political theory were to exert huge influence into the nineteenth century and beyond. Locke's monumental *Essay concerning Human Understanding*, published in 1690, explored the materials and limits of human thinking, setting an agenda that Hume would follow in his similarly titled *Enquiry*. Locke's *Essay* is infused with an empiricist spirit, arguing that all our 'ideas' (i.e. the constituents of our thoughts) derive from experience, as does the overwhelming bulk of our knowledge. Locke starts with a vigorous attack on the theory of 'innate ideas', targeting both scholastic and Cartesian attempts to deduce truths by pure reason based on such supposed ideas (as, for example, in Descartes's argument that the perfection of our innate idea of God implies a perfect cause). Locke then goes on to give a thoroughly empiricist account of the origin of our ideas, taking an atomistic approach in which complex ideas are composed of simples, and the simple ideas themselves are directly derived from experience. This experience can be of the external world or of our own minds: thus the senses yield 'ideas of sensation' (such as the redness of a rose), while introspection yields 'ideas of reflection' (such as desire for the rose, or fear of its thorn). Since all such experience is of particular sensations or feelings, the ideas we derive from these are particular also. General ideas (such as the idea of redness in general) then get generated from ideas of particular instances (e.g. the colour of different red flowers) by 'abstraction', in which the differing details (e.g. the varying brightnesses and hues) are ignored, and notice taken only of what is common to all, leaving an 'abstract idea' which is able to represent any instance whatever.

If all our ideas are derived from experience, then it is natural also to see this as the source of all our knowledge of the world, since only our senses can inform us what kinds of things exist and how they behave. Thus Locke, like Boyle, was far more cautious than Descartes, who had claimed to know the entire essence of matter and mind from his innate ideas of extension and thought respectively. For Locke, the essence of both is hidden from us, and the most we can do is to seek a plausible account of them, which will always remain uncertain and answerable to further experience. It is in this spirit that he endorses the 'corpuscularian hypothesis', that material things are made of corpuscles of 'substance in general' (Boyle's 'universal matter') possessing the geometrical primary properties (size, shape, motion, etc.) together with 'solidity' (Boyle's 'impenetrability'). Since we cannot know the 'real essence' of physical substances—e.g. the underlying corpuscular structure of gold—our science of them has to be based on the manifest properties that we perceive, the 'nominal essence' by which we identify them—e.g. the 'Colour, Weight, Fusibility, and Fixedness, *etc.*' of gold, which 'gives it a right to that Name' (*Essay*, III. iii. 18). Science must therefore proceed by careful observation and experiment, with little point to theorizing about underlying essences. Occasionally Locke seems to go further than these modest principles would allow, suggesting that the mechanical behaviour of the corpuscular world could in principle be predicted without experiment if only we had senses sufficient to inspect it in detail:

> I doubt not but if we could discover the Figure, Size, Texture, and Motion of the minute Constituent parts of any two Bodies, we should know without Trial several of their Operations one upon another, as we do now the Properties of a Square, or a Triangle. (*Essay*, IV. iii. 25)

But this remains at most a theoretical speculation, and unlike Descartes, Locke never expresses any serious ambition to deduce physical laws by pure reason.

Descartes's ambition exceeded his reach, and although his thought remained influential for many years, especially in his native France, its practical value never matched its theoretical elegance. The supposed deduction of precise laws of motion from the pure geometry of extension proved elusive, and Cartesian mechanics was unable to yield convincing predictions either of terrestrial dynamics (e.g. flying projectiles and colliding billiard balls), or the celestial orbits of the planets. Indeed the careful observations and calculations of Tycho Brahe and Johannes Kepler had revealed these orbits to be elliptical rather than circular, and this gave particular difficulties for the Cartesian vortex theory. Its death knell came in 1687, when Isaac Newton was able in his *Principia Mathematica* to prove results indicating the impossibility of a vortex yielding elliptical motion. The *Principia*, perhaps the most influential work of science ever published, went on to displace the Cartesian account by formulating a set of mechanical laws that apparently explained both terrestrial and celestial dynamics in exquisite detail. Newton retained Descartes's concept of inertia as his 'first law' (that objects move uniformly unless acted upon by a force), but followed Boyle in replacing the Cartesian plenum with a universe mainly composed of empty space. He then took the controversial step of positing a force, called 'gravity', acting between bodies across that empty space, proportional to their mass and inversely proportional to the square of the distance between them. Using his newly invented mathematical tool, the calculus, he proved that such a force, acting on bodies in accordance with his second law,[8] would indeed generate elliptical orbital motion amongst bodies in space, and could also explain the parabolic flight and accelerating fall of projectiles near the Earth. Moreover the 'constant of proportionality' required in these two contexts turned out to coincide, strongly confirming both the theory itself and also Galileo's once revolutionary claim that celestial and terrestrial bodies are subject to exactly the same laws.

Despite this success, Newton's postulated gravitational force, acting at a distance and without any intermediate mechanical connexion, seemed to many to be deeply 'unintelligible' and even objectionably 'occult'. Newton's influential response to this objection, in the second edition of *Principia*, was to insist that he 'feigned no hypotheses' (i.e. invented no speculations) about the causes of gravity, and felt no need to do so. If his equations correctly described the observed behaviour of objects, then his theory (including its postulated forces) should be deemed acceptable whatever the underlying reality might be, and speculation about the ultimate cause of gravitational attraction was both unnecessary and inappropriate, unless and until further empirical evidence emerged that might help to throw light on the matter. This somewhat *instrumentalist* position was later to make a deep impression on Hume, whose approach to the metaphysics of causation can be seen as generalizing it to all causes whatever.[9] Amongst natural philosophers, however, although Newton's theory triumphed owing to its sheer accuracy and predictive power, the quest for intelligibility

---

[8] This law states that if a force F acts on a body of mass m, this causes the body to accelerate—i.e. to change its velocity—in the direction of F, the magnitude of that acceleration being F divided by m.

[9] Instrumentalism is the view that theoretical entities such as forces are to be thought of as useful *instruments* for describing and predicting phenomena, whose value does not depend on their actually corresponding to anything in the real world. Strict instrumentalists (e.g. Berkeley) deny such entities' reality. What we might call *methodological instrumentalists* (e.g. Newton in respect of gravity) see the primary criterion of a theory's scientific adequacy as being independent of whether such entities exist. Hume's position on powers and forces is methodologically instrumentalist in spirit, but with a semantic colouring that interprets *what it means* for a power to exist in terms of its instrumentalist adequacy.

continued, and even Newton himself speculated that gravity might be accounted for by some sort of 'etherial active fluid' permeating space (as mentioned by Hume at *E* 7.25 endnote [D]). However, there are also hints in his writings, made louder and more explicit in his followers, that the very unintelligibility of gravity has religious significance as an argument for God's existence, since only the continuous power of an almighty being could keep the world working in conformity with a law for which there is no conceivable mechanical explanation.

4. *Free Will, and the Dangers of Infidelity*

Throughout this period, religion exerted a profound influence over all philosophical and scientific speculation. No philosopher or scientist could afford to ignore the religious implications of his work, and many were attacked on account of their supposed heresy or 'infidelity'. Galileo's punishment by the Inquisition provides the most famous example, deemed heretical for stating that the Earth orbits the Sun and thus contradicting scriptural texts such as 'The Lord . . . has established the world; it shall never be moved' (Psalm 93: 1) and the famous creation story in Genesis (according to which 'the heaven and the earth' are created 'in the beginning', and the Sun is not made until the fourth day). Hearing of Galileo's condemnation, Descartes withheld his own projected treatise *The World*, and took great pains to exclude anything unorthodox from his published writings. But this did not save his works from being added (in 1663) to the Roman Catholic Index of Prohibited Books, a list that came to include almost every significant work of post-medieval Western philosophy. His offence seems to have been an implicit denial of the doctrine of transubstantiation, that in the ceremony of the Eucharist commemorating the Last Supper, consecrated bread and wine are literally changed in substance into the body and blood of Christ. Such a claim made some sense within the Aristotelian scheme, but ceased to be feasible within a physics such as Descartes's or Locke's that saw the perceptible 'secondary' qualities of things (their colour, taste, smell, etc.) as caused directly by their underlying 'primary' or mechanical structure.

Another theological minefield, raising problems for both Roman Catholics and Protestants, concerned the question of free will. The growth of empirical science, and the mechanical philosophy in particular, put increasing emphasis on laws of nature and the clockwork predictability of physical phenomena. Hence most of the great philosophers of the seventeenth and eighteenth centuries (e.g. Descartes, Hobbes, Spinoza, Locke, Leibniz, Hume, and Kant) were attracted to *determinism*, the view that every event is brought about by antecedent causes and is therefore predictable (at least in principle) from knowledge of prior conditions and the relevant causal laws. But while determinism in the physical realm was relatively unproblematic, in the human realm it threatened to undermine freedom and moral responsibility. Punishment seems appropriate only when some wrong is committed freely, by an agent who had some choice in the matter. How then could it be right for any judge (human or divine) to punish a wrongdoer, if the act in question was the product of inexorable causal laws, and could have been foreseen by God with absolute certainty before the sinner had even been born?

Many shied away from facing up to this thorny problem; Descartes, for example, is rather vague about whether determinism applies to the immaterial mind. The classic resolution of the dilemma, *compatibilism*, was most clearly formulated by his contemporary Thomas Hobbes, the first great philosopher to write in the English language and a forthright materialist (who provocatively cited Descartes's mental 'immaterial substance' as a paradigm contradiction in terms). Accepting that the (purely material) world is governed by causal necessitation— what he called 'the doctrine of necessity'—Hobbes preserved moral freedom by asserting its full compatibility with determinism:

LIBERTY, or FREEDOME, signifieth (properly) the absence of Opposition; (by Opposition, I mean external Impediments of motion;) . . . a *FREE-MAN, is he, that in those things, which by his strength and wit he is able to do, is not hindred to doe what he has a will to*. . . . *Liberty* and *Necessity* are Consistent . . . the actions which men voluntarily doe . . . because they proceed from their will, proceed from *liberty*; and yet, because every act of mans will, and every desire, and inclination proceedeth from some cause, and that from another cause, in a continuall chaine, . . . proceed from *necessity*. (*Leviathan*, ch. 21)

Hume is widely seen as following Hobbes here, and indeed uses Hobbesian terminology in Section VIII of the *Enquiry*, 'Of Liberty and Necessity', where he presents his own (subtly different) compatibilist approach.

Compatibilism is now very widely accepted, though it remains controversial, and the nexus of problems surrounding free will—one of the most ancient in metaphysics—is still hotly debated today. However, three hundred years ago it seemed even more intractable, because of the variety of theological issues with which it interlocked. Thus for example not only causal determinism, but also God's creation and sustaining of the world from moment to moment (an idea much emphasized by Descartes), threatens to make Him responsible for everything that happens, including human sin. Denying determinism might ameliorate this difficulty, but would potentially cast doubt on both God's omnipotence (by implying that some things happen by chance, independently of His decrees) and His omniscience (by making it utterly obscure how God could foresee a yet undetermined future). Another related issue involved the theology of grace and justification, sharpened by Protestant Reformers' emphasis on the 'original sin' we inherit from Adam and Eve and our consequent total depravity that makes us all—even the most apparently virtuous—thoroughly deserving of eternal damnation. Following Augustine, the Reformers insisted that we can be saved from this fate only by the grace of God, which generously grants us salvation through faith in Christ, and not through any merit of our own.[10] But how is it that some achieve this saving faith whereas others do not, given that the distinction cannot be founded on their moral virtue? It seems that God must Himself choose on whom to bestow it, but then if He does so, how can this divine grace be anything other than irresistible? Considerations like these led many Protestants—most notably John Calvin—to the doctrine of *predestination*, implying that the choice of who is destined to go to heaven, and who to hell, was made by God from the beginning of time, quite irrespective of human merit. Opponents of Calvinism found this doctrine morally monstrous, whereby most of mankind (including Christians of rival sects) are doomed to inevitable hellfire owing to the sin of Adam, while God—who could very easily spare all of them from this eternal torture simply by granting them saving faith—in fact spares only very few.

With eternal hellfire or salvation at stake, it is not surprising that religious disputes could become impassioned and aggressive. Hume himself, living in Calvinist Scotland, accordingly took care to avoid overt infidelity, for example suppressing his own potentially incendiary

---

[10] The Roman Catholic Jansenists (who make an appearance in Section X of the *Enquiry*) took a similar approach, though most Catholic sects put greater emphasis on good works as also contributing to salvation.

treatment of immortality to be published only posthumously.[11]
Although religious persecution in Britain had greatly declined after
the horrors of the Civil War (1642–51) and the bigotry of Cromwell's
Commonwealth (1649–60), it was still possible in 1697 for Thomas
Aikenhead, a 19-year-old Edinburgh University student, to be hanged
for blasphemous comments made to other students, and even as late
as 1733, the Cambridge theologian Thomas Woolston died in prison,
having been convicted of blasphemy four years earlier. Hume himself experienced prejudice of a less dangerous kind, being rejected as
an applicant for a chair of Philosophy at Edinburgh in 1745 on the
ground that his *Treatise of Human Nature* advocated 'Principles leading to downright Atheism' (*L* 17), even though the *Treatise* (for reasons of prudence) contained no explicit discussion of religion. In 1756,
the General Assembly of the Church of Scotland debated a motion
to excommunicate him (i.e. expel him from the Church), based largely
on the religious sections of the *Enquiry* which had been published in
1748, though the motion was rejected. By then, such a condemnation
might well have made the Church a laughing stock, but it was still
prudent for Hume to tread carefully where Christianity was concerned, and an explicit denial of its central doctrines would be very
likely both to provoke a hostile reaction, and also to upset numerous
friends. Even in eighteenth-century Edinburgh, the 'Athens of the
North' which saw the brilliant flowering of intellectual activity of
which Hume was a leading light, religious orthodoxy remained a
potent force and a centre of allegiance for the vast majority.

5. *God's Design, and Human Reason*

Amongst the more sophisticated classes of this 'Scottish Enlightenment',
however, the nature of religious commitment was profoundly different
from either of the types that had been dominant in the seventeenth
century. Roman Catholicism, with its ornate rites, magical transubstantiation, and saintly miracles, was now commonly dismissed as
'superstition', while the narrow bigotry and fervent 'enthusiasm' of
various Protestant sects was equally despised.[12] Repelled by the vicious

---

[11] For examples of Hume's other methods of hiding or disguising his atheism, see
below pp. 146, 161–2, 202–3.

[12] Accordingly Hume's essay 'Of Superstition and Enthusiasm', in which he critically
discusses them both, could safely be published in 1741.

religious wars that these competing movements had inspired, enlightened intellectuals had moved on to a form of Christianity that fully
embraced the scientific revolution, with an increasing emphasis on
religion as grounded on reason rather than faith. Thus the ancient God
of miracles, grace, exclusive revelations, and inexplicable mysteries
was largely abandoned in favour of the Great Designer. Specifically
Christian doctrines such as the incarnation and resurrection of Jesus
were, as always, based on written revelation, with the miracles reported
in the Bible playing a crucial role in authenticating both Jesus himself and other biblical figures. But any more recent or controversial
revelations (with their divisive doctrinal implications) were downplayed,
in favour of an emphasis on *natural theology*: religion as established
by reason and science. From this perspective, the 'incomparable
Mr. Newton' (as Locke described him) had performed a major service to theology, by revealing the secrets of God's wonderful creation.
Hence the famous epitaph by the poet Alexander Pope:

> Nature and Nature's laws lay hid in night:
> God said, Let Newton be! and all was light.

Unlike many thinkers in both earlier and later centuries, those of the
Enlightenment—at least in Britain—typically saw no conflict between
science and religion, but viewed new discoveries as providing yet
more evidence of the intricacy, wisdom, and benevolence of God's
handiwork. Science became a religiously informed activity, and reading God's works from 'the great book of nature' was judged a worthy
alternative to reading them from the Bible. The Design Argument
for God's existence thus became widely viewed as the strongest pillar
of natural religion.[13]

With God portrayed as the Great Designer, and human reason
demonstrating its own impressive powers in revealing His creation,
this naturally encouraged the thought that our faculty of reason has
a semi-divine quality, substantiating the biblical claim that we are
'made in the image of God'. Much of our behaviour might be instinctive, or driven by bodily appetites and passions, like that of the other
animals. But our reason seemed to be special, providing an insight
into rational truth (most obviously in mathematics) that appears
to approximate to God's transparent perception. Of course we are

---

[13] For one of the most famous and elegant statements of the Design Argument, see
Part ii of Hume's *Dialogues*, in Appendix III, below.

limited creatures, so our pure rational insight may not extend very far, but the apparent success of philosophers in discovering 'intelligible' laws of nature indicated that it was at least partially applicable beyond mathematics, to the operations of the physical world. Locke, typically, was more modest, acknowledging that even our scientific understanding of the world is at best 'probable' and thus inevitably falls short of the 'demonstrative' certainty of mathematics. But even this mere probable judgement is quite sufficient for our practical needs, and our faculty of reason is just as valuable when we use it to perceive probabilities as when we perceive certainties. God has given us faculties suitable for our position in the world, as creatures intermediate between animals and angels. And though our reason might be fallible and limited, it above all is what elevates us above the beasts. In this, at least, most early modern philosophers could agree with Plato, who saw reason as the central function of the immortal soul, and even Aristotle, who defined man as the one distinctive 'rational animal'.

6. *Inertness, Malebranche, and Berkeley*

The Design Argument was not the only way in which the new science could be harnessed to the benefit of religion. Indeed we saw earlier how the 'unintelligible' nature of gravitational attraction—the fact that it seemed inexplicable in mechanistic terms—could be presented as an argument for God's existence. The 'mechanical philosophy' not only encouraged the perception of the world as a clockwork masterpiece (thereby implying the existence of a master clockmaker); it also implied limits on the essence and powers of matter, which could be exploited for theological gain. Descartes was the first to do this, when he claimed to perceive clearly and distinctly that the essence of matter was different from that of the thinking self, so that the soul must be immaterial and hence could potentially survive the body's dissolution. Locke followed, giving an argument for the existence of God which depended on the impossibility of intelligent thought's arising from the mere primary qualities of matter. However, Locke ventured the opinion that God might, if He wished, 'superadd' thought to matter (*Essay*, IV. iii. 6). This provoked a great deal of hostility, since thought was evidently an 'active' power, whereas the mechanical philosophy (inspired by the concept of inertia) encouraged the idea that matter was purely passive or 'inert'. Material things were seen as intricate but lifeless machines, their cogs and levers static until set in motion by some external power. This picture would be undermined if a genuinely active power—such as thought, or possibly gravity—were to be ascribed to matter itself. In that case, the apparent need for an external source of power might be removed, with potentially dangerous implications for the existence of both God and a distinct, immaterial soul. So the inertness of matter became a prominent and theologically charged theme in much philosophical discussion, and was to remain so well into Hume's time (e.g. in the work of Samuel Clarke and Andrew Baxter).

Some metaphysicians took these sorts of considerations much further, to the extent of completely denying the causal relevance of matter, or even its very existence. Nicolas Malebranche, the most influential Cartesian of the late seventeenth century, built on Descartes's idea that continual re-creation by God is necessary to sustain the world from moment to moment, drawing the conclusion that no real causal interaction takes place except through the intervention of God. On this account, when one billiard ball hits another, the second ball moves not because of any force in the first ball, but purely because God then chooses to re-create the second ball in an appropriate sequence of positions. The collision of the balls is not a *cause* of the movement, but an *occasion* for God to bring about the relevant behaviour, in accordance with the behavioural laws that He has decreed. Hence this theory (described and criticized by Hume at E 7.21–5) is called *occasionalism*. Another of Malebranche's arguments for this theory was based on the common assumption—discussed above— that genuine causation should be *intelligible*. Interpreting intelligibility in a particularly strong sense, he insisted that an event can be a real cause only if it makes the subsequent non-occurrence of its effect inconceivable, so that the cause has a (logically) *necessary connexion* with its effect. Hence the collision of the first billiard ball with the second cannot possibly be the real cause of the second ball's motion, because it would be perfectly conceivable for the one event not to be followed by the other. The only cause capable of satisfying this inconceivability requirement turns out to be the will of God, who is omnipotent and whose intentions are therefore infallibly fulfilled. So again we reach Malebranche's desired conclusion, that God is the only true cause.

Malebranche's occasionalism has the peculiar consequence that every event in the world is really brought about by God, and this applies to the operation not only of inanimate things, but also of our own sensory and motor faculties. When we see an apple, for example, or when we stretch to pick it up, it is God who creates our visual perceptions (which are of ideas in His mind) to correspond with the reality, and it is He who moves our arm (or, strictly, re-creates it moment by moment in changing positions) to correspond with our willed movement. But having gone this far, there might now seem little point in postulating a material world at all, since it does not appear to play any part in what we experience or in explaining what happens (e.g. it is not any powers of the billiard balls that explain their movements, but God's decision to re-create them in accordance with the 'laws of motion' to which He has chosen to conform).[14] Thus some philosophers, impressed by the fundamental notion that matter cannot be active, ended up entirely denying its existence, a view called *immaterialism* or *idealism*. On this view, material objects 'exist' only in so far as we have ideas in our mind that appear to represent them, or God has ideas in His mind that are archetypes of the ideas He wills to create in ours.

The most prominent of these immaterialists was George Berkeley, whose overall position is in many respects similar to that of Malebranche, though with a different emphasis due in part to his place within the Lockean rather than Cartesian tradition. Locke had insisted on a distinction between ideas, which are purely in the mind, and material things, which are the presumed external causes of our perceptual ideas. These ideas represent things as having both primary qualities (such as shape, size, and motion) and also secondary qualities (such as colour, taste, and smell), but our best theory of the world— i.e. Boyle's corpuscularianism—indicates that only our ideas of primary qualities resemble genuine qualities of material things. Berkeley agrees with Locke regarding the essentially mental nature of what is immediately perceived, and the main focus of his arguments is to attack the Lockean view that there is something in addition, some supposed material object 'behind' the perceived apple-idea. In particular,

---

[14] In a sense, God's choice of the laws of motion is arbitrary, though Malebranche believed that God would inevitably create the best world consistent with His nature, so that His choice of laws would be determined by His wisdom and goodness.

he emphasizes the inconceivability of anything sensory existing outside a mind, and denies that anything unperceived (such as the supposed primary qualities of an external object) could even *resemble* a sensory idea. He then goes on to attack the basis of the primary-secondary quality distinction itself, arguing that since our ideas of primary qualities are inextricably linked with those of secondary qualities (e.g. we see or imagine an object's shape only by seeing or imagining the extent of its colour), it is impossible to conceive the one without the other.[15] Even if some objects resembling our ideas were to exist outside the mind, since those ideas are 'visibly inactive, [with] nothing of power or agency included in them' (*Principles*, i. 25), any such objects would themselves have to be totally inert, and hence quite unable to cause any perception of them. Thus Berkeley reaches the conclusion that the only active things in the universe are minds, or spirits, while everything that we perceive consists of inactive, inert, ideas.

It seems odd that a line of thought inspired by physical science, namely the mechanical philosophy's emphasis on the inertness of matter, should lead to metaphysical positions such as occasionalism and immaterialism that deny physical objects any causal role whatever in the world that we perceive. But Berkeley in particular took pains to develop an account of physical science consistent with his immaterialism, and he did this by taking further the instrumentalism hinted at by Newton. On this account, the aim of science is simply to discover laws that generate true predictions about the perceived phenomena, and it is irrelevant whether the unperceived entities (such as forces) to which those laws appeal actually have any real existence, as long as they provide useful instruments of prediction. If immaterialism is correct, then such forces—and even the material objects that Locke and others suppose to be the causes of our perceptions—do not in fact exist, and the apparent intricacy of the physical world is due not to the interaction of complex material mechanisms, but instead to God's direct action. God benevolently ensures that our perceptions occur in the same patterns as they would if they were caused by such

---

[15] Berkeley links this with an intense attack on Locke's doctrine of 'abstraction', the process by which we supposedly come to form general ideas. In fact it seems that he misunderstood Locke, whose notion of abstraction (involving 'partial consideration' of some aspects of an idea) is rather similar to Berkeley's. Hume's own account of general ideas, developed from Berkeley's, is sketched at *E* 12.20 endnote [P].

material mechanisms, and He does this precisely to enable us to develop methods of predicting what will happen, and to direct our lives accordingly. Our sensory ideas of objects are thus *signs* from God providing us with predictive information, rather than perceptions of real material things. But this metaphysical position makes no difference to the practice or value of science, which can proceed regardless and yield benefits just as great as if it were genuinely descriptive of an objective material world.

7. *The Humean Revolution*

Against all this background, we are now in a position to appreciate the relevance and the revolutionary implications of Hume's philosophy. Put crudely, he follows the spirit of Locke's empiricism with respect to both the origin of ideas (*Enquiry* Section II) and factual discovery, but develops it far more consistently, ruthlessly dismissing all hints of pure rational insight (e.g. into the powers of matter) and deploying powerful sceptical arguments to undermine even the *ideal* of causal intelligibility.

Hume's first such sceptical argument (Section IV Part i) shows that causal laws can be known only by experience, but that experience gives no real insight into what makes them operate. Hence even the supposed intelligibility of causation by mechanical impact (e.g. of billiard balls) is an illusion, generated by familiarity. He then goes on (Sections IV Part ii and V) to consider how we learn from experience, which Locke had attributed to the rational perception of probable evidential connexions. Hume argues against this that all learning from experience, and hence all factual reasoning, is founded on an instinctive assumption for which we can give no rational basis whatever, namely, that what we have observed is a reliable guide to the unobserved. Thus our capacity for factual reasoning, instead of being a manifestation of angelic rational perception, turns out to be different only in degree from that of the animals (Section IX).

Hume's next major argument (Section VII) investigates our very notion of causation, concluding that so far from having anything to do with insight into the world, it instead involves a projection onto the world of our own inferential behaviour. This might seem to imply dismal prospects for science, but Hume turns it to advantage by insisting on the moral that causation—*genuine* causation—is to be understood in conformity with his analysis, and he ends the section by defining 'cause' accordingly. Intelligibility is not to be had, *but nor is it required*, and the proper ideal of science is rather to discover and simplify the laws that describe phenomena (*E* 4.12). Thus *all* causes in science can, and should, be viewed broadly instrumentally, as Newton had done in the case of gravity and Berkeley generalized. This positive message is developed further in Section VIII, where Hume follows Hobbes in advocating a deterministic compatibilism. His new understanding of causation significantly strengthens the case, by showing that a lack of 'intelligibility' in the moral world is no obstacle to genuine causation or determinism concerning human action. Thus moral science—as exemplified in numerous of Hume's essays and other works—is shown to be feasible. He then goes on to attack the rational basis for belief in God (Sections X and XI), and to advocate a 'mitigated scepticism' which does not aspire to certainty, limits our scientific ambitions, and restricts them to subjects within the scope of our experience (Section XII).

From this perspective, both Darwinian biology and the development of science since the dawn of the twentieth century can be seen as vindicating Hume. Darwin emphasized our continuity with the animals, then relativity theory and quantum physics demonstrated conclusively that the apparent intelligibility of the world that so impressed philosophers from Aristotle to Descartes to Kant (and beyond) was largely an illusion. As a result, the rigorously empiricist and methodologically instrumentalist approach that Hume pioneered has become scientifically mainstream, and in this respect the *Enquiry* may today seem relatively innocuous and inoffensive. However, it still has much to teach even modern scientists, who will often stop applying their critical methods outside the laboratory, whereas Hume would advise that we take them more seriously, into the religious and moral assumptions that drive our lives. To better appreciate the force and implications of all this, let us now turn in more detail to the *Enquiry* itself.

8. Section I: The Aims of the *Enquiry*

The first section of the *Enquiry* serves as an introduction, but starts out as a comparison between two species of 'moral philosophy' (i.e. the study of man).[16] The 'easy philosophy' is eloquent and poetic, using immediately striking, easily comprehensible, and imaginatively pleasing reflections on life to paint virtue in alluring colours and thus to improve our manners and behaviour. By contrast, 'abstruse' philosophy aims to satisfy the intellect rather than to please the imagination—its goal is to discover the actual principles of human nature by systematic rational investigation. Initially Hume gives the appearance of preferring the easy philosophy (*E* 1.3–6) as more agreeable and down to earth, but in fact most of the section is devoted to a defence of abstruse metaphysics, spelling out 'what can reasonably be pleaded in their behalf' (*E* 1.7).

Hume's defence of abstruse metaphysics combines two main themes which might be described as the *scientific* and the *critical*. The former highlights the necessity and value of careful, precise thinking in establishing general truths about man and the moral world; thus the abstruse philosophy can help the easy, in much the same way as an anatomist can help a painter, as well as fostering the innocent pleasure of discovery. The main objection to this optimistic picture is that such potential discovery of truth is an illusion, and it is in response to this objection that the critical theme comes to the fore:

Here indeed lies the justest and most plausible objection against a considerable part of metaphysics, that they are not properly a science; but arise either from the fruitless efforts of human vanity, which would penetrate into subjects utterly inaccessible to the understanding, or from the craft of popular superstitions, which, being unable to defend themselves on fair ground, raise these intangling brambles to cover and protect their weakness. . . .

But is this a sufficient reason, why philosophers should desist from such researches . . . ? Is it not proper to draw an opposite conclusion . . . ? . . . The only method of freeing learning . . . from these abstruse questions, is to enquire seriously into the nature of human understanding, and shew, from an exact analysis of its powers and capacity, that it is by no means fitted for such remote and abstruse subjects. We . . . must cultivate true metaphysics with some care, in order to destroy the false and adulterate. . . . Accurate and just reasoning . . . is alone able to subvert that abstruse philosophy and metaphysical jargon, which, being mixed up with popular superstition . . . gives it the air of science and wisdom. (*E* 1.11–12)

---

[16] Here 'moral philosophy' is used in its 18th-century sense, rather than in the modern sense of *ethics*. Note again that unfamiliar or antiquated terms can be consulted in the Glossary below.

His critical salvo delivered, Hume soon turns back to his scientific theme, emphasizing the 'many positive advantages, which result from an accurate scrutiny into the powers and faculties of human nature'. It might be suggested that any such supposed 'science is uncertain and chimerical', but Hume responds to this suggestion by insisting that at least some kind of 'mental geography, or delineation of the distinct parts and powers of the mind' is clearly defensible and well within our grasp (*E* 1.13–14). Moreover our scientific ambitions can legitimately extend deeper than this mere 'ordering and distinguishing [of] the operations of the mind':

May we not hope, that philosophy, if cultivated with care . . . may carry its researches still farther, and discover, at least in some degree, the secret springs and principles, by which the human mind is actuated in its operations? (*E* 1.15)

Just as Brahe, Kepler, and others, by 'ordering and distinguishing' the apparent motions of the planets, had prepared the way for Newton to build on their work and reveal the hidden laws underlying such motion, so philosophers—having established a reliable mental geography— can then aspire to uncover the secret springs and principles that generate the observable behaviour of the mind.

9. *Sections II and III: The Origin and Association of Ideas*

Section II of the *Enquiry* sets out the basic principles of Hume's 'Theory of Ideas', most of which is derivative from Locke's *Essay concerning Human Understanding*. It is perhaps due to the influence of Locke's attack on innatism (cf. §3 above) that the origin of ideas is given such a prominent position by Hume, but this emphasis is rather misleading, for it plays an important role only in one later section of the *Enquiry* (Section VII), and even here in Section II Hume's explicit discussion of the innate ideas controversy merits only a note (*E* 2.9 endnote [A]).

Ideas and Impressions

Locke, like Descartes, had used the vague word 'idea' for 'whatsoever is the object of the understanding when a man thinks' (*Essay*, I. i. 8). Thus according to Locke, anyone who sees the blue sky or feels a pain has in his mind an idea of that colour or of that sensation, and likewise anyone who merely thinks about the sky or contemplates pain also has in his mind corresponding ideas. Hume, however, considers this broad usage to be inappropriate, for it conflates together two quite distinct mental operations—namely the awareness of sensations or feelings, and the consideration of thoughts—and only the latter, in his opinion, can properly be called 'ideas' in the conventional sense. He therefore restricts the scope of 'idea' to refer to thoughts alone, coining the new term 'impression' to refer to sensations and feelings, and the term 'perception' for the general class of objects of the mind, comprising impressions and ideas together (so Lockean 'ideas' become Humean 'perceptions'). In general, impressions are more 'forceful and vivacious' than ideas, though this rule can break down if 'the mind be disordered by disease or madness' (*E* 2.1): a madman's thoughts could be as vivid to him as his sensations, in which case he would presumably be unable to tell the difference.[17]

Some of Hume's discussion suggests a distinction (again derived from Locke) which he had defined explicitly in the *Treatise*:

Simple perceptions or impressions and ideas are such as admit of no distinction nor separation. The complex are the contrary of these, and may be distinguished into parts. Tho' a particular colour, taste, and smell are qualities all united together in this apple, 'tis easy to perceive they are not the same, but are at least distinguishable from each other. (*T* 1.1.1.2)

Presumably the particular ideas of colour, taste, etc. are understood to be simple ideas, while the idea of the apple is a complex idea that combines them, but in the *Enquiry* Hume gives no such clear examples of complexes composed of simples. Instead he gives two instances of complex ideas, namely that of a golden mountain and that of a virtuous horse, each itself composed of two further complex ideas (*E* 2.5). This might suggest that he no longer wishes to commit himself to a view about which ideas, if any, are absolutely simple, though he later hints that ideas of colour seem to be (*E* 2.8).

---

[17] 'Force' and 'vivacity' do not seem to be the best words to capture the distinction between sensory awareness or feelings on the one hand, and thoughts on the other, because thoughts can sometimes be very vivid (e.g. thinking about one's sweetheart, noticing a vital step in a winning chess combination), while sensations can be very dull and boring (e.g. watching paint dry). Fortunately, very little in the *Enquiry* depends on exactly how 'force and vivacity' is interpreted.

The Copy Principle

Hume argues that although our capacity to form ideas may seem completely unbounded, in fact 'all this creative power of the mind amounts to no more than the faculty of compounding, transposing, augmenting, or diminishing the materials afforded us by the senses and experience' (*E* 2.5).[18] In other words, our minds can create new ideas from the components which experience has already given us, by combining together our existing ideas in new ways or by shuffling the components of our existing ideas, but we are quite unable to form any completely new ideas beyond those that have already been given to us by sensation or feeling.

> Or, to express myself in philosophical language, all our ideas or more feeble perceptions are copies of our impressions or more lively ones. (*E* 2.5)

This is widely known as Hume's *Copy Principle*.[19]

Hume gives two arguments (*E* 2.6, 2.7) for the Copy Principle, the first of which simply claims that all of our existing ideas, if examined, will in fact turn out to be copied from impressions. Here the example he gives is deliberately chosen to oppose Descartes:

> The idea of God, as meaning *an infinitely intelligent, wise, and good Being*, arises from reflecting on the operations of our own mind, and augmenting, without limit, those qualities of goodness and wisdom. (*E* 2.6, my italics)

Obviously the Cartesian could persist in claiming that the idea of God is innate, but Hume's rival account of the idea is straightforward and plausible, and carries force given the weight of his generalization. If all our ideas can be accounted for by the Copy Principle, then why should we suppose any mysterious faculty of innate ideas?

Hume ends Section II by suggesting that the Copy Principle provides a potent weapon for eliminating bogus would-be ideas that turn

---

[18] Hume's famous 'missing shade of blue' (*E* 2.8) highlights another way in which the mind might 'compound . . . the materials afforded us by the senses', by mixing ideas to generate intermediates. This casts doubt on the claim that all *simple* ideas must be direct copies of impressions, but it does not pose any sort of difficulty for his general claim that the materials of our thoughts must ultimately derive from impressions.

[19] Without the simple-complex distinction the principle is hard to express precisely (cf. *T* 1.1.1.7), because a complex idea (e.g. of a golden mountain) can perfectly well be formed without being copied from a single corresponding impression. The point is that every *part* of the idea must ultimately be copied from part of some impression—i.e. there is no part of the idea which is not impression-derived.

out to have no corresponding impression (*E* 2.9). However, in the rest of the *Enquiry* he uses it less aggressively, not to reject ideas but as a tool of analysis, a 'new microscope or species of optics' (*E* 7.4) which can make our ideas more clear and precise by discovering the impressions from which they are derived and of which they are copies.[20] As we shall see later, his main application of this 'microscope' comes in Section VII, where he uses it to clarify the idea of necessary connexion, but there are also brief hints of its playing a role in Section XII, as applied to the ideas of extension (*E* 12.15), space, and time (*E* 12.20 endnote [P]).

The Association of Ideas

The present Section III is merely the first three paragraphs of what was originally a much longer essay, which Hume cut down after the 1772 edition by the removal of an extended discussion of the role of the association of ideas in literature (see pp. 178–83). It is very straightforward, first pointing out that our ideas tend to follow each other, and to combine with each other, in regular patterns. He then suggests that all of this associative behaviour reduces to the operation of three relations or 'principles of connexion among ideas, namely, *Resemblance*, *Contiguity* in time or place, and *Cause* or *Effect*'. The section ends rather tamely, with Hume stating that although he can find no other principles of association besides these three, nevertheless he cannot prove that his enumeration is complete. This doesn't seem to be of great concern to him, presumably because nothing of great consequence hangs on it in what follows. Indeed the only significant role of the association of ideas in the *Enquiry* is to provide an analogy with the operation of *custom*. In Part ii of Section V (*E* 5.20), Hume will suggest that custom, an instinctive mechanism that underlies all of our factual reasoning, operates in a somewhat similar way to the association of ideas.

10. *Section IV: Hume's Fork*

In Section IV the serious business of the *Enquiry* begins, and Hume presents his most celebrated argument, the sceptical argument

---

[20] In the *Treatise* Hume had used the Copy Principle to dismiss a fair number of supposedly bogus ideas, for example material substance (*T* 1.1.6.1), existence (*T* 1.2.6.2–5), solidity (*T* 1.4.4.12–14), mental substance (*T* 1.4.5.3–4), and the self 'as something simple and individual' (*Appendix*, 11).

concerning what he calls 'reasoning concerning matter of fact', but we shall call 'factual reasoning' for short. First, however, there is a vital preliminary. In the first two paragraphs of Section IV, Hume introduces a distinction of enormous importance, between 'relations of ideas' and 'matters of fact' (a distinction commonly known as 'Hume's Fork'). Relations of ideas, as the name implies, can be known a priori, simply by inspecting the nature and internal relations between our ideas, and using either immediate 'intuition' (e.g. our direct intellectual grasp that one plus one equals two, or that a square has four sides) or 'demonstration' (i.e. a sequence of 'intuitive' steps, as for example in the proof of Pythagoras' Theorem). Such truths can therefore be known with complete certainty.

Matters of fact, by contrast, can be known only a posteriori (i.e. by consulting past experience), since they do not concern just the internal relations between our ideas, but rather how those ideas go together in the actual world (e.g. it is a matter of fact whether the idea of gold coexists 'externally' with the idea of a mountain, i.e. whether there is in fact a golden mountain). For this reason there is no internal contradiction in supposing any matter of fact to be otherwise—its falsehood is distinctly *conceivable*—and it follows that no matter of fact can be demonstrated a priori to be true. Thus no matter of fact is intuitively or demonstratively certain.

Here are some relatively straightforward examples of the two sides of Hume's distinction:

Relations of Ideas	Pythagoras' Theorem (E 4.1)
	$3 \times 5 = \frac{1}{2} \times 30$ (E 4.1)
	All bachelors are unmarried
	A metre contains 100 centimetres
Matters of Fact	The sun will rise tomorrow (E 4.2)
	The sun will not rise tomorrow (E 4.2)
	Stones fall when released in air
	Impact causes a billiard ball to move

Note that although relations of ideas are a priori, and in *this* sense prior to experience, it does not follow that the ideas they involve are 'innate' and in *that* sense prior to experience. On Hume's principles the idea of a bachelor, like all other ideas, is derived from experience (e.g. a baby wouldn't have the idea): the point is that *having acquired that idea* I can then know for certain, without any empirical investigation, that all bachelors are unmarried. What makes a truth a priori is that it can be *justified* without appeal to experience, purely by thinking about the ideas involved. Matters of fact, by contrast, can be known to be true (or to be false) only by consulting experience.

Demonstrative and Factual Reasoning

A little later in Section IV, Hume draws a related distinction between types of *reasoning*, though he does not spend long explaining it, perhaps because it was already very familiar from the work of John Locke:

All reasonings may be divided into two kinds, namely demonstrative reasoning, or that concerning relations of ideas, and moral reasoning, or that concerning matter of fact and existence. (*E* 4.18)

Demonstrative reasoning is what can be loosely called 'deductive' reasoning,[21] in which the steps of the argument proceed with absolute certainty based on the logical relations between the ideas concerned (e.g. the kind of argument used in mathematics, such as the proof of Pythagoras' Theorem). *Factual* reasoning—which Hume also calls 'moral' and Locke had called 'probable'—is now commonly called 'inductive' inference, encompassing all sorts of everyday reasoning in which we draw apparently reasonable (but less than logically certain) conclusions based on our personal experience, testimony, our understanding of how people and things behave, and so forth.[22]

11. *Sections IV and V: The Basis of Factual Reasoning*

Hume's Fork raises the question of how we can know 'matters of fact' that go beyond our immediate experience of sensation and memory (*E* 4.3). It is in response to this enquiry that Hume develops his

---

[21] Taking 'deductive' here in an *informal* sense, rather than the stricter alternative modern notion which limits it to reasoning within a formal system.

[22] In this very general sense 'induction' is not confined—as the term's Aristotelian origins would suggest—to inferences that move from particular observations (e.g. of many *A*s that are *B*s) to a universal conclusion (e.g. that *all A*s are *B*s); indeed Hume's own examples are usually of particular inferences (e.g. that all observed *A*s have been *B*s, therefore *this A* is *B*). The term is not used by Hume himself in either sense.

argument concerning induction, probably the most famous argument in English language philosophy.

The Sceptical Argument Concerning Induction

Suppose I see one loose billiard ball collide with another. I will naturally expect the second ball to move, but how can I know—or even have any ground for reasonable belief—that it will do so? Hume starts by pointing out that any such belief about the unobserved appears to be based on *causation*: I predict that the second ball will move on the basis of a belief that the collision will *cause* it to do so. Where, then, do such causal beliefs come from? Apparently only from experience, because they cannot be known a priori, a point on which Hume expands at length (*E* 4.6–11). But to learn anything from experience, we must clearly be able to extrapolate beyond it: to draw factual or inductive inferences from what we *have* observed, to what we have *not* (as when we infer that hitherto unobserved billiard balls will behave in the same sorts of ways as those we have experienced, and that the operative causal laws will remain consistent). It follows that all our beliefs about unobserved matters of fact are based on a general principle or supposition of uniformity, *that the future will resemble, or be conformable to, the past* (*E* 4.19, 4.21), and they can be warranted only if this is rationally well founded. The challenge is to identify any such rational foundation:

if you insist, that the inference [from observed to unobserved] is made by a chain of reasoning, I desire you to produce that reasoning. (*E* 4.16)

Hume therefore turns to examine all the potential sources of rational justification for this principle of uniformity. A passage from *A Letter from a Gentleman to his Friend in Edinburgh* (1745), written at about the same time as the *Enquiry*, helps to explain his procedure in what follows:

It is common for Philosophers to distinguish the Kinds of Evidence into *intuitive*, *demonstrative*, *sensible* [i.e. sensory], and *moral* [i.e. inductive]; (*L* 22)

Hume accordingly points out that his uniformity principle cannot be based on rational 'intuition', nor on 'demonstrative argument' from our experience, because we can easily conceive of the future's turning out differently (*E* 4.18). Nor can it be founded on anything that we learn by sensory experience, since this tells us nothing about objects' underlying powers—we learn what powers things have only through practical experience of their effects, not by any perception of their nature (*E* 4.16, 4.21). All this leaves only 'moral' (factual or inductive) argument from experience, but even if experience might reliably tell us what powers objects have had in the past, it cannot justify any inference *beyond* that past experience, except by taking for granted the principle that we are trying to establish, which would be viciously circular (*E* 4.19). Having thus ruled out intuition, demonstration, sensation, and factual inference, the upshot is that *none* of these conventionally accepted sources of evidence can provide any foundation for the principle of uniformity. Hence, Hume concludes, 'it is not reasoning which engages us to suppose the past resembling the future, and to expect similar effects from causes, which are, to appearance, similar' (*E* 4.23). It seems, then, that we can give no solid rational basis whatever for our only method of establishing matters of fact 'beyond the present testimony of our senses, or the records of our memory', and this result is Hume's famous scepticism about induction.

Custom and Belief

Section V of the *Enquiry* starts with a paragraph commending philosophical scepticism, strongly contrasting with the typical view of the time which saw the sceptic as a dangerous enemy of religion and morality.[23] In opposition to this view, Hume goes on to stress that theoretical sceptical doubts, even if founded on impeccable philosophical argument, cannot in practice undermine our natural human tendency to draw inferences and form beliefs:

Though we should conclude . . . as in the foregoing section, that, in all reasonings from experience, there is a step taken by the mind, which is not supported by any argument or process of the understanding; there is no danger, that these reasonings, on which almost all knowledge depends, will ever be affected by such a discovery. If the mind be not engaged by argument to make this step, it must be induced by some other principle of equal weight and authority (*E* 5.2)

---

[23] Hume's *Letter from a Gentleman*, quoted in the previous paragraph, was written to defend himself against a vitriolic pamphlet which had accused him of 'Universal Scepticism . . . downright Atheism . . . denying the Immateriality of the Soul . . . sapping the Foundations of Morality' (*L* 17–18).

Hume calls this principle of factual inference *custom* or *habit*, emphasizing its vital role as 'the great guide of human life', without which
'we should be entirely ignorant of every matter of fact, beyond what
is immediately present to the memory and senses' (*E* 5.6). Custom
provides an answer to the sceptical doubts that Hume has raised not
by addressing them, but by ignoring them. It irresistibly leads us to
make inferences from observed to unobserved immediately, instinc-
tively, and without reflection, but since these inferences are not
founded on reason, they are also immune to scepticism about reason
(*E* 5.8). All this might seem to make Hume an irrationalist, committed to denying any criteria for reasonable belief and to accepting the
equal legitimacy of any inference that seems natural. But as we shall
see later, this is very far from being the case.

Part ii of Section V discusses the nature of belief, though Hume
indicates that this discussion is not central to his views, and 'may . . .
be neglected' without great loss (*E* 5.9). Whereas Part i seems to be
an exercise in what Section I called 'mental geography', identifying
custom as one of the central 'powers and faculties' of the human
mind (*E* 1.14), Part ii seems to provide a cautious sketch of the kind
of deeper study of 'secret springs and principles' (*E* 1.15) that Hume
had also anticipated, speculating about the underlying basis of
custom's operation. The main conclusion of this study is simply that
custom is somewhat analogous to the association of ideas explained in
Section III (*E* 5.20). It therefore provides an illustration of how the
science of the human mind can proceed, aiming 'to reduce the principles' that govern it 'to a greater simplicity, and to resolve the many
particular effects into a few general causes, by means of reasonings
from analogy, experience, and observation' (*E* 4.12). Hume has already
argued that this sort of systematization is 'the utmost effort of human
reason', and is the most that science can aspire to, given the impossibility of achieving a priori insight into why things operate as they do.
Section V Part ii thus provides a brief illustration of Hume's general
philosophy of science, applied to the study of the human mind.

12. *Section VI: 'Of Probability'*

As we saw earlier in Section IV, Hume took over from Locke (*Essay*,
IV. xv. 1) a general distinction between *demonstrative* and *probable* reasoning, though he generally prefers to call the latter 'moral reasoning',

or 'reasoning concerning matter of fact and existence'. On Locke's account, no reasoning from past to future can be more than 'probable', even if it is based on extensive and totally uniform experience (as for example when I predict that an unsupported stone, when released above the ground, will fall). Hume begins Section VI with an important footnote in which he suggests a refinement of Locke's terminology, coining the term 'proof' for these most strongly grounded experiential inferences, and reserving the word 'probability' for inferences in which past experience is less than uniform. Here he is not, of course, retracting anything in his previous argument: what he now calls 'proofs' are still based on instinct rather than on rational insight, but he is pointing out that it seems unnatural to call a conclusion such as *that all men will die* merely 'probable', since our entirely uniform experience in its favour is psychologically entirely compelling, leaving 'no room for doubt'.

Section VI aims to provide a brief explanation of 'probability' in Hume's new narrower sense, showing how the mechanism of causal inference discovered in Section V can be extended to account for our tendency to form beliefs of different degrees of conviction in proportion to mixed evidence. Such an account advances his proposed science of mind, by 'resolving' another form of reasoning into an already identified 'general cause' (cf. *E* 4.12), namely *custom*. Custom typically leads our minds to make associative links whose strength is in proportion to the balance of evidence, and this can explain both the 'probability of chances' (e.g. predicting the falls of a six-sided die) and the 'probability of causes' (e.g. predicting that the next *A* will be a *B* on the grounds that most, but not all, past *A*s have been *B*s, though the underlying causes are unknown).

Hume will later apply this account to the case of miracles in Section X, where it turns out that he intends it to be not only explanatory of how we *do* reason, but also *normative*: prescribing how we *should* reason. His basis for this is not made entirely explicit, but the underlying motive seems to be the *legitimation* of probabilistic reasoning, conferring it with authority and respectability, by showing it to be derivative from a principle which plays such an essential and irresistible role in our mental life. From now on, one of Hume's main aims in the *Enquiry*—and arguably his primary aim—will be to spell out the implications of systematically taking custom, and custom alone, as our touchstone of empirical rationality.

13. *Section VII: 'Of the Idea of Necessary Connexion'*

Hume starts Section VII by emphasizing the importance of clarifying our philosophical ideas, focusing particularly on 'those of *power*,
force, *energy*, or *necessary connexion*' (*E* 7.3) which are so intimately
connected with the vital concept of *causation*, itself the basis of all reasoning from experience (as we saw in Section IV). Hume's method of
clarifying obscure ideas is to make use of the 'new microscope or
species of optics' (*E* 7.4) which the Copy Principle of Section II
provides, by inspecting the impression(s) from which those ideas
are derived. Thus begins the hunt for the impression of necessary
connexion.[24]

PART I: A Fruitless Search

Hume begins with his favourite example of the two billiard balls. We
see one billiard ball striking another, see the second one move, no
doubt hear a sound; but what we do not perceive in any way through
the senses is the *necessity* that we assume connects the two events
together (in that the one event *had to be* followed by the other). All
we see is a sequence of events—we do not see the causal glue that
(we assume) binds them, or the *power* in the one ball's movement by
which it communicates motion to the other.

Hume proceeds to back up this claim with an important argument,
several variations on which will be used in the pages to come:

> From the first appearance of an object, we never can conjecture what effect
> will result from it. But were the power or energy of any cause discoverable
> by the mind, we could foresee the effect, even without experience; and
> might, at first, pronounce with certainty concerning it, by the mere dint of
> thought and reasoning. (*E* 7.7)

This builds on the sceptical argument of Section IV Part i, which
established that all causal knowledge is a posteriori, that nothing
about causes and effects can be known in advance of experience.

---

[24] Hume consistently treats 'power' and 'necessary connexion' as equivalent, sometimes abbreviates the latter to just 'connexion' (*E* 7.28), and also equates these with other
terms such as 'force' and 'energy'. This suggests that the key idea whose source he is
seeking is not strictly that of *necessary* connexion, but rather the wider notion of *connexion*
in general, or a *consequential* link from one thing to another. This also fits with his view,
implied by Section VI, that the notion of probability is derived from the same source.

If we perceived an impression of necessary connexion between *A* and *B*, he reasons, *then* we could know a priori that *A* causes *B*. But we cannot know a priori that *A* causes *B*. So it follows that we perceive no such impression of their necessary connexion.

Having ruled out any sensory source for the impression of necessary connexion, Hume moves on to consider the possibility that it might instead be an impression of reflection acquired from our awareness of the mind's powers, or consciousness of the actions of our will (*E* 7.9–20). But he denies that this can be so, using the same style of argument. He examines the operation of our will first in moving our body (*E* 7.10–15), and then in forming and processing ideas (*E* 7.16–20), emphasizing how both types of power can be known only by experience.

Hume then takes time off from his search for the impression of necessity, to mount a vigorous attack upon Malebranche's doctrine of *occasionalism* (explained in §6, above). Malebranche had used arguments somewhat similar to Hume's, to maintain that we have no idea of power in objects, and he concluded that only God can exert genuine power. Hume starts his critique by mischievously suggesting that occasionalism has superstitious origins (*E* 7.21). He then dismisses it with two characteristic objections (*E* 7.24–5), first, that it is too bold and bizarre to be credible (cf. *E* 12.25), and secondly, that it is inconsistent, since the same reasoning that the occasionalists use to show that power in objects is inconceivable shows equally that power in minds, even in a divine mind, is also inconceivable.

Although Hume's hunt for the elusive impression of necessary connexion has so far been in vain, his arguments of Section VII Part i have succeeded in other ways. He has attacked the foundation of Cartesian science, based as it is on the ideal of clear and distinct perception of nature's workings, by denying outright that any causal interactions at all—even those of God—are in any way 'intelligible'. We cannot 'understand' how billiard balls communicate motion by impulse, nor how the mind has command over the body, nor even how any mind, whether human or divine, has command over itself. And the fact that we cannot understand these operations proves that we cannot perceive the necessity which supposedly governs them. All are equally unintelligible, equally opaque to 'clear and distinct' perception.

PART II: Cause Successfully Defined

The first paragraph of Part ii provides a useful summary of Part i, pointing towards the sceptical conclusion that the idea of necessary connexion is entirely bogus and the term meaningless. But Hume then suggests an alternative which proves to be more fruitful. Perhaps the impression of necessary connexion is not one that we perceive in *particular* instances of causal interactions (whether these be external or internal, physical or mental), but is instead an impression that arises *from repetition* when it leads us, through the operation of custom, to make causal inferences:

> This connexion, therefore, which we *feel* in the mind, this customary transition of the imagination from one object to its usual attendant, is the sentiment or impression, from which we form the idea of power or necessary connexion. (*E* 7.28)

Thus the idea of necessary connexion is derived from our own awareness of making causal inferences. Having seen *A* and *B* constantly conjoined in the past, when we see an *A*, we just find ourselves expecting a *B*, and we are aware of having made this transition of thought or inference. It is the inference itself that then gives content to our idea of connexion, 'that inference of the understanding, which is the only connexion, that we can have any comprehension of' (*E* 8.25). When we say that *A* is the cause of *B*, we naturally think of this causal link—this supposed necessary connexion—as the basis of our inference from *A* to *B*. But the central core of Hume's message is that *this is the wrong way round*: it is our tendency to infer *B* from *A* that gives content to the causal claim, and so, as he put it in the *Treatise*, 'the necessary connexion depends on the inference, instead of the inference's depending on the necessary connexion' (*T* 1.3.6.3).

The idea of necessary connexion has now been vindicated as a bona fide idea, but shown to be copied from something internal, which Hume—in line with his Copy Principle—calls an 'impression', but which would perhaps be more accurately described as a reflexive awareness of our own inferential behaviour. It seems to follow that we have no real idea of any sort of 'power' or 'necessity' that might be supposed to reside in objects, leading Hume to his famous—indeed notorious—subjectivist conclusion about necessity and hence causation:

> When we say, therefore, that one object is connected with another, we mean only, that they have acquired a connexion in our thought (*E* 7.28)

The necessity of any action, whether of matter or of mind, is not, properly speaking, a quality in the agent, but in any thinking or intelligent being, who may consider the action. (*E* 8.22 endnote [F])

Some recent interpreters have cast doubt on the extent to which passages such as these reflect a genuine subjectivism on Hume's part.[25] But in terms of its influence on epistemology, metaphysics, and the philosophy of science, this 'anti-realism' about causation, along with his inductive scepticism, constitutes his most prominent legacy.

Having finally tracked down the impression of necessary connexion, Hume sets about clarifying the notion of 'cause', of which necessary connexion is the central component. He gives two 'definitions of *cause*', also adding a gloss on the first of them:

[1] *an object, followed by another,*[26] *and where all the objects, similar to the first, are followed by objects similar to the second.*

Or in other words

[1′] *where, if the first object had not been, the second never had existed.*[27]

[2] *an object followed by another, and whose appearance always conveys the thought to that other.* (*E* 7.29)

Since Hume has already argued that the idea of necessity cannot literally be *defined* in the sense of a conceptual analysis or dictionary definition (i.e. through 'enumeration of those parts . . . that compose' the idea, *E* 7.4), his two definitions must be understood as doing something rather different. They seem to be intended to capture the circumstances under which we come to ascribe causal connexion, with the first definition focusing on the kind of observation that leads someone to believe in such a connexion (namely, the observation of what appears to that person to be a constant conjunction), while the second definition focuses instead on what the student of human

[25] The main contributions to this ongoing debate are most easily accessible in Rupert Read and Kenneth A. Richman (eds.), *The New Hume Debate* (Routledge, 2nd edn., 2007), to which I have also contributed an essay.

[26] In the *Treatise* (*T* 1.3.14.31), Hume had insisted that a cause must be contiguous with its effect as well as temporally prior, but he dropped this condition from the *Enquiry* (cf. p. 207), presumably to allow for the possibility of gravitational action at a distance, or perhaps causation between mental events that have no spatial location.

[27] This gloss cannot possibly be equivalent to (1) even if it is interpreted as a straightforward past tense conditional, meaning 'where, if the first object *was not*, the second *was not* either'. Definition (1) states that the first object has never appeared without the second, which implies that if the *second* object was not, the *first* was not either. So Hume's gloss is puzzling, seeming to get things the wrong way round.

nature will observe in the believer once the causal belief has taken hold, and which gives that belief its characteristic content (namely, the operation of a certain type of associative mechanism). Hume acknowledges that his definitions fall short of what might be wished for: neither of them identifies anything about the specific cause in itself that connects it with its effect, for it is only in virtue of the *pattern of events*— the conjunction in other instances, or the consequent tendency to draw inferences—that the causal link can be ascribed. We are naturally inclined to want more, to try to grasp 'that circumstance in the cause, which gives it a connexion with its effect'. But on Hume's subjectivist principles, even this wish is incoherent: 'We have no idea of this connexion; nor even any distinct notion what it is we desire to know, when we endeavour at a conception of it' (*E* 7.29). So Hume's two definitions capture everything that we can coherently mean in ascribing causal connexions. Though we hanker after a deeper and more substantial conception of causation, some notion of the supposed causal glue that binds events together, we cannot achieve this, nor even any coherent understanding of what it is that we thus seek! This does not, however, undermine the notion of 'cause'; rather, it shows that the notion is to be ascribed purely on the basis of Hume's two definitions (cf. *T* 1.4.5.32).

14. *Section VIII: 'Of Liberty and Necessity'*

In Section VIII Hume pursues 'a reconciling project' (*E* 8.23), presenting a *compatibilist* solution to the ancient problem of free will and determinism. As briefly discussed in §4, above, he follows Hobbes in claiming that *the doctrine of necessity*—i.e. universal determinism— is compatible with *the doctrine of liberty*—i.e. the claim that some of our actions are *free* and therefore morally accountable. Hobbes had based his compatibilism on a definition of 'freedom' as being *able to do what one wills without hindrance*, and Hume's definition of 'liberty' is in the same spirit:

By liberty, then, we can only mean *a power of acting or not acting, according to the determinations of the will*; that is, if we chuse to remain at rest, we may; if we chuse to move, we also may. (*E* 8.23)

Liberty so defined is obviously compatible with determinism: if our actions follow our will, then we do have such liberty, even if our will itself is entirely causally determined. Hobbes had maintained that our will is indeed thus determined, and Hume agrees, but his distinctive contribution to the debate is to provide a new argument for this claim, appealing to the understanding of 'necessity' reached in Section VII:

Our idea . . . of necessity and causation arises entirely from the uniformity, observable in the operations of nature; where similar objects are constantly conjoined together, and the mind is determined by custom to infer the one from the appearance of the other. . . . Beyond the constant *conjunction* of similar objects, and the consequent *inference* from one to the other, we have no notion of any necessity, or connexion. (*E* 8.5)

Most of Part i of Section VIII is devoted to making the case that human actions manifest such uniformity, that they are generally recognized as doing so, and that people standardly perform inductive inferences accordingly. Hence 'all mankind . . . have . . . acknowledged the doctrine of necessity, in their whole practice and reasoning', even while 'profess[ing] the contrary opinion' (*E* 8.21). Hume attributes this mismatch to men's 'propensity to believe, that they penetrate farther into the powers of nature, and perceive something like a necessary connexion between the cause and the effect'. Such penetration is, of course, an illusion (as shown in Sections IV and VII), and it is this recognition that provides the key to properly understanding the necessity of human actions. In learning that the necessity of *physical* operations amounts to no more than constant conjunction and consequent inference, we come to see that *human* actions too are subject to the same necessity.

While making this case, Hume in passing develops his view of inductive science, as sketched earlier in Section IV (*E* 4.12). We should look for causal relations that are entirely constant (*E* 8.13), seeking for deeper laws that underlie superficial irregularities. And we should do this not only in natural philosophy but in the human realm also, with equal expectation of success.

In Part ii of Section VIII, Hume turns to address the consequences of his determinist world-view for morality and religion. He starts (*E* 8.27) by re-emphasizing that his most distinctive contribution is to undermine the supposed metaphysical necessity of the *physical* world, rather than to propose any novel understanding of human action. He then goes on to argue for another distinctive claim (*E* 8.28–30): that viewing human behaviour as causally determined, so far from being contrary to morality, is actually essential to it, since blame and punishment are appropriate only where actions are caused by the agent's durable character and disposition. This argument, however, even if accepted, does little to resolve the widely felt tension between determinism and moral responsibility: if everything that I do was 'pre-ordained' before I was even born, then how can I be *genuinely* responsible? It might now seem that the notion of moral responsibility has turned out to be incoherent, both requiring and yet being incompatible with determinism. Hume sketches his solution to this conundrum when discussing the religious implications of his views (*E* 8.34–5), a solution based on his moral theory which is *sentimentalist* (i.e. based on the emotions or passions) rather than *rationalist*:

A man, who is robbed of a considerable sum; does he find his vexation for the loss any wise diminished by these sublime reflections? Why then should his moral resentment against the crime be supposed incompatible with them? (*E* 8.35)

If morality is founded on emotions of blame (etc.) that naturally arise within us in certain circumstances—for example when a crime is committed—then we should not expect that these emotions will disappear, just because we reflect on the inexorable chain of causation which led to the criminal's action. Here Hume does little more than drop this hint; the full development of his sentimentalist moral theory comes in the companion work, his *Enquiry concerning the Principles of Morals*.

15. *Section IX: 'Of the Reason of Animals'*

In the wake of the Darwinian revolution, it is no surprise that there should be similarities between animal and human thinking, but in the eighteenth century the suggestion was potentially quite shocking.[28] Human reason was commonly thought to be quasi-divine or angelic rather than beastlike, a faculty expressing the essence of our unique immaterial soul, capable of providing transparent insight into the nature of things and operating quite independently of brute animal

---

[28] Darwin's notebooks of 1838–9 record that he read Hume's section on the reason of animals just at the time that he was developing his theory of evolution.

instincts. Perhaps for this reason Hume's discussion is quite short, and steers clear of the dangerous implications made explicit in his essay 'Of the Immortality of the Soul' (included in this volume as Appendix II).

The main point Hume emphasizes here is a corollary of his inductive approach to science: since all our factual reasonings are founded on an assumption of uniformity or resemblance, their strength can be expected to depend on the *degree* of resemblance involved. Though Hume illustrates this point by the analogy between humans and animals—appealing to the instinctive nature of animal reasoning to corroborate his claim (from Sections IV and V) that human reasoning is instinctive also—his methodological message is more general. This is, that reasoning from analogy is a natural extension of inference based on custom, just as probabilistic reasoning was shown to be in Section VI.

16. *Section X: 'Of Miracles'*

Though mainly concerned with miracles, Section X has a far wider significance, because here we see how Hume's theory of induction based on custom has a critical edge, helping us to weigh up conflicting evidence appropriately, particularly in the case of evidence from testimony. Hume starts (*E* 10.3–4) by recalling his account of probability from Section VI, making its normative implications very explicit:

> A wise man, therefore, proportions his belief to the evidence. . . . All probability, then, supposes an opposition of experiments and observations, where the one side is found to overbalance the other, and to produce a degree of evidence, proportioned to the superiority. (*E* 10.4)

He goes on to argue that this general principle should be applied equally in the case of testimony, hence the credit that we give to reports of witnesses should be proportioned to their experienced reliability. However experience indicates that the reliability of witnesses varies, depending on a number of factors such as 'the opposition of contrary testimony; . . . the character or number of the witnesses; . . . the manner of their delivering their testimony; or . . . the union of all these circumstances' (*E* 10.7). These are all factors that we naturally—and rightly—take into account when assessing the overall credibility of testimony, which will depend in each case on the balance between the positive and negative factors involved.

Hume's main point in Part i of Section X is that there is another factor to put into this balancing operation, which does not depend on the nature of the *witnesses*, but rather, on the nature of the *reported event*. If this supposed event is quite contrary to our uniform experience or even apparently miraculous, then that experience itself provides strong inductive evidence against the event's occurrence.[29] Hence in assessing the overall credibility of the testimony, we must balance whatever experience we might have in favour of the reliability of the witnesses, against this contrary evidence:

The plain consequence is (and it is a general maxim worthy of our attention), 'That no testimony is sufficient to establish a miracle, unless the testimony be of such a kind, that its falsehood would be more miraculous, than the fact, which it endeavours to establish: And even in that case, there is a mutual destruction of arguments, and the superior only gives us an assurance suitable to that degree of force, which remains, after deducting the inferior.' (*E* 10.13)

Hume can here be seen as anticipating a result that is now very familiar to theoreticians, but all too often ignored more widely: that when assessing the evidence for some event, it is important to take into account the *background probability* of the event itself.[30]

Hume's 'general maxim' sets a demanding requirement for testimony to establish a miracle. Then in Part ii, he gives four arguments to suggest that this requirement is, in practice, never likely to be satisfied, especially in the case of miracles associated with a religion. First, no miracle in history has in fact been sufficiently well attested by sufficiently many reliable witnesses (*E* 10.15). Secondly, the pleasant passion of surprise and wonder makes miracle stories particularly

---

[29] As we saw above in Section VI, Hume coins the term 'proof' for this strongest type of inductive argument, based on totally uniform experience. However, such proofs are not necessarily irresistible, and his discussion of miracles makes very clear that they can differ in strength and potentially conflict (see also his letter at p. 165, below).

[30] Suppose, for example, that I am worried about a genetic disease that afflicts one in a million people, and take a test for it which has a 99.9% chance of giving the 'correct' result (i.e. if I have the disease, it is 99.9% likely to come out positive, and if I don't, it is only 0.1% likely to come out positive). Most people would naturally take a positive result as showing that I very probably have the disease. However the one in a million 'background probability' outweighs the one in a thousand chance of the test's getting it wrong, leaving an overall probability that I have the disease, based on this evidence, of only 1 in 1,002. Thus a false test is far more likely than the disease itself.

prone to invention and fantasy, all the more so if they are propagated to promote religion (*E* 10.16–19). As the history of forged miracles amply demonstrates, a religious person may lie 'for the sake of promoting so holy a cause', or out of vanity, or he may be gullible or swayed by eloquence (since many renounce their reason in questions of religion). Thirdly, miracle stories almost all 'abound amongst ignorant and barbarous nations', suggesting that they are indeed products of imagination rather than provable fact (*E* 10.20–3). Finally, if a miracle is supposed to establish the religion (or sect) to which it is attributed, and since the various religions are incompatible, it follows that the evidence for any miracle will be opposed by the evidence in favour of the far greater number of miracles reported in other religions. Hume illustrates this point (*E* 10.25–7) with some apparently well-evidenced miracles that he is confident his readers will reject, thus suggesting that the dismissive attitude they naturally feel towards miracles associated with the Roman emperor Vespasian (for example) should equally be extended to the Christian miracles they are inclined to accept.

Putting all these points together, 'Upon the whole . . . it appears, that no testimony for any kind of miracle has ever amounted to a probability, much less to a proof'. Moreover because of the distinctive tendency of religions to propagate bogus miracle stories and to generate fanciful testimony for them, 'no human testimony can have such force as to prove a miracle, and make it a just foundation for any [popular] system of religion' (*E* 10.35). Outside a religious context, there *could* conceivably be sufficient evidence for some kinds of miracles (though perhaps not for a resurrection—*E* 10.37), but if a miracle 'be ascribed to any new system of religion, . . . this very circumstance would be a full proof of a cheat' (*E* 10.38). 'Proof' here does not imply that religious miracles are logically impossible (cf. n. 29, above); it is simply that our extensive experience of the hopeless unreliability of religiously inspired miracle stories counts decisively against their credibility. An omnipotent deity *could*, of course, bring about whatever the stories report. But even if God exists, experience remains our only guide to His ways of working, and hence in assessing the stories we are still reduced to comparing the reliability of testimony with the reliability of the apparent laws of nature (*E* 10.38). Even for the theist, custom and induction provide the only route to factual discovery.

17. Section XI: 'Of a Particular Providence, and of a Future State'

Most of the argument of Section XI is put in the mouth of 'a friend who loves sceptical paradoxes', and placed in a classical context, to enable Hume to distance himself from his controversial critique of the Design Argument for a Christian God, which when he wrote was the most respected weapon in the theist's arsenal (cf. §5, above). Hume's main point against that argument is that it can never prove the existence of a being with more impressive qualities (e.g. power, wisdom, or goodness) than are actually manifested in the world. So we can never argue first from the world to God, and then back from the nature of that inferred God to draw *new* conclusions about the world—for example that there is an afterlife in which the good will be rewarded and the evil punished.

Just as in Section X, therefore, Hume is working out the implications of basing our knowledge of the world on induction. 'Experimental theists' claim to provide a solid rational foundation for their belief in God, based not on speculative metaphysics, nor on special divine revelation, but on the relatively down-to-earth methods of inductive science, reasonably 'drawing inferences from effects to causes'.[31] Hume counters that

they have aided the ascent of reason by the wings of imagination; otherwise they could not thus change their manner of inference, and argue from causes to effects; presuming, that a more perfect production than the present world would be more suitable to such perfect beings as the gods, and forgetting that they have no reason to ascribe to these celestial beings any perfection or any attribute, but what can be found in the present world. (*E* 11.16)

Again Hume attacks a theistic argument, and in doing so uses—and highlights—principles that are of far broader application. As well as this principle of *proportionality*, that we should proportion hypothesized causes to their observed effects, Section XI also re-emphasizes the principle of *analogy* from Section IX, that an inductive argument's strength varies with the degree of similarity between the objects involved, so that any inference from human purposes to those

---

[31] In the excerpt from Hume's *Dialogues* (see Appendix III), Cleanthes expresses this preference very clearly. It is instructive to read Section XI of the *Enquiry* alongside both the *Dialogues* and the essay 'Of the Immortality of the Soul' (see Appendix II).

of a god is bound to be weak (*E* 11.25–7). Hume also hints at two other general principles, that it is problematic to draw conclusions about any supposed cause that is known only through a single manifestation (*E* 11.25–6), and—even more so—any supposed cause of a unique type (*E* 11.30).

18. Section XII: 'Of the Academical or Sceptical Philosophy'

In Section XII, Hume discusses a wide array of sceptical arguments, clarifying his own finely balanced attitude to them. While acknowledging many of them to be irrefutable, he nevertheless resists, on practical rather than purely theoretical grounds, being forced by them into 'excessive' scepticism. This approach is typified by his short treatment of *antecedent* scepticism at *E* 12.3–4, where he contrasts the futile and self-defeating extremes of Cartesian doubt with a more moderate caution and modesty that he fully endorses.[32] He then moves on to discuss several varieties of *consequent* scepticism— scepticism arising from specific considerations rather than generalized a priori distrust of our faculties—and these occupy most of Part i and all of Part ii.

Turning first to our sensory belief in the external world, Hume attributes this to a 'blind and powerful instinct of nature' (*E* 12.8), which, however, leads us to identify physical objects with the very images that appear to our minds. This identification raises obvious problems, because the perceptions of the mind are so fleeting (*E* 12.9); hence to maintain our instinctive belief in a durable external world, modern philosophers such as Locke adopt the theory of *representative realism*: postulating physical objects that are distinct from, and causes of, those perceptions. Drawing on his theory of causation, Hume now emphasizes the impossibility of establishing any such theory. If we are only ever directly acquainted with our perceptions, and never with their supposed causes, then no connexion between the two—no 'constant conjunction' (cf. *E* 7.28, 8.5)—can ever be observed. Even worse, an argument derived from Berkeley (*E* 12.15) suggests that the Lockean theory is not only groundless but vacuous or incoherent.

---

[32] Descartes used extreme scepticism as a tool for sweeping away traditional views, and claimed to establish his own first principles as 'clearly and distinctly perceived', supposedly immune even to the most radical doubt.

For Locke's understanding of perception depends on a distinction between *primary* and *secondary* qualities, where the former (e.g. length, movement, solidity) are supposed to be in the objects themselves in a way that resembles our ideas of them, while the latter (e.g. felt hardness, temperature, colour) are not. But Hume agrees with Berkeley that our ideas of primary qualities are entirely dependent on those of secondary qualities; for example we acquire an idea of an extended area by seeing it differently coloured from its surroundings. Hence if we try to imagine an external object as independent of our perceptions, distinct from all mind-dependent qualities, then we are forced to 'bereave matter of all its intelligible qualities, both primary and secondary', and we are left only with 'a certain unknown, inexplicable *something*, as the cause of our perceptions; a notion so imperfect, that no sceptic will think it worth while to contend against it' (*E* 12.16). One important upshot of this discussion is that any attempt to penetrate the essence of physical objects—so popular amongst theological metaphysicians intent on proving matter's inertness (cf. §6, above)—is doomed to failure.

Part ii of Section XII turns to scepticism about our reasoning faculties, starting with some of the notorious paradoxes of infinite divisibility. Hume describes and seems to endorse them, though in a note (*E* 12.20 endnote [P]) he suggests that it may be possible 'to avoid these absurdities and contradictions', by appeal to a non-abstractionist theory of general ideas (as developed more fully in *Treatise* 1.1.7). He then moves on to scepticism about factual reasoning, first dismissing—on practical grounds—an 'excessive' *popular* variant which takes our inconsistent judgements to undermine all inductive reasoning:

The great subverter of *Pyrrhonism* or the excessive principles of scepticism, is action, and employment, and the occupations of common life. These principles may flourish and triumph in the schools; where it is, indeed difficult, if not impossible, to refute them. But as soon as they leave the shade, and by the presence of the real objects, which actuate our passions, and sentiments, are put in opposition to the more powerful principles of our nature, they vanish like smoke (*E* 12.21)

More substantial is a *philosophical* variant of scepticism about induction, Hume's own argument from Section IV in summary form (*E* 12.22). This too can be criticized as excessive if it goes to the Pyrrhonian extreme of attempting to undermine all belief, but fortunately for our survival, human nature is too strong to make such avoidance of belief a genuine possibility. We simply cannot help forming beliefs through custom, as Hume has already explained in Section V, even though we have no rational basis for the assumption of uniformity on which such beliefs are founded.

This appeal to the unavoidability of belief can be used to dismiss total scepticism—i.e. 'undistinguished doubts' (*E* 12.24) about everything—but it need not imply an indiscriminate *acceptance* of whatever we are inclined to believe. Indeed Hume suggests that a sceptical appreciation of the weakness of our faculties, combined with a recognition of the practical inevitability of belief, can lead us to a form of undogmatic *mitigated* scepticism in which our doubts and beliefs are cautiously assessed and 'corrected by common sense and reflection'. It is also natural to combine this caution with a modest restriction of our enquiries to 'such subjects as are best adapted to the narrow capacity of human understanding' (*E* 12.25), given that even in common life, we cannot provide any solid reason for supposing our faculties to be reliable. Empirical science can comfortably be accommodated by this approach, in so far as it is simply a more systematic application of everyday inductive reasoning, that is, 'the reflections of common life, methodized and corrected'. Moreover the earlier sections of the *Enquiry* have already shown what such methodizing and correction involves, and how custom can ground such procedures as the explanation of phenomena by relatively simple and potentially quantifiable laws (*E* 4.12–13, 7.25 endnote [D], 7.29 endnote [E]), the calculation of probabilities by past frequencies (*E* 6.2–4, 10.3–7), the systematic search for hidden causes (*E* 8.13–15), the use of analogy (*E* 9.1, 11.24–6), proportionate inference (*E* 11.12–16), and so on.

The overall shape of this defence of inductive science is most concisely sketched by Philo in Hume's posthumous *Dialogues concerning Natural Religion*. Scepticism may be theoretically irrefutable, but even the sceptic must 'act . . . and live, and converse, like other men', since human nature gives him no choice. Reasonings of common life are thus vindicated, but we may well be driven further by curiosity, in which case our scientific speculations can also share in this vindication if they proceed in the same spirit, as a systematic extension of everyday inductive thinking:

[The sceptic] considers . . . that every one, even in common life, is constrained to have more or less of this philosophy; that from our earliest infancy we make continual advances in forming more general principles of conduct and reasoning; that the larger experience we acquire, and the stronger reason we are endued with, we always render our principles the more general and comprehensive; and that what we call *philosophy* [i.e. natural philosophy or science] is nothing but a more regular and methodical operation of the same kind. To philosophise on such subjects is nothing essentially different from reasoning on common life; and we may only expect greater stability, if not greater truth, from our philosophy, on account of its exacter and more scrupulous method of proceeding. (*D* 134, pp. 154–5 below)

Hume's scepticism thus leaves room for a scientific approach founded on modest inductive systematization, but the sceptical thrust remains in what is *excluded*. All knowledge of matter of fact beyond what we immediately perceive and remember depends on causation (*E* 4.4), while causal laws—whether concerning the operations of matter (*E* 4.6–13, 7.6–8) or mind (*E* 7.9–20)—are discoverable only by experience. 'If we reason *à priori*, any thing may appear able to produce any thing' (*E* 12.29). Hence rational insight into the nature of things is a hopeless fantasy, and it is impossible a priori to prove the existence of God, or indeed of anything else (*E* 12.13, 12.28–9).

Thus a priori demonstration is limited to the abstract realm of ideas, but only in mathematics are our ideas sufficiently precise to make demonstrative argument genuinely fruitful (*E* 12.27). The upshot of all this is to limit the worthwhile fields of investigation to mathematics (which is a priori but concerns only relations of ideas) and inductive empirical science (which concerns matters of fact but is uncertain and empirical). Any work that purports to transcend these limits, by establishing matters of fact with demonstrative certainty—what Immanuel Kant would later call 'synthetic a priori knowledge'—can therefore be roundly condemned, as Hume expresses in his famous concluding paragraph:

When we run over libraries, persuaded of these principles, what havoc must we make? If we take in our hand any volume; of divinity or school metaphysics, for instance; let us ask, *Does it contain any abstract reasoning containing quantity or number?* No. *Does it contain any experimental reasoning concerning matter of fact and existence?* No. Commit it then to the flames: for it can contain nothing but sophistry and illusion. (*E* 12.34)

NOTE ON THE TEXT

WHAT is now known as Hume's first *Enquiry* was originally published in 1748, by Andrew Millar of the Strand, London, under the title *Philosophical Essays concerning Human Understanding*. A second edition appeared in 1750, and this was reprinted in 1751 and 1753, the latter in the form of volume ii of Hume's four-volume *Essays and Treatises on Several Subjects*. This arrangement was retained in the third edition of 1756, at which point volume ii was the only one of the four to be reissued. The next edition of the *Essays and Treatises*, in 1758, combined the constituent works into a single volume, and here Hume permanently changed the title of his *Philosophical Essays* to *An Enquiry concerning Human Understanding*. In the four-volume 1760 and 1770 editions of the *Essays and Treatises*, the *Enquiry* appeared in volume iii with *A Dissertation on the Passions*. In the two-volume editions of 1764, 1767, 1768, 1772, and 1777, it appeared at the beginning of volume ii, followed in order by *A Dissertation on the Passions*, *An Enquiry concerning the Principles of Morals*, and *The Natural History of Religion*.

The Final 1772 and 1777 Editions

Hume took great pains over correcting his texts, and there is no doubt that the last two editions of the *Enquiry* that he prepared, of 1772 and 1777, are the most authoritative. The latter incorporates corrections made shortly before his death in 1776, most notably a substantial deletion from Section III (well-motivated in my view, since the deleted material distracts from, rather than contributing to, the central thrust of the work). What was for many years the standard modern edition, by Selby-Bigge and later Nidditch (Clarendon Press, 3rd edn., 1975), like the previously standard Green and Grose edition, follows the posthumous 1777 text, though with well over a thousand editorial intrusions or errors (mainly of punctuation). Tom Beauchamp's recent Clarendon critical edition (2000) is vastly superior, but he instead takes the 1772 edition as his copytext on the basis that this was 'the last edition to be seen through the press with

Hume's supervision' (and he accordingly includes the deleted Section III material). While not disputing Beauchamp's general editorial principles and practice (which included properly consulting the 1777 text 'for evidence of late authorial changes', p. cv), I have reverted to the traditionally preferred 1777 edition, partly in accordance with Hume's own expressed satisfaction with his final editorial changes (including the Section III deletion), and partly to remedy the lack hitherto of a genuinely reliable published text of that edition. For this reason, the text here very carefully follows the 1777 edition, with minimal editorial intervention except as explained below. My aim, in other words, has been to create not a *critical* edition, but an entirely *accurate* edition, of which no other currently exists except in facsimile (and very expensive) form. Hence in this so-called 'diplomatic' edition, even the inconsistencies in Hume's original, for example in spellings or capitalization (e.g. between the table of contents and the chapter headings) have been preserved, as of potential interest to scholars and readers. Likewise the wording of the running headers has been retained, though here the font style—which in every case followed that of the chapter heading—has been modernized, and the terminating full stops removed. The full stops which originally followed all the headings within the text have also been removed. Only in three cases have substantive changes been made, where typographical corrections were clearly required and could be identified by reference to other editions: these involve the insertion of '[is]' within 3.3 n. 6, '[and]' within endnote [B], and the substitution of 'reasoning' for 'reasonings' in the first line of endnote [H]. My text was prepared from the copy of the 1777 edition in the Brotherton Library at the University of Leeds, and checked also against the facsimile edition published by Thoemmes Press in 2002.

Treatment of Hume's Notes

In Hume's editions, both footnotes and endnotes are indicated by symbols rather than numbers, typically* for the first on each page, then †, ‡ and § as necessary (e.g. in paragraph 3 of Section III). Since Hume's original pagination is almost never referenced by the secondary literature, and these symbols have no other significance, I have replaced them by numbers, so as to correspond with the footnote numbering in Beauchamp's critical edition. This causes one small complication: Beauchamp's note 5 from the 1772 edition is absent from the 1777 text followed here, and hence appears only in the textual variant of Section III: p. 179 below.

Apart from the change of symbolic indicators, Hume's original footnotes remain here in exactly their original form (including the placement of the indicators). The endnote references have, however, been slightly changed to ease navigation. Thus for example the bottom line of page 174 in Hume's 1777 edition was '* See NOTE [Q].', with the endnote itself, on page 486, being headed 'NOTE [Q], p. 174.' In this edition these two lines, on pages 120 and 131 respectively, have been changed to:

^{35} See endnote [Q], p. 131.

Endnote [Q] to 12.29, p. 120^{35}

thus making cross-referring easier, and incorporating the Beauchamp note numbers as superscripts (in this case note 35, the last of the book).

In editions prior to 1770, all notes appeared as footnotes, and Beauchamp's edition follows the same practice (unfortunately without indicating what form each note took in the subsequent editions). That Hume took an interest in such matters is clear from his letters, notably to his printer William Strahan on 8 April 1776:

I am very much taken with Mr Gibbon's Roman History which came from your press . . . I intended to have given him my Advice with regard to the manner of printing it . . . One is . . . plagued with his Notes, according to the present Method of printing the Book: When a note is announced, you turn to the End of the Volume; and there you often find nothing but the Reference to an Authority. All these Authorities ought only to be printed at the Margin on the Bottom of the Page. I desire, that a Copy of my new Edition [i.e. the posthumous edition then in preparation] should be sent to Mr Gibbon, as wishing that a Gentleman, whom I so highly value, shoud peruse me in the form the least imperfect, to which I can bring my work. (*HL* ii. 313)

In another letter to Strahan of 8 June, Hume reports the seriousness of his illness, and makes some last requests concerning the printing of 'My Own Life' in his forthcoming edition, and the future publication of the *Dialogues concerning Natural Religion*. Here again he expresses enthusiasm for the quality of what would become the 1777

edition of the *Essays and Treatises on Several Subjects* (including the
first *Enquiry*), and the 1778 edition of the *History of England*:

I am glad to find, that you have been able to set about this New Edition in
earnest. I have made it extremely correct; at least I believe that, if I were to live
twenty Years longer, I shoud never be able to give it any further
Improvements. (*HL* ii. 322)

Hence the policy followed here, of carefully reproducing that 1777
edition, including its distinction between footnotes and endnotes,
with footnotes being used for references to 'Authorities' and other
relatively short comments, and endnotes generally containing the
longer material. Whether the distinction has any deeper significance
is now open for the reader to judge, but since the footnotes at *E* 5.17
and *E* 7.8 are both longer than one or more of the endnotes, this at
least suggests that length was not Hume's only criterion.

References to Other Editions

The vast majority of the existing secondary literature on Hume refers
to the *Enquiry* using page numbers from the Selby-Bigge and Nidditch
editions (*Enquiries concerning Human Understanding and concerning
the Principles of Morals* (Clarendon Press, 1888, 1902, and 1975)).
Hence page references to the 1975 edition have been indicated throughout this text, using numbers in the outer margin. Beauchamp's recent
Clarendon edition has moved to a different method of reference, using
section and paragraph numbers, which seems likely to become standard and is used here in the editorial material. Accordingly, paragraph
numbers are also provided throughout the text, preceding every
paragraph except the first of each section. Use of both methods of
reference is already standard amongst Hume scholars, and required
by the Hume Society's journal *Hume Studies*. Hence this edition has
been designed to accommodate both.

I should like to take this opportunity to acknowledge the debt that
I and other Hume scholars owe to Tom Beauchamp, for the painstak-
ing work that he put into his excellent critical edition of the *Enquiry*.

SELECT BIBLIOGRAPHY

MY 2002 collection, *Reading Hume on Human Understanding: Essays on the First Enquiry* (OUP) contains a sixty-page 'Critical Survey of the Literature on Hume and the First *Enquiry*' (pp. 413–74), summarizing and discussing around 250 selected books and papers, all organized according to the relevant topics. There is also a Web version of this Critical Survey at *www.davidhume.org* together with other relevant resources. Hence this small bibliography makes no attempt to identify specialist treatments of particular topics from the *Enquiry*.

Hume's Life and the Intellectual Background

Mossner, E. C., *The Life of David Hume* (OUP, 2nd edn. 1980) is the standard biography.

Gribbin, John, *Science: A History* (Penguin, 2002), chs. 1–5 cover the development of science from Copernicus to Newton.

Craig, Edward, *The Mind of God and the Works of Man* (OUP, 1987), chs. 1–2 suggest that Hume's primary aim was to oppose a widespread view of reason as 'the Image of God'.

Books on the Enquiry

Millican, Peter, *Reading Hume on Human Understanding: Essays on the First Enquiry* (OUP, 2002) contains a general overview of the *Enquiry*, followed by papers from noted Hume scholars on each of its main sections. The papers are also summarized in an introduction.

Penelhum, Terence, *David Hume: An Introduction to his Philosophical System* (Purdue University Press, 1992) includes selections from the *Enquiry*, together with helpful commentary.

Buckle, Stephen, *Hume's Enlightenment Tract* (OUP, 2001) is devoted to the *Enquiry*, giving historical background and a significantly different perspective from that presented here.

Flew, Antony, *Hume's Philosophy of Belief* (Routledge & Kegan Paul, 1961) was the first major book on the *Enquiry*—dated and difficult, but still rewarding.

Approachable Discussions of Specific Topics from the Enquiry

Craig, Edward, 'Hume on Thought and Belief', in Godfrey Vesey (ed.), *Philosophers Ancient and Modern* (CUP, 1986), 93–110.

Salmon, Wesley, 'An Encounter with David Hume', in Joel Feinberg (ed.), *Reason and Responsibility* (Dickenson, 3rd edn. 1975), 190–208 (on induction).

Stroud, Barry, *Hume* (Routledge & Kegan Paul, 1977), ch. 4 (on necessary connexion).

Botterill, George, 'Hume on Liberty and Necessity', in Millican (ed.), *Reading Hume*, 277–300.

Gaskin, J. C. A., *Hume's Philosophy of Religion* (Macmillan, 2nd edn. 1988).

Norton, David Fate, 'Of the Academical or Sceptical Philosophy', in Millican (ed.), *Reading Hume*, 371–92.

General Introductory Books on Hume's Epistemology

Dicker, Georges, *Hume's Epistemology and Metaphysics* (Routledge, 1998).

Noonan, Harold W., *Hume on Knowledge* (Routledge, 1999).

Stroud, Barry, *Hume* (Routledge & Kegan Paul, 1977).

Advanced General Books

Bennett, Jonathan, *Learning from Six Philosophers*, vol. ii (OUP, 2001).

Garrett, Don, *Cognition and Commitment in Hume's Philosophy* (OUP, 1997).

Noxon, James, *Hume's Philosophical Development* (OUP, 1973).

Passmore, John, *Hume's Intentions* (Duckworth, 3rd edn. 1980).

Wright, John P., *The Sceptical Realism of David Hume* (Manchester University Press, 1983).

Multi-Authored Collections

Norton, David Fate (ed.), *The Cambridge Companion to Hume* (CUP, 1993).

Owen, David W. D. (ed.), *Hume: General Philosophy* (Ashgate, 2000).

Read, Rupert, and Richman, Kenneth A. (eds), *The New Hume Debate* (Routledge, 2nd edn. 2007).

Stewart M. A and Wright, John P. (eds), *Hume and Hume's Connexions* (Edinburgh University Press, 1994).

Traiger, Saul (ed.), *The Blackwell Guide to Hume's Treatise* (Blackwell, 2006).

Tweyman, Stanley (ed.), *David Hume: Critical Assessments*, 6 vols. (Routledge, 1995).

Further Reading in Oxford World's Classics

Berkeley, George, *Principles of Human Knowledge and Three Dialogues*, ed. Howard Robinson.

Descartes, René, *A Discourse on the Method*, trans. Ian Maclean.

Hobbes, Thomas, *The Elements of Law Natural and Politic*, ed. J. C. A. Gaskin.

—— *Leviathan*, ed. J. C. A. Gaskin.

Hume, David, *Dialogues concerning Natural Religion and The Natural History of Religion*, ed. J. C. A. Gaskin.

—— *Selected Essays*, ed. Stephen Copley and Andrew Edgar.

A CHRONOLOGY OF DAVID HUME

1707   Acts of Union of the Kingdoms of England and Scotland, to create the new Kingdom of Great Britain with a single parliament, under Queen Anne.

1711   Birth of David Hume (originally Home) in Edinburgh on 26 April, after which his boyhood is spent mainly at Ninewells, the family house at Chirnside in the Scottish Borders, near Berwick upon Tweed.

1713   Death of Hume's father, Joseph Home, leaving his young wife Katherine and three children, John, Katherine, and David.

1714   Accession of George I to the British throne establishes the Protestant House of Hanover.

1715   First Scottish Jacobite Rebellion on behalf of James Francis Edward Stuart, the Roman Catholic son of James II commonly known as 'The Old Pretender'.

1723   Hume matriculates at Edinburgh University where he remains until 1725 or 1726 without taking a degree.

1726-33 Studies Law until 1729, then is captivated by 'a new Scene of Thought' and devotes his time to Philosophy.

1734   After a long period of poor health, Hume briefly attempts a career in banking at Bristol. He changes the spelling of his surname from 'Home' to 'Hume', to ensure that the English will pronounce it correctly.

1734-7 Lives in France, for the first year at Rheims and then at La Flèche in Anjou, writing the *Treatise of Human Nature*.

1739-40 *A Treatise of Human Nature* is published anonymously, Books I and II ('Of the Understanding' and 'Of the Passions') in January 1739, Book III ('Of Morals') in November 1740. Meanwhile the *Abstract* appears in March 1740.

1741-2 First edition of *Essays, Moral and Political* is published in two volumes, and is very soon more successful than the neglected *Treatise*.

1745   Hume fails to obtain the Chair of Ethics and Pneumatical Philosophy at Edinburgh University, his candidature damaged by an anonymous pamphlet accusing him of 'Universal Scepticism' and 'Principles leading to downright Atheism', to which he replies in *A Letter from a Gentleman to his Friend in Edinburgh*. He then becomes tutor to the mad Marquess of Annandale for a year, an unhappy experience.

1745   Second Scottish Jacobite Rebellion on behalf of Charles Edward Stuart, 'Bonnie Prince Charlie' or 'The Young Pretender' (son of 'The Old Pretender' of 1715). Observing from London, Hume does not support the Jacobite cause.

1746   Hume joins General St Clair, in the role of Judge Advocate, on a farcical military expedition to Brittany as part of the War of the Austrian Succession.

1748   The first *Enquiry* is published in April, under its original title *Philosophical Essays concerning Human Understanding*. Meanwhile Hume is appointed as secretary to General St Clair on diplomatic missions to Vienna and Turin.

1750   Second edition of the *Philosophical Essays*, with the third edition appearing in 1756.

1751   After two years living back in Edinburgh, Hume publishes *An Enquiry concerning the Principles of Morals*—the second *Enquiry*.

1752   *Political Discourses* published, enjoying much wider success than Hume's philosophical works, and helping to establish the new science of Economics. Meanwhile, he fails to obtain the Chair of Moral Philosophy at Glasgow University.

1752–7 Hume is appointed Keeper of the Advocates' Library, Edinburgh, facilitating work on his *History of England*, whose six volumes are published between 1754 and 1762.

1756   An attempt is made to excommunicate Hume from the Church of Scotland.

1757   Publication of *Four Dissertations*, containing *The Natural History of Religion*, *A Dissertation on the Passions*, 'Of Tragedy', and 'Of the Standard of Taste' (the last of these replaced 'Of Suicide' and 'Of the Immortality of the Soul', which Hume had planned to include but now suppressed for posthumous publication).

1758   *Philosophical Essays* renamed as *An Enquiry concerning Human Understanding*, its fourth edition appearing as part of the *Essays and Treatises on Several Subjects*.

1763–5 Hume is appointed Secretary to Lord Hertford, British Ambassador in Paris, being lionized in the salons and by the French *philosophes*.

1766   Invites Jean-Jacques Rousseau to England, escaping persecution in his native Geneva. But the pathologically suspicious Rousseau accuses Hume of treachery, prompting him to publish an account of the affair to clear his name.

1767–8   Appointed Under-Secretary of State, Northern Department, after which he remains in London before returning to Edinburgh in 1769.

1776   Death of Hume on 25 August, probably from cancer.

1779   *Dialogues concerning Natural Religion* published on the authority of Hume's nephew, David Hume the younger, in accordance with Hume's instructions.

AN ENQUIRY
CONCERNING
HUMAN UNDERSTANDING

ADVERTISEMENT*

M ost of the principles, and reasonings, contained in this volume, were published in a work in three volumes, called *A Treatise of Human Nature*: A work which the Author had projected before he left College, and which he wrote and published not long after. But not finding it successful, he was sensible of his error in going to the press too early, and he cast the whole anew in the following pieces, where some negligences in his former reasoning and more in the expression, are, he hopes, corrected. Yet several writers, who have honoured the Author's Philosophy with answers, have taken care to direct all their batteries against that juvenile work, which the Author never acknowledged,* and have affected to triumph in any advantages, which, they imagined, they had obtained over it: A practice very contrary to all rules of candour and fair-dealing, and a strong instance of those polemical artifices, which a bigotted zeal thinks itself authorised to employ. Henceforth, the Author desires, that the following Pieces* may alone be regarded as containing his philosophical sentiments and principles.

SECTION I

Of the DIFFERENT SPECIES of PHILOSOPHY

MORAL philosophy,* or the science of human nature, may be treated after two different manners;* each of which has its peculiar merit, and may contribute to the entertainment, instruction, and reformation of mankind. The one considers man chiefly as born for action; and as influenced in his measures by taste and sentiment; pursuing one object, and avoiding another, according to the value which these objects seem to possess, and according to the light in which they present themselves. As virtue, of all objects, is allowed to be the most valuable, this species of philosophers paint her in the most amiable colours; borrowing all helps from poetry and eloquence, and treating their subject in an easy and obvious manner, and such as is best fitted to please the imagination, and engage the affections. They select the most striking observations and instances from common life; place opposite characters in a proper contrast; and alluring us into the paths of virtue by the views of glory and happiness, direct our steps in these paths by the soundest precepts and most illustrious examples. 6 They make us *feel* the difference between vice and virtue; they excite and regulate our sentiments; and so they can but bend our hearts to the love of probity and true honour, they think, that they have fully attained the end of all their labours.

[2] The other species of philosophers consider man in the light of a reasonable rather than an active being, and endeavour to form his understanding* more than cultivate his manners. They regard human nature as a subject of speculation; and with a narrow scrutiny examine it, in order to find those principles, which regulate our understanding, excite our sentiments, and make us approve or blame any particular object, action, or behaviour. They think it a reproach to all literature, that philosophy should not yet have fixed, beyond controversy, the foundation of morals, reasoning, and criticism; and should for ever talk of truth and falsehood, vice and virtue, beauty and deformity, without being able to determine the source of these distinctions. While they attempt this arduous task, they are deterred by no difficulties; but proceeding from particular instances to general

principles, they still push on their enquiries to principles more general, and rest not satisfied till they arrive at those original principles,
by which, in every science, all human curiosity must be bounded.
Though their speculations seem abstract, and even unintelligible to
common readers, they aim at the approbation of the learned and the
wise; and think themselves sufficiently compensated for the labour of
their whole lives, if they can discover some hidden truths, which may
contribute to the instruction of posterity.

[3] It is certain that the easy and obvious philosophy will always,
with the generality of mankind, have the preference above the accurate
and abstruse; and by many will be recommended, not only as more
agreeable, but more useful than the other. It enters more into common
life; moulds the heart and affections; and, by touching those principles
which actuate men, reforms their conduct, and brings them nearer to
that model of perfection which it describes. On the contrary, the
abstruse philosophy, being founded on a turn of mind, which cannot
enter into business and action, vanishes when the philosopher leaves
the shade, and comes into open day; nor can its principles easily retain
any influence over our conduct and behaviour. The feelings of our
heart, the agitation of our passions, the vehemence of our affections,
dissipate all its conclusions, and reduce the profound philosopher to a
mere plebeian.*

[4] This also must be confessed, that the most durable, as well as
justest fame, has been acquired by the easy philosophy, and that
abstract reasoners seem hitherto to have enjoyed only a momentary
reputation, from the caprice or ignorance of their own age, but have
not been able to support their renown with more equitable posterity.
It is easy for a profound philosopher to commit a mistake in his subtile reasonings; and one mistake is the necessary parent of another,
while he pushes on his consequences, and is not deterred from embracing any conclusion, by its unusual appearance, or its contradiction to
popular opinion. But a philosopher, who purposes only to represent
the common sense of mankind in more beautiful and more engaging
colours, if by accident he falls into error, goes no farther; but renew-
ing his appeal to common sense, and the natural sentiments of the
mind, returns into the right path, and secures himself from any dangerous illusions. The fame of CICERO flourishes at present; but that
of ARISTOTLE is utterly decayed. LA BRUYERE passes the seas, and
still maintains his reputation: But the glory of MALEBRANCHE

is confined to his own nation, and to his own age. And ADDISON, perhaps, will be read with pleasure, when LOCKE* shall be entirely forgotten.

[5] The mere philosopher is a character, which is commonly but little 8 acceptable in the world, as being supposed to contribute nothing either to the advantage or pleasure of society; while he lives remote from communication with mankind, and is wrapped up in principles and notions equally remote from their comprehension. On the other hand, the mere ignorant is still more despised; nor is any thing deemed a surer sign of an illiberal genius in an age and nation where the sciences flourish, than to be entirely destitute of all relish for those noble entertainments. The most perfect character is supposed to lie between those extremes; retaining an equal ability and taste for books, company, and business; preserving in conversation that discernment and delicacy which arise from polite letters; and in business, that probity and accuracy which are the natural result of a just philosophy. In order to diffuse and cultivate so accomplished a character, nothing can be more useful than compositions of the easy style and manner, which draw not too much from life, require no deep application or retreat to be comprehended, and send back the student among mankind full of noble sentiments and wise precepts, applicable to every exigence of human life. By means of such compositions, virtue becomes amiable, science agreeable, company instructive, and retirement entertaining.

[6] Man is a reasonable being; and as such, receives from science his proper food and nourishment: But so narrow are the bounds of human understanding, that little satisfaction can be hoped for in this particular, either from the extent or security of his acquisitions. Man is a sociable, no less than a reasonable being: But neither can he always enjoy company agreeable and amusing, or preserve the proper relish for them. Man is also an active being; and from that disposition, as well as from the various necessities of human life, must submit to business and occupation: But the mind requires some relaxation, and 9 cannot always support its bent to care and industry. It seems, then, that nature has pointed out a mixed kind of life as most suitable to human race, and secretly admonished them to allow none of these biasses to *draw* too much, so as to incapacitate them for other occupations and entertainments. Indulge your passion for science, says she, but let your science be human, and such as may have a direct reference to action and society. Abstruse thought and profound researches I prohibit, and

will severely punish, by the pensive melancholy which they introduce, by the endless uncertainty in which they involve you, and by the cold reception which your pretended discoveries shall meet with, when communicated.* Be a philosopher; but, amidst all your philosophy, be still a man.*

[7] Were the generality of mankind contented to prefer the easy philosophy to the abstract and profound, without throwing any blame or contempt on the latter, it might not be improper, perhaps, to comply with this general opinion, and allow every man to enjoy, without opposition, his own taste and sentiment. But as the matter is often carried farther, even to the absolute rejecting of all profound reasonings, or what is commonly called *metaphysics*, we shall now proceed to consider what can reasonably be pleaded in their behalf.

[8] We may begin with observing, that one considerable advantage, which results from the accurate and abstract philosophy, is, its subserviency to the easy and humane; which, without the former, can never attain a sufficient degree of exactness in its sentiments, precepts, or reasonings. All polite letters are nothing but pictures* of human life in various attitudes and situations; and inspire us with different sentiments, of praise or blame, admiration or ridicule, according to the qualities of the object, which they set before us. An artist must be better qualified to succeed in this undertaking, who, besides a delicate taste and a quick apprehension, possesses an accurate knowledge of the internal fabric, the operations of the understanding, the workings of the passions, and the various species of sentiment which discriminate vice and virtue. How painful soever this inward search or enquiry may appear, it becomes, in some measure, requisite to those, who would describe with success the obvious and outward appearances of life and manners. The anatomist presents to the eye the most hideous and disagreeable objects; but his science is useful to the painter in delineating even a VENUS or an HELEN.* While the latter employs all the richest colours of his art, and gives his figures the most graceful and engaging airs; he must still carry his attention to the inward structure of the human body, the position of the muscles, the fabric of the bones, and the use and figure of every part or organ. Accuracy is, in every case, advantageous to beauty, and just reasoning to delicate sentiment. In vain would we exalt the one by depreciating the other.

[9] Besides, we may observe, in every art or profession, even those which most concern life or action, that a spirit of accuracy, however

acquired, carries all of them nearer their perfection, and renders them more subservient to the interests of society. And though a philosopher may live remote from business, the genius of philosophy, if carefully cultivated by several, must gradually diffuse itself throughout the whole society, and bestow a similar correctness on every art and calling. The politician will acquire greater foresight and subtility, in the subdividing and balancing of power; the lawyer more method and finer principles in his reasonings; and the general more regularity in his discipline, and more caution in his plans and operations. The stability of modern governments above the ancient, and the accuracy of modern philosophy, have improved, and probably will still improve, by similar gradations.

[10] Were there no advantage to be reaped from these studies, 11 beyond the gratification of an innocent curiosity, yet ought not even this to be despised; as being one accession to those few safe and harmless pleasures, which are bestowed on human race. The sweetest and most inoffensive path of life leads through the avenues of science and learning; and whoever can either remove any obstructions in this way, or open up any new prospect, ought so far to be esteemed a benefactor to mankind. And though these researches may appear painful and fatiguing, it is with some minds as with some bodies, which being endowed with vigorous and florid health, require severe exercise, and reap a pleasure from what, to the generality of mankind, may seem burdensome and laborious. Obscurity, indeed, is painful to the mind as well as to the eye; but to bring light from obscurity, by whatever labour, must needs be delightful and rejoicing.

[11] But this obscurity in the profound and abstract philosophy, is objected to, not only as painful and fatiguing, but as the inevitable source of uncertainty and error. Here indeed lies the justest and most plausible objection against a considerable part of metaphysics, that they are not properly a science; but arise either from the fruitless efforts of human vanity, which would penetrate into subjects utterly inaccessible to the understanding, or from the craft of popular superstitions,* which, being unable to defend themselves on fair ground, raise these intangling brambles to cover and protect their weakness. Chaced from the open country, these robbers fly into the forest, and lie in wait to break in upon every unguarded avenue of the mind, and overwhelm it with religious fears and prejudices. The stoutest antagonist, if he remit his watch a moment, is oppressed. And many, through cowardice and

folly, open the gates to the enemies, and willingly receive them with
reverence and submission, as their legal sovereigns.

12   [12] But is this a sufficient reason, why philosophers should desist
from such researches, and leave superstition still in possession of her
retreat? Is it not proper to draw an opposite conclusion, and perceive
the necessity of carrying the war into the most secret recesses of the
enemy? In vain do we hope, that men, from frequent disappointment,
will at last abandon such airy sciences, and discover the proper
province of human reason. For, besides, that many persons find too
sensible an interest* in perpetually recalling such topics; besides this,
I say, the motive of blind despair can never reasonably have place in
the sciences; since, however unsuccessful former attempts may have
proved, there is still room to hope, that the industry, good fortune, or
improved sagacity of succeeding generations may reach discoveries
unknown to former ages. Each adventurous genius will still leap at the
arduous prize, and find himself stimulated, rather than discouraged,
by the failures of his predecessors; while he hopes that the glory of
atchieving so hard an adventure is reserved for him alone. The only
method of freeing learning, at once, from these abstruse questions, is
to enquire seriously into the nature of human understanding, and
shew, from an exact analysis of its powers and capacity, that it is by
no means fitted for such remote and abstruse subjects. We must
submit to this fatigue, in order to live at ease ever after: And must
cultivate true metaphysics with some care, in order to destroy the
false and adulterate. Indolence, which, to some persons, affords a safe-
guard against this deceitful philosophy, is, with others, overbalanced
by curiosity; and despair, which, at some moments, prevails, may give
place afterwards to sanguine hopes and expectations. Accurate and just
reasoning is the only catholic remedy,* fitted for all persons and all
dispositions; and is alone able to subvert that abstruse philosophy and
metaphysical jargon, which, being mixed up with popular superstition,
13   renders it in a manner impenetrable to careless* reasoners, and gives it
the air of science and wisdom.

[13] Besides this advantage of rejecting, after deliberate enquiry,
the most uncertain and disagreeable part of learning, there are many
positive advantages, which result from an accurate scrutiny into the
powers and faculties of human nature. It is remarkable concerning
the operations of the mind, that, though most intimately present
to us, yet, whenever they become the object of reflection, they seem

involved in obscurity; nor can the eye readily find those lines and boundaries, which discriminate and distinguish them. The objects are too fine to remain long in the same aspect or situation; and must be apprehended in an instant, by a superior penetration, derived from nature, and improved by habit and reflection. It becomes, therefore, no inconsiderable part of science barely to know the different operations of the mind, to separate them from each other, to class them under their proper heads, and to correct all that seeming disorder, in which they lie involved, when made the object of reflection and enquiry. This task of ordering and distinguishing, which has no merit, when performed with regard to external bodies, the objects of our senses, rises in its value, when directed towards the operations of the mind, in proportion to the difficulty and labour, which we meet with in performing it. And if we can go no farther than this mental geography,* or delineation of the distinct parts and powers of the mind, it is at least a satisfaction to go so far; and the more obvious this science may appear (and it is by no means obvious) the more contemptible still must the ignorance of it be esteemed, in all pretenders to learning and philosophy.

[14] Nor can there remain any suspicion, that this science is uncertain and chimerical; unless we should entertain such a scepticism as is entirely subversive of all speculation, and even action. It cannot be doubted, that the mind is endowed with several powers and faculties, that these powers are distinct from each other, that what is really distinct to the immediate perception may be distinguished by reflection; and consequently, that there is a truth and falsehood in all propositions on this subject, and a truth and falsehood, which lie not beyond the compass of human understanding.* There are many obvious distinctions of this kind, such as those between the will and understanding, the imagination and passions, which fall within the comprehension of every human creature; and the finer and more philosophical distinctions are no less real and certain, though more difficult to be comprehended. Some instances, especially late ones, of success in these enquiries, may give us a juster notion of the certainty and solidity of this branch of learning. And shall we esteem it worthy the labour of a philosopher to give us a true system of the planets, and adjust the position and order of those remote bodies; while we affect to overlook those, who, with so much success, delineate the parts of the mind, in which we are so intimately concerned?*

[15] But may we not hope, that philosophy, if cultivated with care, and encouraged by the attention of the public, may carry its researches still farther, and discover, at least in some degree, the secret springs and principles,* by which the human mind is actuated in its operations? Astronomers had long contented themselves with proving, from the phaenomena, the true motions, order, and magnitude of the heavenly bodies: Till a philosopher,* at last, arose, who seems, from the happiest reasoning, to have also determined the laws and forces, by which the revolutions of the planets are governed and directed. The like has been performed with regard to other parts of nature. And there is no reason to despair of equal success in our enquiries concerning the mental powers and oeconomy, if prosecuted with equal capacity and caution. It is probable, that one operation and principle of the mind depends on another; which, again, may be resolved into one more general and universal: And how far these researches may possibly be carried, it will be difficult for us, before, or even after, a careful trial, exactly to determine. This is certain, that attempts of this kind are every day made even by those who philosophize the most negligently: And nothing can be more requisite than to enter upon the enterprize with thorough care and attention; that, if it lie within the compass of human understanding, it may at last be happily atchieved; if not, it may, however, be rejected with some confidence and security. This last conclusion, surely, is not desirable; nor ought it to be embraced too rashly. For how much must we diminish from the beauty and value of this species of philosophy, upon such a supposition? Moralists have hitherto been accustomed, when they considered the vast multitude and diversity of those actions that excite our approbation or dislike, to search for some common principle, on which this variety of sentiments might depend. And though they have sometimes carried the matter too far, by their passion for some one general principle; it must, however, be confessed, that they are excusable in expecting to find some general principles, into which all the vices and virtues were justly to be resolved. The like has been the endeavour of critics, logicians, and even politicians: Nor have their attempts been wholly unsuccessful; though perhaps longer time, greater accuracy, and more ardent application may bring these sciences still nearer their perfection. To throw up at once all pretensions of this kind may justly be deemed more rash, precipitate, and dogmatical, than even the boldest and most affirmative philosophy, that has ever attempted to impose its crude dictates and principles on mankind.

[16] What though these reasonings concerning human nature seem abstract, and of difficult comprehension? This affords no presumption of their falsehood. On the contrary, it seems impossible, that what has hitherto escaped so many wise and profound philosophers can be very obvious and easy. And whatever pains these researches may cost us, we may think ourselves sufficiently rewarded, not only in point of profit but of pleasure, if, by that means, we can make any addition to our stock of knowledge, in subjects of such unspeakable importance.

[17] But as, after all, the abstractedness of these speculations is no recommendation, but rather a disadvantage to them, and as this difficulty may perhaps be surmounted by care and art, and the avoiding of all unnecessary detail, we have, in the following enquiry, attempted to throw some light upon subjects, from which uncertainty has hitherto deterred the wise, and obscurity the ignorant. Happy, if we can unite the boundaries of the different species of philosophy, by reconciling profound enquiry with clearness, and truth with novelty! And still more happy, if, reasoning in this easy manner, we can undermine the foundations of an abstruse philosophy, which seems to have hitherto served only as a shelter to superstition, and a cover to absurdity and error!

SECTION II

Of the ORIGIN of IDEAS*

EVERY one will readily allow, that there is a considerable difference between the perceptions of the mind,* when a man feels the pain of excessive heat, or the pleasure of moderate warmth, and when he afterwards recalls to his memory this sensation, or anticipates it by his imagination. These faculties* may mimic or copy the perceptions of the senses; but they never can entirely reach the force and vivacity of the original sentiment. The utmost we say of them, even when they operate with greatest vigour, is, that they represent their object in so lively a manner, that we could *almost* say we feel or see it: But, except the mind be disordered by disease or madness, they never can arrive at such a pitch of vivacity, as to render these perceptions altogether undistinguishable. All the colours of poetry, however splendid, can never paint natural objects in such a manner as to make the description be taken for a real landskip. The most lively thought is still inferior to the dullest sensation.

[2] We may observe a like distinction to run through all the other perceptions of the mind. A man in a fit of anger, is actuated in a very different manner from one who only thinks of that emotion. If you tell me, that any person is in love, I easily understand your meaning, and form a just conception of his situation; but never can mistake that conception for the real disorders and agitations of the passion. When we reflect on our past sentiments and affections, our thought is a faithful mirror, and copies its objects truly; but the colours which it employs are faint and dull, in comparison of those in which our original perceptions were clothed. It requires no nice discernment or metaphysical head to mark the distinction between them.

[3] Here therefore we may divide all the perceptions of the mind into two classes or species, which are distinguished by their different degrees of force and vivacity.* The less forcible and lively are commonly denominated THOUGHTS or IDEAS. The other species want a name in our language, and in most others; I suppose, because it was not requisite for any, but philosophical purposes, to rank them under a general term or appellation. Let us, therefore, use a little freedom,

and call them IMPRESSIONS; employing that word in a sense some-what different from the usual. By the term *impression*, then, I mean all our more lively perceptions, when we hear, or see, or feel, or love, or hate, or desire, or will. And impressions are distinguished from ideas, which are the less lively perceptions, of which we are conscious, when we reflect on any of those sensations or movements above mentioned.

[4] Nothing, at first view, may seem more unbounded than the thought of man, which not only escapes all human power and author-ity, but is not even restrained within the limits of nature and reality. To form monsters, and join incongruous shapes and appearances, costs the imagination no more trouble than to conceive the most natu-ral and familiar objects. And while the body is confined to one planet, along which it creeps with pain and difficulty; the thought can in an instant transport us into the most distant regions of the universe; or even beyond the universe, into the unbounded chaos, where nature is supposed to lie in total confusion. What never was seen, or heard of, may yet be conceived; nor is any thing beyond the power of thought, except what implies an absolute contradiction.

[5] But though our thought seems to possess this unbounded 19 liberty, we shall find, upon a nearer examination, that it is really confined within very narrow limits, and that all this creative power of the mind amounts to no more than the faculty of compounding, transposing, augmenting, or diminishing the materials afforded us by the senses and experience. When we think of a golden mountain, we only join two consistent ideas, *gold*, and *mountain*, with which we were formerly acquainted. A virtuous horse we can conceive; because, from our own feeling, we can conceive virtue; and this we may unite to the figure and shape of a horse, which is an animal familiar to us. In short, all the materials of thinking are derived either from our outward or inward sentiment: The mixture and composition of these belongs alone to the mind and will. Or, to express myself in philo-sophical language, all our ideas or more feeble perceptions are copies of our impressions or more lively ones.*

[6] To prove this, the two following arguments will, I hope, be sufficient. First, when we analyse our thoughts or ideas, however com-pounded or sublime, we always find, that they resolve themselves into such simple ideas as were copied from a precedent feeling or senti-ment. Even those ideas, which, at first view, seem the most wide of this origin, are found, upon a nearer scrutiny, to be derived from it.

The idea of God, as meaning an infinitely intelligent, wise, and good
Being, arises from reflecting on the operations of our own mind, and
augmenting, without limit, those qualities of goodness and wisdom.
We may prosecute this enquiry to what length we please; where we
shall always find, that every idea which we examine is copied from a
similar impression. Those who would assert, that this position is not
universally true nor without exception, have only one, and that an
easy method of refuting it; by producing that idea, which, in their
20 opinion, is not derived from this source. It will then be incumbent on
us, if we would maintain our doctrine, to produce the impression or
lively perception, which corresponds to it.

[7] Secondly. If it happen, from a defect of the organ, that a man
is not susceptible of any species of sensation, we always find, that he
is as little susceptible of the correspondent ideas. A blind man can
form no notion of colours; a deaf man of sounds. Restore either of
them that sense, in which he is deficient; by opening this new inlet
for his sensations, you also open an inlet for the ideas; and he finds
no difficulty in conceiving these objects. The case is the same, if the
object, proper for exciting any sensation, has never been applied to
the organ. A LAPLANDER or NEGROE* has no notion of the relish of
wine. And though there are few or no instances of a like deficiency in
the mind, where a person has never felt or is wholly incapable of a
sentiment or passion, that belongs to his species; yet we find the same
observation to take place in a less degree. A man of mild manners can
form no idea of inveterate revenge or cruelty; nor can a selfish heart
easily conceive the heights of friendship and generosity. It is readily
allowed, that other beings may possess many senses of which we can
have no conception; because the ideas of them have never been introduced to us, in the only manner, by which an idea can have access to
the mind, to wit, by the actual feeling and sensation.

[8] There is, however, one contradictory phaenomenon,* which
may prove, that it is not absolutely impossible for ideas to arise, independent of their correspondent impressions. I believe it will readily be
allowed, that the several distinct ideas of colour, which enter by the eye,
or those of sound, which are conveyed by the ear, are really different
from each other; though, at the same time, resembling. Now if this be
true of different colours, it must be no less so of the different shades of
21 the same colour; and each shade produces a distinct idea, independent
of the rest. For if this should be denied, it is possible, by the continual
gradation of shades, to run a colour insensibly into what is most remote

from it; and if you will not allow any of the means to be different, you cannot, without absurdity, deny the extremes to be the same. Suppose, therefore, a person to have enjoyed his sight for thirty years, and to have become perfectly acquainted with colours of all kinds, except one particular shade of blue, for instance, which it never has been his fortune to meet with. Let all the different shades of that colour, except that single one, be placed before him, descending gradually from the deepest to the lightest; it is plain, that he will perceive a blank, where that shade is wanting, and will be sensible, that there is a greater distance in that place between the contiguous colours than in any other. Now I ask, whether it be possible for him, from his own imagination, to supply this deficiency, and raise up to himself the idea of that particular shade, though it had never been conveyed to him by his senses? I believe there are few but will be of opinion that he can: And this may serve as a proof, that the simple ideas are not always, in every instance, derived from the correspondent impressions; though this instance is so singular, that it is scarcely worth our observing, and does not merit, that for it alone we should alter our general maxim.

[9] Here, therefore, is a proposition, which not only seems, in itself, simple and intelligible; but, if a proper use were made of it, might render every dispute equally intelligible, and banish all that jargon, which has so long taken possession of metaphysical reasonings, and drawn disgrace upon them. All ideas, especially abstract ones, are naturally faint and obscure: The mind has but a slender hold of them: They are apt to be confounded with other resembling ideas; and when we have often employed any term, though without a distinct meaning, we are apt to imagine it has a determinate idea, annexed to it. On the contrary, all impressions, that is, all sensations, either outward or inward, are strong and vivid: The limits between them are more exactly determined: Nor is it easy to fall into any error or mistake with regard to them. When we entertain, therefore, any suspicion, that a philosophical term is employed without any meaning or idea (as is but too frequent), we need but enquire, *from what impression is that supposed idea derived?** And if it be impossible to assign any, this will serve to confirm our suspicion. By bringing ideas into so clear a light, we may reasonably hope to remove all dispute, which may arise, concerning their nature and reality[1].

---

[1] See endnote [A], p. 121.

SECTION III

Of the Association of Ideas*

IT is evident, that there is a principle of connexion between the different thoughts or ideas of the mind, and that, in their appearance to the memory or imagination, they introduce each other with a certain degree of method and regularity. In our more serious thinking or discourse, this is so observable, that any particular thought, which breaks in upon the regular tract or chain of ideas, is immediately remarked and rejected. And even in our wildest and most wandering reveries, nay in our very dreams, we shall find, if we reflect, that the imagination ran not altogether at adventures, but that there was still a connexion upheld among the different ideas, which succeeded each other. Were the loosest and freest conversation to be transcribed, there would immediately be observed something, which connected it in all its transitions. Or where this is wanting, the person, who broke the thread of discourse, might still inform you, that there had secretly revolved in his mind a succession of thought, which had gradually led him from the subject of conversation. Among different languages, even where we cannot suspect the least connexion or communication, it is found, that the words, expressive of ideas, the most compounded, do yet nearly correspond to each other: A certain proof, that the simple ideas, comprehended in the compound ones, were bound together by some universal principle, which had an equal influence on all mankind.

24 [2] Though it be too obvious to escape observation, that different ideas are connected together; I do not find, that any philosopher has attempted to enumerate or class all the principles of association; a subject, however, that seems worthy of curiosity. To me, there appear to be only three principles of connexion among ideas, namely, *Resemblance, Contiguity* in time or place, and *Cause* or *Effect*.

[3] That these principles serve to connect ideas will not, I believe, be much doubted. A picture naturally leads our thoughts to the original[2]: The mention of one apartment in a building naturally introduces an

---

[2] Resemblance.

enquiry or discourse concerning the others[3]: And if we think of a wound, we can scarcely forbear reflecting on the pain which follows it[4]. But that this enumeration is compleat, and that there are no other principles of association, except these, may be difficult to prove to the satisfaction of the reader, or even to a man's own satisfaction. All we can do, in such cases, is to run over several instances, and examine carefully the principle, which binds the different thoughts to each other, never stopping till we render the principle as general as possible[6].* The more instances we examine, and the more care we employ, the more assurance shall we acquire, that the enumeration, which we form from the whole, is compleat and entire.*

[3] Contiguity.

[4] Cause and effect.

[6] For instance, Contrast or Contrariety is also a connexion among Ideas: But it may, perhaps, be considered as a mixture of *Causation* and *Resemblance*. Where two objects are contrary, the one destroys the other; that is, [is] the cause of its annihilation, and the idea of the annihilation of an object, implies the idea of its former existence.

SECTION IV

Sceptical Doubts concerning the Operations of the Understanding

PART I

ALL the objects of human reason or enquiry may naturally be divided into two kinds, to wit, *Relations of Ideas*, and *Matters of Fact*.* Of the first kind are the sciences of Geometry, Algebra, and Arithmetic; and in short, every affirmation, which is either intuitively or demonstratively certain. *That the square of the hypothenuse is equal to the square of the two sides*, is a proposition, which expresses a relation between these figures. *That three times five is equal to the half of thirty*, expresses a relation between these numbers. Propositions of this kind are discoverable by the mere operation of thought, without dependence on what is any where existent in the universe. Though there never were a circle or triangle in nature, the truths, demonstrated by EUCLID,* would for ever retain their certainty and evidence.

[2] Matters of fact, which are the second objects of human reason, are not ascertained in the same manner; nor is our evidence of their truth, however great, of a like nature with the foregoing. The contrary of every matter of fact is still possible;* because it can never imply a contradiction, and is conceived by the mind with the same facility and distinctness, as if ever so conformable to reality. *That the sun will not rise to-morrow* is no less intelligible a proposition, and implies no more contradiction, than the affirmation, *that it will rise*. We should in vain, therefore, attempt to demonstrate its falsehood. Were it demonstratively false, it would imply a contradiction, and could never be distinctly conceived by the mind.

[3] It may, therefore, be a subject worthy of curiosity, to enquire what is the nature of that evidence, which assures us of any real existence and matter of fact, beyond the present testimony of our senses, or the records of our memory. This part of philosophy, it is observable, has been little cultivated, either by the ancients or moderns; and therefore our doubts and errors, in the prosecution of so important an enquiry, may be the more excusable; while we march through such difficult

paths, without any guide or direction. They may even prove useful, by exciting curiosity, and destroying that implicit faith and security, which is the bane of all reasoning and free enquiry. The discovery of defects in the common philosophy, if any such there be, will not, I presume, be a discouragement, but rather an incitement, as is usual, to attempt something more full and satisfactory, than has yet been proposed to the public.

[4] All reasonings concerning matter of fact seem to be founded on the relation of *Cause and Effect*. By means of that relation alone we can go beyond the evidence of our memory and senses. If you were to ask a man, why he believes any matter of fact, which is absent; for instance, that his friend is in the country, or in FRANCE; he would give you a reason; and this reason would be some other fact; as a letter received from him, or the knowledge of his former resolutions and promises. A man, finding a watch or any other machine in a desart island, would conclude, that there had once been men in that island. All our reasonings concerning fact are of the same nature. And here it is constantly supposed, that there is a connexion between the present fact and that which is inferred from it. Were there nothing to bind them together, the inference would be entirely precarious. The hearing of an articulate voice and rational discourse in the dark assures us of the presence of some person: Why? because these are the effects of the human make and fabric, and closely connected with it. If we anatomize all the other reasonings of this nature, we shall find, that they are founded on the relation of cause and effect, and that this relation is either near or remote, direct or collateral. Heat and light are collateral effects of fire, and the one effect may justly be inferred from the other.

[5] If we would satisfy ourselves, therefore, concerning the nature of that evidence, which assures us of matters of fact, we must enquire how we arrive at the knowledge of cause and effect.

[6] I shall venture to affirm, as a general proposition, which admits of no exception, that the knowledge of this relation is not, in any instance, attained by reasonings *à priori*;* but arises entirely from experience, when we find, that any particular objects are constantly conjoined with each other. Let an object be presented to a man of ever so strong natural reason and abilities; if that object be entirely new to him, he will not be able, by the most accurate examination of its sensible qualities, to discover any of its causes or effects. ADAM,* though

his rational faculties be supposed, at the very first, entirely perfect, could not have inferred from the fluidity, and transparency of water, that it would suffocate him, or from the light and warmth of fire, that it would consume him. No object ever discovers,* by the qualities which appear to the senses, either the causes which produced it, or the effects which will arise from it; nor can our reason, unassisted by experience, ever draw any inference concerning real existence and matter of fact.

28   [7] This proposition, *that causes and effects are discoverable, not by reason, but by experience*, will readily be admitted with regard to such objects, as we remember to have once been altogether unknown to us; since we must be conscious of the utter inability, which we then lay under, of foretelling, what would arise from them. Present two smooth pieces of marble to a man, who has no tincture of natural philosophy; he will never discover, that they will adhere together, in such a manner as to require great force to separate them in a direct line, while they make so small a resistance to a lateral pressure. Such events, as bear little analogy to the common course of nature, are also readily confessed to be known only by experience; nor does any man imagine that the explosion of gunpowder, or the attraction of a loadstone,* could ever be discovered by arguments *à priori*. In like manner, when an effect is supposed to depend upon an intricate machinery or secret structure of parts, we make no difficulty in attributing all our knowledge of it to experience. Who will assert, that he can give the ultimate reason, why milk or bread is proper nourishment for a man, not for a lion or a tyger?

[8] But the same truth may not appear, at first sight, to have the same evidence with regard to events, which have become familiar to us from our first appearance in the world, which bear a close analogy to the whole course of nature, and which are supposed to depend on the simple qualities of objects, without any secret structure of parts. We are apt to imagine, that we could discover these effects by the mere operation of our reason, without experience. We fancy, that were we brought, on a sudden, into this world, we could at first have inferred, that one Billiard-ball would communicate motion to another upon impulse;* and that we needed not to have waited for the event, in order to pronounce with certainty concerning it. Such is the influence of custom, that, where it is strongest, it not only
29 covers our natural ignorance, but even conceals itself, and seems not to take place, merely because it is found in the highest degree.

[9] But to convince us, that all the laws of nature, and all the operations of bodies without exception, are known only by experience, the following reflections may, perhaps, suffice. Were any object presented to us, and were we required to pronounce concerning the effect, which will result from it, without consulting past observation; after what manner, I beseech you, must the mind proceed in this operation? It must invent or imagine some event, which it ascribes to the object as its effect; and it is plain that this invention must be entirely arbitrary. The mind can never possibly find the effect in the supposed cause, by the most accurate scrutiny and examination. For the effect is totally different from the cause, and consequently can never be discovered in it. Motion in the second Billiard-ball is a quite distinct event from motion in the first; nor is there any thing in the one to suggest the smallest hint of the other. A stone or piece of metal raised into the air, and left without any support, immediately falls: But to consider the matter *à priori*, is there any thing we discover in this situation, which can beget the idea of a downward, rather than an upward, or any other motion, in the stone or metal?

[10] And as the first imagination or invention of a particular effect, in all natural operations, is arbitrary, where we consult not experience; so must we also esteem the supposed tye or connexion between the cause and effect, which binds them together, and renders it impossible, that any other effect could result from the operation of that cause. When I see, for instance, a Billiard-ball moving in a straight line towards another; even suppose motion in the second ball should by accident be suggested to me, as the result of their contact or impulse; may I not conceive,* that a hundred different events might as well follow from that cause? May not both these balls remain at absolute rest? May not the first ball return in a straight line, or leap off from the second in any line or direction? All these suppositions are consistent and conceivable. Why then should we give the preference to one, which is no more consistent or conceivable than the rest? All our reasonings *à priori* will never be able to shew us any foundation for this preference.

[11] In a word, then, every effect is a distinct event from its cause. It could not, therefore, be discovered in the cause, and the first invention or conception of it, *à priori*, must be entirely arbitrary. And even after it is suggested, the conjunction of it with the cause must appear equally arbitrary; since there are always many other effects, which, to

reason, must seem fully as consistent and natural. In vain, therefore, should we pretend to determine any single event, or infer any cause or effect, without the assistance of observation and experience.

[12] Hence we may discover the reason, why no philosopher, who is rational and modest, has ever pretended to assign the ultimate cause of any natural operation, or to show distinctly the action of that power, which produces any single effect in the universe. It is confessed, that the utmost effort of human reason is, to reduce the principles, productive of natural phaenomena, to a greater simplicity, and to resolve the many particular effects into a few general causes, by means of reasonings from analogy, experience, and observation.* But as to the causes of these general causes, we should in vain attempt their discovery; nor shall we ever be able to satisfy ourselves, by any particular explication of them. These ultimate springs and principles are totally shut up from human curiosity and enquiry. Elasticity, gravity, cohesion of parts, communication of motion by impulse; these are probably the ultimate causes and principles which we shall ever discover in nature; and we may esteem ourselves sufficiently happy, if, by accurate enquiry and reasoning, we can trace up the particular phaenomena to, or near to, these general principles. The most perfect philosophy of the natural kind only staves off our ignorance a little longer: As perhaps the most perfect philosophy of the moral or metaphysical kind serves only to discover larger portions of it. Thus the observation of human blindness and weakness is the result of all philosophy, and meets us, at every turn, in spite of our endeavours to elude or avoid it.

[13] Nor is geometry, when taken into the assistance of natural philosophy, ever able to remedy this defect, or lead us into the knowledge of ultimate causes, by all that accuracy of reasoning, for which it is so justly celebrated. Every part of mixed mathematics* proceeds upon the supposition, that certain laws are established by nature in her operations; and abstract reasonings are employed, either to assist experience in the discovery of these laws, or to determine their influence in particular instances, where it depends upon any precise degree of distance and quantity. Thus, it is a law of motion, discovered by experience, that the moment or force of any body in motion* is in the compound ratio or proportion of its solid contents and its velocity; and consequently, that a small force may remove the greatest obstacle or raise the greatest weight, if, by any contrivance or machinery, we can encrease the velocity of that force, so as to make it an overmatch for

its antagonist. Geometry assists us in the application of this law, by giving us the just dimensions of all the parts and figures, which can enter into any species of machine; but still the discovery of the law itself is owing merely to experience,* and all the abstract reasonings in the world could never lead us one step towards the knowledge of it. When we reason *à priori*, and consider merely any object or cause, as it appears to the mind, independent of all observation, it never could suggest to us the notion of any distinct object, such as its effect; much less, shew us the inseparable and inviolable connection between them. A man must be very sagacious, who could discover by reasoning, that crystal is the effect of heat, and ice of cold, without being previously acquainted with the operation of these qualities. 32

PART II

[14] But we have not, yet, attained any tolerable satisfaction with regard to the question first proposed. Each solution still gives rise to a new question as difficult as the foregoing, and leads us on to farther enquiries. When it is asked, *What is the nature of all our reasonings concerning matter of fact?* the proper answer seems to be, that they are founded on the relation of cause and effect. When again it is asked, *What is the foundation of all our reasonings and conclusions concerning that relation?* it may be replied in one word, EXPERIENCE. But if we still carry on our sifting humour,* and ask, *What is the foundation of all conclusions from experience?* this implies a new question, which may be of more difficult solution and explication. Philosophers, that give themselves airs of superior wisdom and sufficiency, have a hard task, when they encounter persons of inquisitive dispositions, who push them from every corner, to which they retreat, and who are sure at last to bring them to some dangerous dilemma. The best expedient to prevent this confusion, is to be modest in our pretensions; and even to discover the difficulty ourselves before it is objected to us. By this means, we may make a kind of merit of our very ignorance.

[15] I shall content myself, in this section, with an easy task, and shall pretend* only to give a negative answer to the question here proposed. I say then, that, even after we have experience of the operations of cause and effect, our conclusions from that experience are *not* founded on reasoning, or any process of the understanding. This answer we must endeavour, both to explain and to defend.

[16] It must certainly be allowed, that nature has kept us at a great
33 distance from all her secrets, and has afforded us only the knowledge
of a few superficial qualities of objects; while she conceals from us
those powers and principles, on which the influence of these objects
entirely depends. Our senses inform us of the colour, weight, and
consistence of bread; but neither sense nor reason can ever inform us
of those qualities, which fit it for the nourishment and support of a
human body. Sight or feeling conveys an idea of the actual motion of
bodies; but as to that wonderful force or power, which would carry
on a moving body for ever in a continued change of place, and which
bodies never lose but by communicating it to others;* of this we
cannot form the most distant conception. But notwithstanding this
ignorance of natural powers[7] and principles, we always presume,
when we see like sensible qualities, that they have like secret powers,
and expect, that effects, similar to those which we have experienced,
will follow from them. If a body of like colour and consistence with
that bread, which we have formerly eat, be presented to us, we make
no scruple of repeating the experiment, and foresee, with certainty,
like nourishment and support. Now this is a process of the mind
or thought, of which I would willingly know the foundation. It is
allowed on all hands, that there is no known connexion between the
sensible qualities and the secret powers; and consequently, that the
mind is not led to form such a conclusion concerning their constant
and regular conjunction, by any thing which it knows of their nature.
As to past *Experience*, it can be allowed to give *direct* and *certain* information of those precise objects only, and that precise period of time,
which fell under its cognizance: But why this experience should be
extended to future times, and to other objects, which for aught we
34 know, may be only in appearance similar; this is the main question on
which I would insist. The bread, which I formerly eat, nourished me;
that is, a body of such sensible qualities, was, at that time, endued
with such secret powers: But does it follow, that other bread must also
nourish me at another time, and that like sensible qualities must
always be attended with like secret powers? The consequence seems
nowise necessary. At least, it must be acknowledged, that there is
here a consequence drawn by the mind; that there is a certain step

---

[7] The word, Power, is here used in a loose and popular sense. The more accurate
explication of it would give additional evidence to this argument. See Sect. 7.*

taken; a process of thought, and an inference, which wants to be explained. These two propositions are far from being the same, *I have found that such an object has always been attended with such an effect*, and *I foresee, that other objects, which are, in appearance, similar, will be attended with similar effects*. I shall allow, if you please, that the one proposition may justly be inferred from the other: I know in fact, that it always is inferred. But if you insist, that the inference is made by a chain of reasoning, I desire you to produce that reasoning. The connexion between these propositions is not intuitive. There is required a medium,* which may enable the mind to draw such an inference, if indeed it be drawn by reasoning and argument. What that medium is, I must confess, passes my comprehension; and it is incumbent on those to produce it, who assert, that it really exists, and is the origin of all our conclusions concerning matter of fact.

[17] This negative argument must certainly, in process of time, become altogether convincing, if many penetrating and able philosophers shall turn their enquiries this way; and no one be ever able to discover any connecting proposition or intermediate step, which supports the understanding in this conclusion. But as the question is yet new, every reader may not trust so far to his own penetration, as to conclude, because an argument escapes his enquiry, that therefore it does not really exist. For this reason it may be requisite to venture 35 upon a more difficult task; and enumerating all the branches of human knowledge, endeavour to shew, that none of them can afford such an argument.

[18] All reasonings may be divided into two kinds, namely demonstrative reasoning, or that concerning relations of ideas, and moral reasoning,* or that concerning matter of fact and existence. That there are no demonstrative arguments* in the case, seems evident; since it implies no contradiction, that the course of nature may change, and that an object, seemingly like those which we have experienced, may be attended with different or contrary effects. May I not clearly and distinctly conceive, that a body, falling from the clouds, and which, in all other respects, resembles snow, has yet the taste of salt or feeling of fire? Is there any more intelligible proposition than to affirm, that all the trees will flourish in DECEMBER and JANUARY, and decay in MAY and JUNE? Now whatever is intelligible, and can be distinctly conceived, implies no contradiction, and can never be proved false by any demonstrative argument or abstract reasoning *à priori*.

[19] If we be, therefore, engaged by arguments to put trust in past experience, and make it the standard of our future judgment, these arguments must be probable only, or such as regard matter of fact and real existence, according to the division above mentioned. But that there is no argument of this kind, must appear, if our explication of that species of reasoning be admitted as solid and satisfactory. We have said, that all arguments concerning existence are founded on the relation of cause and effect; that our knowledge of that relation is derived entirely from experience; and that all our experimental conclusions* proceed upon the supposition, that the future will be conformable to the past. To endeavour, therefore, the proof of this last supposition by probable arguments, or arguments regarding existence, must be evidently going in a circle, and taking that for granted, which is the very point in question.

[20] In reality, all arguments from experience are founded on the similarity, which we discover among natural objects, and by which we are induced to expect effects similar to those, which we have found to follow from such objects. And though none but a fool or madman will ever pretend to dispute the authority of experience, or to reject that great guide of human life; it may surely be allowed a philosopher to have so much curiosity at least, as to examine the principle of human nature, which gives this mighty authority to experience, and makes us draw advantage from that similarity, which nature has placed among different objects. From causes, which appear *similar*, we expect similar effects. This is the sum of all our experimental conclusions. Now it seems evident, that, if this conclusion were formed by reason, it would be as perfect at first, and upon one instance, as after ever so long a course of experience. But the case is far otherwise. Nothing so like as eggs; yet no one, on account of this appearing similarity, expects the same taste and relish in all of them. It is only after a long course of uniform experiments in any kind, that we attain a firm reliance and security with regard to a particular event. Now where is that process of reasoning, which, from one instance, draws a conclusion, so different from that which it infers from a hundred instances, that are nowise different from that single one? This question I propose as much for the sake of information, as with an intention of raising difficulties. I cannot find, I cannot imagine any such reasoning.* But I keep my mind still open to instruction, if any one will vouchsafe to bestow it on me.

[21] Should it be said, that, from a number of uniform experiments, we *infer* a connexion between the sensible qualities and the secret powers; this, I must confess, seems the same difficulty, couched in 37 different terms. The question still recurs, on what process of argument this *inference* is founded? Where is the medium, the interposing ideas,* which join propositions so very wide of each other? It is confessed, that the colour, consistence, and other sensible qualities of bread appear not, of themselves, to have any connexion with the secret powers of nourishment and support. For otherwise we could infer these secret powers from the first appearance of these sensible qualities, without the aid of experience; contrary to the sentiment of all philosophers, and contrary to plain matter of fact. Here then is our natural state of ignorance with regard to the powers and influence of all objects. How is this remedied by experience? It only shews us a number of uniform effects, resulting from certain objects, and teaches us, that those particular objects, at that particular time, were endowed with such powers and forces. When a new object, endowed with similar sensible qualities, is produced, we expect similar powers and forces, and look for a like effect. From a body of like colour and consistence with bread, we expect like nourishment and support. But this surely is a step or progress of the mind, which wants to be explained. When a man says, *I have found, in all past instances, such sensible qualities conjoined with such secret powers:* And when he says, *similar sensible qualities will always be conjoined with similar secret powers*; he is not guilty of a tautology, nor are these propositions in any respect the same. You say that the one proposition is an inference from the other. But you must confess that the inference is not intuitive; neither is it demonstrative: Of what nature is it then? To say it is experimental, is begging the question. For all inferences from experience suppose, as their foundation, that the future will resemble the past, and that similar powers will be conjoined with similar sensible qualities. If there be any suspicion, that the course of nature may change, and that the past may be no rule for 38 the future, all experience becomes useless, and can give rise to no inference or conclusion. It is impossible, therefore, that any arguments from experience can prove this resemblance of the past to the future; since all these arguments are founded on the supposition of that resemblance. Let the course of things be allowed hitherto ever so regular; that alone, without some new argument or inference, proves not, that, for the future, it will continue so. In vain do you pretend to

have learned the nature of bodies from your past experience. Their secret nature, and consequently, all their effects and influence, may change, without any change in their sensible qualities. This happens sometimes, and with regard to some objects: Why may it not happen always, and with regard to all objects? What logic, what process of argument secures you against this supposition? My practice, you say, refutes my doubts. But you mistake the purport of my question. As an agent, I am quite satisfied in the point; but as a philosopher, who has some share of curiosity, I will not say scepticism, I want to learn the foundation of this inference. No reading, no enquiry has yet been able to remove my difficulty, or give me satisfaction in a matter of such importance. Can I do better than propose the difficulty to the public, even though, perhaps, I have small hopes of obtaining a solution? We shall at least, by this means, be sensible of our ignorance, if we do not augment our knowledge.

[22] I must confess, that a man is guilty of unpardonable arrogance, who concludes, because an argument has escaped his own investigation, that therefore it does not really exist. I must also confess, that, though all the learned, for several ages, should have employed themselves in fruitless search upon any subject, it may still, perhaps, be rash to conclude positively, that the subject must, therefore, pass all human 39 comprehension. Even though we examine all the sources of our knowledge, and conclude them unfit for such a subject, there may still remain a suspicion, that the enumeration is not compleat, or the examination not accurate. But with regard to the present subject, there are some considerations, which seem to remove all this accusation of arrogance or suspicion of mistake.

[23] It is certain, that the most ignorant and stupid peasants, nay infants, nay even brute beasts, improve by experience, and learn the qualities of natural objects, by observing the effects, which result from them. When a child has felt the sensation of pain from touching the flame of a candle, he will be careful not to put his hand near any candle; but will expect a similar effect from a cause, which is similar in its sensible qualities and appearance. If you assert, therefore, that the understanding of the child is led into this conclusion by any process of argument or ratiocination, I may justly require you to produce that argument; nor have you any pretence to refuse so equitable a demand. You cannot say, that the argument is abstruse, and may possibly escape your enquiry; since you confess, that it is obvious to the capacity of

a mere infant. If you hesitate, therefore, a moment, or if, after reflection, you produce any intricate or profound argument, you, in a manner, give up the question, and confess, that it is not reasoning which engages us to suppose the past resembling the future, and to expect similar effects from causes, which are, to appearance, similar. This is the proposition which I intended to enforce in the present section. If I be right, I pretend not to have made any mighty discovery. And if I be wrong, I must acknowledge myself to be indeed a very backward scholar; since I cannot now discover an argument, which, it seems, was perfectly familiar to me, long before I was out of my cradle.

SECTION V

SCEPTICAL SOLUTION of these DOUBTS

PART I

THE passion for philosophy, like that for religion, seems liable to this inconvenience, that, though it aims at the correction of our manners, and extirpation of our vices, it may only serve, by imprudent management, to foster a predominant inclination, and push the mind, with more determined resolution, towards that side, which already *draws* too much, by the biass and propensity of the natural temper. It is certain, that, while we aspire to the magnanimous firmness of the philosophic sage, and endeavour to confine our pleasures altogether within our own minds, we may, at last, render our philosophy like that of EPICTETUS, and other *Stoics*,* only a more refined system of selfishness, and reason ourselves out of all virtue, as well as social enjoyment. While we study with attention the vanity of human life, and turn all our thoughts towards the empty and transitory nature of riches and honours, we are, perhaps, all the while, flattering our natural indolence, which, hating the bustle of the world, and drudgery of business, seeks a pretence of reason, to give itself a full and uncontrouled indulgence. There is, however, one species of philosophy, which seems little liable to this inconvenience, and that because it strikes in with no disorderly passion of the human mind, nor can mingle itself with any natural affection or propensity; and that is the ACADEMIC or SCEPTICAL philosophy.* The academics always talk of doubt and suspense of judgment, of danger in hasty determinations, of confining to very narrow bounds the enquiries of the understanding, and of renouncing all speculations which lie not within the limits of common life and practice. Nothing, therefore, can be more contrary than such a philosophy to the supine indolence of the mind, its rash arrogance, its lofty pretensions, and its superstitious credulity. Every passion is mortified by it, except the love of truth; and that passion never is, nor can be carried to too high a degree. It is surprising, therefore, that this philosophy, which, in almost every instance, must be harmless and innocent, should be the subject of so much groundless reproach and obloquy. But, perhaps, the very circumstance, which renders it so innocent, is what chiefly exposes it to the public hatred and resentment. By flattering no irregular passion, it gains few partizans: By opposing so many vices and follies, it raises to itself abundance of enemies, who stigmatize it as libertine, profane, and irreligious.

[2] Nor need we fear, that this philosophy, while it endeavours to limit our enquiries to common life, should ever undermine the reasonings of common life, and carry its doubts so far as to destroy all action, as well as speculation. Nature will always maintain her rights, and prevail in the end over any abstract reasoning whatsoever. Though we should conclude, for instance, as in the foregoing section, that, in all reasonings from experience, there is a step taken by the mind, which is not supported by any argument or process of the understanding; there is no danger, that these reasonings, on which almost all knowledge depends, will ever be affected by such a discovery. If the mind be not engaged by argument to make this step, it must be induced by some other principle of equal weight and authority; and that principle will preserve its influence as long as human nature remains the same. What 42 that principle is, may well be worth the pains of enquiry.

[3] Suppose a person, though endowed with the strongest faculties of reason and reflection, to be brought on a sudden into this world;* he would, indeed, immediately observe a continual succession of objects, and one event following another; but he would not be able to discover any thing farther. He would not, at first, by any reasoning, be able to reach the idea of cause and effect; since the particular powers, by which all natural operations are performed, never appear to the senses; nor is it reasonable to conclude, merely because one event, in one instance, precedes another, that therefore the one is the cause, the other the effect. Their conjunction may be arbitrary and casual. There may be no reason to infer the existence of one from the appearance of the other. And in a word, such a person, without more experience, could never employ his conjecture or reasoning concerning any matter of fact, or be assured of any thing beyond what was immediately present to his memory and senses.

[4] Suppose again, that he has acquired more experience, and has lived so long in the world as to have observed similar objects or events to be constantly conjoined together; what is the consequence of this experience? He immediately infers the existence of one object from the appearance of the other. Yet he has not, by all his experience,

acquired any idea or knowledge of the secret power, by which the one object produces the other; nor is it, by any process of reasoning, he is engaged to draw this inference. But still he finds himself determined to draw it: And though he should be convinced, that his understanding has no part in the operation, he would nevertheless continue in the same course of thinking. There is some other principle, which determines him to form such a conclusion.

43   [5] This principle is CUSTOM or HABIT.* For wherever the repetition of any particular act or operation produces a propensity to renew the same act or operation, without being impelled by any reasoning or process of the understanding; we always say, that this propensity is the effect of *Custom*. By employing that word, we pretend not to have given the ultimate reason of such a propensity. We only point out a principle of human nature, which is universally acknowledged, and which is well known by its effects. Perhaps, we can push our enquiries no farther, or pretend to give the cause of this cause; but must rest contented with it as the ultimate principle, which we can assign, of all our conclusions from experience. It is sufficient satisfaction, that we can go so far; without repining at the narrowness of our faculties, because they will carry us no farther. And it is certain we here advance a very intelligible proposition at least, if not a true one, when we assert, that, after the constant conjunction of two objects, heat and flame, for instance, weight and solidity, we are determined by custom alone to expect the one from the appearance of the other. This hypothesis seems even the only one, which explains the difficulty, why we draw, from a thousand instances, an inference, which we are not able to draw from one instance, that is, in no respect, different from them. Reason is incapable of any such variation. The conclusions, which it draws from considering one circle, are the same which it would form upon surveying all the circles in the universe. But no man, having seen only one body move after being impelled by another, could infer, that every other body will move after a like impulse. All inferences from experience, therefore, are effects of custom, not of reasoning[8].

44   [6] Custom, then, is the great guide of human life.* It is that principle alone, which renders our experience useful to us, and makes us expect, for the future, a similar train of events with those which have
45   appeared in the past. Without the influence of custom, we should be

entirely ignorant of every matter of fact, beyond what is immediately present to the memory and senses. We should never know how to adjust means to ends, or to employ our natural powers in the production of any effect. There would be an end at once of all action, as well as of the chief part of speculation.

[7] But here it may be proper to remark, that though our conclusions from experience carry us beyond our memory and senses, and assure us of matters of fact, which happened in the most distant places and most remote ages; yet some fact must always be present to the senses or memory, from which we may first proceed in drawing these conclusions. A man, who should find in a desert country the remains of pompous buildings, would conclude, that the country had, in ancient times, been cultivated by civilized inhabitants; but did nothing of this nature occur to him, he could never form such an 46 inference. We learn the events of former ages from history; but then we must peruse the volumes, in which this instruction is contained, and thence carry up our inferences from one testimony to another, till we arrive at the eye-witnesses and spectators of these distant events. In a word, if we proceed not upon some fact, present to the memory or senses, our reasonings would be merely hypothetical; and however the particular links might be connected with each other, the whole chain of inferences would have nothing to support it, nor could we ever, by its means, arrive at the knowledge of any real existence. If I ask, why you believe any particular matter of fact, which you relate, you must tell me some reason; and this reason will be some other fact, connected with it. But as you cannot proceed after this manner, *in infinitum*, you must at last terminate in some fact, which is present to your memory or senses; or must allow that your belief is entirely without foundation.

[8] What then is the conclusion of the whole matter?* A simple one; though, it must be confessed, pretty remote from the common theories of philosophy. All belief of matter of fact or real existence is derived merely from some object, present to the memory or senses, and a customary conjunction between that and some other object. Or in other words; having found, in many instances, that any two kinds of objects, flame and heat, snow and cold, have always been conjoined together; if flame or snow be presented anew to the senses, the mind is carried by custom to expect heat or cold, and to *believe*, that such a quality does exist, and will discover itself upon a nearer approach.

This belief is the necessary result of placing the mind in such circumstances. It is an operation of the soul,* when we are so situated, as unavoidable as to feel the passion of love, when we receive benefits; or hatred, when we meet with injuries. All these operations are a species 47 of natural instincts, which no reasoning or process of the thought and understanding is able, either to produce, or to prevent.

[9] At this point, it would be very allowable for us to stop our philosophical researches. In most questions, we can never make a single step farther; and in all questions, we must terminate here at last, after our most restless and curious enquiries. But still our curiosity will be pardonable, perhaps commendable, if it carry us on to still farther researches, and make us examine more accurately the nature of this *belief*, and of the *customary conjunction*, whence it is derived. By this means we may meet with some explications and analogies, that will give satisfaction; at least to such as love the abstract sciences, and can be entertained with speculations, which, however accurate, may still retain a degree of doubt and uncertainty. As to readers of a different taste; the remaining part of this section is not calculated for them, and the following enquiries may well be understood, though it be neglected.*

PART II

[10] Nothing is more free than the imagination of man; and though it cannot exceed that original stock of ideas, furnished by the internal and external senses, it has unlimited power of mixing, compounding, separating, and dividing these ideas, in all the varieties of fiction and vision. It can feign a train of events, with all the appearance of reality, ascribe to them a particular time and place, conceive them as existent, and paint them out to itself with every circumstance, that belongs to any historical fact, which it believes with the greatest certainty. Wherein, therefore, consists the difference between such a fiction and belief? It lies not merely in any peculiar idea, which is annexed to such a conception as commands our assent, and which is wanting to every known fiction. For as the mind has authority over all its ideas, it could 48 voluntarily annex this particular idea to any fiction, and consequently be able to believe whatever it pleases; contrary to what we find by daily experience. We can, in our conception, join the head of a man to the body of a horse; but it is not in our power to believe, that such an animal has ever really existed.

[11] It follows, therefore, that the difference between *fiction* and *belief* lies in some sentiment or feeling, which is annexed to the latter, not to the former, and which depends not on the will, nor can be commanded at pleasure. It must be excited by nature, like all other sentiments; and must arise from the particular situation, in which the mind is placed at any particular juncture. Whenever any object is presented to the memory or senses, it immediately, by the force of custom, carries the imagination to conceive that object, which is usually conjoined to it; and this conception is attended with a feeling or sentiment, different from the loose reveries of the fancy. In this consists the whole nature of belief. For as there is no matter of fact which we believe so firmly, that we cannot conceive the contrary, there would be no difference between the conception assented to, and that which is rejected, were it not for some sentiment, which distinguishes the one from the other. If I see a billiard-ball moving towards another, on a smooth table, I can easily conceive it to stop upon contact. This conception implies no contradiction; but still it feels very differently from that conception, by which I represent to myself the impulse, and the communication of motion from one ball to another.

[12] Were we to attempt a *definition* of this sentiment,* we should, perhaps, find it a very difficult, if not an impossible task; in the same manner as if we should endeavour to define the feeling of cold or passion of anger, to a creature who never had any experience of these sentiments. BELIEF is the true and proper name of this feeling; and no one is ever at a loss to know the meaning of that term; because every man is every moment conscious of the sentiment represented by it. It may not, however, be improper to attempt a *description* of this sentiment; in hopes we may, by that means, arrive at some analogies, which may afford a more perfect explication of it. I say then, that belief is nothing but a more vivid, lively, forcible, firm, steady conception of an object, than what the imagination alone is ever able to attain. This variety of terms, which may seem so unphilosophical, is intended only to express that act of the mind, which renders realities, or what is taken for such, more present to us than fictions, causes them to weigh more in the thought, and gives them a superior influence on the passions and imagination. Provided we agree about the thing, it is needless to dispute about the terms. The imagination has the command over all its ideas, and can join and mix and vary them, in all the ways possible. It may conceive fictitious

objects with all the circumstances of place and time. It may set them, in a manner, before our eyes, in their true colours, just as they might have existed. But as it is impossible, that this faculty of imagination can ever, of itself, reach belief, it is evident, that belief consists not in the peculiar nature or order of ideas, but in the *manner* of their conception, and in their *feeling* to the mind. I confess, that it is impossible perfectly to explain this feeling or manner of conception. We may make use of words, which express something near it. But its true and proper name, as we observed before, is *belief*; which is a term, that every one sufficiently understands in common life. And in philosophy, we can go no farther than assert, that *belief* is something felt by the mind, which distinguishes the ideas of the judgment from the fictions of the imagination. It gives them more weight and influence; makes them appear of greater importance; inforces them in the mind; and renders them the governing principle of our actions. I hear at present, for instance, a person's voice, with whom I am acquainted; and the sound comes as from the next room. This impression of my senses immediately conveys my thought to the person, together with all the surrounding objects. I paint them out to myself as existing at present, with the same qualities and relations, of which I formerly knew them possessed. These ideas take faster hold of my mind, than ideas of an enchanted castle. They are very different to the feeling, and have a much greater influence of every kind, either to give pleasure or pain, joy or sorrow.

[13] Let us, then, take in the whole compass of this doctrine, and allow, that the sentiment of belief is nothing but a conception more intense and steady than what attends the mere fictions of the imagination, and that this *manner* of conception arises from a customary conjunction of the object with something present to the memory or senses: I believe that it will not be difficult, upon these suppositions, to find other operations of the mind analogous to it, and to trace up these phaenomena to principles still more general.

[14] We have already observed, that nature has established connexions among particular ideas, and that no sooner one idea occurs to our thoughts than it introduces its correlative, and carries our attention towards it, by a gentle and insensible movement. These principles of connexion or association we have reduced to three, namely, *Resemblance*, *Contiguity*, and *Causation*; which are the only bonds, that unite our thoughts together, and beget that regular train

of reflection or discourse, which, in a greater or less degree, takes place among all mankind. Now here arises a question, on which the solution of the present difficulty will depend. Does it happen, in all these relations, that, when one of the objects is presented to the senses ₅₁ or memory, the mind is not only carried to the conception of the correlative, but reaches a steadier and stronger conception of it than what otherwise it would have been able to attain? This seems to be the case with that belief, which arises from the relation of cause and effect. And if the case be the same with the other relations or principles of association, this may be established as a general law, which takes place in all the operations of the mind.

[15] We may, therefore, observe, as the first experiment to our present purpose, that, upon the appearance of the picture of an absent friend, our idea of him is evidently enlivened by the *resemblance*, and that every passion, which that idea occasions, whether of joy or sorrow, acquires new force and vigour. In producing this effect, there concur both a relation and a present impression. Where the picture bears him no resemblance, at least was not intended for him, it never so much as conveys our thought to him: And where it is absent, as well as the person; though the mind may pass from the thought of the one to that of the other; it feels its idea to be rather weakened than enlivened by that transition. We take a pleasure in viewing the picture of a friend, when it is set before us; but when it is removed, rather chuse to consider him directly, than by reflection in an image, which is equally distant and obscure.

[16] The ceremonies of the ROMAN CATHOLIC religion may be considered as instances of the same nature. The devotees of that superstition usually plead in excuse for the mummeries, with which they are upbraided, that they feel the good effect of those external motions, and postures, and actions, in enlivening their devotion and quickening their fervour, which otherwise would decay, if directed entirely to distant and immaterial objects. We shadow out* the objects of our faith, say they, in sensible types and images, and render them ₅₂ more present to us by the immediate presence of these types, than it is possible for us to do, merely by an intellectual view and contemplation. Sensible objects have always a greater influence on the fancy than any other; and this influence they readily convey to those ideas, to which they are related, and which they resemble. I shall only infer from these practices, and this reasoning, that the effect of resemblance

in enlivening the ideas is very common; and as in every case a resemblance and a present impression must concur, we are abundantly supplied with experiments to prove the reality of the foregoing principle.

[17] We may add force to these experiments by others of a different kind, in considering the effects of *contiguity* as well as of *resemblance*. It is certain, that distance diminishes the force of every idea, and that, upon our approach to any object; though it does not discover itself to our senses; it operates upon the mind with an influence, which imitates an immediate impression. The thinking on any object readily transports the mind to what is contiguous; but it is only the actual presence of an object, that transports it with a superior vivacity. When I am a few miles from home, whatever relates to it touches me more nearly than when I am two hundred leagues distant; though even at that distance the reflecting on any thing in the neighbourhood of my friends or family naturally produces an idea of them. But as in this latter case, both the objects of the mind are ideas; notwithstanding there is an easy transition between them; that transition alone is not able to give a superior vivacity to any of the ideas, for want of some immediate impression[9].

53   [18] No one can doubt but causation has the same influence as the other two relations of resemblance and contiguity. Superstitious people are fond of the reliques of saints and holy men, for the same reason, that they seek after types or images, in order to enliven their devotion, and give them a more intimate and strong conception of those exemplary lives, which they desire to imitate. Now it is evident, that one of the best reliques, which a devotee could procure, would be the handywork of a saint; and if his cloaths and furniture are ever to be considered in this light, it is because they were once at his disposal, and were moved and affected by him; in which respect they are to be considered as imperfect effects, and as connected with

[9] "Naturane nobis, inquit, datum dicam, an errore quodam, ut, cum ea loca videamus, in quibus memoria dignos viros acceperimus multum esse versatos, magis moveamur, quam siquando eorum ipsorum aut facta audiamus aut scriptum aliquod legamus? Velut ego nunc moveor. Venit enim mihi PLATONIS in mentem, quem accepimus primum hîc disputare solitum: Cujus etiam illi hortuli propinqui non memoriam solum mihi afferunt, sed ipsum videntur in conspectu meo hîc ponere. Hic SPEUSIPPUS, hic XENOCRATES, hic ejus auditor POLEMO; cujus ipsa illa sessio fuit, quam videamus. Equidem etiam curiam nostram, HOSTILIAM dico, non hanc novam, quae mihi minor esse videtur postquam est major, solebam intuens, SCIPIONEM, CATONEM, LAELIUM, nostrum vero in primis avum cogitare. Tanta vis admonitionis est in locis; ut non sine causa ex his memoriae deducta sit disciplina."* CICERO *de Finibus.* Lib. v.

him by a shorter chain of consequences than any of those, by which we learn the reality of his existence.

[19] Suppose, that the son of a friend, who had been long dead or absent, were presented to us; it is evident, that this object would instantly revive its correlative idea, and recal to our thoughts all past intimacies and familiarities, in more lively colours than they would otherwise have appeared to us. This is another phaenomenon, which seems to prove the principle above-mentioned.

[20] We may observe, that, in these phaenomena, the belief of the correlative object is always presupposed;* without which the relation could have no effect. The influence of the picture supposes, that we *believe* our friend to have once existed. Contiguity to home can never excite our ideas of home, unless we *believe* that it really exists. Now I assert, that this belief, where it reaches beyond the memory or senses, is of a similar nature, and arises from similar causes, with the transition of thought and vivacity of conception here explained. When I throw a piece of dry wood into a fire, my mind is immediately carried to conceive, that it augments, not extinguishes the flame. This transition of thought from the cause to the effect proceeds not from reason. It derives its origin altogether from custom and experience. And as it first begins from an object, present to the senses, it renders the idea or conception of flame more strong and lively than any loose, floating reverie of the imagination. That idea arises immediately. The thought moves instantly towards it, and conveys to it all that force of conception, which is derived from the impression present to the senses. When a sword is levelled at my breast, does not the idea of wound and pain strike me more strongly, than when a glass of wine is presented to me, even though by accident this idea should occur after the appearance of the latter object? But what is there in this whole matter to cause such a strong conception, except only a present object and a customary transition to the idea of another object, which we have been accustomed to conjoin with the former? This is the whole operation of the mind, in all our conclusions concerning matter of fact and existence; and it is a satisfaction to find some analogies, by which it may be explained. The transition from a present object does in all cases give strength and solidity to the related idea.

[21] Here, then, is a kind of pre-established harmony* between the course of nature and the succession of our ideas; and though the powers

and forces, by which the former is governed, be wholly unknown to us; yet our thoughts and conceptions have still, we find, gone on in the same train with the other works of nature. Custom is that principle, by which this correspondence has been effected; so necessary to the subsistence of our species, and the regulation of our conduct, in every circumstance and occurrence of human life. Had not the presence of an object instantly excited the idea of those objects, commonly conjoined with it, all our knowledge must have been limited to the narrow sphere of our memory and senses; and we should never have been able to adjust means to ends, or employ our natural powers, either to the producing of good, or avoiding of evil. Those, who delight in the discovery and contemplation of *final causes,** have here ample subject to employ their wonder and admiration.

[22] I shall add, for a further confirmation of the foregoing theory, that, as this operation of the mind, by which we infer like effects from like causes, and *vice versa*, is so essential to the subsistence of all human creatures, it is not probable, that it could be trusted to the fallacious deductions of our reason, which is slow in its operations; appears not, in any degree, during the first years of infancy; and at best is, in every age and period of human life, extremely liable to error and mistake. It is more conformable to the ordinary wisdom of nature to secure so necessary an act of the mind, by some instinct or mechanical tendency, which may be infallible in its operations, may discover itself at the first appearance of life and thought, and may be independent of all the laboured deductions of the understanding. As nature has taught us the use of our limbs, without giving us the knowledge of the muscles and nerves, by which they are actuated; so has she implanted in us an instinct, which carries forward the thought in a correspondent course to that which she has established among external objects; though we are ignorant of those powers and forces, on which this regular course and succession of objects totally depends.

SECTION VI

Of Probability[10]

THOUGH there be no such thing as *Chance* in the world;* our ignorance of the real cause of any event has the same influence on the understanding, and begets a like species of belief or opinion.

[2] There is certainly a probability, which arises from a superiority of chances on any side; and according as this superiority encreases, and surpasses the opposite chances, the probability receives a proportionable encrease, and begets still a higher degree of belief or assent to that side, in which we discover the superiority. If a dye were marked with one figure or number of spots on four sides, and with another figure or number of spots on the two remaining sides, it would be more probable, that the former would turn up than the latter; though, if it had a thousand sides marked in the same manner, and only one side different, the probability would be much higher, and our belief or expectation of the event more steady and secure. This process of the thought or reasoning may seem trivial and obvious; but to those who consider it more narrowly, it may, perhaps, afford matter for curious speculation.

[3] It seems evident, that, when the mind looks forward to discover the event, which may result from the throw of such a dye, it considers the turning up of each particular side as alike probable; and this is the very nature of chance, to render all the particular events, comprehended in it, entirely equal. But finding a greater number of sides concur in the one event than in the other, the mind is carried more frequently to that event, and meets it oftener, in revolving the various possibilities or chances, on which the ultimate result depends. This concurrence of several views in one particular event begets immediately, by an inexplicable contrivance of nature,* the sentiment of belief, and gives that event the advantage over its antagonist, which is supported by a smaller number of views, and recurs less frequently

---

[10] Mr. LOCKE divides all arguments into demonstrative and probable. In this view, we must say, that it is only probable all men must die, or that the sun will rise to-morrow. But to conform our language more to common use, we ought to divide arguments into *demonstrations*, *proofs*, and *probabilities*.* By proofs meaning such arguments from experience as leave no room for doubt or opposition.

to the mind. If we allow, that belief is nothing but a firmer and stronger conception of an object than what attends the mere fictions of the imagination, this operation may, perhaps, in some measure, be accounted for. The concurrence of these several views or glimpses imprints the idea more strongly on the imagination; gives it superior force and vigour; renders its influence on the passions and affections more sensible; and in a word, begets that reliance or security, which constitutes the nature of belief and opinion.

[4] The case is the same with the probability of causes, as with that of chance. There are some causes, which are entirely uniform and constant in producing a particular effect; and no instance has ever yet been found of any failure or irregularity in their operation. Fire has always burned, and water suffocated every human creature: The production of motion by impulse and gravity is an universal law, which has hitherto admitted of no exception. But there are other causes, which have been found more irregular and uncertain; nor has rhubarb always proved a purge, or opium a soporific* to every one, who has taken these medicines. It is true, when any cause fails of producing its usual effect, philosophers ascribe not this to any irregularity in nature; but suppose, that some secret causes, in the particular structure of parts, have prevented the operation. Our reasonings, however, and conclusions concerning the event are the same as if this principle had no place. Being determined by custom to transfer the past to the future, in all our inferences; where the past has been entirely regular and uniform, we expect the event with the greatest assurance, and leave no room for any contrary supposition. But where different effects have been found to follow from causes, which are to *appearance* exactly similar, all these various effects must occur to the mind in transferring the past to the future, and enter into our consideration, when we determine the probability of the event. Though we give the preference to that which has been found most usual, and believe that this effect will exist, we must not overlook the other effects, but must assign to each of them a particular weight and authority, in proportion as we have found it to be more or less frequent. It is more probable, in almost every country of EUROPE, that there will be frost sometime in JANUARY, than that the weather will continue open throughout that whole month; though this probability varies according to the different climates, and approaches to a certainty in the more northern kingdoms. Here then it seems evident, that, when

we transfer the past to the future, in order to determine the effect, which will result from any cause, we transfer all the different events, in the same proportion as they have appeared in the past, and conceive one to have existed a hundred times, for instance, another ten times, and another once. As a great number of views do here concur in one event, they fortify and confirm it to the imagination, beget that sentiment which we call *belief*, and give its object the preference above the contrary event, which is not supported by an equal number of experiments, and recurs not so frequently to the thought in transferring the past to the future. Let any one try to account for this operation of the mind upon any of the received systems of philosophy, and he will be sensible of the difficulty.* For my part, I shall think it sufficient, if the present hints excite the curiosity of philosophers, and make them sensible how defective all common theories are in treating of such curious and such sublime subjects.

SECTION VII

Of the IDEA of NECESSARY CONNEXION*

PART I

THE great advantage of the mathematical sciences above the moral consists in this, that the ideas of the former, being sensible, are always clear and determinate, the smallest distinction between them is immediately perceptible, and the same terms are still expressive of the same ideas, without ambiguity or variation. An oval is never mistaken for a circle, nor an hyperbola for an ellipsis. The isosceles and scalenum are distinguished by boundaries more exact than vice and virtue, right and wrong. If any term be defined in geometry, the mind readily, of itself, substitutes, on all occasions, the definition for the term defined: Or even when no definition is employed, the object itself may be presented to the senses, and by that means be steadily and clearly apprehended. But the finer sentiments of the mind, the operations of the understanding, the various agitations of the passions, though really in themselves distinct, easily escape us, when surveyed by reflection; nor is it in our power to recal the original object, as often as we have occasion to contemplate it. Ambiguity, by this means, is gradually introduced into our reasonings: Similar objects are readily taken to be the same: And the conclusion becomes at last very wide of the premises.

[2] One may safely, however, affirm, that, if we consider these sciences in a proper light, their advantages and disadvantages nearly compensate each other, and reduce both of them to a state of equality. If the mind, with greater facility, retains the ideas of geometry clear and determinate, it must carry on a much longer and more intricate chain of reasoning, and compare ideas much wider of each other, in order to reach the abstruser truths of that science. And if moral ideas are apt, without extreme care, to fall into obscurity and confusion, the inferences are always much shorter in these disquisitions, and the intermediate steps, which lead to the conclusion, much fewer than in the sciences which treat of quantity and number. In reality, there is scarcely a proposition in EUCLID* so simple, as not to consist

of more parts, than are to be found in any moral reasoning which runs not into chimera and conceit.* Where we trace the principles of the human mind through a few steps, we may be very well satisfied with our progress; considering how soon nature throws a bar to all our enquiries concerning causes, and reduces us to an acknowledgment of our ignorance. The chief obstacle, therefore, to our improvement in the moral or metaphysical sciences is the obscurity of the ideas, and ambiguity of the terms. The principal difficulty in the mathematics is the length of inferences and compass of thought, requisite to the forming of any conclusion. And, perhaps, our progress in natural philosophy is chiefly retarded by the want of proper experiments and phaenomena, which are often discovered by chance, and cannot always be found, when requisite, even by the most diligent and prudent enquiry. As moral philosophy seems hitherto to have received less improvement than either geometry or physics, we may conclude, that, if there be any difference in this respect among these sciences, the difficulties, which obstruct the progress of the former, require superior care and capacity to be surmounted.

[3] There are no ideas, which occur in metaphysics, more obscure 62 and uncertain, than those of *power, force, energy,* or *necessary connexion,* of which it is every moment necessary for us to treat in all our disquisitions. We shall, therefore, endeavour, in this section, to fix, if possible, the precise meaning of these terms, and thereby remove some part of that obscurity, which is so much complained of in this species of philosophy.

[4] It seems a proposition, which will not admit of much dispute, that all our ideas are nothing but copies of our impressions,* or, in other words, that it is impossible for us to *think* of any thing, which we have not antecedently *felt*, either by our external or internal senses. I have endeavoured[11] to explain and prove this proposition, and have expressed my hopes, that, by a proper application of it, men may reach a greater clearness and precision in philosophical reasonings, than what they have hitherto been able to attain. Complex ideas may, perhaps, be well known by definition, which is nothing but an enumeration of those parts or simple ideas, that compose them. But when we have pushed up definitions to the most simple ideas, and find still some ambiguity and obscurity; what resource are we

---

[11] Section II.

then possessed of? By what invention can we throw light upon these ideas, and render them altogether precise and determinate to our intellectual view? Produce the impressions or original sentiments, from which the ideas are copied. These impressions are all strong and sensible. They admit not of ambiguity. They are not only placed in a full light themselves, but may throw light on their correspondent ideas, which lie in obscurity. And by this means, we may, perhaps, attain a new microscope or species of optics, by which, in the moral sciences, the most minute, and most simple ideas may be so enlarged as to fall readily under our apprehension, and be equally known with the grossest and most sensible ideas, that can be the object of our enquiry.

63   [5] To be fully acquainted, therefore, with the idea of power or necessary connexion, let us examine its impression; and in order to find the impression with greater certainty, let us search for it in all the sources, from which it may possibly be derived.*

[6] When we look about us towards external objects, and consider the operation of causes, we are never able, in a single instance, to discover any power or necessary connexion; any quality, which binds the effect to the cause, and renders the one an infallible consequence of the other. We only find, that the one does actually, in fact, follow the other. The impulse of one billiard-ball is attended with motion in the second. This is the whole that appears to the *outward* senses. The mind feels no sentiment or *inward* impression* from this succession of objects: Consequently, there is not, in any single, particular instance of cause and effect, any thing which can suggest the idea of power or necessary connexion.

[7] From the first appearance of an object, we never can conjecture what effect will result from it. But were the power or energy of any cause discoverable by the mind, we could foresee the effect, even without experience; and might, at first, pronounce with certainty concerning it, by the mere dint of thought and reasoning.

[8] In reality, there is no part of matter, that does ever, by its sensible qualities, discover any power or energy, or give us ground to imagine, that it could produce any thing, or be followed by any other object, which we could denominate its effect. Solidity, extension, motion; these qualities are all complete in themselves, and never point out any other event which may result from them. The scenes of the universe are continually shifting, and one object follows another in an uninterrupted succession; but the power or force, which actuates

the whole machine, is entirely concealed from us, and never discovers itself in any of the sensible qualities of body. We know, that, in fact, 64 heat is a constant attendant of flame; but what is the connexion between them, we have no room so much as to conjecture or imagine. It is impossible, therefore, that the idea of power can be derived from the contemplation of bodies, in single instances of their operation; because no bodies ever discover any power, which can be the original of this idea[12].

[9] Since, therefore, external objects as they appear to the senses, give us no idea of power or necessary connexion, by their operation in particular instances, let us see, whether this idea be derived from reflection on the operations of our own minds, and be copied from any internal impression. It may be said, that we are every moment conscious of internal power; while we feel, that, by the simple command of our will, we can move the organs of our body, or direct the faculties of our mind. An act of volition produces motion in our limbs, or raises a new idea in our imagination. This influence of the will we know by consciousness. Hence we acquire the idea of power or energy; and are certain, that we ourselves and all other intelligent beings are possessed of power. This idea, then, is an idea of reflection, since it arises from reflecting on the operations of our own mind, and on the command which is exercised by will, both over the organs of the body and faculties of the soul.

[10] We shall proceed to examine this pretension; and first with regard to the influence of volition over the organs of the body. This influence, we may observe, is a fact, which, like all other natural events, can be known only by experience, and can never be foreseen from any apparent energy or power in the cause, which connects it with 65 the effect, and renders the one an infallible consequence of the other. The motion of our body follows upon the command of our will. Of this we are every moment conscious. But the means, by which this is effected; the energy, by which the will performs so extraordinary an operation; of this we are so far from being immediately conscious, that it must for ever escape our most diligent enquiry.

[12] Mr. LOCKE,* in his chapter of power, says, that, finding from experience, that there are several new productions in matter, and concluding that there must somewhere be a power capable of producing them, we arrive at last by this reasoning at the idea of power. But no reasoning can ever give us a new, original, simple idea;* as this philosopher himself confesses. This, therefore, can never be the origin of that idea.

[11] For *first*; is there any principle in all nature more mysterious than the union of soul with body; by which a supposed spiritual substance acquires such an influence over a material one, that the most refined thought is able to actuate the grossest matter? Were we empowered, by a secret wish, to remove mountains, or control the planets in their orbit; this extensive authority would not be more extraordinary, nor more beyond our comprehension. But if by consciousness we perceived any power or energy in the will, we must know this power; we must know its connexion with the effect; we must know the secret union of soul and body, and the nature of both these substances; by which the one is able to operate, in so many instances, upon the other.

[12] *Secondly*, We are not able to move all the organs of the body with a like authority; though we cannot assign any reason besides experience, for so remarkable a difference between one and the other. Why has the will an influence over the tongue and fingers, not over the heart or liver? This question would never embarrass us, were we conscious of a power in the former case, not in the latter. We should then perceive, independent of experience, why the authority of will over the organs of the body is circumscribed within such particular limits. Being in that case fully acquainted with the power or force, by which it operates, we should also know, why its influence reaches precisely to such boundaries, and no farther.

66   [13] A man, suddenly struck with a palsy* in the leg or arm, or who had newly lost those members, frequently endeavours, at first, to move them, and employ them in their usual offices. Here he is as much conscious of power to command such limbs, as a man in perfect health is conscious of power to actuate any member which remains in its natural state and condition. But consciousness never deceives. Consequently, neither in the one case nor in the other, are we ever conscious of any power. We learn the influence of our will from experience alone. And experience only teaches us, how one event constantly follows another; without instructing us in the secret connexion, which binds them together, and renders them inseparable.

[14] *Thirdly*, We learn from anatomy, that the immediate object of power in voluntary motion, is not the member itself which is moved, but certain muscles, and nerves, and animal spirits,* and, perhaps, something still more minute and more unknown, through which the motion is successively propagated, ere it reach the member itself whose motion is the immediate object of volition. Can there be

a more certain proof, that the power, by which this whole operation is performed, so far from being directly and fully known by an inward sentiment or consciousness, is, to the last degree, mysterious and unintelligible? Here the mind wills a certain event: Immediately another event, unknown to ourselves, and totally different from the one intended, is produced: This event produces another, equally unknown: Till at last, through a long succession, the desired event is produced. But if the original power were felt, it must be known: Were it known, its effect must also be known; since all power is relative to its effect. And *vice versa*, if the effect be not known, the power cannot be known nor felt. How indeed can we be conscious of a power to move our limbs, when we have no such power; but only that to move certain animal spirits, which, though they produce at last the motion of our limbs, yet operate in such a manner as is wholly 67 beyond our comprehension?

[15] We may, therefore, conclude from the whole, I hope, without any temerity, though with assurance; that our idea of power is not copied from any sentiment or consciousness of power within ourselves, when we give rise to animal motion, or apply our limbs to their proper use and office. That their motion follows the command of the will is a matter of common experience, like other natural events: But the power or energy by which this is effected, like that in other natural events, is unknown and inconceivable[13].

[16] Shall we then assert, that we are conscious of a power or energy in our own minds, when, by an act or command of our will, we raise up a new idea, fix the mind to the contemplation of it, turn it on all sides, and at last dismiss it for some other idea, when we think that we have surveyed it with sufficient accuracy? I believe the same arguments will prove, that even this command of the will gives us no real idea of force or energy.

[17] *First*, It must be allowed, that, when we know a power, we know that very circumstance in the cause, by which it is enabled 68 to produce the effect: For these are supposed to be synonimous. We must, therefore, know both the cause and effect, and the relation between them. But do we pretend to be acquainted with the nature of the human soul and the nature of an idea, or the aptitude of the one to produce the other? This is a real creation; a production of

---

[13] See endnote [C], p. 123.

something out of nothing: Which implies a power so great, that it may seem, at first sight, beyond the reach of any being, less than infinite. At least it must be owned, that such a power is not felt, nor known, nor even conceivable by the mind. We only feel the event, namely, the existence of an idea, consequent to a command of the will: But the manner, in which this operation is performed; the power, by which it is produced; is entirely beyond our comprehension.

[18] *Secondly*, The command of the mind over itself is limited, as well as its command over the body; and these limits are not known by reason, or any acquaintance with the nature of cause and effect; but only by experience and observation, as in all other natural events and in the operation of external objects. Our authority over our sentiments and passions is much weaker than that over our ideas; and even the latter authority is circumscribed within very narrow boundaries. Will any one pretend to assign the ultimate reason of these boundaries, or show why the power is deficient in one case not in another.

[19] *Thirdly*, This self-command is very different at different times. A man in health possesses more of it, than one languishing with sickness. We are more master of our thoughts in the morning than in the evening: Fasting, than after a full meal. Can we give any reason for these variations, except experience? Where then is the power, of which we pretend to be conscious? Is there not here, either in a spiritual or material substance, or both, some secret mechanism or structure of parts, upon which the effect depends, and which, being entirely unknown to us, renders the power or energy of the will equally unknown and incomprehensible?

[20] Volition is surely an act of the mind, with which we are sufficiently acquainted. Reflect upon it. Consider it on all sides. Do you find any thing in it like this creative power, by which it raises from nothing a new idea, and with a kind of FIAT, imitates the omnipotence of its Maker, if I may be allowed so to speak, who called forth into existence all the various scenes of nature? So far from being conscious of this energy in the will, it requires as certain experience, as that of which we are possessed, to convince us, that such extraordinary effects do ever result from a simple act of volition.

[21] The generality of mankind never find any difficulty in accounting for the more common and familiar operations of nature; such as the descent of heavy bodies, the growth of plants, the generation of animals, or the nourishment of bodies by food: But suppose, that, in

all these cases, they perceive the very force or energy of the cause, by which it is connected with its effect, and is for ever infallible in its operation. They acquire, by long habit, such a turn of mind, that, upon the appearance of the cause, they immediately expect with assurance its usual attendant, and hardly conceive it possible, that any other event could result from it. It is only on the discovery of extraordinary phaenomena, such as earthquakes, pestilence, and prodigies of any kind, that they find themselves at a loss to assign a proper cause, and to explain the manner, in which the effect is produced by it. It is usual for men, in such difficulties, to have recourse to some invisible intelligent principle[14], as the immediate cause of that event, which surprises them, and which, they think, cannot be accounted for from the common powers of nature. But philosophers, who carry their scrutiny a little farther, immediately perceive, that, even in the most familiar events, the energy of the cause is as unintelligible as in the most unusual, and that we only learn by experience the frequent CONJUNCTION of objects, without being ever able to comprehend any thing like CONNEXION between them. Here then, many philosophers* think themselves obliged by reason to have recourse, on all occasions, to the same principle, which the vulgar never appeal to but in cases, that appear miraculous and supernatural. They acknowledge mind and intelligence to be, not only the ultimate and original cause of all things, but the immediate and sole cause of every event, which appears in nature. They pretend, that those objects, which are commonly denominated *causes*, are in reality nothing but *occasions*; and that the true and direct principle of every effect is not any power or force in nature, but a volition of the Supreme Being, who wills, that such particular objects should, for ever, be conjoined with each other. Instead of saying, that one billiard-ball moves another, by a force, which it has derived from the author of nature; it is the Deity himself, they say, who, by a particular volition, moves the second ball, being determined to this operation by the impulse of the first ball; in consequence of those general laws, which he has laid down to himself in the government of the universe. But philosophers advancing still in their enquiries, discover, that, as we are totally ignorant of the power, on which depends the mutual operation of bodies, we are no less ignorant of that power, on which depends the operation of

[14] Θεος απο μηχανης.*

mind on body, or of body on mind; nor are we able, either from our senses or consciousness, to assign the ultimate principle in one case, more than in the other. The same ignorance, therefore, reduces them to the same conclusion. They assert, that the Deity is the immediate cause of the union between soul and body; and that they are not the organs of sense, which, being agitated by external objects, produce

71 sensations in the mind; but that it is a particular volition of our omnipotent Maker, which excites such a sensation, in consequence of such a motion in the organ. In like manner, it is not any energy in the will, that produces local motion in our members: It is God himself, who is pleased to second our will, in itself impotent, and to command that motion, which we erroneously attribute to our own power and efficacy. Nor do philosophers stop at this conclusion. They sometimes extend the same inference to the mind itself, in its internal operations. Our mental vision or conception of ideas is nothing but a revelation made to us by our Maker. When we voluntarily turn our thoughts to any object, and raise up its image in the fancy; it is not the will which creates that idea: It is the universal Creator, who discovers it to the mind, and renders it present to us.

[22] Thus, according to these philosophers, every thing is full of God. Not content with the principle, that nothing exists but by his will, that nothing possesses any power but by his concession: They rob nature, and all created beings, of every power, in order to render their dependence on the Deity still more sensible and immediate. They consider not, that, by this theory, they diminish, instead of magnifying, the grandeur of those attributes, which they affect so much to celebrate. It argues surely more power in the Deity to delegate a certain degree of power to inferior creatures, than to produce every thing by his own immediate volition. It argues more wisdom to contrive at first the fabric of the world with such perfect foresight, that, of itself, and by its proper operation, it may serve all the purposes of providence, than if the great Creator were obliged every moment to adjust its parts, and animate by his breath all the wheels of that stupendous machine.

[23] But if we would have a more philosophical confutation of this theory, perhaps the two following reflections may suffice.

72 [24] *First*, It seems to me, that this theory of the universal energy and operation of the Supreme Being, is too bold ever to carry conviction with it to a man, sufficiently apprized of the weakness of human

reason, and the narrow limits, to which it is confined in all its operations. Though the chain of arguments, which conduct to it, were ever so logical, there must arise a strong suspicion, if not an absolute assurance, that it has carried us quite beyond the reach of our faculties, when it leads to conclusions so extraordinary, and so remote from common life and experience. We are got into fairy land, long ere we have reached the last steps of our theory; and *there* we have no reason to trust our common methods of argument, or to think that our usual analogies and probabilities have any authority. Our line is too short to fathom such immense abysses. And however we may flatter ourselves, that we are guided, in every step which we take, by a kind of verisimilitude and experience; we may be assured, that this fancied experience has no authority, when we thus apply it to subjects, that lie entirely out of the sphere of experience. But on this we shall have occasion to touch afterwards[15].

[25] *Secondly*, I cannot perceive any force in the arguments, on which this theory is founded. We are ignorant, it is true, of the manner in which bodies operate on each other: Their force or energy is entirely incomprehensible: But are we not equally ignorant of the manner or force by which a mind, even the supreme mind, operates either on itself or on body? Whence, I beseech you, do we acquire any idea of it? We have no sentiment or consciousness of this power in ourselves. We have no idea of the Supreme Being but what we learn from reflection on our own faculties. Were our ignorance, therefore, a good reason for rejecting any thing, we should be led into that principle of denying all energy in the Supreme Being as much as in the grossest matter. We surely comprehend as little the operations of one as of the other. Is it more difficult to conceive, that motion may arise from impulse, than that it may arise from volition? All we know is our profound ignorance in both cases[16].

PART II

[26] But to hasten to a conclusion of this argument, which is already drawn out to too great a length: We have sought in vain for an idea of power or necessary connexion, in all the sources from which we could suppose it to be derived. It appears, that, in single instances of

---

[15] Section XII.
[16] See endnote [D], p. 123.

the operation of bodies, we never can, by our utmost scrutiny, discover any thing but one event following another; without being able to comprehend any force or power, by which the cause operates, or any connexion between it and its supposed effect. The same difficulty occurs in contemplating the operations of mind on body; where we observe the motion of the latter to follow upon the volition of the former; but are not able to observe or conceive the tye, which binds together the motion and volition, or the energy by which the mind produces this effect. The authority of the will over its own faculties and ideas is not a whit more comprehensible: So that, upon the whole, there appears not, throughout all nature, any one instance of connexion, which is conceivable by us. All events seem entirely loose and separate. One event follows another; but we never can observe any tye between them. They seem *conjoined*, but never *connected*. And as we can have no idea of any thing, which never appeared to our outward sense or inward sentiment, the necessary conclusion *seems* to be, that we have no idea of connexion or power at all, and that these words are absolutely without any meaning, when employed either in philosophical reasonings, or common life.

[27] But there still remains one method of avoiding this conclusion, and one source which we have not yet examined. When any natural object or event is presented, it is impossible for us, by any sagacity or penetration, to discover, or even conjecture, without experience, what event will result from it, or to carry our foresight beyond that object, which is immediately present to the memory and senses. Even after one instance or experiment, where we have observed a particular event to follow upon another, we are not entitled to form a general rule, or foretel what will happen in like cases; it being justly esteemed an unpardonable temerity to judge of the whole course of nature from one single experiment, however accurate or certain. But when one particular species of event has always, in all instances, been conjoined with another, we make no longer any scruple of foretelling one upon the appearance of the other, and of employing that reasoning, which can alone assure us of any matter of fact or existence. We then call the one object, *Cause*; the other, *Effect*. We suppose, that there is some connexion between them; some power in the one, by which it infallibly produces the other, and operates with the greatest certainty and strongest necessity.

[28] It appears, then, that this idea of a necessary connexion* among events arises from a number of similar instances, which occur,

of the constant conjunction of these events; nor can that idea ever be suggested by any one of these instances, surveyed in all possible lights and positions. But there is nothing in a number of instances, different from every single instance, which is supposed to be exactly similar; except only, that after a repetition of similar instances, the mind is carried by habit, upon the appearance of one event, to expect its usual attendant, and to believe, that it will exist. This connexion, therefore, which we *feel* in the mind, this customary transition of the imagination from one object to its usual attendant, is the sentiment or impression, from which we form the idea of power or necessary connexion. Nothing farther is in the case. Contemplate the subject on all sides; you will never find any other origin of that idea. This is the sole difference between one instance, from which we can never receive the idea of connexion, and a number of similar instances, by which it is suggested. The first time a man saw the communication of motion by impulse, as by the shock of two billiard-balls, he could not pronounce that the one event was *connected:* but only that it was *conjoined* with the other. After he has observed several instances of this nature, he then pronounces them to be *connected*. What alteration has happened to give rise to this new idea of *connexion*? Nothing but that he now *feels* these events to be *connected* in his imagination, and can readily foretel the existence of one from the appearance of the other. When we say, therefore, that one object is connected with another, we mean only, that they have acquired a connexion in our thought, and give rise to this inference, by which they become proofs of each other's existence: A conclusion, which is somewhat extraordinary; but which seems founded on sufficient evidence. Nor will its evidence be weakened by any general diffidence of the understanding, or sceptical suspicion concerning every conclusion, which is new and extraordinary. No conclusions can be more agreeable to scepticism than such as make discoveries concerning the weakness and narrow limits of human reason and capacity.

[29] And what stronger instance can be produced of the surprising ignorance and weakness of the understanding, than the present? For surely, if there be any relation among objects, which it imports to us to know perfectly, it is that of cause and effect. On this are founded all our reasonings concerning matter of fact or existence. By means of it alone we attain any assurance concerning objects, which are removed from the present testimony of our memory and senses.

The only immediate utility of all sciences, is to teach us, how to control and regulate future events by their causes. Our thoughts and enquiries are, therefore, every moment, employed about this relation: Yet so imperfect are the ideas which we form concerning it, that it is impossible to give any just definition of cause, except what is drawn from something extraneous and foreign to it. Similar objects are always conjoined with similar. Of this we have experience. Suitably to this experience, therefore, we may define a cause* to be *an object, followed by another, and where all the objects, similar to the first, are followed by objects similar to the second.* Or in other words, *where, if the first object had not been, the second never had existed.* The

77 appearance of a cause always conveys the mind, by a customary transition, to the idea of the effect. Of this also we have experience. We may, therefore, suitably to this experience, form another definition of cause; and call it, *an object followed by another, and whose appearance always conveys the thought to that other.* But though both these definitions be drawn from circumstances foreign to the cause, we cannot remedy this inconvenience, or attain any more perfect definition, which may point out that circumstance in the cause, which gives it a connexion with its effect. We have no idea of this connexion; nor even any distinct notion what it is we desire to know, when we endeavour at a conception of it. We say, for instance, that the vibration of this string is the cause of this particular sound. But what do we mean by that affirmation? We either mean, *that this vibration is followed by this sound, and that all similar vibrations have been followed by similar sounds:* Or, *that this vibration is followed by this sound, and that upon the appearance of one, the mind anticipates the senses, and forms immediately an idea of the other.* We may consider the relation of cause and effect in either of these two lights; but beyond these, we have no idea of it[17].

78 [30] To recapitulate, therefore, the reasonings of this section: Every idea is copied from some preceding impression or sentiment; and where we cannot find any impression, we may be certain that there is no idea. In all single instances of the operation of bodies or minds, there is nothing that produces any impression, nor consequently can suggest any idea, of power or necessary connexion. But when many uniform instances appear, and the same object is always followed by

[17] See endnote [E], p. 124.

the same event; we then begin to entertain the notion of cause and connexion. We then *feel* a new sentiment or impression, to wit, a customary connexion in the thought or imagination between one object and its usual attendant; and this sentiment is the original of that idea which we seek for. For as this idea arises from a number of similar instances, and not from any single instance; it must arise from that circumstance, in which the number of instances differ from every individual instance. But this customary connexion or transition of the imagination is the only circumstance, in which they differ. In every other particular they are alike. The first instance which we saw of motion, communicated by the shock of two billiard-balls (to return to this obvious illustration) is exactly similar to any instance that may, at present, occur to us; except only, that we could not, at first, *infer* one event from the other; which we are enabled to do at present, after so long a course of uniform experience. I know not, whether the reader will readily apprehend this reasoning. I am afraid, that, should I multiply words about it, or throw it into a greater variety of lights, it would only become more obscure and intricate. In all abstract reasonings, there is one point of view, which, if we can happily hit, we shall go farther towards illustrating the subject, than by all the eloquence and copious expression in the world. This point of view we should endeavour to reach, and reserve the flowers of rhetoric for subjects which are more adapted to them.

SECTION VIII

Of LIBERTY and NECESSITY

PART I

IT might reasonably be expected, in questions, which have been canvassed and disputed with great eagerness, since the first origin of science and philosophy, that the meaning of all the terms, at least, should have been agreed upon among the disputants; and our enquiries, in the course of two thousand years, been able to pass from words to the true and real subject of the controversy. For how easy may it seem to give exact definitions of the terms employed in reasoning, and make these definitions, not the mere sound of words, the object of future scrutiny and examination? But if we consider the matter more narrowly, we shall be apt to draw a quite opposite conclusion. From this circumstance alone, that a controversy has been long kept on foot, and remains still undecided, we may presume, that there is some ambiguity in the expression, and that the disputants affix different ideas to the terms employed in the controversy. For as the faculties of the mind are supposed to be naturally alike in every individual; otherwise nothing could be more fruitless than to reason or dispute together; it were impossible, if men affix the same ideas to their terms, that they could so long form different opinions of the same subject; especially when they communicate their views, and each party turn themselves on all sides, in search of arguments, which may give them the victory over their antagonists. It is true; if men attempt the discussion of questions, which lie entirely beyond the reach of human capacity, such as those concerning the origin of worlds, or the oeconomy of the intellectual system or region of spirits, they may long beat the air in their fruitless contests, and never arrive at any determinate conclusion. But if the question regard any subject of common life and experience; nothing, one would think, could preserve the dispute so long undecided, but some ambiguous expressions, which keep the antagonists still at a distance, and hinder them from grappling with each other.

[2] This has been the case in the long disputed question concerning liberty and necessity;* and to so remarkable a degree, that, if I be not

much mistaken, we shall find, that all mankind, both learned and ignorant, have always been of the same opinion with regard to this subject, and that a few intelligible definitions would immediately have put an end to the whole controversy. I own, that this dispute has been so much canvassed on all hands, and has led philosophers into such a labyrinth of obscure sophistry, that it is no wonder, if a sensible reader indulge his ease so far as to turn a deaf ear to the proposal of such a question, from which he can expect neither instruction nor entertainment. But the state of the argument here proposed may, perhaps, serve to renew his attention; as it has more novelty, promises at least some decision of the controversy, and will not much disturb his ease by any intricate or obscure reasoning.

[3] I hope, therefore, to make it appear, that all men have ever agreed in the doctrine both of necessity and of liberty,* according to any reasonable sense, which can be put on these terms; and that the whole controversy has hitherto turned merely upon words. We shall begin with examining the doctrine of necessity.

[4] It is universally allowed,* that matter, in all its operations, is 82 actuated by a necessary force, and that every natural effect is so precisely determined by the energy of its cause, that no other effect, in such particular circumstances, could possibly have resulted from it. The degree and direction of every motion is, by the laws of nature, prescribed with such exactness, that a living creature may as soon arise from the shock of two bodies, as motion, in any other degree or direction than what is actually produced by it. Would we, therefore, form a just and precise idea of *necessity*, we must consider whence that idea arises, when we apply it to the operation of bodies.

[5] It seems evident, that, if all the scenes of nature were continually shifted in such a manner, that no two events bore any resemblance to each other, but every object was entirely new, without any similitude to whatever had been seen before, we should never, in that case, have attained the least idea of necessity, or of a connexion among these objects. We might say, upon such a supposition, that one object or event has followed another; not that one was produced by the other. The relation of cause and effect must be utterly unknown to mankind. Inference and reasoning concerning the operations of nature would, from that moment, be at an end; and the memory and senses remain the only canals, by which the knowledge of any real existence could possibly have access to the mind. Our idea, therefore, of necessity and

causation arises entirely from the uniformity, observable in the operations of nature; where similar objects are constantly conjoined together, and the mind is determined by custom to infer the one from the appearance of the other. These two circumstances form the whole of that necessity, which we ascribe to matter. Beyond the constant *conjunction* of similar objects, and the consequent *inference* from one to the other, we have no notion of any necessity, or connexion.*

83 [6] If it appear, therefore, that all mankind have ever allowed, without any doubt or hesitation, that these two circumstances take place in the voluntary actions of men, and in the operations of mind; it must follow, that all mankind have ever agreed in the doctrine of necessity, and that they have hitherto disputed, merely for not understanding each other.

[7] As to the first circumstance, the constant and regular conjunction of similar events; we may possibly satisfy ourselves by the following considerations. It is universally acknowledged, that there is a great uniformity among the actions of men, in all nations and ages, and that human nature remains still the same, in its principles and operations. The same motives always produce the same actions: The same events follow from the same causes. Ambition, avarice, self-love, vanity, friendship, generosity, public spirit; these passions, mixed in various degrees, and distributed through society, have been, from the beginning of the world, and still are, the source of all the actions and enterprizes, which have ever been observed among mankind. Would you know the sentiments, inclinations, and course of life of the GREEKS and ROMANS? Study well the temper and actions of the FRENCH and ENGLISH: You cannot be much mistaken in transferring to the former *most* of the observations, which you have made with regard to the latter. Mankind are so much the same, in all times and places, that history informs us of nothing new or strange in this particular. Its chief use is only to discover the constant and universal principles of human nature, by shewing men in all varieties of circumstances and situations, and furnishing us with materials, from which we may form our observations, and become acquainted with the regular springs of human action and behaviour. These records of wars, intrigues, factions, and revolutions, are so many collections of

84 experiments, by which the politician or moral philosopher fixes the principles of his science; in the same manner as the physician or natural philosopher becomes acquainted with the nature of plants,

minerals, and other external objects, by the experiments, which he forms concerning them. Nor are the earth, water, and other elements, examined by ARISTOTLE, and HIPPOCRATES,* more like to those, which at present lie under our observation, than the men, described by POLYBIUS and TACITUS,* are to those who now govern the world.

[8] Should a traveller, returning from a far country, bring us an account of men, wholly different from any, with whom we were ever acquainted; men, who were entirely divested of avarice, ambition, or revenge; who knew no pleasure but friendship, generosity, and public spirit; we should immediately, from these circumstances, detect the falsehood, and prove him a liar, with the same certainty as if he had stuffed his narration with stories of centaurs and dragons, miracles and prodigies. And if we would explode any forgery in history, we cannot make use of a more convincing argument, than to prove, that the actions, ascribed to any person, are directly contrary to the course of nature, and that no human motives, in such circumstances, could ever induce him to such a conduct. The veracity of QUINTUS CURTIUS is as much to be suspected, when he describes the supernatural courage of ALEXANDER,* by which he was hurried on singly to attack multitudes, as when he describes his supernatural force and activity, by which he was able to resist them. So readily and universally do we acknowledge a uniformity in human motives and actions as well as in the operations of body.

[9] Hence likewise the benefit of that experience, acquired by long life and a variety of business and company, in order to instruct us in the principles of human nature, and regulate our future conduct, as well as speculation. By means of this guide, we mount up to the knowledge of men's inclinations and motives, from their actions, 85 expressions, and even gestures; and again, descend to the interpretation of their actions from our knowledge of their motives and inclinations. The general observations, treasured up by a course of experience, give us the clue of human nature, and teach us to unravel all its intricacies. Pretexts and appearances no longer deceive us. Public declarations pass for the specious colouring of a cause.* And though virtue and honour be allowed their proper weight and authority, that perfect disinterestedness, so often pretended to, is never expected in multitudes and parties; seldom in their leaders; and scarcely even in individuals of any rank or station. But were there no uniformity in human actions, and were every experiment, which we could form of this

kind, irregular and anomalous, it were impossible to collect any general observations concerning mankind; and no experience, however accurately digested by reflection, would ever serve to any purpose. Why is the aged husbandman more skilful in his calling than the young beginner, but because there is a certain uniformity in the operation of the sun, rain, and earth, towards the production of vegetables; and experience teaches the old practitioner the rules, by which this operation is governed and directed?

[10] We must not, however, expect, that this uniformity of human actions should be carried to such a length, as that all men, in the same circumstances, will always act precisely in the same manner, without making any allowance for the diversity of characters, prejudices, and opinions. Such a uniformity in every particular, is found in no part of nature. On the contrary, from observing the variety of conduct in different men, we are enabled to form a greater variety of maxims, which still suppose a degree of uniformity and regularity.

86   [11] Are the manners of men different in different ages and countries? We learn thence the great force of custom and education, which mould the human mind from its infancy, and form it into a fixed and established character. Is the behaviour and conduct of the one sex very unlike that of the other? It is thence we become acquainted with the different characters, which nature has impressed upon the sexes, and which she preserves with constancy and regularity. Are the actions of the same person much diversified in the different periods of his life, from infancy to old age? This affords room for many general observations concerning the gradual change of our sentiments and inclinations, and the different maxims, which prevail in the different ages of human creatures. Even the characters, which are peculiar to each individual, have a uniformity in their influence; otherwise our acquaintance with the persons and our observation of their conduct, could never teach us their dispositions, or serve to direct our behaviour with regard to them.

[12] I grant it possible to find some actions, which seem to have no regular connexion with any known motives, and are exceptions to all the measures of conduct, which have ever been established for the government of men. But if we would willingly know, what judgment should be formed of such irregular and extraordinary actions; we may consider the sentiments, commonly entertained with regard to those irregular events, which appear in the course of nature, and the operations of external objects. All causes are not conjoined to their

usual effects, with like uniformity. An artificer, who handles only dead matter, may be disappointed of his aim, as well as the politician, who directs the conduct of sensible and intelligent agents.

[13] The vulgar, who take things according to their first appearance,* attribute the uncertainty of events to such an uncertainty in the causes as makes the latter often fail of their usual influence; though they meet with no impediment in their operation. But philosophers, observing, that, almost in every part of nature, there is contained a 87 vast variety of springs and principles, which are hid, by reason of their minuteness or remoteness, find, that it is at least possible the contrariety of events may not proceed from any contingency in the cause, but from the secret operation of contrary causes. This possibility is converted into certainty by farther observation; when they remark, that, upon an exact scrutiny, a contrariety of effects always betrays a contrariety of causes, and proceeds from their mutual opposition. A peasant can give no better reason for the stopping of any clock or watch than to say that it does not commonly go right: But an artist easily perceives, that the same force in the spring or pendulum has always the same influence on the wheels; but fails of its usual effect, perhaps by reason of a grain of dust, which puts a stop to the whole movement. From the observation of several parallel instances, philosophers form a maxim, that the connexion between all causes and effects is equally necessary, and that its seeming uncertainty in some instances proceeds from the secret opposition of contrary causes.

[14] Thus for instance, in the human body, when the usual symptoms of health or sickness disappoint our expectation; when medicines operate not with their wonted powers; when irregular events follow from any particular cause; the philosopher and physician are not surprized at the matter, nor are ever tempted to deny, in general, the necessity and uniformity of those principles, by which the animal oeconomy is conducted. They know, that a human body is a mighty complicated machine: That many secret powers lurk in it, which are altogether beyond our comprehension: That to us it must often appear very uncertain in its operations: And that therefore the irregular events, which outwardly discover themselves, can be no proof, that the laws of nature are not observed with the greatest regularity in its internal operations and government.

[15] The philosopher, if he be consistent, must apply the same 88 reasoning to the actions and volitions of intelligent agents. The most

irregular and unexpected resolutions of men may frequently be accounted for by those, who know every particular circumstance of their character and situation. A person of an obliging disposition gives a peevish answer: But he has the toothake, or has not dined. A stupid fellow discovers an uncommon alacrity in his carriage:* But he has met with a sudden piece of good fortune. Or even when an action, as sometimes happens, cannot be particularly accounted for, either by the person himself or by others; we know, in general, that the characters of men are, to a certain degree, inconstant and irregular. This is, in a manner, the constant character of human nature; though it be applicable, in a more particular manner, to some persons, who have no fixed rule for their conduct, but proceed in a continued course of caprice and inconstancy. The internal principles and motives may operate in a uniform manner, notwithstanding these seeming irregularities; in the same manner as the winds, rain, clouds, and other variations of the weather are supposed to be governed by steady principles; though not easily discoverable by human sagacity and enquiry.

[16] Thus it appears, not only that the conjunction between motives and voluntary actions is as regular and uniform, as that between the cause and effect in any part of nature;* but also that this regular conjunction has been universally acknowledged among mankind, and has never been the subject of dispute, either in philosophy or common life. Now, as it is from past experience, that we draw all inferences concerning the future, and as we conclude, that objects will always be conjoined together, which we find to have always been conjoined; it may seem superfluous to prove, that this experienced uniformity in human actions is a source, whence we draw *inferences* concerning them. But in order to throw the argument into a greater variety of lights, we shall also insist, though briefly, on this latter topic.

[17] The mutual dependence of men is so great, in all societies, that scarce any human action is entirely compleat in itself, or is performed without some reference to the actions of others, which are requisite to make it answer fully the intention of the agent. The poorest artificer, who labours alone, expects at least the protection of the magistrate, to ensure him the enjoyment of the fruits of his labour. He also expects, that, when he carries his goods to market, and offers them at a reasonable price, he shall find purchasers; and shall be able, by the money he acquires, to engage others to supply him with those commodities, which are requisite for his subsistence. In proportion

as men extend their dealings, and render their intercourse with others more complicated, they always comprehend, in their schemes of life, a greater variety of voluntary actions, which they expect, from the proper motives, to co-operate with their own. In all these conclusions, they take their measures from past experience, in the same manner as in their reasonings concerning external objects; and firmly believe, that men, as well as all the elements, are to continue, in their operations, the same, that they have ever found them. A manufacturer reckons upon the labour of his servants, for the execution of any work, as much as upon the tools, which he employs, and would be equally surprized, were his expectations disappointed. In short, this experimental inference and reasoning concerning the actions of others enters so much into human life, that no man, while awake, is ever a moment without employing it. Have we not reason, therefore, to affirm, that all mankind have always agreed in the doctrine of necessity, according to the foregoing definition and explication of it?

[18] Nor have philosophers ever entertained a different opinion from the people in this particular. For not to mention, that almost every action of their life supposes that opinion; there are even few of the speculative parts of learning, to which it is not essential. What would become of *history*, had we not a dependence on the veracity of the historian, according to the experience, which we have had of mankind? How could *politics* be a science,* if laws and forms of government had not a uniform influence upon society? Where would be the foundation of *morals*, if particular characters had no certain or determinate power to produce particular sentiments, and if these sentiments had no constant operation on actions? And with what pretence could we employ our *criticism* upon any poet or polite author, if we could not pronounce the conduct and sentiments of his actors, either natural or unnatural, to such characters, and in such circumstances? It seems almost impossible, therefore, to engage, either in science or action of any kind, without acknowledging the doctrine of necessity, and this *inference* from motives to voluntary actions; from characters to conduct.

[19] And indeed, when we consider how aptly *natural* and *moral* evidence link together, and form only one chain of argument, we shall make no scruple to allow, that they are of the same nature, and derived from the same principles. A prisoner, who has neither money nor interest,* discovers the impossibility of his escape, as well when

he considers the obstinacy of the gaoler, as the walls and bars, with which he is surrounded; and, in all attempts for his freedom, chuses rather to work upon the stone and iron of the one, than upon the inflexible nature of the other. The same prisoner, when conducted to the scaffold, foresees his death as certainly from the constancy and fidelity of his guards, as from the operation of the ax or wheel.* His mind runs along a certain train of ideas: The refusal of the soldiers to consent to his escape; the action of the executioner; the separation of the head and body; bleeding, convulsive motions, and death. Here is a connected chain of natural causes and voluntary actions; but the mind feels no difference between them, in passing from one link to another: Nor is less certain of the future event than if it were connected with the objects present to the memory or senses, by a train of causes, cemented together by what we are pleased to call a *physical* necessity. The same experienced union has the same effect on the mind, whether the united objects be motives, volition, and actions; or figure and motion. We may change the names of things; but their nature and their operation on the understanding never change.

[20] Were a man, whom I know to be honest and opulent, and with whom I live in intimate friendship, to come into my house, where I am surrounded with my servants, I rest assured, that he is not to stab me before he leaves it, in order to rob me of my silver standish; and I no more suspect this event, than the falling of the house itself which is new, and solidly built and founded.—*But he may have been seized with a sudden and unknown frenzy.*—So may a sudden earthquake arise, and shake and tumble my house about my ears. I shall therefore change the suppositions. I shall say, that I know with certainty, that he is not to put his hand into the fire, and hold it there, till it be consumed: And this event, I think I can foretell with the same assurance, as that, if he throw himself out at the window, and meet with no obstruction, he will not remain a moment suspended in the air. No suspicion of an unknown frenzy can give the least possibility to the former event, which is so contrary to all the known principles of human nature. A man who at noon leaves his purse full of gold on the pavement at Charing-Cross,* may as well expect that it will fly away like a feather, as that he will find it untouched an hour after. Above one half of human reasonings contain inferences of a similar nature, attended with more or less degrees of certainty, proportioned to our experience of the usual conduct of mankind in such particular situations.

[21] I have frequently considered, what could possibly be the 92 reason,* why all mankind, though they have ever, without hesitation, acknowledged the doctrine of necessity, in their whole practice and reasoning, have yet discovered such a reluctance to acknowledge it in words, and have rather shewn a propensity, in all ages, to profess the contrary opinion. The matter, I think, may be accounted for, after the following manner. If we examine the operations of body, and the production of effects from their causes, we shall find, that all our faculties can never carry us farther in our knowledge of this relation, than barely to observe, that particular objects are *constantly conjoined* together, and that the mind is carried, by a *customary transition*, from the appearance of one to the belief of the other. But though this conclusion concerning human ignorance be the result of the strictest scrutiny of this subject, men still entertain a strong propensity to believe, that they penetrate farther into the powers of nature, and perceive something like a necessary connexion between the cause and the effect. When again they turn their reflections towards the operations of their own minds, and *feel* no such connexion of the motive and the action; they are thence apt to suppose, that there is a difference between the effects, which result from material force, and those which arise from thought and intelligence. But being once convinced, that we know nothing farther of causation of any kind, than merely the *constant conjunction* of objects, and the consequent *inference* of the mind from one to another, and finding, that these two circumstances are universally allowed to have place in voluntary actions; we may be more easily led to own the same necessity common to all causes. And though this reasoning may contradict the systems of many philosophers, in ascribing necessity to the determinations of the will, we shall find, upon reflection, that they dissent from it in words only, not in their real sentiment. Necessity, according to the sense, in which it is here taken, has never yet been rejected, nor can 93 ever, I think, be rejected by any philosopher. It may only, perhaps, be pretended, that the mind can perceive, in the operations of matter, some farther connexion between the cause and effect; and a connexion that has not place in the voluntary actions of intelligent beings. Now whether it be so or not, can only appear upon examination; and it is incumbent on these philosophers to make good their assertion, by defining or describing that necessity, and pointing it out to us in the operations of material causes.

[22] It would seem, indeed, that men begin at the wrong end of this question concerning liberty and necessity, when they enter upon it by examining the faculties of the soul, the influence of the understanding, and the operations of the will. Let them first discuss a more simple question, namely, the operations of body and of brute unintelligent matter; and try whether they can there form any idea of causation and necessity, except that of a constant conjunction of objects, and subsequent inference of the mind from one to another. If these circumstances form, in reality, the whole of that necessity, which we conceive in matter, and if these circumstances be also universally acknowledged to take place in the operations of the mind, the dispute is at an end; at least, must be owned to be thenceforth merely verbal. But as long as we will rashly suppose, that we have some farther idea of necessity and causation in the operations of external objects; at the same time, that we can find nothing farther, in the voluntary actions of the mind; there is no possibility of bringing the question to any determinate issue, while we proceed upon so erroneous a supposition. The only method of undeceiving us, is, to mount up higher; to examine the narrow extent of science when applied to material causes; and to convince ourselves, that all we know of them, is, the constant conjunction and inference above mentioned. We may, perhaps, find, that it is with difficulty we are induced to fix such narrow limits to human understanding: But we can afterwards find no difficulty when we come to apply this doctrine to the actions of the will. For as it is evident, that these have a regular conjunction with motives and circumstances and characters, and as we always draw inferences from one to the other, we must be obliged to acknowledge in words, that necessity, which we have already avowed, in every deliberation of our lives, and in every step of our conduct and behaviour[18].

[23] But to proceed in this reconciling project with regard to the question of liberty and necessity; the most contentious question, of metaphysics, the most contentious science; it will not require many words to prove, that all mankind have ever agreed in the doctrine of liberty as well as in that of necessity, and that the whole dispute, in this respect also, has been hitherto merely verbal. For what is meant by liberty, when applied to voluntary actions? We cannot surely mean,

---

[18] See endnote [F], p. 124.

that actions have so little connexion with motives, inclinations, and circumstances, that one does not follow with a certain degree of uniformity from the other, and that one affords no inference by which we can conclude the existence of the other. For these are plain and acknowledged matters of fact. By liberty, then, we can only mean *a power of acting or not acting, according to the determinations of the will;** that is, if we chuse to remain at rest, we may; if we chuse to move, we also may. Now this hypothetical liberty is universally allowed to belong to every one, who is not a prisoner and in chains.* Here then is no subject of dispute.

[24] Whatever definition we may give of liberty, we should be careful to observe two requisite circumstances; *first*, that it be consistent with plain matter of fact; *secondly*, that it be consistent with itself. If we observe these circumstances, and render our definition intelligible, I am persuaded that all mankind will be found of one opinion with regard to it.

[25] It is universally allowed, that nothing exists without a cause of its existence,* and that chance, when strictly examined, is a mere negative word, and means not any real power, which has any where, a being in nature. But it is pretended, that some causes are necessary, some not necessary. Here then is the advantage of definitions. Let any one *define* a cause, without comprehending, as a part of the definition, a *necessary connexion* with its effect; and let him shew distinctly the origin of the idea, expressed by the definition; and I shall readily give up the whole controversy. But if the foregoing explication of the matter be received, this must be absolutely impracticable. Had not objects a regular conjunction with each other, we should never have entertained any notion of cause and effect; and this regular conjunction produces that inference of the understanding, which is the only connexion, that we can have any comprehension of. Whoever attempts a definition of cause, exclusive of these circumstances, will be obliged, either to employ unintelligible terms, or such as are synonimous to the term, which he endeavours to define[19]. And if the definition above mentioned be admitted; liberty, when opposed to necessity, not to constraint, is the same thing with chance; which is universally allowed to have no existence.

---

[19] See endnote [G], p. 125.

PART II

[26] There is no method of reasoning more common, and yet none more blameable, than, in philosophical disputes, to endeavour the refutation of any hypothesis, by a pretence of its dangerous consequences to religion and morality. When any opinion leads to absurdities, it is certainly false; but it is not certain that an opinion is false, because it is of dangerous consequence. Such topics, therefore, ought entirely to be forborne; as serving nothing to the discovery of truth, but only to make the person of an antagonist odious. This I observe in general, 97 without pretending to draw any advantage from it. I frankly submit to an examination of this kind, and shall venture to affirm, that the doctrines, both of necessity and of liberty, as above explained, are not only consistent with morality,* but are absolutely essential to its support.

[27] Necessity may be defined two ways, conformably to the two definitions of *cause*,* of which it makes an essential part. It consists either in the constant conjunction of like objects, or in the inference of the understanding from one object to another. Now necessity, in both these senses, (which, indeed, are, at bottom, the same) has universally, though tacitly, in the schools, in the pulpit, and in common life, been allowed to belong to the will of man; and no one has ever pretended to deny, that we can draw inferences concerning human actions, and that those inferences are founded on the experienced union of like actions, with like motives, inclinations, and circumstances. The only particular, in which any one can differ, is, that either, perhaps, he will refuse to give the name of necessity to this property of human actions: But as long as the meaning is understood, I hope the word can do no harm: Or that he will maintain it possible to discover something farther in the operations of matter. But this, it must be acknowledged, can be of no consequence to morality or religion, whatever it may be to natural philosophy or metaphysics. We may here be mistaken in asserting, that there is no idea of any other necessity or connexion in the actions of body: But surely we ascribe nothing to the actions of the mind, but what every one does, and must readily allow of. We change no circumstance in the received orthodox system with regard to the will, but only in that with regard to material objects and causes. Nothing therefore can be more innocent, at least, than this doctrine.

[28] All laws being founded on rewards and punishments, it is sup-98 posed as a fundamental principle, that these motives have a regular

and uniform influence on the mind,* and both produce the good and prevent the evil actions. We may give to this influence what name we please; but, as it is usually conjoined with the action, it must be esteemed a *cause*, and be looked upon as an instance of that necessity, which we would here establish.

[29] The only proper object of hatred or vengeance, is a person or creature, endowed with thought and consciousness; and when any criminal or injurious actions excite that passion, it is only by their relation to the person, or connexion with him. Actions are, by their very nature, temporary and perishing; and where they proceed not from some *cause* in the character and disposition of the person who performed them, they can neither redound to his honour, if good; nor infamy, if evil. The actions themselves may be blameable; they may be contrary to all the rules of morality and religion: But the person is not answerable for them; and as they proceeded from nothing in him, that is durable and constant, and leave nothing of that nature behind them, it is impossible he can, upon their account, become the object of punishment or vengeance. According to the principle, therefore, which denies necessity, and consequently causes, a man is as pure and untainted, after having committed the most horrid crime, as at the first moment of his birth, nor is his character any wise concerned in his actions; since they are not derived from it, and the wickedness of the one can never be used as a proof of the depravity of the other.

[30] Men are not blamed for such actions, as they perform ignorantly and casually, whatever may be the consequences. Why? but because the principles of these actions are only momentary, and terminate in them alone. Men are less blamed for such actions as they perform hastily and unpremeditately, than for such as proceed from deliberation. For what reason? but because a hasty temper, though a constant cause or principle in the mind, operates only by intervals, 99 and infects not the whole character. Again, repentance wipes off every crime, if attended with a reformation of life and manners. How is this to be accounted for? but by asserting, that actions render a person criminal, merely as they are proofs of criminal principles in the mind; and when, by an alteration of these principles, they cease to be just proofs, they likewise cease to be criminal. But, except upon the doctrine of necessity, they never were just proofs, and consequently never were criminal.

[31] It will be equally easy to prove, and from the same arguments, that *liberty*, according to that definition above mentioned, in which all men agree, is also essential to morality, and that no human actions, where it is wanting, are susceptible of any moral qualities, or can be the objects either of approbation or dislike. For as actions are objects of our moral sentiment, so far only as they are indications of the internal character, passions, and affections; it is impossible that they can give rise either to praise or blame, where they proceed not from these principles, but are derived altogether from external violence.

[32] I pretend not to have obviated or removed all objections to this theory, with regard to necessity and liberty. I can foresee other objections, derived from topics, which have not here been treated of. It may be said, for instance, that, if voluntary actions be subjected to the same laws of necessity with the operations of matter, there is a continued chain of necessary causes, pre-ordained and pre-determined, reaching from the original cause of all, to every single volition of every human creature. No contingency any where in the universe; no indifference; no liberty.* While we act, we are, at the same time, acted upon. The ultimate Author of all our volitions is the Creator of the world, who first bestowed motion on this immense machine, and, placed all beings in that particular position, whence every subsequent event, by an inevitable necessity, must result. Human actions, therefore, either can have no moral turpitude at all, as proceeding from so good a cause; or if they have any turpitude, they must involve our Creator in the same guilt, while he is acknowledged to be their ultimate cause and author. For as a man, who fired a mine, is answerable for all the consequences whether the train* he employed be long or short; so wherever a continued chain of necessary causes is fixed, that Being, either finite or infinite, who produces the first, is likewise the author of all the rest, and must both bear the blame and acquire the praise, which belong to them. Our clear and unalterable ideas of morality establish this rule, upon unquestionable reasons, when we examine the consequences of any human action; and these reasons must still have greater force, when applied to the volitions and intentions of a Being, infinitely wise and powerful. Ignorance or impotence may be pleaded for so limited a creature as man; but those imperfections have no place in our Creator. He foresaw, he ordained, he intended all those actions of men, which we so rashly pronounce criminal. And we must therefore conclude, either that they are not criminal, or that

the Deity, not man, is accountable for them. But as either of these positions is absurd and impious, it follows, that the doctrine, from which they are deduced, cannot possibly be true, as being liable to all the same objections. An absurd consequence, if necessary, proves the original doctrine to be absurd; in the same manner as criminal actions render criminal the original cause, if the connexion between them be necessary and inevitable.

[33] This objection consists of two parts, which we shall examine separately; *First*, that, if human actions can be traced up, by a necessary chain, to the Deity, they can never be criminal; on account of the infinite perfection of that Being, from whom they are derived, and who can intend nothing but what is altogether good and laudable. Or, *Secondly*, if they be criminal, we must retract the attribute of perfection, which we ascribe to the Deity, and must acknowledge him to be the ultimate author of guilt and moral turpitude in all his creatures.

[34] The answer to the first objection seems obvious and convincing. There are many philosophers, who, after an exact scrutiny of all the phaenomena of nature, conclude, that the WHOLE, considered as one system, is, in every period of its existence, ordered with perfect benevolence; and that the utmost possible happiness will, in the end, result to all created beings, without any mixture of positive or absolute ill and misery. Every physical ill, say they, makes an essential part of this benevolent system, and could not possibly be removed, even by the Deity himself, considered as a wise agent, without giving entrance to greater ill, or excluding greater good, which will result from it. From this theory, some philosophers, and the ancient *Stoics* * among the rest, derived a topic of consolation under all afflictions, while they taught their pupils, that those ills, under which they laboured, were, in reality, goods to the universe; and that to an enlarged view, which could comprehend the whole system of nature, every event became an object of joy and exultation. But though this topic be specious and sublime, it was soon found in practice weak and ineffectual. You would surely more irritate, than appease a man, lying under the racking pains of the gout, by preaching up to him the rectitude of those general laws, which produced the malignant humours* in his body, and led them through the proper canals, to the sinews and nerves, where they now excite such acute torments. These enlarged views may, for a moment, please the imagination of a speculative man, who is placed in ease and security; but neither can they dwell with constancy on his mind, even

102 though undisturbed by the emotions of pain or passion; much less can they maintain their ground, when attacked by such powerful antagonists. The affections take a narrower and more natural survey of their object; and by an oeconomy, more suitable to the infirmity of human minds, regard alone the beings around us, and are actuated by such events as appear good or ill to the private system.

[35] The case is the same with *moral* as with *physical* ill. It cannot reasonably be supposed, that those remote considerations, which are found of so little efficacy with regard to one, will have a more powerful influence with regard to the other. The mind of man is so formed by nature, that, upon the appearance of certain characters, dispositions, and actions, it immediately feels the sentiment of approbation or blame;* nor are there any emotions more essential to its frame and constitution. The characters, which engage our approbation, are chiefly such as contribute to the peace and security of human society; as the characters, which excite blame, are chiefly such as tend to public detriment and disturbance: Whence it may reasonably be presumed, that the moral sentiments arise, either mediately or immediately, from a reflection on these opposite interests. What though philosophical meditations establish a different opinion or conjecture; that every thing is right with regard to the WHOLE, and that the qualities, which disturb society, are, in the main, as beneficial, and are as suitable to the primary intention of nature, as those which more directly promote its happiness and welfare? Are such remote and uncertain speculations able to counterbalance the sentiments, which arise from the natural and immediate view of the objects? A man who is robbed of a considerable sum; does he find his vexation for the loss any wise diminished by these sublime reflections? Why then should his moral resentment against the crime be supposed incompatible with them? Or why should not the acknowledgment of a
103 real distinction between vice and virtue be reconcileable to all speculative systems of philosophy, as well as that of a real distinction between personal beauty and deformity? Both these distinctions are founded in the natural sentiments of the human mind: And these sentiments are not to be controuled or altered by any philosophical theory or speculation whatsoever.

[36] The *second* objection admits not of so easy and satisfactory an answer; nor is it possible to explain distinctly, how the Deity can be the mediate cause of all the actions of men, without being the author of sin and moral turpitude. These are mysteries,* which mere natural

and unassisted reason is very unfit to handle; and whatever system she embraces, she must find herself involved in inextricable difficulties, and even contradictions, at every step which she takes with regard to such subjects. To reconcile the indifference and contingency of human actions with prescience;* or to defend absolute decrees, and yet free the Deity from being the author of sin,* has been found hitherto to exceed all the power of philosophy. Happy, if she be thence sensible of her temerity, when she pries into these sublime mysteries; and leaving a scene so full of obscurities and perplexities, return, with suitable modesty, to her true and proper province, the examination of common life; where she will find difficulties enow to employ her enquiries, without launching into so boundless an ocean of doubt, uncertainty, and contradiction!

SECTION IX

Of the REASON of ANIMALS

A LL our reasonings concerning matter of fact are founded on a species of ANALOGY,* which leads us to expect from any cause the same events, which we have observed to result from similar causes. Where the causes are entirely similar, the analogy is perfect, and the inference, drawn from it, is regarded as certain and conclusive: Nor does any man ever entertain a doubt, where he sees a piece of iron, that it will have weight and cohesion of parts; as in all other instances, which have ever fallen under his observation. But where the objects have not so exact a similarity, the analogy is less perfect, and the inference is less conclusive; though still it has some force, in proportion to the degree of similarity and resemblance. The anatomical observations, formed upon one animal, are, by this species of reasoning, extended to all animals; and it is certain, that when the circulation of the blood, for instance, is clearly proved to have place in one creature, as a frog, or fish, it forms a strong presumption, that the same principle has place in all. These analogical observations may be carried farther, even to this science, of which we are now treating; and any theory, by which we explain the operations of the understanding, or the origin and connexion of the passions in man, will acquire additional authority, if we find, that the same theory is requisite to explain the same phaenomena in all other animals. We shall make trial of this, with regard to the hypothesis, by which, we have, in the foregoing discourse, endeavoured to account for all experimental reasonings; and it is hoped, that this new point of view will serve to confirm all our former observations.

[2] *First*, It seems evident, that animals, as well as men learn many things from experience, and infer, that the same events will always follow from the same causes. By this principle they become acquainted with the more obvious properties of external objects, and gradually, from their birth, treasure up a knowledge of the nature of fire, water, earth, stones, heights, depths, &c. and of the effects, which result from their operation. The ignorance and inexperience of the young are here plainly distinguishable from the cunning and sagacity of the old, who have learned, by long observation, to avoid what hurt them,

and to pursue what gave ease or pleasure. A horse, that has been accustomed to the field, becomes acquainted with the proper height, which he can leap, and will never attempt what exceeds his force and ability. An old greyhound will trust the more fatiguing part of the chace to the younger, and will place himself so as to meet the hare in her doubles;* nor are the conjectures, which he forms on this occasion, founded in any thing but his observation and experience.

[3] This is still more evident from the effects of discipline and education on animals, who, by the proper application of rewards and punishments, may be taught any course of action, the most contrary to their natural instincts and propensities. Is it not experience, which renders a dog apprehensive of pain, when you menace him, or lift up the whip to beat him? Is it not even experience, which makes him answer to his name, and infer, from such an arbitrary sound, that you mean him rather than any of his fellows, and intend to call him, when you pronounce it in a certain manner, and with a certain tone and accent?

[4] In all these cases, we may observe, that the animal infers some 106 fact beyond what immediately strikes his senses; and that this inference is altogether founded on past experience, while the creature expects from the present object the same consequences, which it has always found in its observation to result from similar objects.

[5] *Secondly*, It is impossible, that this inference of the animal can be founded on any process of argument or reasoning, by which he concludes, that like events must follow like objects, and that the course of nature will always be regular in its operations. For if there be in reality any arguments of this nature, they surely lie too abstruse for the observation of such imperfect understandings; since it may well employ the utmost care and attention of a philosophic genius to discover and observe them. Animals, therefore, are not guided in these inferences by reasoning: Neither are children: Neither are the generality of mankind, in their ordinary actions and conclusions: Neither are philosophers themselves, who, in all the active parts of life, are, in the main, the same with the vulgar, and are governed by the same maxims. Nature must have provided some other principle, of more ready, and more general use and application; nor can an operation of such immense consequence in life, as that of inferring effects from causes, be trusted to the uncertain process of reasoning and argumentation. Were this doubtful with regard to men, it seems

to admit of no question with regard to the brute creation; and the conclusion being once firmly established in the one, we have a strong presumption, from all the rules of analogy, that it ought to be universally admitted, without any exception or reserve. It is custom alone, which engages animals, from every object, that strikes their senses, to infer its usual attendant, and carries their imagination, from the appearance of the one, to conceive the other, in that particular manner, which we denominate *belief*. No other explication can be given of this

107 operation, in all the higher, as well as lower classes of sensitive beings, which fall under our notice and observation[20].

108   [6] But though animals learn many parts of their knowledge from observation, there are also many parts of it, which they derive from the original hand of nature; which much exceed the share of capacity they possess on ordinary occasions; and in which they improve, little or nothing, by the longest practice and experience. These we denominate INSTINCTS, and are so apt to admire, as something very extraordinary, and inexplicable by all the disquisitions of human understanding. But our wonder will, perhaps, cease or diminish; when we consider, that the experimental reasoning itself, which we possess in common with beasts,* and on which the whole conduct of life depends, is nothing but a species of instinct or mechanical power, that acts in us unknown to ourselves; and in its chief operations, is not directed by any such relations or comparisons of ideas, as are the proper objects of our intellectual faculties. Though the instinct be different, yet still it is an instinct, which teaches a man to avoid the fire; as much as that, which teaches a bird, with such exactness, the art of incubation, and the whole oeconomy and order of its nursery.

[20] See endnote [H], p. 125.

Of Miracles

PART I

THERE is, in Dr. TILLOTSON'S writings,* an argument against the *real presence*, which is as concise, and elegant, and strong as any argument can possibly be supposed against a doctrine, so little worthy of a serious refutation. It is acknowledged on all hands, says that learned prelate, that the authority, either of the scripture or of tradition, is founded merely in the testimony of the apostles, who were eye-witnesses to those miracles of our Saviour, by which he proved his divine mission. Our evidence, then, for the truth of the *Christian* religion is less than the evidence for the truth of our senses; because, even in the first authors of our religion, it was no greater; and it is evident it must diminish in passing from them to their disciples; nor can any one rest such confidence in their testimony, as in the immediate object of his senses. But a weaker evidence can never destroy a stronger; and therefore, were the doctrine of the real presence ever so clearly revealed in scripture, it were directly contrary to the rules of just reasoning to give our assent to it. It contradicts sense, though both the scripture and tradition, on which it is supposed to be built, carry not such evidence with them as sense; when they are considered merely as external evidences, and are not brought home to every one's breast, by the immediate operation of the Holy Spirit.

[2] Nothing is so convenient as a decisive argument of this kind, 110 which must at least *silence* the most arrogant bigotry and superstition, and free us from their impertinent solicitations. I flatter myself, that I have discovered an argument of a like nature, which, if just, will, with the wise and learned, be an everlasting check to all kinds of superstitious delusion, and consequently, will be useful as long as the world endures. For so long, I presume, will the accounts of miracles and prodigies be found in all history, sacred and profane.

[3] Though experience be our only guide in reasoning concerning matters of fact; it must be acknowledged, that this guide is not altogether infallible, but in some cases is apt to lead us into errors.

One, who in our climate, should expect better weather in any week of
JUNE than in one of DECEMBER, would reason justly, and conformably
to experience; but it is certain, that he may happen, in the event, to
find himself mistaken. However, we may observe, that, in such a
case, he would have no cause to complain of experience; because it
commonly informs us beforehand of the uncertainty, by that contrariety of events, which we may learn from a diligent observation. All
effects follow not with like certainty from their supposed causes. Some
events are found, in all countries and all ages, to have been constantly
conjoined together: Others are found to have been more variable, and
sometimes to disappoint our expectations; so that, in our reasonings
concerning matter of fact, there are all imaginable degrees of assurance,
from the highest certainty to the lowest species of moral evidence.*

[4] A wise man, therefore, proportions his belief to the evidence.*
In such conclusions as are founded on an infallible experience, he
expects the event with the last degree of assurance, and regards his
past experience as a full *proof* of the future existence of that event.
In other cases, he proceeds with more caution: He weighs the opposite
experiments:* He considers which side is supported by the greater
number of experiments: To that side he inclines, with doubt and hesitation; and when at last he fixes his judgment, the evidence exceeds
not what we properly call *probability*. All probability, then, supposes
an opposition of experiments and observations, where the one side is
found to overbalance the other, and to produce a degree of evidence,
proportioned to the superiority. A hundred instances or experiments
on one side, and fifty on another, afford a doubtful expectation of any
event; though a hundred uniform experiments, with only one that is
contradictory, reasonably beget a pretty strong degree of assurance.
In all cases, we must balance the opposite experiments, where they are
opposite, and deduct the smaller number from the greater, in order to
know the exact force of the superior evidence.

[5] To apply these principles to a particular instance; we may
observe, that there is no species of reasoning more common, more
useful, and even necessary to human life, than that which is derived
from the testimony of men, and the reports of eye-witnesses and
spectators. This species of reasoning, perhaps, one may deny to be
founded on the relation of cause and effect. I shall not dispute about
a word. It will be sufficient to observe, that our assurance in any
argument of this kind is derived from no other principle than our

observation of the veracity of human testimony, and of the usual conformity of facts to the reports of witnesses. It being a general maxim,
that no objects have any discoverable connexion together, and that all
the inferences, which we can draw from one to another, are founded
merely on our experience of their constant and regular conjunction;
it is evident, that we ought not to make an exception to this maxim
in favour of human testimony, whose connexion with any event seems,
in itself, as little necessary as any other. Were not the memory tenacious   112
to a certain degree; had not men commonly an inclination to truth and
a principle of probity; were they not sensible to shame, when detected
in a falsehood: Were not these, I say, discovered by *experience* to be
qualities, inherent in human nature, we should never repose the least
confidence in human testimony. A man delirious, or noted for falsehood and villany, has no manner of authority with us.

[6] And as the evidence, derived from witnesses and human testimony, is founded on past experience, so it varies with the experience,
and is regarded either as a *proof* * or a *probability*, according as the conjunction between any particular kind of report and any kind of object
has been found to be constant or variable. There are a number of circumstances to be taken into consideration in all judgments of this kind;
and the ultimate standard, by which we determine all disputes, that
may arise concerning them, is always derived from experience and
observation. Where this experience is not entirely uniform on any side,
it is attended with an unavoidable contrariety in our judgments, and
with the same opposition and mutual destruction of argument as in
every other kind of evidence. We frequently hesitate concerning the
reports of others. We balance the opposite circumstances, which cause
any doubt or uncertainty; and when we discover a superiority on any
side, we incline to it; but still with a diminution of assurance, in proportion to the force of its antagonist.

[7] This contrariety of evidence, in the present case, may be derived
from several different causes; from the opposition of contrary testimony;
from the character or number of the witnesses; from the manner of
their delivering their testimony; or from the union of all these circumstances. We entertain a suspicion concerning any matter of fact, when
the witnesses contradict each other; when they are but few, or of a
doubtful character; when they have an interest in what they affirm;   113
when they deliver their testimony with hesitation, or on the contrary,
with too violent asseverations. There are many other particulars of

the same kind, which may diminish or destroy the force of any argument, derived from human testimony.

[8] Suppose, for instance, that the fact, which the testimony endeavours to establish, partakes of the extraordinary and the marvellous; in that case, the evidence, resulting from the testimony, admits of a diminution, greater or less, in proportion as the fact is more or less unusual. The reason, why we place any credit in witnesses and historians, is not derived from any *connexion*, which we perceive *à priori*, between testimony and reality, but because we are accustomed to find a conformity between them. But when the fact attested is such a one as has seldom fallen under our observation, here is a contest of two opposite experiences; of which the one destroys the other, as far as its force goes, and the superior can only operate on the mind by the force, which remains. The very same principle of experience, which gives us a certain degree of assurance in the testimony of witnesses, gives us also, in this case, another degree of assurance against the fact, which they endeavour to establish; from which contradiction there necessarily arises a counterpoize, and mutual destruction of belief and authority.

[9] *I should not believe such a story were it told me by* CATO;* was a proverbial saying in ROME, even during the lifetime of that philosophical patriot[21]. The incredibility of a fact, it was allowed, might invalidate so great an authority.

[10] The INDIAN prince,* who refused to believe the first relations concerning the effects of frost, reasoned justly; and it naturally required very strong testimony to engage his assent to facts, that arose from a state of nature, with which he was unacquainted, and which bore so little analogy to those events, of which he had had constant and uniform experience. Though they were not contrary to his experience, they were not conformable to it[22].

[11] But in order to encrease the probability against the testimony of witnesses, let us suppose, that the fact, which they affirm, instead of being only marvellous, is really miraculous; and suppose also, that the testimony, considered apart and in itself, amounts to an entire proof; in that case, there is proof against proof, of which the strongest must prevail, but still with a diminution of its force, in proportion to that of its antagonist.

---

[21] PLUTARCH, in vita Catonis.
[22] See endnote [I], p. 127.

[12] A miracle is a violation of the laws of nature;* and as a firm and unalterable experience has established these laws, the proof against a miracle, from the very nature of the fact, is as entire as any argument from experience can possibly be imagined. Why is it more than probable, that all men must die; that lead cannot, of itself, remain suspended in the air; that fire consumes wood, and is extinguished by water; unless it be, that these events are found agreeable to the laws of nature, and there is required a violation of these laws, or in other words, a miracle to prevent them? Nothing is esteemed a miracle, if it ever happen in the common course of nature. It is no miracle that a man, seemingly in good health, should die on a sudden: because such a kind of death, though more unusual than any other, has yet been frequently observed to happen. But it is a miracle, that a dead man should come to life; because that has never been observed, in any age or country. There must, therefore, be a uniform experience against every miraculous event, otherwise the event would not merit that appellation. And as an uniform experience amounts to a proof, there is here a direct and full *proof*, from the nature of the fact, against the existence of any miracle; nor can such a proof be destroyed, or the miracle rendered credible, but by an opposite proof, which is superior[23]. 115

[13] The plain consequence is (and it is a general maxim worthy of our attention), "That no testimony is sufficient to establish a miracle, unless the testimony be of such a kind, that its falsehood would be more miraculous, than the fact, which it endeavours to establish: And even in that case there is a mutual destruction of arguments, and the superior only gives us an assurance suitable to that degree of force, which remains, after deducting the inferior."* When any one tells me, that he saw a dead man restored to life, I immediately consider with myself, whether it be more probable, that this person should either deceive or be deceived, or that the fact, which he relates, should really have happened. I weigh the one miracle against the other; and according to the superiority, which I discover, I pronounce my decision, and always reject the greater miracle. If the falsehood of his testimony would be more miraculous, than the event which he relates; then, and not till then, can he pretend to command my belief or opinion. 116

---

[23] See endnote [K], p. 127.

PART II

[14] In the foregoing reasoning we have supposed, that the testimony, upon which a miracle is founded, may possibly amount to an entire proof, and that the falsehood of that testimony would be a real prodigy: But it is easy to shew, that we have been a great deal too liberal in our concession, and that there never was a miraculous event established on so full an evidence.

[15] For *first*, there is not to be found, in all history, any miracle attested by a sufficient number of men, of such unquestioned goodsense, education, and learning, as to secure us against all delusion in themselves; of such undoubted integrity, as to place them beyond all suspicion of any design to deceive others; of such credit and reputation in the eyes of mankind, as to have a great deal to lose in case of their being detected in any falsehood; and at the same time, attesting facts, performed in such a public manner, and in so celebrated a part of the world, as to render the detection unavoidable: All which circumstances are requisite to give us a full assurance in the testimony of men.

[16] *Secondly.* We may observe in human nature a principle, which, if strictly examined, will be found to diminish extremely the assurance, which we might, from human testimony, have, in any kind of prodigy. The maxim, by which we commonly conduct ourselves in our reasonings, is, that the objects, of which we have no experience, resemble those, of which we have; that what we have found to be most usual is always most probable; and that where there is an opposition of arguments, we ought to give the preference to such as are founded on the greatest number of past observations. But though, in proceeding by this rule, we readily reject any fact which is unusual and incredible in an ordinary degree; yet in advancing farther, the mind observes not always the same rule; but when any thing is affirmed utterly absurd and miraculous, it rather the more readily admits of such a fact, upon account of that very circumstance, which ought to destroy all its authority. The passion of *surprize* and *wonder*, arising from miracles, being an agreeable emotion, gives a sensible tendency towards the belief of those events, from which it is derived. And this goes so far, that even those who cannot enjoy this pleasure immediately, nor can believe those miraculous events, of which they are informed, yet love to partake of the satisfaction at second-hand or by rebound, and place a pride and delight in exciting the admiration of others.

[17] With what greediness are the miraculous accounts of travellers received, their descriptions of sea and land monsters, their relations of wonderful adventures, strange men, and uncouth manners? But if the spirit of religion join itself to the love of wonder, there is an end of common sense; and human testimony, in these circumstances, loses all pretensions to authority. A religionist may be an enthusiast,* and imagine he sees what has no reality: He may know his narrative 118 to be false, and yet persevere in it, with the best intentions in the world, for the sake of promoting so holy a cause: Or even where this delusion has not place, vanity, excited by so strong a temptation, operates on him more powerfully than on the rest of mankind in any other circumstances; and self-interest with equal force. His auditors may not have, and commonly have not, sufficient judgment to canvass his evidence: What judgment they have, they renounce by principle, in these sublime and mysterious subjects: Or if they were ever so willing to employ it, passion and a heated imagination disturb the regularity of its operations. Their credulity encreases his impudence: And his impudence overpowers their credulity.

[18] Eloquence, when at its highest pitch, leaves little room for reason or reflection; but addressing itself entirely to the fancy or the affections, captivates the willing hearers, and subdues their understanding. Happily, this pitch it seldom attains. But what a TULLY or a DEMOSTHENES* could scarcely effect over a ROMAN or ATHENIAN audience, every *Capuchin*,* every itinerant or stationary teacher can perform over the generality of mankind, and in a higher degree, by touching such gross and vulgar passions.

[19] The many instances of forged miracles, and prophecies, and supernatural events, which, in all ages, have either been detected by contrary evidence, or which detect themselves by their absurdity, prove sufficiently the strong propensity of mankind to the extraordinary and the marvellous, and ought reasonably to beget a suspicion against all relations of this kind. This is our natural way of thinking, even with regard to the most common and most credible events. For instance: There is no kind of report, which rises so easily, and spreads so quickly, especially in country places and provincial towns, as those concerning marriages; insomuch that two young persons of equal condition never see each other twice, but the whole neighbourhood 119 immediately join them together. The pleasure of telling a piece of news so interesting, of propagating it, and of being the first reporters

of it, spreads the intelligence. And this is so well known, that no man of sense gives attention to these reports, till he find them confirmed by some greater evidence. Do not the same passions, and others still stronger, incline the generality of mankind to believe and report, with the greatest vehemence and assurance, all religious miracles?

[20] *Thirdly*. It forms a strong presumption against all supernatural and miraculous relations, that they are observed chiefly to abound among ignorant and barbarous nations; or if a civilized people has ever given admission to any of them, that people will be found to have received them from ignorant and barbarous ancestors, who transmitted them with that inviolable sanction and authority, which always attend received opinions. When we peruse the first histories of all nations, we are apt to imagine ourselves transported into some new world; where the whole frame of nature is disjointed, and every element performs its operations in a different manner, from what it does at present. Battles, revolutions, pestilence, famine, and death, are never the effect of those natural causes, which we experience. Prodigies, omens, oracles, judgments, quite obscure the few natural events, that are intermingled with them. But as the former grow thinner every page, in proportion as we advance nearer the enlightened ages, we soon learn, that there is nothing mysterious or supernatural in the case, but that all proceeds from the usual propensity of mankind towards the marvellous, and that, though this inclination may at intervals receive a check from sense and learning, it can never be thoroughly extirpated from human nature.

[21] *It is strange*, a judicious reader is apt to say, upon the perusal of 120 these wonderful historians,* *that such prodigious events never happen in our days*. But it is nothing strange, I hope, that men should lie in all ages. You must surely have seen instances enow of that frailty. You have yourself heard many such marvellous relations started, which, being treated with scorn by all the wise and judicious, have at last been abandoned even by the vulgar. Be assured, that those renowned lies, which have spread and flourished to such a monstrous height, arose from like beginnings; but being sown in a more proper soil, shot up at last into prodigies almost equal to those which they relate.

[22] It was a wise policy in that false prophet, ALEXANDER, who, though now forgotten, was once so famous, to lay the first scene of his impostures in PAPHLAGONIA, where, as LUCIAN* tells us, the people were extremely ignorant and stupid, and ready to swallow even the grossest delusion. People at a distance, who are weak enough to think

the matter at all worth enquiry, have no opportunity of receiving better information. The stories come magnified to them by a hundred circumstances. Fools are industrious in propagating the imposture; while the wise and learned are contented, in general, to deride its absurdity, without informing themselves of the particular facts, by which it may be distinctly refuted. And thus the impostor above-mentioned was enabled to proceed, from his ignorant PAPHLAGONIANS, to the enlisting of votaries, even among the GRECIAN philosophers, and men of the most eminent rank and distinction in ROME: Nay, could engage the attention of that sage emperor MARCUS AURELIUS;* so far as to make him trust the success of a military expedition to his delusive prophecies.

[23] The advantages are so great, of starting an imposture among an ignorant people, that, even though the delusion should be too gross to impose on the generality of them (*which, though seldom, is sometimes the case*) it has a much better chance for succeeding in remote countries, than if the first scene had been laid in a city renowned for arts and knowledge. The most ignorant and barbarous of these barbarians 121 carry the report abroad. None of their countrymen have a large correspondence, or sufficient credit and authority to contradict and beat down the delusion. Men's inclination to the marvellous has full opportunity to display itself. And thus a story, which is universally exploded in the place where it was first started, shall pass for certain at a thousand miles distance. But had ALEXANDER fixed his residence at ATHENS, the philosophers of that renowned mart of learning had immediately spread, throughout the whole ROMAN empire, their sense of the matter; which, being supported by so great authority, and displayed by all the force of reason and eloquence, had entirely opened the eyes of mankind. It is true; LUCIAN, passing by chance through PAPHLAGONIA, had an opportunity of performing this good office. But, though much to be wished, it does not always happen, that every ALEXANDER meets with a LUCIAN, ready to expose and detect his impostures.*

[24] I may add as a *fourth* reason, which diminishes the authority of prodigies, that there is no testimony for any, even those which have not been expressly detected, that is not opposed by an infinite number of witnesses; so that not only the miracle destroys the credit of testimony, but the testimony destroys itself. To make this the better understood, let us consider, that, in matters of religion, whatever is

different is contrary; and that it is impossible the religions of ancient
ROME, of TURKEY, of SIAM, and of CHINA should, all of them, be
established on any solid foundation. Every miracle, therefore, pretended to have been wrought in any of these religions (and all of them
abound in miracles), as its direct scope is to establish the particular
system to which it is attributed; so has it the same force, though more
indirectly, to overthrow every other system. In destroying a rival
system, it likewise destroys the credit of those miracles, on which
that system was established; so that all the prodigies of different religions are to be regarded as contrary facts, and the evidences of these
prodigies, whether weak or strong, as opposite to each other. According
to this method of reasoning, when we believe any miracle of MAHOMET*
or his successors, we have for our warrant the testimony of a few barbarous ARABIANS: And on the other hand, we are to regard the
authority of TITUS LIVIUS, PLUTARCH, TACITUS,* and, in short, of
all the authors and witnesses, GRECIAN, CHINESE, and ROMAN
CATHOLIC, who have related any miracle in their particular religion;
I say, we are to regard their testimony in the same light as if they had
mentioned that MAHOMETAN miracle, and had in express terms
contradicted it, with the same certainty as they have for the miracle
they relate. This argument may appear over subtile and refined; but
is not in reality different from the reasoning of a judge, who supposes,
that the credit of two witnesses, maintaining a crime against any one,
is destroyed by the testimony of two others, who affirm him to have
been two hundred leagues distant, at the same instant when the crime
is said to have been committed.

[25] One of the best attested miracles in all profane history, is that
which TACITUS reports of VESPASIAN,* who cured a blind man in
ALEXANDRIA, by means of his spittle, and a lame man by the mere
touch of his foot; in obedience to a vision of the god SERAPIS, who
had enjoined them to have recourse to the Emperor, for these miraculous cures. The story may be seen in that fine historian[24]; where
every circumstance seems to add weight to the testimony, and might
be displayed at large with all the force of argument and eloquence,
if any one were now concerned to enforce the evidence of that exploded
and idolatrous superstition. The gravity, solidity, age, and probity of
so great an emperor, who, through the whole course of his life, conversed

[24] Hist. lib. v. cap. 8. SUETONIUS* gives nearly the same account *in vita* VESP.

in a familiar manner with his friends and courtiers, and never affected those extraordinary airs of divinity assumed by ALEXANDER and DEMETRIUS.* The historian, a cotemporary writer, noted for candour and veracity, and withal, the greatest and most penetrating genius, perhaps, of all antiquity; and so free from any tendency to credulity, that he even lies under the contrary imputation, of atheism and profaneness: The persons, from whose authority he related the miracle, of established character for judgment and veracity, as we may well presume; eye-witnesses of the fact, and confirming their testimony, after the FLAVIAN family was despoiled of the empire, and could no longer give any reward, as the price of a lie. *Utrumque, qui interfuere, nunc quoque memorant, postquam nullum mendacio pretium.* To which if we add the public nature of the facts, as related, it will appear, that no evidence can well be supposed stronger for so gross and so palpable a falsehood.

[26] There is also a memorable story related by Cardinal DE RETZ,* which may well deserve our consideration. When that intriguing politician fled into SPAIN, to avoid the persecution of his enemies, he passed through SARAGOSSA, the capital of ARRAGON, where he was shewn, in the cathedral, a man, who had served seven years as a doorkeeper, and was well known to every body in town, that had ever paid his devotions at that church. He had been seen, for so long a time, wanting a leg; but recovered that limb by the rubbing of holy oil upon the stump; and the cardinal assures us that he saw him with two legs. This miracle was vouched by all the canons of the church;* and the whole company in town were appealed to for a confirmation of the fact; whom the cardinal found, by their zealous devotion, to be thorough believers of the miracle. Here the relater was also cotemporary to the supposed prodigy, of an incredulous and libertine character, as well as of great genius; the miracle of so *singular* a nature as could scarcely admit of a counterfeit, and the witnesses very numerous, and all of them, in a manner, spectators of the fact, to which they gave their testimony. And what adds mightily to the force of the evidence, and may double our surprize on this occasion, is, that the cardinal himself, who relates the story, seems not to give any credit to it, and consequently cannot be suspected of any concurrence in the holy fraud. He considered justly, that it was not requisite, in order to reject a fact of this nature, to be able accurately to disprove the testimony, and to trace its falsehood, through all the circumstances of knavery and credulity which

produced it. He knew, that, as this was commonly altogether impossible at any small distance of time and place; so was it extremely difficult, even where one was immediately present, by reason of the bigotry, ignorance, cunning, and roguery of a great part of mankind. He therefore concluded, like a just reasoner, that such an evidence carried falsehood upon the very face of it, and that a miracle, supported by any human testimony, was more properly a subject of derision than of argument.

[27] There surely never was a greater number of miracles ascribed to one person, than those, which were lately said to have been wrought in FRANCE upon the tomb of Abbé PARIS, the famous JANSENIST,* with whose sanctity the people were so long deluded. The curing of the sick, giving hearing to the deaf, and sight to the blind, were every where talked of as the usual effects of that holy sepulchre. But what is more extraordinary; many of the miracles were immediately proved upon the spot, before judges of unquestioned integrity, attested by witnesses of credit and distinction, in a learned age, and on the most eminent theatre that is now in the world. Nor is this all: A relation of them was published and dispersed every where; nor were the *Jesuits*,* though a learned body, supported by the civil magistrate, and determined enemies to those opinions, in whose favour the miracles were said to have been wrought, ever able distinctly to refute or detect them[25]. Where shall we find such a number of circumstances, agreeing to the corroboration of one fact? And what have we to oppose to such a cloud of witnesses, but the absolute impossibility or miraculous nature of the events, which they relate? And this surely, in the eyes of all reasonable people, will alone be regarded as a sufficient refutation.

[28] Is the consequence just, because some human testimony has the utmost force and authority in some cases, when it relates the battle of PHILIPPI or PHARSALIA for instance; that therefore all kinds of testimony must, in all cases, have equal force and authority? Suppose that the CAESAREAN and POMPEIAN* factions had, each of them, claimed the victory in these battles, and that the historians of each party had uniformly ascribed the advantage to their own side; how could mankind, at this distance, have been able to determine between them? The contrariety is equally strong between the miracles related by HERODOTUS* or PLUTARCH, and those delivered by MARIANA, BEDE,* or any monkish historian.

---

[25] See endnote [L], p. 128.

[29] The wise lend a very academic faith to every report which favours the passion of the reporter; whether it magnifies his country, his family, or himself, or in any other way strikes in with his natural inclinations and propensities. But what greater temptation than to appear a missionary, a prophet, an ambassador from heaven? Who would not encounter many dangers and difficulties, in order to attain so sublime a character? Or if, by the help of vanity and a heated imagination, a man has first made a convert of himself, and entered seriously into the delusion; who ever scruples to make use of pious frauds, in support of so holy and meritorious a cause?

[30] The smallest spark may here kindle into the greatest flame; 126 because the materials are always prepared for it. The *avidum genus auricularum*[26],* the gazing populace, receive greedily, without examination, whatever sooths superstition, and promotes wonder.

[31] How many stories of this nature, have, in all ages, been detected and exploded in their infancy? How many more have been celebrated for a time, and have afterwards sunk into neglect and oblivion? Where such reports, therefore, fly about, the solution of the phaenomenon is obvious; and we judge in conformity to regular experience and observation, when we account for it by the known and natural principles of credulity and delusion. And shall we, rather than have a recourse to so natural a solution, allow of a miraculous violation of the most established laws of nature?

[32] I need not mention the difficulty of detecting a falsehood in any private or even public history, at the place, where it is said to happen; much more when the scene is removed to ever so small a distance. Even a court of judicature, with all the authority, accuracy, and judgment, which they can employ, find themselves often at a loss to distinguish between truth and falsehood in the most recent actions. But the matter never comes to any issue, if trusted to the common method of altercation and debate and flying rumours; especially when men's passions have taken part on either side.

[33] In the infancy of new religions, the wise and learned commonly esteem the matter too inconsiderable to deserve their attention or regard. And when afterwards they would willingly detect the cheat, in order to undeceive the deluded multitude, the season is now past,

---

[26] LUCRET.

and the records and witnesses, which might clear up the matter, have perished beyond recovery.

127   [34] No means of detection remain, but those which must be drawn from the very testimony itself of the reporters: And these, though always sufficient with the judicious and knowing, are commonly too fine to fall under the comprehension of the vulgar.

[35] Upon the whole, then, it appears, that no testimony for any kind of miracle has ever amounted to* a probability, much less to a proof; and that, even supposing it amounted to a proof, it would be opposed by another proof; derived from the very nature of the fact, which it would endeavour to establish. It is experience only, which gives authority to human testimony; and it is the same experience, which assures us of the laws of nature. When, therefore, these two kinds of experience are contrary, we have nothing to do but substract the one from the other, and embrace an opinion, either on one side or the other, with that assurance which arises from the remainder. But according to the principle here explained, this substraction, with regard to all popular religions, amounts to an entire annihilation; and therefore we may establish it as a maxim, that no human testimony can have such force as to prove a miracle, and make it a just foundation for any such system of religion.

[36] I beg the limitations here made may be remarked, when I say, that a miracle can never be proved, so as to be the foundation of a system of religion. For I own, that otherwise, there may possibly be miracles, or violations of the usual course of nature, of such a kind as to admit of proof from human testimony; though, perhaps, it will be impossible to find any such in all the records of history. Thus, suppose, all authors, in all languages, agree, that, from the first of JANUARY 1600, there was a total darkness over the whole earth for eight days: Suppose that the tradition of this extraordinary event is still strong and lively among the people: That all travellers, who return from 128 foreign countries, bring us accounts of the same tradition, without the least variation or contradiction: It is evident, that our present philosophers, instead of doubting the fact, ought to receive it as certain, and ought to search for the causes whence it might be derived. The decay, corruption, and dissolution of nature, is an event rendered probable by so many analogies, that any phaenomenon, which seems to have a tendency towards that catastrophe, comes within the reach of human testimony, if that testimony be very extensive and uniform.

[37] But suppose, that all the historians who treat of ENGLAND, should agree, that, on the first of JANUARY 1600, Queen ELIZABETH*

died; that both before and after her death she was seen by her physicians and the whole court, as is usual with persons of her rank; that her successor was acknowledged and proclaimed by the parliament; and that, after being interred a month, she again appeared, resumed the throne, and governed ENGLAND for three years: I must confess that I should be surprized at the concurrence of so many odd circumstances, but should not have the least inclination to believe so miraculous an event. I should not doubt of her pretended death, and of those other public circumstances that followed it: I should only assert it to have been pretended, and that it neither was, nor possibly could be real. You would in vain object to me the difficulty, and almost impossibility of deceiving the world in an affair of such consequence; the wisdom and solid judgment of that renowned queen; with the little or no advantage which she could reap from so poor an artifice: All this might astonish me; but I would still reply, that the knavery and folly of men are such common phaenomena, that I should rather believe the most extraordinary events to arise from their concurrence, than admit of so signal a violation of the laws of nature.

[38] But should this miracle be ascribed to any new system of religion; men, in all ages, have been so much imposed on by ridiculous stories of that kind, that this very circumstance would be a full proof of a cheat, and sufficient, with all men of sense, not only to make them reject the fact, but even reject it without farther examination. Though the Being to whom the miracle is ascribed, be, in this case, Almighty, it does not, upon that account, become a whit more probable; since it is impossible for us to know the attributes or actions of such a Being, otherwise than from the experience which we have of his productions, in the usual course of nature. This still reduces us to past observation, and obliges us to compare the instances of the violation of truth in the testimony of men, with those of the violation of the laws of nature by miracles, in order to judge which of them is most likely and probable. As the violations of truth are more common in the testimony concerning religious miracles, than in that concerning any other matter of fact; this must diminish very much the authority of the former testimony, and make us form a general resolution, never to lend any attention to it, with whatever specious pretence it may be covered.

[39] Lord BACON* seems to have embraced the same principles of reasoning. "We ought", says he, "to make a collection or particular history of all monsters and prodigious births or productions, and in a

word of every thing new, rare, and extraordinary in nature. But this must be done with the most severe scrutiny, lest we depart from truth. Above all, every relation must be considered as suspicious, which depends in any degree upon religion, as the prodigies of LIVY:* And no less so, every thing that is to be found in the writers of natural magic or alchimy, or such authors, who seem, all of them, to have an unconquerable appetite for falsehood and fable[27]."

[40] I am the better pleased with the method of reasoning here delivered, as I think it may serve to confound those dangerous friends or disguised enemies to the *Christian Religion*, who have undertaken to defend it by the principles of human reason. Our most holy religion is founded on *Faith*, not on reason; and it is a sure method of exposing it to put it to such a trial as it is, by no means, fitted to endure. To make this more evident, let us examine those miracles, related in scripture; and not to lose ourselves in too wide a field, let us confine ourselves to such as we find in the *Pentateuch*,* which we shall examine, according to the principles of these pretended Christians, not as the word or testimony of God himself, but as the production of a mere human writer and historian. Here then we are first to consider a book, presented to us by a barbarous and ignorant people, written in an age when they were still more barbarous, and in all probability long after the facts which it relates, corroborated by no concurring testimony, and resembling those fabulous accounts, which every nation gives of its origin. Upon reading this book, we find it full of prodigies and miracles. It gives an account of a state of the world and of human nature entirely different from the present: Of our fall from that state: Of the age of man, extended to near a thousand years: Of the destruction of the world by a deluge: Of the arbitrary choice of one people, as the favourites of heaven; and that people the countrymen of the author: Of their deliverance from bondage by prodigies the most astonishing imaginable: I desire any one to lay his hand upon his heart, and after a serious consideration declare, whether he thinks that the falsehood of such a book, supported by such a testimony, would be more extraordinary and miraculous than all the miracles it relates; which is, however, necessary to make it be received, according to the measures of probability above established.

130

---

[27] Nov. Org. lib. ii. aph. 29.

[41] What we have said of miracles may be applied, without any variation, to prophecies; and indeed, all prophecies are real miracles, 131 and as such only, can be admitted as proofs of any revelation. If it did not exceed the capacity of human nature to foretel future events, it would be absurd to employ any prophecy as an argument for a divine mission or authority from heaven. So that, upon the whole, we may conclude, that the *Christian Religion* not only was at first attended with miracles, but even at this day cannot be believed by any reasonable person without one. Mere reason is insufficient to convince us of its veracity: And whoever is moved by *Faith* to assent to it,* is conscious of a continued miracle in his own person, which subverts all the principles of his understanding, and gives him a determination to believe what is most contrary to custom and experience.

SECTION XI

Of a PARTICULAR PROVIDENCE and of a FUTURE STATE*

I WAS lately engaged in conversation with a friend who loves sceptical paradoxes; where, though he advanced many principles, of
which I can by no means approve,* yet as they seem to be curious,
and to bear some relation to the chain of reasoning carried on
throughout this enquiry, I shall here copy them from my memory as
accurately as I can, in order to submit them to the judgment of the
reader.

[2] Our conversation began with my admiring the singular good
fortune of philosophy, which, as it requires entire liberty above all
other privileges, and chiefly flourishes from the free opposition of
sentiments and argumentation, received its first birth in an age and
country of freedom and toleration, and was never cramped, even in
its most extravagant principles, by any creeds, confessions, or penal
statutes. For, except the banishment of PROTAGORAS, and the death
of SOCRATES,* which last event proceeded partly from other
motives, there are scarcely any instances to be met with, in ancient
history, of this bigotted jealousy, with which the present age is so
much infested. EPICURUS lived at ATHENS to an advanced age, in
peace and tranquillity: EPICUREANS[28]* were even admitted to receive
the sacerdotal character, and to officiate at the altar, in the most sacred
rites of the established religion: And the public encouragement[29] of
133 pensions and salaries was afforded equally, by the wisest of all the
ROMAN emperors[30],* to the professors of every sect of philosophy.
How requisite such kind of treatment was to philosophy, in her early
youth, will easily be conceived, if we reflect, that, even at present,
when she may be supposed more hardy and robust, she bears with
much difficulty the inclemency of the seasons, and those harsh winds
of calumny and persecution, which blow upon her.

---

[28] LUCIANI συμπ. η, λαπιθαι.
[29] LUCIANI ευνουχος.
[30] Id. & Dio.

[3] You admire, says my friend, as the singular good fortune of philosophy, what seems to result from the natural course of things, and to be unavoidable in every age and nation. This pertinacious bigotry, of which you complain, as so fatal to philosophy, is really her offspring, who, after allying with superstition, separates himself entirely from the interest of his parent, and becomes her most inveterate enemy and persecutor. Speculative dogmas of religion, the present occasions of such furious dispute, could not possibly be conceived or admitted in the early ages of the world; when mankind, being wholly illiterate, formed an idea of religion more suitable to their weak apprehension, and composed their sacred tenets of such tales chiefly as were the objects of traditional belief, more than of argument or disputation. After the first alarm, therefore, was over, which arose from the new paradoxes and principles of the philosophers; these teachers seem ever after, during the ages of antiquity, to have lived in great harmony with the established superstition, and to have made a fair partition of mankind between them; the former claiming all the learned and wise, the latter possessing all the vulgar and illiterate.

[4] It seems then, say I, that you leave politics entirely out of the question, and never suppose, that a wise magistrate* can justly be jealous of certain tenets of philosophy, such as those of EPICURUS, which, denying a divine existence, and consequently a providence and a future state, seem to loosen, in a great measure, the ties of morality, and may 134 be supposed, for that reason, pernicious to the peace of civil society.

[5] I know, replied he, that in fact these persecutions never, in any age, proceeded from calm reason, or from experience of the pernicious consequences of philosophy; but arose entirely from passion and prejudice. But what if I should advance farther, and assert, that, if EPICURUS had been accused before the people, by any of the *sycophants* or informers of those days, he could easily have defended his cause, and proved his principles of philosophy to be as salutary as those of his adversaries, who endeavoured, with such zeal, to expose him to the public hatred and jealousy?

[6] I wish, said I, you would try your eloquence upon so extraordinary a topic, and make a speech for EPICURUS, which might satisfy, not the mob of ATHENS, if you will allow that ancient and polite city to have contained any mob, but the more philosophical part of his audience, such as might be supposed capable of comprehending his arguments.

[7] The matter would not be difficult, upon such conditions, replied he: And if you please, I shall suppose myself EPICURUS for a moment, and make you stand for the ATHENIAN people, and shall deliver you such an harangue as will fill all the urn with white beans,* and leave not a black one to gratify the malice of my adversaries.

[8] Very well: Pray proceed upon these suppositions.

[9] I come hither, O ye ATHENIANS, to justify in your assembly what I maintained in my school, and I find myself impeached by furious antagonists, instead of reasoning with calm and dispassionate enquirers. Your deliberations, which of right should be directed to questions of public good, and the interest of the commonwealth, are diverted to the disquisitions of speculative philosophy; and these magnificent, but perhaps fruitless enquiries, take place of your more familiar but more useful occupations. But so far as in me lies, I will prevent this abuse. We shall not here dispute concerning the origin and government of worlds. We shall only enquire how far such questions concern the public interest. And if I can persuade you, that they are entirely indifferent to the peace of society and security of government, I hope that you will presently send us back to our schools, there to examine, at leisure, the question, the most sublime, but, at the same time, the most speculative of all philosophy.

[10] The religious philosophers, not satisfied with the tradition of your forefathers, and doctrine of your priests (in which I willingly acquiesce), indulge a rash curiosity, in trying how far they can establish religion upon the principles of reason; and they thereby excite, instead of satisfying, the doubts, which naturally arise from a diligent and scrutinous enquiry. They paint, in the most magnificent colours, the order, beauty, and wise arrangement of the universe; and then ask, if such a glorious display of intelligence could proceed from the fortuitous concourse of atoms, or if chance could produce what the greatest genius can never sufficiently admire. I shall not examine the justness of this argument. I shall allow it to be as solid as my antagonists and accusers can desire. It is sufficient, if I can prove, from this very reasoning, that the question is entirely speculative, and that, when, in my philosophical disquisitions, I deny a providence and a future state, I undermine not the foundations of society, but advance principles, which they themselves, upon their own topics, if they argue consistently, must allow to be solid and satisfactory.

[11] You then, who are my accusers, have acknowledged, that the chief or sole argument for a divine existence (which I never questioned)

is derived from the order of nature; where there appear such marks
of intelligence and design, that you think it extravagant to assign for
its cause, either chance, or the blind and unguided force of matter.
You allow, that this is an argument drawn from effects to causes.* 136
From the order of the work, you infer, that there must have been
project and forethought in the workman. If you cannot make out this
point, you allow, that your conclusion fails; and you pretend not to
establish the conclusion in a greater latitude than the phaenomena of
nature will justify. These are your concessions. I desire you to mark
the consequences.

[12] When we infer any particular cause from an effect, we must
proportion the one to the other, and can never be allowed to ascribe
to the cause any qualities, but what are exactly sufficient to produce
the effect. A body of ten ounces raised in any scale may serve as a
proof, that the counterbalancing weight exceeds ten ounces; but can
never afford a reason that it exceeds a hundred. If the cause, assigned
for any effect, be not sufficient to produce it, we must either reject
that cause, or add to it such qualities as will give it a just proportion
to the effect. But if we ascribe to it farther qualities, or affirm it capable
of producing other effects, we can only indulge the licence of conjecture, and arbitrarily suppose the existence of qualities and energies,
without reason or authority.

[13] The same rule holds, whether the cause assigned be brute
unconscious matter, or a rational intelligent being. If the cause be
known only by the effect, we never ought to ascribe to it any qualities, beyond what are precisely requisite to produce the effect: Nor
can we, by any rules of just reasoning, return back from the cause, and
infer other effects from it, beyond those by which alone it is known to
us. No one, merely from the sight of one of ZEUXIS'S* pictures, could
know, that he was also a statuary or architect, and was an artist no less
skilful in stone and marble than in colours. The talents and taste, displayed in the particular work before us; these we may safely conclude
the workman to be possessed of. The cause must be proportioned to
the effect; and if we exactly and precisely proportion it, we shall 137
never find in it any qualities, that point farther, or afford an inference
concerning any other design or performance. Such qualities must be
somewhat beyond what is merely requisite for producing the effect,
which we examine.

[14] Allowing, therefore, the gods to be the authors of the existence
or order of the universe; it follows, that they possess that precise

degree of power, intelligence, and benevolence, which appears in their workmanship; but nothing farther can ever be proved, except we call in the assistance of exaggeration and flattery to supply the defects of argument and reasoning. So far as the traces of any attributes, at present, appear, so far may we conclude these attributes to exist. The supposition of farther attributes is mere hypothesis; much more the supposition, that, in distant regions of space or periods of time, there has been, or will be, a more magnificent display of these attributes, and a scheme of administration more suitable to such imaginary virtues. We can never be allowed to mount up from the universe, the effect, to JUPITER,* the cause; and then descend downwards, to infer any new effect from that cause; as if the present effects alone were not entirely worthy of the glorious attributes, which we ascribe to that deity. The knowledge of the cause being derived solely from the effect, they must be exactly adjusted to each other; and the one can never refer to any thing farther, or be the foundation of any new inference and conclusion.

[15] You find certain phaenomena in nature. You seek a cause or author. You imagine that you have found him. You afterwards become so enamoured of this offspring of your brain, that you imagine it impossible, but he must produce something greater and more perfect than the present scene of things, which is so full of ill and disorder. You forget, that this superlative intelligence and benevolence are entirely imaginary, or, at least, without any foundation in reason; and that you have no ground to ascribe to him any qualities, but what you see he has actually exerted and displayed in his productions. Let your gods, therefore, O philosophers, be suited to the present appearances of nature: And presume not to alter these appearances by arbitrary suppositions, in order to suit them to the attributes, which you so fondly ascribe to your deities.

[16] When priests and poets, supported by your authority, O ATHENIANS, talk of a golden or silver age, which preceded the present state of vice and misery, I hear them with attention and with reverence. But when philosophers, who pretend to neglect authority, and to cultivate reason, hold the same discourse, I pay them not, I own, the same obsequious submission and pious deference. I ask; who carried them into the celestial regions, who admitted them into the councils of the gods, who opened to them the book of fate, that they thus rashly affirm, that their deities have executed, or will execute, any purpose

beyond what has actually appeared? If they tell me, that they have mounted on the steps or by the gradual ascent of reason, and by drawing inferences from effects to causes, I still insist, that they have aided the ascent of reason by the wings of imagination; otherwise they could not thus change their manner of inference, and argue from causes to effects; presuming, that a more perfect production than the present world would be more suitable to such perfect beings as the gods, and forgetting that they have no reason to ascribe to these celestial beings any perfection or any attribute, but what can be found in the present world.

[17] Hence all the fruitless industry to account for the ill appearances of nature,* and save the honour of the gods; while we must acknowledge the reality of that evil and disorder, with which the world so much abounds. The obstinate and intractable qualities of matter, we are told, or the observance of general laws, or some such 139 reason, is the sole cause, which controlled the power and benevolence of JUPITER, and obliged him to create mankind and every sensible creature so imperfect and so unhappy. These attributes, then, are, it seems, beforehand, taken for granted, in their greatest latitude. And upon that supposition, I own, that such conjectures may, perhaps, be admitted as plausible solutions of the ill phaenomena. But still I ask; Why take these attributes for granted, or why ascribe to the cause any qualities but what actually appear in the effect? Why torture your brain to justify the course of nature upon suppositions, which, for aught you know, may be entirely imaginary, and of which there are to be found no traces in the course of nature?

[18] The religious hypothesis, therefore, must be considered only as a particular method of accounting for the visible phaenomena of the universe: But no just reasoner will ever presume to infer from it any single fact, and alter or add to the phaenomena, in any single particular. If you think, that the appearances of things prove such causes, it is allowable for you to draw an inference concerning the existence of these causes. In such complicated and sublime subjects, every one should be indulged in the liberty of conjecture and argument. But here you ought to rest. If you come backward, and arguing from your inferred causes, conclude, that any other fact has existed, or will exist, in the course of nature, which may serve as a fuller display of particular attributes; I must admonish you, that you have departed from the method of reasoning, attached to the present subject, and have

certainly added something to the attributes of the cause, beyond
what appears in the effect; otherwise you could never, with tolerable
sense or propriety, add any thing to the effect, in order to render it
more worthy of the cause.

140   [19] Where, then, is the odiousness of that doctrine, which I teach
in my school, or rather, which I examine in my gardens? Or what do
you find in this whole question, wherein the security of good morals,
or the peace and order of society is in the least concerned?

[20] I deny a providence, you say, and supreme governour of the
world, who guides the course of events, and punishes the vicious with
infamy and disappointment, and rewards the virtuous with honour and
success, in all their undertakings. But surely, I deny not the course itself
of events, which lies open to every one's enquiry and examination.
I acknowledge, that, in the present order of things, virtue is attended
with more peace of mind than vice, and meets with a more favourable
reception from the world. I am sensible, that, according to the past
experience of mankind, friendship is the chief joy of human life, and
moderation the only source of tranquillity and happiness. I never
balance between the virtuous and the vicious course of life; but am
sensible, that, to a well disposed mind, every advantage is on the
side of the former. And what can you say more, allowing all your
suppositions and reasonings? You tell me, indeed, that this disposition of things proceeds from intelligence and design. But whatever it
proceeds from, the disposition itself, on which depends our happiness or misery, and consequently our conduct and deportment in
life, is still the same. It is still open for me, as well as you, to regulate
my behaviour, by my experience of past events. And if you affirm,
that, while a divine providence is allowed, and a supreme distributive
justice in the universe, I ought to expect some more particular
reward of the good, and punishment of the bad, beyond the ordinary
course of events; I here find the same fallacy, which I have before
endeavoured to detect. You persist in imagining, that, if we grant
that divine existence, for which you so earnestly contend, you
141   may safely infer consequences from it, and add something to the
experienced order of nature, by arguing from the attributes which
you ascribe to your gods. You seem not to remember, that all your
reasonings on this subject can only be drawn from effects to causes;
and that every argument, deduced from causes to effects, must of
necessity be a gross sophism; since it is impossible for you to know

any thing of the cause, but what you have antecedently, not inferred, but discovered to the full, in the effect.

[21] But what must a philosopher think of those vain reasoners, who, instead of regarding the present scene of things as the sole object of their contemplation, so far reverse the whole course of nature, as to render this life merely a passage to something farther; a porch,* which leads to a greater, and vastly different building; a prologue, which serves only to introduce the piece, and give it more grace and propriety? Whence, do you think, can such philosophers derive their idea of the gods? From their own conceit and imagination surely. For if they derived it from the present phaenomena, it would never point to any thing farther, but must be exactly adjusted to them. That the divinity may *possibly* be endowed with attributes, which we have never seen exerted; may be governed by principles of action, which we cannot discover to be satisfied: All this will freely be allowed. But still this is mere *possibility* and hypothesis. We never can have reason to *infer* any attributes, or any principles of action in him, but so far as we know them to have been exerted and satisfied.

[22] *Are there any marks of a distributive justice in the world?* If you answer in the affirmative, I conclude, that, since justice here exerts itself, it is satisfied. If you reply in the negative, I conclude, that you have then no reason to ascribe justice, in our sense of it, to the gods. If you hold a medium between affirmation and negation, by saying, 142 that the justice of the gods, at present, exerts itself in part, but not in its full extent; I answer, that you have no reason to give it any particular extent, but only so far as you see it, *at present*, exert itself.

[23] Thus I bring the dispute, O ATHENIANS, to a short issue with my antagonists. The course of nature lies open to my contemplation as well as to theirs. The experienced train of events is the great standard, by which we all regulate our conduct. Nothing else can be appealed to in the field, or in the senate. Nothing else ought ever to be heard of in the school, or in the closet.* In vain would our limited understanding break through those boundaries, which are too narrow for our fond imagination. While we argue from the course of nature, and infer a particular intelligent cause, which first bestowed, and still preserves order in the universe, we embrace a principle, which is both uncertain and useless. It is uncertain; because the subject lies entirely beyond the reach of human experience. It is useless; because our knowledge of this cause being derived entirely from the course of

nature, we can never, according to the rules of just reasoning, return back from the cause with any new inference, or making additions to the common and experienced course of nature, establish any new principles of conduct and behaviour.

[24] I observe (said I, finding he had finished his harangue) that you neglect not the artifice of the demagogues of old; and as you were pleased to make me stand for the people, you insinuate yourself into my favour by embracing those principles, to which, you know, I have always expressed a particular attachment. But allowing you to make experience (as indeed I think you ought) the only standard of our judgment concerning this, and all other questions of fact; I doubt not but, from the very same experience, to which you appeal, it may be possible to refute this reasoning, which you have put into the mouth of Epicurus. If you saw, for instance, a half-finished building, surrounded with heaps of brick and stone and mortar, and all the instruments of masonry; could you not *infer* from the effect, that it was a work of design and contrivance? And could you not return again, from this inferred cause, to infer new additions to the effect, and conclude, that the building would soon be finished, and receive all the further improvements, which art could bestow upon it? If you saw upon the sea-shore the print of one human foot, you would conclude, that a man had passed that way, and that he had also left the traces of the other foot, though effaced by the rolling of the sands or inundation of the waters. Why then do you refuse to admit the same method of reasoning with regard to the order of nature? Consider the world and the present life only as an imperfect building, from which you can infer a superior intelligence; and arguing from that superior intelligence, which can leave nothing imperfect; why may you not infer a more finished scheme or plan, which will receive its completion in some distant point of space or time? Are not these methods of reasoning exactly similar? And under what pretence can you embrace the one, while you reject the other?

[25] The infinite difference of the subjects, replied he, is a sufficient foundation for this difference in my conclusions. In works of *human* art and contrivance, it is allowable to advance from the effect to the cause, and returning back from the cause, to form new inferences concerning the effect, and examine the alterations, which it has probably undergone, or may still undergo. But what is the foundation of this method of reasoning? Plainly this; that man is a

being, whom we know by experience, whose motives and designs we are acquainted with, and whose projects and inclinations have a certain connexion and coherence, according to the laws which nature 144 has established for the government of such a creature. When, therefore, we find, that any work has proceeded from the skill and industry of man; as we are otherwise acquainted with the nature of the animal, we can draw a hundred inferences concerning what may be expected from him; and these inferences will all be founded in experience and observation. But did we know man only from the single work or production which we examine, it were impossible for us to argue in this manner; because our knowledge of all the qualities, which we ascribe to him, being in that case derived from the production, it is impossible they could point to any thing farther, or be the foundation of any new inference. The print of a foot in the sand can only prove, when considered alone, that there was some figure adapted to it, by which it was produced: But the print of a human foot proves likewise, from our other experience, that there was probably another foot, which also left its impression, though effaced by time or other accidents. Here we mount from the effect to the cause; and descending again from the cause, infer alterations in the effect; but this is not a continuation of the same simple chain of reasoning. We comprehend in this case a hundred other experiences and observations, concerning the *usual* figure and members of that species of animal, without which this method of argument must be considered as fallacious and sophistical.

[26] The case is not the same with our reasonings from the works of nature. The Deity is known to us only by his productions, and is a single being in the universe, not comprehended under any species or genus, from whose experienced attributes or qualities, we can, by analogy, infer any attribute or quality in him. As the universe shews wisdom and goodness, we infer wisdom and goodness. As it shews a particular degree of these perfections, we infer a particular degree of 145 them, precisely adapted to the effect which we examine. But farther attributes or farther degrees of the same attributes, we can never be authorised to infer or suppose, by any rules of just reasoning. Now, without some such licence of supposition, it is impossible for us to argue from the cause, or infer any alteration in the effect, beyond what has immediately fallen under our observation. Greater good produced by this Being must still prove a greater degree of goodness: A more impartial distribution of rewards and punishments must proceed

from a greater regard to justice and equity. Every supposed addition to the works of nature makes an addition to the attributes of the Author of nature; and consequently, being entirely unsupported by any reason or argument, can never be admitted but as mere conjecture and hypothesis[31].

[27] The great source of our mistake in this subject, and of the unbounded licence of conjecture, which we indulge, is, that we tacitly consider ourselves, as in the place of the Supreme Being, and conclude, that he will, on every occasion, observe the same conduct, which we ourselves, in his situation, would have embraced as reasonable and eligible. But, besides that the ordinary course of nature may convince us, that almost every thing is regulated by principles and maxims very different from ours; besides this, I say, it must evidently appear contrary to all rules of analogy to reason, from the intentions and projects of men, to those of a Being so different, and so much superior. In human nature, there is a certain experienced coherence of designs and inclinations; so that when, from any fact, we have discovered one intention of any man, it may often be reasonable, from experience, to infer another, and draw a long chain of conclusions concerning his past or future conduct. But this method of reasoning can never have place with regard to a Being, so remote and incomprehensible, who bears much less analogy to any other being in the universe than the sun to a waxen taper, and who discovers himself* only by some faint traces or outlines, beyond which we have no authority to ascribe to him any attribute or perfection. What we imagine to be a superior perfection, may really be a defect. Or were it ever so much a perfection, the ascribing of it to the Supreme Being, where it appears not to have been really exerted, to the full, in his works, savours more of flattery and panegyric, than of just reasoning and sound philosophy. All the philosophy, therefore, in the world, and all the religion, which is nothing but a species of philosophy, will never be able to carry us beyond the usual course of experience, or give us measures of conduct and behaviour different from those which are furnished by reflections on common life. No new fact can ever be inferred from the religious hypothesis; no event foreseen or foretold; no reward or punishment expected or dreaded, beyond what is already known by practice and observation. So that my apology for

---

[31] See endnote [M], p. 130.

EPICURUS* will still appear solid and satisfactory; nor have the political 147
interests of society any connexion with the philosophical disputes
concerning metaphysics and religion.

[28] There is still one circumstance, replied I, which you seem to
have overlooked. Though I should allow your premises, I must deny
your conclusion. You conclude, that religious doctrines and reasonings
can have no influence on life, because they *ought* to have no influence;
never considering, that men reason not in the same manner you do,
but draw many consequences from the belief of a divine Existence, and
suppose that the Deity will inflict punishments on vice, and bestow
rewards on virtue, beyond what appear in the ordinary course of
nature. Whether this reasoning of theirs be just or not, is no matter. Its
influence on their life and conduct must still be the same. And, those,
who attempt to disabuse them of such prejudices, may, for aught
I know, be good reasoners, but I cannot allow them to be good citizens
and politicians; since they free men from one restraint upon their passions, and make the infringement of the laws of society, in one respect,
more easy and secure.

[29] After all, I may, perhaps, agree to your general conclusion in
favour of liberty, though upon different premises from those, on
which you endeavour to found it. I think, that the state ought to
tolerate every principle of philosophy; nor is there an instance, that
any government has suffered in its political interests by such indulgence. There is no enthusiasm* among philosophers; their doctrines
are not very alluring to the people; and no restraint can be put upon
their reasonings, but what must be of dangerous consequence to the
sciences, and even to the state, by paving the way for persecution and
oppression in points, where the generality of mankind are more deeply
interested and concerned.

[30] But there occurs to me (continued I) with regard to your main 148
topic, a difficulty, which I shall just propose to you, without insisting
on it; lest it lead into reasonings of too nice and delicate a nature. In a
word, I much doubt whether it be possible for a cause to be known only
by its effect (as you have all along supposed) or to be of so singular and
particular a nature as to have no parallel and no similarity with any
other cause or object, that has ever fallen under our observation. It is
only when two *species* of objects are found to be constantly conjoined,
that we can infer the one from the other; and were an effect presented,
which was entirely singular, and could not be comprehended under

any known *species,* I do not see, that we could form any conjecture or inference at all concerning its cause. If experience and observation and analogy be, indeed, the only guides which we can reasonably follow in inferences of this nature; both the effect and cause must bear a similarity and resemblance to other effects and causes, which we know, and which we have found, in many instances, to be conjoined with each other. I leave it to your own reflection to pursue the consequences of this principle. I shall just observe, that, as the antagonists of EPICURUS always suppose the universe, an effect quite singular and unparalleled, to be the proof of a Deity, a cause no less singular and unparalleled; your reasonings, upon that supposition, seem, at least, to merit our attention. There is, I own, some difficulty, how we can ever return from the cause to the effect, and, reasoning from our ideas of the former, infer any alteration on the latter, or any addition to it.

Of the ACADEMICAL or SCEPTICAL PHILOSOPHY

PART I

THERE is not a greater number of philosophical reasonings, displayed upon any subject, than those, which prove the existence
of a Deity, and refute the fallacies of *Atheists*;* and yet the most religious philosophers still dispute whether any man can be so blinded
as to be a speculative atheist. How shall we reconcile these contradictions? The knights-errant, who wandered about to clear the world of
dragons and giants, never entertained the least doubt with regard to
the existence of these monsters.

[2] The *Sceptic* is another enemy of religion, who naturally pro-
vokes the indignation of all divines and graver philosophers; though
it is certain, that no man ever met with any such absurd creature, or
conversed with a man, who had no opinion or principle concerning
any subject, either of action or speculation. This begets a very natural question; What is meant by a sceptic? And how far it is possible
to push these philosophical principles of doubt and uncertainty?

[3] There is a species of scepticism, *antecedent** to all study and
philosophy, which is much inculcated by DES CARTES* and others,
as a sovereign preservative against error and precipitate judgment.
It recommends an universal doubt, not only of all our former opinions
and principles, but also of our very faculties; of whose veracity, say they,
we must assure ourselves, by a chain of reasoning, deduced from some 150
original principle, which cannot possibly be fallacious or deceitful. But
neither is there any such original principle, which has a prerogative above
others, that are self-evident and convincing: Or if there were, could we
advance a step beyond it, but by the use of those very faculties, of which
we are supposed to be already diffident.* The CARTESIAN doubt, therefore, were it ever possible to be attained by any human creature (as it
plainly is not) would be entirely incurable; and no reasoning could
ever bring us to a state of assurance and conviction upon any subject.

[4] It must, however, be confessed, that this species of scepticism,
when more moderate, may be understood in a very reasonable sense,

and is a necessary preparative to the study of philosophy, by preserving a proper impartiality in our judgments, and weaning our mind from all those prejudices, which we may have imbibed from education or rash opinion.* To begin with clear and self-evident principles, to advance by timorous and sure steps, to review frequently our conclusions, and examine accurately all their consequences; though by these means we shall make both a slow and a short progress in our systems; are the only methods, by which we can ever hope to reach truth, and attain a proper stability and certainty in our determinations.

[5] There is another species of scepticism, *consequent* to science and enquiry, when men are supposed to have discovered, either the absolute fallaciousness of their mental faculties, or their unfitness to reach any fixed determination in all those curious subjects of speculation, about which they are commonly employed. Even our very senses are brought into dispute, by a certain species of philosophers; and the maxims of common life are subjected to the same doubt as the most profound principles or conclusions of metaphysics and theology. As these paradoxical tenets (if they may be called tenets) are to be met with in some philosophers, and the refutation of them in several, they naturally excite our curiosity, and make us enquire into the arguments, on which they may be founded.

[6] I need not insist upon the more trite topics, employed by the sceptics in all ages, against the evidence of *sense*;* such as those which are derived from the imperfection and fallaciousness of our organs, on numberless occasions; the crooked appearance of an oar in water; the various aspects of objects, according to their different distances; the double images which arise from the pressing one eye; with many other appearances of a like nature. These sceptical topics, indeed, are only sufficient to prove, that the senses alone are not implicitly to be depended on; but that we must correct their evidence by reason, and by considerations, derived from the nature of the medium, the distance of the object, and the disposition of the organ, in order to render them, within their sphere, the proper *criteria* of truth and falsehood. There are other more profound arguments against the senses, which admit not of so easy a solution.

[7] It seems evident, that men are carried, by a natural instinct or prepossession, to repose faith in their senses; and that, without any reasoning, or even almost before the use of reason, we always suppose an external universe, which depends not on our perception, but would exist, though we and every sensible creature were absent or annihilated.

Even the animal creation are governed by a like opinion, and preserve this belief of external objects, in all their thoughts, designs, and actions.

[8] It seems also evident, that, when men follow this blind and powerful instinct of nature, they always suppose the very images, presented by the senses, to be the external objects, and never entertain any suspicion, that the one are nothing but representations of the other. This very table, which we see white, and which we feel hard, is believed to exist, independent of our perception, and to be something external to 152 our mind, which perceives it. Our presence bestows not being on it: Our absence does not annihilate it. It preserves its existence uniform and entire, independent of the situation of intelligent beings, who perceive or contemplate it.

[9] But this universal and primary opinion of all men is soon destroyed by the slightest philosophy, which teaches us, that nothing can ever be present to the mind but an image or perception, and that the senses are only the inlets, through which these images are conveyed, without being able to produce any immediate intercourse between the mind and the object. The table, which we see, seems to diminish, as we remove farther from it: But the real table, which exists independent of us, suffers no alteration: It was, therefore, nothing but its image, which was present to the mind. These are the obvious dictates of reason; and no man, who reflects, ever doubted, that the existences, which we consider, when we say, *this house* and *that tree*, are nothing but perceptions in the mind, and fleeting copies or representations of other existences, which remain uniform and independent.

[10] So far, then, are we necessitated by reasoning to contradict or depart from the primary instincts of nature, and to embrace a new system with regard to the evidence of our senses. But here philosophy finds herself extremely embarrassed, when she would justify this new system, and obviate the cavils* and objections of the sceptics. She can no longer plead the infallible and irresistible instinct of nature: For that led us to a quite different system, which is acknowledged fallible and even erroneous. And to justify this pretended philosophical system, by a chain of clear and convincing argument, or even any appearance of argument, exceeds the power of all human capacity.

[11] By what argument can it be proved, that the perceptions of 153 the mind must be caused by external objects, entirely different from them, though resembling them (if that be possible) and could not arise either from the energy of the mind itself, or from the suggestion of some

invisible and unknown spirit, or from some other cause still more unknown to us? It is acknowledged, that, in fact, many of these perceptions arise not from any thing external, as in dreams, madness, and other diseases. And nothing can be more inexplicable than the manner, in which body should so operate upon mind as ever to convey an image of itself to a substance, supposed of so different, and even contrary a nature.

[12] It is a question of fact, whether the perceptions of the senses be produced by external objects, resembling them: How shall this question be determined? By experience surely; as all other questions of a like nature. But here experience is, and must be entirely silent. The mind has never any thing present to it but the perceptions, and cannot possibly reach any experience of their connexion with objects. The supposition of such a connexion is, therefore, without any foundation in reasoning.

[13] To have recourse to the veracity of the supreme Being, in order to prove the veracity of our senses, is surely making a very unexpected circuit.* If his veracity were at all concerned in this matter, our senses would be entirely infallible; because it is not possible that he can ever deceive. Not to mention, that, if the external world be once called in question, we shall be at a loss to find arguments, by which we may prove the existence of that Being or any of his attributes.

[14] This is a topic, therefore, in which the profounder and more philosophical sceptics will always triumph, when they endeavour to introduce an universal doubt into all subjects of human knowledge and enquiry. Do you follow the instincts and propensities of nature, 154 may they say, in assenting to the veracity of sense? But these lead you to believe, that the very perception or sensible image is the external object. Do you disclaim this principle, in order to embrace a more rational opinion, that the perceptions are only representations of something external? You here depart from your natural propensities and more obvious sentiments; and yet are not able to satisfy your reason, which can never find any convincing argument from experience to prove, that the perceptions are connected with any external objects.

[15] There is another sceptical topic* of a like nature, derived from the most profound philosophy; which might merit our attention, were it requisite to dive so deep, in order to discover arguments and reasonings, which can so little serve to any serious purpose. It is universally allowed by modern enquirers, that all the sensible qualities of objects, such as hard, soft, hot, cold, white, black, &c. are merely secondary,*

and exist not in the objects themselves, but are perceptions of the mind, without any external archetype or model, which they represent. If this be allowed, with regard to secondary qualities, it must also follow, with regard to the supposed primary qualities of extension and solidity; nor can the latter be any more entitled to that denomination than the former. The idea of extension is entirely acquired from the senses of sight and feeling; and if all the qualities, perceived by the senses, be in the mind, not in the object, the same conclusion must reach the idea of extension, which is wholly dependent on the sensible ideas or the ideas of secondary qualities. Nothing can save us from this conclusion, but the asserting, that the ideas of those primary qualities are attained by *Abstraction*;* an opinion, which, if we examine it accurately, we shall find to be unintelligible, and even absurd. An extension, that is neither tangible nor visible, cannot possibly be conceived: And a tangible or visible extension, which is neither hard nor soft, black nor white, is equally beyond the reach of human conception. Let any man try to conceive a triangle in general, which is neither *Isoceles* nor *Scalenum*,* nor has any particular length or proportion of sides; and he will soon perceive the absurdity of all the scholastic notions with regard to abstraction and general ideas[32].

[16] Thus the first philosophical objection to the evidence of sense or to the opinion of external existence consists in this, that such an opinion, if rested on natural instinct, is contrary to reason, and if referred to reason, is contrary to natural instinct, and at the same time carries no rational evidence with it, to convince an impartial enquirer. The second objection goes farther, and represents this opinion as contrary to reason: at least, if it be a principle of reason, that all sensible qualities are in the mind, not in the object. Bereave matter of all its intelligible qualities, both primary and secondary, you in a manner annihilate it, and leave only a certain unknown, inexplicable *something*, as the cause of our perceptions; a notion so imperfect, that no sceptic will think it worth while to contend against it.*

PART II

[17] It may seem a very extravagant attempt of the sceptics to destroy *reason* by argument and ratiocination; yet is this the grand scope of all

[32] See endnote [N], p. 130.

156   their enquiries and disputes. They endeavour to find objections, both
to our abstract reasonings, and to those which regard matter of fact
and existence.

[18] The chief objection against all *abstract* reasonings is derived from
the ideas of space and time; ideas, which, in common life and to a careless view, are very clear and intelligible, but when they pass through the
scrutiny of the profound sciences (and they are the chief object of these
sciences) afford principles, which seem full of absurdity and contradiction. No priestly *dogmas*, invented on purpose to tame and subdue the
rebellious reason of mankind, ever shocked common sense more than
the doctrine of the infinite divisibility of extension, with its consequences;
as they are pompously displayed by all geometricians and metaphysicians, with a kind of triumph and exultation. A real quantity, infinitely
less than any finite quantity, containing quantities infinitely less than
itself, and so on *in infinitum*; this is an edifice so bold and prodigious,
that it is too weighty for any pretended demonstration to support,
because it shocks the clearest and most natural principles of human
reason[33]. But what renders the matter more extraordinary, is, that these
seemingly absurd opinions are supported by a chain of reasoning, the
clearest and most natural; nor is it possible for us to allow the premises
without admitting the consequences. Nothing can be more convincing
157   and satisfactory than all the conclusions concerning the properties of
circles and triangles; and yet, when these are once received, how can we
deny, that the angle of contact between a circle and its tangent is
infinitely less than any rectilineal angle, that as you may encrease the
diameter of the circle *in infinitum*, this angle of contact becomes still
less, even *in infinitum*, and that the angle of contact between other
curves and their tangents may be infinitely less than those between any
circle and its tangent, and so on, *in infinitum?* The demonstration of
these principles seems as unexceptionable as that which proves the
three angles of a triangle to be equal to two right ones, though the latter
opinion be natural and easy, and the former big with contradiction and
absurdity. Reason here seems to be thrown into a kind of amazement
and suspence, which, without the suggestions of any sceptic, gives her
a diffidence of herself, and of the ground on which she treads. She sees
a full light, which illuminates certain places; but that light borders upon
the most profound darkness. And between these she is so dazzled and

---

[33] See endnote [O], p. 131.

confounded, that she scarcely can pronounce with certainty and assurance concerning any one object.

[19] The absurdity of these bold determinations of the abstract sciences seems to become, if possible, still more palpable with regard to time than extension. An infinite number of real parts of time, passing in succession, and exhausted one after another, appears so evident a contradiction, that no man, one should think, whose judgment is not corrupted, instead of being improved, by the sciences, would ever be able to admit of it.

[20] Yet still reason must remain restless, and unquiet, even with regard to that scepticism, to which she is driven by these seeming absurdities and contradictions. How any clear, distinct idea can contain circumstances, contradictory to itself, or to any other clear, distinct idea, is absolutely incomprehensible; and is, perhaps, as absurd as any proposition, which can be formed. So that nothing can be | 158 more sceptical, or more full of doubt and hesitation, than this scepticism itself, which arises from some of the paradoxical conclusions of geometry or the science of quantity[34].

[21] The sceptical objections to *moral* evidence, or to the reasonings concerning matter of fact, are either *popular* or *philosophical*. The popular objections are derived from the natural weakness of human understanding; the contradictory opinions, which have been entertained in different ages and nations; the variations of our judgment in sickness and health, youth and old age, prosperity and adversity; the perpetual contradiction of each particular man's opinions and sentiments; with many other topics of that kind. It is needless to insist farther on this head. These objections are but weak. For as, in common life, we reason every moment concerning fact and existence, and cannot possibly subsist, without continually employing this species of argument, any popular objections, derived from thence, must be insufficient to destroy that evidence. The great subverter of *Pyrrhonism** or the excessive principles of scepticism, is action, and employment, and the | 159 occupations of common life. These principles may flourish and triumph in the schools; where it is, indeed, difficult, if not impossible, to refute them. But as soon as they leave the shade, and by the presence of the real objects, which actuate our passions and sentiments, are put in opposition to the more powerful principles of our nature,

[34] See endnote [P], p. 131.

they vanish like smoke, and leave the most determined sceptic in the same condition as other mortals.

[22] The sceptic, therefore, had better keep within his proper sphere, and display those *philosophical* objections, which arise from more profound researches.* Here he seems to have ample matter of triumph; while he justly insists, that all our evidence for any matter of fact, which lies beyond the testimony of sense or memory, is derived entirely from the relation of cause and effect; that we have no other idea of this relation than that of two objects, which have been frequently *conjoined* together; that we have no argument to convince us, that objects, which have, in our experience, been frequently conjoined, will likewise, in other instances, be conjoined in the same manner; and that nothing leads us to this inference but custom or a certain instinct of our nature; which it is indeed difficult to resist, but which, like other instincts, may be fallacious and deceitful. While the sceptic insists upon these topics, he shews his force, or rather, indeed, his own and our weakness; and seems, for the time at least, to destroy all assurance and conviction. These arguments might be displayed at greater length, if any durable good or benefit to society could ever be expected to result from them.

[23] For here is the chief and most confounding objection to *excessive* scepticism, that no durable good can ever result from it; while it remains in its full force and vigour. We need only ask such a sceptic, *What his meaning is? And what he proposes by all these curious researches?* He is immediately at a loss, and knows not what to answer. A COPERNICAN or PTOLEMAIC,* who supports each his different system of astronomy, may hope to produce a conviction, which will remain constant and durable, with his audience. A STOIC or EPICUREAN* displays principles, which may not only be durable, but which have an effect on conduct and behaviour. But a PYRRHONIAN cannot expect, that his philosophy will have any constant influence on the mind: Or if it had, that its influence would be beneficial to society. On the contrary, he must acknowledge, if he will acknowledge any thing, that all human life must perish, were his principles universally and steadily to prevail. All discourse, all action would immediately cease; and men remain in a total lethargy, till the necessities of nature, unsatisfied, put an end to their miserable existence. It is true; so fatal an event is very little to be dreaded. Nature is always too strong for principle. And though a PYRRHONIAN may throw himself or others into a momentary

amazement and confusion by his profound reasonings; the first and most trivial event in life will put to flight all his doubts and scruples, and leave him the same, in every point of action and speculation, with the philosophers of every other sect, or with those who never concerned themselves in any philosophical researches. When he awakes from his dream, he will be the first to join in the laugh against himself, and to confess, that all his objections are mere amusement, and can have no other tendency than to show the whimsical condition of mankind, who must act and reason and believe; though they are not able, by their most diligent enquiry, to satisfy themselves concerning the foundation of these operations, or to remove the objections, which may be raised against them.

PART III

[24] There is, indeed, a more *mitigated* scepticism or *academical* philosophy, which may be both durable and useful, and which may, in part, be the result of this PYRRHONISM,* or *excessive* scepticism, when its undistinguished doubts are, in some measure, corrected by common sense and reflection. The greater part of mankind are naturally apt to be affirmative and dogmatical in their opinions; and while they see objects only on one side, and have no idea of any counterpoising argument, they throw themselves precipitately into the principles, to which they are inclined; nor have they any indulgence for those who entertain opposite sentiments. To hesitate or balance perplexes their understanding, checks their passion, and suspends their action. They are, therefore, impatient till they escape from a state, which to them is so uneasy; and they think, that they can never remove themselves far enough from it, by the violence of their affirmations and obstinacy of their belief. But could such dogmatical reasoners become sensible of the strange infirmities of human understanding, even in its most perfect state, and when most accurate and cautious in its determinations; such a reflection would naturally inspire them with more modesty and reserve, and diminish their fond opinion of themselves, and their prejudice against antagonists. The illiterate may reflect on the disposition of the learned, who, amidst all the advantages of study and reflection, are commonly still diffident in their determinations: And if any of the learned be inclined, from their natural temper, to haughtiness and obstinacy, a small tincture of PYRRHONISM might abate

their pride, by shewing them, that the few advantages, which they may have attained over their fellows, are but inconsiderable, if compared with the universal perplexity and confusion, which is inherent in
162 human nature. In general, there is a degree of doubt, and caution, and modesty, which, in all kinds of scrutiny and decision, ought for ever to accompany a just reasoner.

[25] Another species of *mitigated* scepticism, which may be of advantage to mankind, and which may be the natural result of the PYRRHONIAN doubts and scruples, is the limitation of our enquiries* to such subjects as are best adapted to the narrow capacity of human understanding. The *imagination* of man is naturally sublime, delighted with whatever is remote and extraordinary, and running, without controul, into the most distant parts of space and time in order to avoid the objects, which custom has rendered too familiar to it. A correct *Judgment* observes a contrary method, and avoiding all distant and high enquiries, confines itself to common life, and to such subjects as fall under daily practice and experience; leaving the more sublime topics to the embellishment of poets and orators, or to the arts of priests and politicians. To bring us to so salutary a determination, nothing can be more serviceable, than to be once thoroughly convinced of the force of the PYRRHONIAN doubt, and of the impossibility, that any thing, but the strong power of natural instinct, could free us from it. Those who have a propensity to philosophy, will still continue their researches; because they reflect, that, besides the immediate pleasure, attending such an occupation, philosophical decisions are nothing but the reflections of common life, methodized and corrected.* But they will never be tempted to go beyond common life, so long as they consider the imperfection of those faculties which they employ, their narrow reach, and their inaccurate operations. While we cannot give a satisfactory reason, why we believe, after a thousand experiments, that a stone will fall, or fire burn; can we ever satisfy ourselves concerning any determination, which we may form, with regard to the origin of worlds, and the situation of nature, from, and to eternity?

163 [26] This narrow limitation, indeed, of our enquiries, is, in every respect, so reasonable, that it suffices to make the slightest examination into the natural powers of the human mind, and to compare them with their objects, in order to recommend it to us. We shall then find what are the proper subjects of science and enquiry.

[27] It seems to me, that the only objects of the abstract sciences or of demonstration are quantity and number, and that all attempts to extend this more perfect species of knowledge beyond these bounds are mere sophistry and illusion. As the component parts of quantity and number are entirely similar,* their relations become intricate and involved; and nothing can be more curious, as well as useful, than to trace, by a variety of mediums, their equality or inequality, through their different appearances. But as all other ideas are clearly distinct and different from each other, we can never advance farther, by our outmost scrutiny, than to observe this diversity, and, by an obvious reflection, pronounce one thing not to be another. Or if there be any difficulty in these decisions, it proceeds entirely from the undeterminate meaning of words, which is corrected by juster definitions. That *the square of the hypothenuse* * *is equal to the squares of the other two sides*, cannot be known, let the terms be ever so exactly defined, without a train of reasoning and enquiry. But to convince us of this proposition, *that where there is no property, there can be no injustice*, it is only necessary to define the terms, and explain injustice to be a violation of property. This proposition is, indeed, nothing but a more imperfect definition. It is the same case with all those pretended syllogistical reasonings, which may be found in every other branch of learning, except the sciences of quantity and number; and these may safely, I think, be pronounced the only proper objects of knowledge and demonstration.

[28] All other enquiries of men regard only matter of fact and existence; and these are evidently incapable of demonstration. Whatever *is* may *not be*. No negation of a fact can involve a contradiction. The non-existence of any being, without exception, is as clear and distinct an idea as its existence. The proposition, which affirms it not to be, however false, is no less conceivable and intelligible, than that which affirms it to be. The case is different with the sciences, properly so called. Every proposition, which is not true, is there confused and unintelligible. That the cube root of 64 is equal to the half of 10, is a false proposition, and can never be distinctly conceived. But that CAESAR,* or the angel GABRIEL,* or any being never existed, may be a false proposition, but still is perfectly conceivable, and implies no contradiction.

[29] The existence, therefore, of any being can only be proved by arguments from its cause or its effect; and these arguments are founded entirely on experience. If we reason *à priori*, any thing may appear able to produce any thing. The falling of a pebble may, for

ought we know, extinguish the sun; or the wish of a man controul the planets in their orbits. It is only experience,* which teaches us the nature and bounds of cause and effect, and enables us to infer the existence of one object from that of another[35]. Such is the foundation of moral reasoning, which forms the greater part of human knowledge, and is the source of all human action and behaviour.

[30] Moral reasonings are either concerning particular or general facts. All deliberations in life regard the former; as also all disquisitions in history, chronology, geography, and astronomy.

165   [31] The sciences, which treat of general facts, are politics, natural philosophy, physic, chymistry, *&c.* where the qualities, causes and effects of a whole species of objects are enquired into.

[32] Divinity or Theology, as it proves the existence of a Deity, and the immortality of souls, is composed partly of reasonings concerning particular, partly concerning general facts. It has a foundation in *reason*, so far as it is supported by experience. But its best and most solid foundation is *faith* and divine revelation.*

[33] Morals and criticism are not so properly objects of the understanding as of taste and sentiment.* Beauty, whether moral or natural, is felt, more properly than perceived. Or if we reason concerning it, and endeavour to fix its standard, we regard a new fact, to wit, the general taste of mankind, or some such fact, which may be the object of reasoning and enquiry.

[34] When we run over libraries, persuaded of these principles, what havoc must we make? If we take in our hand any volume; of divinity or school metaphysics, for instance; let us ask, *Does it contain any abstract reasoning concerning quantity or number?* No. *Does it contain any experimental reasoning concerning matter of fact and existence?* No. Commit it then to the flames:* For it can contain nothing but sophistry and illusion.

[35] See endnote [Q], p. 131.

HUME'S ENDNOTES

[*For the editorial principles applied here, please see the Note on the Text, above.*]

Endnote [A] to 2.9, p. 15[1]

IT is probable that no more was meant by those, who denied innate ideas, 22 than that all ideas were copies of our impressions; though it must be confessed, that the terms, which they employed, were not chosen with such caution, nor so exactly defined, as to prevent all mistakes about their doctrine. For what is meant by *innate*? If innate be equivalent to natural, then all the perceptions and ideas of the mind must be allowed to be innate or natural, in whatever sense we take the latter word, whether in opposition to what is uncommon, artificial, or miraculous. If by innate be meant, cotemporary to our birth, the dispute seems to be frivolous; nor is it worth while to enquire at what time thinking begins, whether before, at, or after our birth. Again, the word *idea*, seems to be commonly taken in a very loose sense, by LOCKE* and others; as standing for any of our perceptions, our sensations and passions, as well as thoughts. Now in this sense, I should desire to know, what can be meant by asserting, that self-love, or resentment of injuries, or the passion between the sexes is not innate?

But admitting these terms, *impressions* and *ideas*, in the sense above explained, and understanding by *innate*, what is original or copied from no precedent perception, then may we assert, that all our impressions are innate, and our ideas not innate.

To be ingenuous, I must own it to be my opinion, that LOCKE was betrayed into this question by the schoolmen,* who, making use of undefined terms, draw out their disputes to a tedious length, without ever touching the point in question. A like ambiguity and circumlocution seem to run through that philosopher's reasonings on this as well as most other subjects.

Endnote [B] to 5.5, p. 32[8]

NOTHING is more usual than for writers, even, on *moral, political*, or 43 *physical* subjects, to distinguish between *reason* and *experience*, and to suppose, that these species of argumentation are entirely different from 44 each other. The former are taken for the mere result of our intellectual faculties, which, by considering *à priori* the nature of things, and examining the effects, that must follow from their operation, establish particular principles of science and philosophy. The latter are supposed to be derived entirely from sense and observation, by which we learn what has actually resulted from the operation of particular objects, and are thence able to infer, what will, for the future, result from them. Thus, for instance, the limitations and restraints of civil government, and a legal constitution, may be defended, either from *reason*, which reflecting on the great frailty and corruption of human nature, teaches, that no man can safely be trusted with unlimited authority; or from *experience* and history, which inform us of the enormous abuses, that ambition, in every age and country, has been found to make of so imprudent a confidence.

The same distinction between reason and experience is maintained in all our deliberations concerning the conduct of life; while the experienced statesman, general, physician, or merchant is trusted and followed; and the unpractised novice, with whatever natural talents endowed, neglected and despised. Though it be allowed, that reason may form very plausible conjectures with regard to the consequences of such a particular conduct in such particular circumstances; it is still supposed imperfect, without the assistance of experience, which is alone able to give stability and certainty to the maxims, derived from study and reflection.

But notwithstanding that this distinction be thus universally received, both in the active [and] speculative scenes of life, I shall not scruple to pronounce, that it is, at bottom, erroneous, at least, superficial.

If we examine those arguments, which, in any of the sciences above-mentioned, are supposed to be the mere effects of reasoning and reflection, they will be found to terminate, at last, in some general principle or conclusion, for which we can assign no reason but observation and experience. The only difference between them and those maxims, which are vulgarly esteemed the result of pure experience, is, that the former cannot be established without some process of thought, and some reflection on what we have observed, in order to distinguish its circumstances, and trace its consequences: Whereas in the latter, the experienced event is exactly and fully similar to that which we infer as the result of any particular situation. The history of a TIBERIUS or a NERO* makes us dread a like tyranny, were our monarchs freed from the restraints of laws and senates: But the observation of any fraud or cruelty in private life is sufficient, with the aid of a little thought, to give us the same apprehension; while it serves as an instance of the general corruption of human nature, and shews us the danger which we must incur by reposing an entire confidence in mankind. In both cases, it is experience which is ultimately the foundation of our inference and conclusion.

There is no man so young and unexperienced, as not to have formed, from observation, many general and just maxims concerning human affairs and the conduct of life; but it must be confessed, that, when a man comes to put these in practice, he will be extremely liable to error, till time and farther experience both enlarge these maxims, and teach him their proper use and application. In every situation or incident, there are many particular and seemingly minute circumstances, which the man of greatest talents is, at first, apt to overlook, though on them the justness of his conclusions, and consequently the prudence of his conduct, entirely depend. Not to mention, that, to a young beginner, the general observations and maxims occur not always on the proper occasions, nor can be immediately applied with due calmness and distinction. The truth is, an unexperienced reasoner could be no reasoner at all, were he absolutely unexperienced; and when we assign that character to any one, we mean it only in a comparative sense, and suppose him possessed of experience, in a smaller and more imperfect degree.

Endnote [C] to 7.15, p. 49[13]

IT may be pretended, that the resistance which we meet with in bodies, 67 obliging us frequently to exert our force, and call up all our power, this gives us the idea of force and power. It is this *nisus* or strong endeavour, of which we are conscious, that is the original impression from which this idea is copied. But, first, we attribute power to a vast number of objects, where we never can suppose this resistance or exertion of force to take place; to the Supreme Being, who never meets with any resistance; to the mind in its command over its ideas and limbs, in common thinking and motion, where the effect follows immediately upon the will, without any exertion or summoning up of force; to inanimate matter, which is not capable of this sentiment. *Secondly*, This sentiment of an endeavour to overcome resistance has no known connexion with any event: What follows it, we know by experience; but could not know it *à priori*. It must, however, be confessed, that the animal *nisus*, which we experience, though it can afford no accurate precise idea of power, enters very much into that vulgar, inaccurate idea, which is formed of it.

Endnote [D] to 7.25, p. 53[16]

I NEED not examine at length the *vis inertiae** which is so much talked of 73 in the new philosophy, and which is ascribed to matter. We find by experience, that a body at rest or in motion continues for ever in its present state, till put from it by some new cause; and that a body impelled takes as much motion from the impelling body as it acquires itself. These are facts. When we call this a *vis inertiae*, we only mark these facts,* without pretending to have any idea of the inert power; in the same manner as, when we talk of gravity, we mean certain effects, without comprehending that active power. It was never the meaning of Sir ISAAC NEWTON to rob second causes* of all force or energy; though some of his followers have endeavoured to establish that theory upon his authority. On the contrary, that great philosopher had recourse to an etherial active fluid to explain his universal attraction; though he was so cautious and modest as to allow, that it was a mere hypothesis, not to be insisted on, without more experiments. I must confess, that there is something in the fate of opinions a little extraordinary. DES CARTES insinuated that doctrine of the universal and sole efficacy of the Deity, without insisting on it. MALEBRANCHE and other CARTESIANS made it the foundation of all their philosophy. It had, however, no authority in ENGLAND. LOCKE,* CLARKE, and CUDWORTH,* never so much as take notice of it, but suppose all along, that matter has a real, though subordinate and derived power. By what means has it become so prevalent among our modern metaphysicians?

Endnote [E] to 7.29, p. 56[17]

77 ACCORDING to these explications and definitions, the idea of *power* is relative as much as that of *cause*; and both have a reference to an effect, or some other event constantly conjoined with the former. When we consider the *unknown* circumstance of an object, by which the degree or quantity of its effect is fixed and determined, we call that its power: And accordingly, it is allowed by all philosophers, that the effect is the measure of the power. But if they had any idea of power, as it is in itself, why could not they measure it in itself? The dispute* whether the force of a body in motion be as its velocity, or the square of its velocity; this dispute, I say, needed not be decided by comparing its effects in equal or unequal times; but by a direct mensuration* and comparison.

As to the frequent* use of the words, Force, Power, Energy, &c. which every where occur in common conversation, as well as in philosophy; that is no proof, that we are acquainted, in any instance, with the connecting principle between cause and effect, or can account ultimately for the production
78 of one thing by another. These words, as commonly used, have very loose meanings annexed to them; and their ideas are very uncertain and confused. No animal can put external bodies in motion without the sentiment of a *nisus* or endeavour; and every animal has a sentiment or feeling from the stroke or blow of an external object, that is in motion. These sensations, which are merely animal, and from which we can *à priori* draw no inference, we are apt to transfer to inanimate objects, and to suppose, that they have some such feelings, whenever they transfer or receive motion. With regard to energies, which are exerted, without our annexing to them any idea of communicated motion, we consider only the constant experienced conjunction of the events; and as we *feel* a customary connexion between the ideas, we transfer that feeling to the objects; as nothing is more usual than to apply to external bodies every internal sensation, which they occasion.

Endnote [F] to 8.22, p. 68[18]

94 THE prevalence of the doctrine of liberty may be accounted for, from another cause, *viz.* a false sensation or seeming experience which we

have, or may have, of liberty or indifference, in many of our actions. The necessity of any action, whether of matter or of mind, is not, properly speaking, a quality in the agent, but in any thinking or intelligent being, who may consider the action; and it consists chiefly in the determination of his thoughts to infer the existence of that action from some preceding objects; as liberty, when opposed to necessity, is nothing but the want of that determination, and a certain looseness or indifference, which we feel, in passing, or not passing, from the idea of one object to that of any succeeding one. Now we may observe, that, though, in *reflecting* on human actions, we seldom feel such a looseness or indifference, but are commonly able to infer them with considerable certainty from their motives, and from the dispositions of the agent; yet it frequently happens, that, in *performing* the actions themselves, we are sensible of something like it: And as all resembling objects are readily taken for each other, this has been employed as a demonstrative and even intuitive proof of human liberty. We feel, that our actions are subject to our will, on most occasions; and imagine we feel, that the will itself is subject to nothing, because, when by a denial of it we are provoked to try, we feel, that it moves easily every way, and produces an image of itself, (or a *Velleïty*, as it is called in the schools) even on that side, on which it did not settle. This image, or faint motion, we persuade ourselves, could, at that time, have been compleated into the thing itself; because, should that be denied, we find, upon a second trial, that, at present, it can. We consider not, that the fantastical desire of shewing liberty, is here the motive of our actions. And it seems certain, that, however we may imagine we feel a liberty within ourselves, a spectator can commonly infer our actions from our motives and character; and even where he cannot, he concludes in general, that he might, were he perfectly acquainted with every circumstance of our situation and temper, and the most secret springs of our complexion and disposition. Now this is the very essence of necessity, according to the foregoing doctrine.

Endnote [G] to 8.25, p. 69[19]

THUS, if a cause be defined, *that which produces any thing*; it is easy to observe, that *producing* is synonimous to *causing*. In like manner, if a cause be defined, *that by which any thing exists*; this is liable to the same objection. For what is meant by these words, *by which*? Had it been said, that a cause is *that* after which *any thing constantly exists*; we should have understood the terms. For this is, indeed, all we know of the matter. And this constancy forms the very essence of necessity, nor have we any other idea of it. 96

Endnote [H] to 9.5, p. 78[20]

SINCE all reasoning concerning facts or causes is derived merely from custom, it may be asked how it happens, that men so much surpass 107 animals in reasoning, and one man so much surpasses another? Has not the same custom the same influence on all?

We shall here* endeavour briefly to explain the great difference in human understandings: After which the reason of the difference between men and animals will easily be comprehended.

1. When we have lived any time, and have been accustomed to the uniformity of nature, we acquire a general habit, by which we always transfer the known to the unknown, and conceive the latter to resemble the former. By means of this general habitual principle, we regard even one experiment as the foundation of reasoning, and expect a similar event with some degree of certainty, where the experiment has been made accurately, and free from all foreign circumstances. It is therefore considered as a matter of great importance to observe the consequences of things; and as one man may very much surpass another in attention and memory and observation, this will make a very great difference in their reasoning.

2. Where there is a complication of causes to produce any effect, one mind may be much larger than another, and better able to comprehend the whole system of objects, and to infer justly their consequences.

3. One man is able to carry on a chain of consequences to a greater length than another.

4. Few men can think long without running into a confusion of ideas, and mistaking one for another; and there are various degrees of this infirmity.

5. The circumstance, on which the effect depends, is frequently involved in other circumstances, which are foreign and extrinsic. The separation of it often requires great attention, accuracy, and subtilty.

6. The forming of general maxims from particular observation is a very nice operation; and nothing is more usual, from haste or a narrowness of mind, which sees not on all sides, than to commit mistakes in this particular.

7. When we reason from analogies, the man, who has the greater experience or the greater promptitude of suggesting analogies, will be the better reasoner.

8. Byasses from prejudice, education, passion, party, &c. hang more upon one mind than another.

9. After we have acquired a confidence in human testimony, books and conversation enlarge much more the sphere of one man's experience and thought than those of another.

It would be easy to discover many other circumstances that make a difference in the understandings of men.

Endnote [I] to 10.10, p. 82[22]

N° INDIAN, it is evident, could have experience that water did not 114 freeze in cold climates. This is placing nature in a situation quite unknown to him; and it is impossible for him to tell *à priori* what will result from it. It is making a new experiment, the consequence of which is always uncertain. One may sometimes conjecture from analogy what will follow; but still this is but conjecture. And it must be confessed, that, in the present case of freezing, the event follows contrary to the rules of analogy, and is such as a rational INDIAN would not look for. The operations of cold upon water are not gradual, according to the degrees of cold; but whenever it comes to the freezing point, the water passes in a moment, from the utmost liquidity to perfect hardness. Such an event, therefore, may be denominated *extraordinary*, and requires a pretty strong testimony, to render it credible to people in a warm climate: But still it is not *miraculous*, nor contrary to uniform experience of the course of nature in cases where all the circumstances are the same. The inhabitants of SUMATRA have always seen water fluid in their own climate, and the freezing of their rivers ought to be deemed a prodigy: But they never saw water in MUSCOVY during the winter; and therefore they cannot reasonably be positive what would there be the consequence.

Endnote [K] to 10.12, p. 83[23]

SOMETIMES an event may not, *in itself, seem* to be contrary to the laws 115 of nature, and yet, if it were real, it might, by reason of some circumstances, be denominated a miracle; because, in *fact*, it is contrary to these laws. Thus if a person, claiming a divine authority, should command a sick person to be well, a healthful man to fall down dead, the clouds to pour rain, the winds to blow, in short, should order many natural events, which immediately follow upon his command; these might justly be esteemed miracles, because they are really, in this case, contrary to the laws of nature. For if any suspicion remain, that the event and command concurred by accident, there is no miracle and no transgression of the laws of nature. If this suspicion be removed, there is evidently a miracle, and a transgression of these laws; because nothing can be more contrary to nature than that the voice or command of a man should have such an influence. A miracle may be accurately defined, *a transgression of a law of nature by a particular volition of the Deity, or by the interposition of some invisible agent.* A miracle may either be discoverable by men or not. This alters not its nature and essence. The raising of a house or ship into the air is a visible miracle. The raising of a feather, when the wind wants ever so little of a force requisite for that purpose, is as real a miracle, though not so sensible with regard to us.

Endnote [L] to 10.27, p. 90[25]

344   THIS book was writ by Mons. MONTGERON,* counsellor or judge of
       the parliament of PARIS, a man of figure and character, who was also
a martyr to the cause, and is now said to be somewhere in a dungeon on
account of his book.

There is another book in three volumes (called *Recueil des Miracles de
l'Abbé* PARIS*) giving an account of many of these miracles, and accompanied with prefatory discourses, which are very well written. There runs,
however, through the whole of these a ridiculous comparison between the
miracles of our Saviour and those of the Abbé; wherein it is asserted, that
the evidence for the latter is equal to that for the former: As if the testimony
of men could ever be put in the balance with that of God himself, who
conducted the pen of the inspired writers. If these writers, indeed, were
to be considered merely as human testimony, the FRENCH author is very
moderate in his comparison; since he might, with some appearance of
reason, pretend, that the JANSENIST miracles much surpass the other in
evidence and authority. The following circumstances are drawn from
authentic papers, inserted in the above-mentioned book.

Many of the miracles of Abbé PARIS were proved immediately by
witnesses before the officiality or bishop's court at PARIS, under the eye of
cardinal NOAILLES,* whose character for integrity and capacity was never
contested even by his enemies.

His successor in the archbishopric was an enemy to the JANSENISTS,
and for that reason promoted to the see by the court. Yet 22 rectors or *cures*
of PARIS, with infinite earnestness, press him to examine those miracles,
which they assert to be known to the whole world, and undisputably
certain: But he wisely forbore.

The MOLINIST party had tried to discredit these miracles in one
instance, that of Mademoiselle le FRANC.* But, besides that their proceed-
ings were in many respects the most irregular in the world, particularly in
345   citing only a few of the JANSENIST witnesses, whom they tampered with:
Besides this, I say, they soon found themselves overwhelmed by a cloud of
new witnesses, one hundred and twenty in number, most of them persons
of credit and substance in PARIS, who gave oath for the miracle. This was
accompanied with a solemn and earnest appeal to the parliament. But the
parliament were forbidden by authority to meddle in the affair. It was at
last observed, that where men are heated by zeal and enthusiasm, there is
no degree of human testimony so strong as may not be procured for the
greatest absurdity: And those who will be so silly as to examine the affair
by that medium, and seek particular flaws in the testimony, are almost sure
to be confounded. It must be a miserable imposture, indeed, that does not
prevail in that contest.

All who have been in FRANCE about that time have heard of the reputation of Mons. HERAUT, the *lieutenant de Police*, whose vigilance, penetration, activity, and extensive intelligence have been much talked of. This magistrate, who by the nature of his office is almost absolute, was invested with full powers, on purpose to suppress or discredit these miracles; and he frequently seized immediately, and examined the witnesses and subjects of them: But never could reach any thing satisfactory against them.

In the case of Madamoiselle THIBAUT he sent the famous DE SYLVA* to examine her; whose evidence is very curious. The physician declares, that it was impossible she could have been so ill as was proved by witnesses; because it was impossible she could, in so short a time, have recovered so perfectly as he found her. He reasoned, like a man of sense, from natural causes; but the opposite party told him, that the whole was a miracle, and that his evidence was the very best proof of it.

The MOLINISTS were in a sad dilemma. They durst not assert the absolute insufficiency of human evidence, to prove a miracle. They were obliged to say, that these miracles were wrought by witchcraft and the devil. But they were told, that this was the resource of the JEWS* of old.

No JANSENIST was ever embarrassed to account for the cessation of the miracles, when the church-yard was shut up by the king's edict. It was the touch of the tomb, which produced these extraordinary effects; and when no one could approach the tomb, no effects could be expected. God, indeed, could have thrown down the walls in a moment; but he is master of his own graces and works, and it belongs not to us to account for them. He did not throw down the walls of every city like those of JERICHO, on the sounding of 346 the rams horns, nor break up the prison of every apostle, like that of St. PAUL.*

No less a man, than the Duc de CHATILLON,* a duke and peer of FRANCE, of the highest rank and family, gives evidence of a miraculous cure, performed upon a servant of his, who had lived several years in his house with a visible and palpable infirmity.

I shall conclude with observing, that no clergy are more celebrated for strictness of life and manners than the secular clergy of FRANCE, particularly the rectors or curés of PARIS, who bear testimony to these impostures.

The learning, genius, and probity of the gentlemen, and the austerity of the nuns of PORT-ROYAL,* have been much celebrated all over EUROPE. Yet they all give evidence for a miracle, wrought on the niece of the famous PASCAL,* whose sanctity of life, as well as extraordinary capacity, is well known. The famous RACINE* gives an account of this miracle in his famous history of PORT ROYAL, and fortifies it with all the proofs, which a multitude of nuns, priests, physicians, and men of the world, all of them of undoubted credit, could bestow upon it. Several men of letters, particularly the bishop of TOURNAY,* thought this miracle so certain, as to employ it in

the refutation of atheists and free-thinkers. The queen-regent of FRANCE,*
who was extremely prejudiced against the PORT-ROYAL, sent her own
physician to examine the miracle, who returned an absolute convert. In
short, the supernatural cure was so uncontestable, that it saved, for a time,
that famous monastery from the ruin with which it was threatened by the
JESUITS. Had it been a cheat, it had certainly been detected by such sagacious
and powerful antagonists, and must have hastened the ruin of the contrivers.
Our divines, who can build up a formidable castle from such despicable
materials; what a prodigious fabric could they have reared from these and
many other circumstances, which I have not mentioned! How often would
the great names of PASCAL, RACINE, ARNAUD, NICOLE, have resounded
in our ears? But if they be wise, they had better adopt the miracle, as being
more worth, a thousand times, than all the rest of their collection. Besides,
it may serve very much to their purpose. For that miracle was really performed by the touch of an authentic holy prickle of the holy thorn, which
composed the holy crown, which, &c.

Endnote [M] to 11.26, p. 106[31]

145   IN general, it may, I think, be established as a maxim, that where any
        cause is known only by its particular effects, it must be impossible to
infer any new effects from that cause; since the qualities, which are requisite
to produce these new effects along with the former, must either be
different, or superior, or of more extensive operation, than those which
simply produced the effect, whence alone the cause is supposed to be
known to us. We can never, therefore, have any reason to suppose the existence of these qualities. To say, that the new effects proceed only from a
continuation of the same energy, which is already known from the first
effects, will not remove the difficulty. For even granting this to be the case
(which can seldom be supposed), the very continuation and exertion of a
like energy (for it is impossible it can be absolutely the same), I say, this
exertion of a like energy, in a different period of space and time, is a very
arbitrary supposition, and what there cannot possibly be any traces of in
the effects, from which all our knowledge of the cause is originally derived.
Let the *inferred* cause be exactly proportioned (as it should be) to the
known effect; and it is impossible that it can possess any qualities, from
which new or different effects can be *inferred*.

Endnote [N] to 12.15, p. 113[32]

155   THIS argument is drawn from Dr. BERKLEY; and indeed most of the
        writings of that very ingenious author form the best lessons of scepti-
cism, which are to be found either among the ancient or modern philosophers, BAYLE* not excepted. He professes, however, in his title-page
(and undoubtedly with great truth) to have composed his book against the

sceptics as well as against the atheists and free-thinkers. But that all his arguments, though otherwise intended, are, in reality, merely sceptical, appears from this, *that they admit of no answer and produce no conviction.* Their only effect is to cause that momentary amazement and irresolution and confusion, which is the result of scepticism.

Endnote [O] to 12.18, p. 114[33]

WHATEVER disputes there may be about mathematical points,* we 156 must allow that there are physical points; that is, parts of extension, which cannot be divided or lessened, either by the eye or imagination. These images, then, which are present to the fancy or senses, are absolutely indivisible, and consequently must be allowed by mathematicians to be infinitely less than any real part of extension; and yet nothing appears more certain to reason, than that an infinite number of them composes an infinite extension. How much more an infinite number of those infinitely small parts of extension, which are still supposed infinitely divisible.*

Endnote [P] to 12.20, p. 115[34]

IT seems to me not impossible to avoid these absurdities and contradic- 158 tions, if it be admitted, that there is no such thing as abstract or general ideas, properly speaking; but that all general ideas are, in reality, particular ones, attached to a general term,* which recalls, upon occasion, other particular ones, that resemble, in certain circumstances, the idea, present to the mind. Thus when the term Horse, is pronounced, we immediately figure to ourselves the idea of a black or a white animal, of a particular size or figure: But as that term is also usually applied to animals of other colours, figures and sizes, these ideas, though not actually present to the imagination, are easily recalled; and our reasoning and conclusion proceed in the same way, as if they were actually present. If this be admitted (as seems reasonable) it follows that all the ideas of quantity, upon which mathematicians reason, are nothing but particular, and such as are suggested by the senses and imagination, and consequently, cannot be infinitely divisible. It is sufficient to have dropped this hint at present, without prosecuting it any farther. It certainly concerns all lovers of science not to expose themselves to the ridicule and contempt of the ignorant* by their conclusions; and this seems the readiest solution of these difficulties.

Endnote [Q] to 12.29, p. 120[35]

THAT impious maxim of the ancient philosophy, *Ex nihilo, nihil fit,** by 164 which the creation of matter was excluded, ceases to be a maxim, according to this philosophy. Not only the will of the supreme Being may create matter; but, for aught we know *à priori,* the will of any other being might create it, or any other cause, that the most whimsical imagination can assign.

APPENDIX I

Abstract of *A Treatise of Human Nature* (1740)

[*THIS abstract, now generally agreed to have been composed by Hume himself, was published anonymously in 1740 in an attempt to promote and explicate Books I and II of the* Treatise of Human Nature, *which had been published in January 1739. A valuable resource with elegant and concise presentations of some of Hume's principal arguments, it also indicates which of them he took to be most central and important to his philosophical project. It is striking and significant that the structure, focus, and ordering of the* Abstract, *though ostensibly describing the* Treatise, *actually bears much closer resemblance to a quite different work, the first* Enquiry, *which was still eight years away. For detailed discussion of this matter, setting it in a wider context, see my essay 'The Context, Aims, and Structure of Hume's First Enquiry' (chapter 1 of Peter Millican (ed.),* Reading Hume on Human Understanding, *OUP, 2002).*

The text here is taken from the original edition, with marginal numbers corresponding to the pages of the standard Selby-Bigge and Nidditch edition of the Treatise and Abstract *(OUP, 2nd edn., 1978).*]

AN ABSTRACT OF A BOOK lately PUBLISHED; ENTITULED,   641
A TREATISE OF *Human Nature*, &c. WHEREIN The CHIEF
ARGUMENT of that BOOK is farther ILLUSTRATED and EXPLAINED

PREFACE   643

M Y expectations in this small performance may seem somewhat extra-ordinary, when I declare that my intentions are to render a larger work more intelligible to ordinary capacities, by abridging it. 'Tis however certain, that those who are not accustomed to abstract reasoning, are apt to lose the thread of argument, where it is drawn out to a great length, and each part fortified with all the arguments, guarded against all the objections, and illustrated with all the views, which occur to a writer in the diligent survey of his subject. Such Readers will more readily apprehend a chain of reasoning, that is more single and concise, where the chief propositions only are linkt on to each other, illustrated by some simple examples, and confirmed by a few of the more forcible arguments. The parts lying nearer together can better be compared, and the connexion be more easily traced from the first principles to the last conclusion.

The work, of which I here present the Reader with an abstract, has been complained of as obscure and difficult to be comprehended, and I am apt to *think, that this proceeded as much from the length as from the abstractedness of the argument. If I have remedy'd this inconvenience in any degree, I have attain'd my end. The book seem'd to me to have such an air of singularity, and novelty as claim'd the attention of the public; especially if it be found, as the Author seems to insinuate, that were his philosophy receiv'd, we must alter from the foundation the greatest part of the sciences. Such bold attempts are always advantageous in the republic of letters, because they shake off the yoke of authority, accustom men to think for themselves, give new hints, which men of genius may carry farther, and by the very opposition, illustrate points, wherein no one before suspected any difficulty.*

644

The Author must be contented to wait with patience for some time before the learned world can agree in their sentiments of his performance. 'Tis his misfortune, that he cannot make an appeal to the people, who in all matters of common reason and eloquence are found so infallible a tribunal. He must be judg'd by the Few, whose verdict is more apt to be corrupted by partiality and prejudice, especially as no one is a proper judge in these subjects, who has not often thought of them; and such are apt to form to themselves systems of their own, which they resolve not to relinquish. I hope the Author will excuse me for intermeddling in this affair, since my aim is only to encrease his auditory, by removing some difficulties, which have kept many from apprehending his meaning. I have chosen one simple argument, which I have carefully traced from the beginning to the end. This is the only point I have taken care to finish. The rest is only hints of particular passages, which seem'd to me curious and remarkable.

645   AN ABSTRACT OF A BOOK lately PUBLISHED; ENTITULED,
A Treatise of Human Nature, &c.

THIS book seems to be wrote upon the same plan with several other works that have had a great vogue of late years in *England*. The philosophical spirit, which has been so much improved all over *Europe* within these last fourscore years, has been carried to as great a length in this kingdom as in any other. Our writers seem even to have started a new kind of philosophy, which promises more both to the entertainment and advantage of mankind, than any other with which the world has been yet acquainted. Most of the philosophers of antiquity, who treated of human nature, have shewn more of a delicacy of sentiment, a just sense of morals, or a greatness of soul, than a depth of reasoning and reflection. They content themselves with representing the common sense of mankind in the strongest lights, and with the best turn of thought and expression, without following out steadily a chain of propositions, or forming the several truths into a regular science. But 'tis at least worth while to try if the science of *man* will not admit of the same accuracy which several parts of natural philosophy are found susceptible of. There seems to be all the reason in the world to imagine that it may be carried to the greatest degree of exactness. 646 If, in examining several phaenomena, we find that they resolve themselves into one common principle, and can trace this principle into another, we shall at last arrive at those few simple principles, on which all the rest depend. And tho' we can never arrive at the ultimate principles, 'tis a satisfaction to go as far as our faculties will allow us.

[2] This seems to have been the aim of our late philosophers, and, among the rest, of this author. He proposes to anatomize human nature in a regular manner, and promises to draw no conclusions but where he is authorized by experience. He talks with contempt of hypotheses; and insinuates, that such of our countrymen as have banished them from moral philosophy, have done a more signal service to the world, than *my Lord Bacon*, whom he considers as the father of experimental physicks. He mentions, on this occasion, *Mr. Locke, my Lord Shaftesbury, Dr. Mandeville, Mr. Hutcheson, Dr. Butler*, who, tho' they differ in many points among themselves, seem all to agree in founding their accurate disquisitions of human nature entirely upon experience.

[3] Beside the satisfaction of being acquainted with what most nearly concerns us, it may be safely affirmed, that almost all the sciences are comprehended in the science of human nature, and are dependent on it. *The sole end of logic is to explain the principles and operations of our reasoning faculty, and the nature of our ideas*; morals *and* criticism *regard our tastes and sentiments; and* politics *consider men as united in society, and dependent on each other*. This treatise therefore of human nature seems intended for a system of the sciences. The author has finished what regards logic, and has laid the foundations of the other parts in his account of the passions.

[4] The celebrated *Monsieur Leibnitz* has observed it to be a defect in the common systems of logic, that they are very copious when they explain the 647 operations of the understanding in the forming of demonstrations, but are too concise when they treat of probabilities, and those other measures of evidence on which life and action entirely depend, and which are our guides even in most of our philosophical speculations. In this censure, he comprehends the *Essay on human understanding, Le Recherche de la verité*, and *L'Art de penser*. The author of the *Treatise of human nature* seems to have been sensible of this defect in these philosophers, and has endeavoured, as much as he can, to supply it. As his book contains a great number of speculations very new and remarkable, it will be impossible to give the reader a just notion of the whole. We shall therefore chiefly confine ourselves to his explication of our reasonings from cause and effect. If we can make this intelligible to the reader, it may serve as a specimen of the whole.

[5] Our author begins with some definitions. He calls a *perception* whatever can be present to the mind, whether we employ our senses, or are actuated with passion, or exercise our thought and reflection. He divides our perceptions into two kinds, *viz. impressions* and *ideas*. When we feel a passion or emotion of any kind, or have the images of external objects conveyed by our senses; the perception of the mind is what he calls an *impression*, which is a word that he employs in a new sense. When we reflect on a passion or an object which is not present, this perception is an *idea*. *Impressions*, therefore, are our lively and strong perceptions; *ideas* are the fainter and weaker. This distinction is evident; as evident as that betwixt feeling and thinking.

[6] The first proposition he advances, is, that all our ideas, or weak perceptions, are derived from our impressions, or strong perceptions, and that we can never think of any thing which we have not seen without us, or felt in our own minds. This proposition seems to be equivalent to that which Mr. *Locke* has taken such pains to establish, *viz. that no ideas are innate.* Only it may be observed, as an inaccuracy of that famous philosopher, that he comprehends all our perceptions under the term of idea, in which sense it is false, that we have no innate ideas. For it is evident our stronger perceptions or impressions are innate, and that natural affection, love of virtue, resentment, and all the other passions, arise immediately from nature. I am perswaded, whoever would take the question in this light, would be easily able to reconcile all parties. *Father Malebranche* would find himself at a loss to point out any thought of the mind, which did not represent something antecedently felt by it, either internally, or by means of the external senses, and must allow, that however we may compound, and mix, and augment, and diminish our ideas, they are all derived from these sources. *Mr. Locke*, on the other hand, would readily acknowledge, that all our passions are a kind of natural instincts, derived from nothing but the original constitution of the human mind.

[7] Our author thinks, "that no discovery cou'd have been made more happily for deciding all controversies concerning ideas than this, that impressions always take the precedency of them, and that every idea, with which the imagination is furnish'd, first makes its appearance in a correspondent impression. These latter perceptions are all so clear and evident, that they admit of no controversy; tho' many of our ideas are so obscure, that 'tis almost impossible even for the mind, which forms them, to tell exactly their nature and composition." Accordingly, wherever any idea is ambiguous, he has always recourse to the impression, which must render it clear and precise. And when he suspects that any philosophical term has no idea annexed to it (as is too common) he always asks *from what impression that pretended idea is derived?* And if no impression can be produced, he concludes

that the term is altogether insignificant. 'Tis after this manner he examines our idea of *substance* and *essence*; and it were to be wished, that this rigorous method were more practised in all philosophical debates.

[8] 'Tis evident, that all reasonings concerning *matter of fact* are founded on the relation of cause and effect, and that we can never infer the existence of one object from another, unless they be connected together, either mediately or immediately. In order therefore to understand these reasonings, we must be perfectly acquainted with the idea of a cause; and in order to that, must look about us to find something that is the cause of another.

[9] Here is a billiard-ball lying on the table, and another ball moving towards it with rapidity. They strike; and the ball, which was formerly at rest, now acquires a motion. This is as perfect an instance of the relation of cause and effect as any which we know, either by sensation or reflection. Let us therefore examine it. 'Tis evident, that the two balls touched one another before the motion was communicated, and that there was no interval betwixt the shock and the motion. *Contiguity* in time and place is therefore a requisite circumstance to the operation of all causes. 'Tis evident likewise, that the motion, which was the cause, is prior to the motion, which was the effect. *Priority* in time is therefore another requisite circumstance in every cause. But this is not all. Let us try any other balls of the same kind in a like situation, and we shall always find, that the impulse of the one produces motion in the other. Here therefore is a *third* circumstance, *viz.* that of a *constant conjunction* betwixt the cause and effect. Every object like the cause, produces always some object like the effect. Beyond these three circumstances of contiguity, priority, and constant conjunction, I can discover 650 nothing in this cause. The first ball is in motion; touches the second; immediately the second is in motion: and when I try the experiment with the same or like balls, in the same or like circumstances, I find, that upon the motion and touch of the one ball, motion always follows in the other. In whatever shape I turn this matter, and however I examine it, I can find nothing farther.

[10] This is the case when both the cause and effect are present to the senses. Let us now see upon what our inference is founded, when we conclude from the one that the other has existed or will exist. Suppose I see a ball moving in a streight line towards another, I immediately conclude, that they will shock, and that the second will be in motion. This is the inference from cause to effect; and of this nature are all our reasonings in the conduct of life: on this is founded all our belief in history: and from hence is derived all philosophy, excepting only geometry and arithmetic. If we can explain the inference from the shock of two balls, we shall be able to account for this operation of the mind in all instances.

[11] Were a man, such as *Adam*, created in the full vigour of understanding, without experience, he would never be able to infer motion in the second

ball from the motion and impulse of the first. It is not any thing that reason sees in the cause, which makes us *infer* the effect. Such an inference, were it possible, would amount to a demonstration, as being founded merely on the comparison of ideas. But no inference from cause to effect amounts to a demonstration. Of which there is this evident proof. The mind can always *conceive* any effect to follow from any cause, and indeed any event to follow upon another: whatever we *conceive* is possible, at least in a metaphysical sense: but wherever a demonstration takes place, the contrary is impossible, and implies a contradiction. There is no demonstration, therefore, for any conjunction of cause and effect. And this is a principle, which is generally allowed by philosophers.

651

[12] It would have been necessary, therefore, for *Adam* (if he was not inspired) to have had *experience* of the effect, which followed upon the impulse of these two balls. He must have seen, in several instances, that when the one ball struck upon the other, the second always acquired motion. If he had seen a sufficient number of instances of this kind, whenever he saw the one ball moving towards the other, he would always conclude without hesitation, that the second would acquire motion. His understanding would anticipate his sight, and form a conclusion suitable to his past experience.

[13] It follows, then, that all reasonings concerning cause and effect, are founded on experience, and that all reasonings from experience are founded on the supposition, that the course of nature will continue uniformly the same. We conclude, that like causes, in like circumstances, will always produce like effects. It may now be worth while to consider, what determines us to form a conclusion of such infinite consequence.

[14] 'Tis evident, that *Adam* with all his science, would never have been able to *demonstrate*, that the course of nature must continue uniformly the same, and that the future must be conformable to the past. What is possible can never be demonstrated to be false; and 'tis possible the course of nature may change, since we can conceive such a change. Nay, I will go farther, and assert, that he could not so much as prove by any *probable* arguments, that the future must be conformable to the past. All probable arguments are built on the supposition, that there is this conformity betwixt the future and the past, and therefore can never prove it. This conformity is a *matter of fact*, and if it must be proved, will admit of no proof but from experience. But our experience in the past can be a proof of nothing for the future, but upon a supposition, that there is a resemblance betwixt them. This therefore is a point, which can admit of no proof at all, and which we take for granted without any proof.

652

[15] We are determined by CUSTOM alone to suppose the future conformable to the past. When I see a billiard-ball moving towards another, my mind is immediately carry'd by habit to the usual effect, and anticipates my sight

by conceiving the second ball in motion. There is nothing in these objects, abstractly considered, and independent of experience, which leads me to form any such conclusion: and even after I have had experience of many repeated effects of this kind, there is no argument, which determines me to suppose, that the effect will be conformable to past experience. The powers, by which bodies operate, are entirely unknown. We perceive only their sensible qualities: and what *reason* have we to think, that the same powers will always be conjoined with the same sensible qualities?

[16] 'Tis not, therefore, reason, which is the guide of life, but custom. That alone determines the mind, in all instances, to suppose the future conformable to the past. However easy this step may seem, reason would never, to all eternity, be able to make it.

[17] This is a very curious discovery, but leads us to others, that are still more curious. *When I see a billiard-ball moving towards another, my mind is immediately carry'd by habit to the usual effect, and anticipates my sight by conceiving the second ball in motion.* But is this all? Do I nothing but CONCEIVE the motion of the second ball? No surely. I also BELIEVE that it will move. What then is this *belief*? And how does it differ from the simple conception of any thing? Here is a new question unthought of by philosophers.

[18] When a demonstration convinces me of any proposition, it not only   653
makes me conceive the proposition, but also makes me sensible, that 'tis impossible to conceive any thing contrary. What is demonstratively false implies a contradiction; and what implies a contradiction cannot be conceived. But with regard to any matter of fact, however strong the proof may be from experience, I can always conceive the contrary, tho' I cannot always believe it. The belief, therefore, makes some difference betwixt the conception to which we assent, and that to which we do not assent.

[19] To account for this, there are only two hypotheses. It may be said, that belief joins some new idea to those which we may conceive without assenting to them. But this hypothesis is false. For *first*, no such idea can be produced. When we simply conceive an object, we conceive it in all its parts. We conceive it as it might exist, tho' we do not believe it to exist. Our belief of it would discover no new qualities. We may paint out the entire object in imagination without believing it. We may set it, in a manner, before our eyes, with every circumstance of time and place. 'Tis the very object conceived as it might exist; and when we believe it, we can do no more.

[20] *Secondly,* The mind has a faculty of joining all ideas together, which involve not a contradiction; and therefore if belief consisted in some idea, which we add to the simple conception, it would be in a man's power, by adding this idea to it, to believe any thing, which he can conceive.

[21] Since therefore belief implies a conception, and yet is something more; and since it adds no new idea to the conception; it follows, that it is

a different MANNER of conceiving an object; *something* that is distinguishable to the feeling, and depends not upon our will, as all our ideas do. My mind runs by habit from the visible object of one ball moving towards another, to the usual effect of motion in the second ball. It not only conceives that motion, but *feels* something different in the conception of it from a mere reverie of the imagination. The presence of this visible object, and the constant conjunction of that particular effect, render the idea different to the *feeling* from those loose ideas, which come into the mind without any introduction. This conclusion seems a little surprizing; but we are led into it by a chain of propositions, which admit of no doubt. To ease the reader's memory I shall briefly resume them. No matter of fact can be proved but from its cause or its effect. Nothing can be known to be the cause of another but by experience. We can give no reason for extending to the future our experience in the past; but are entirely determined by custom, when we conceive an effect to follow from its usual cause. But we also believe an effect to follow, as well as conceive it. This belief joins no new idea to the conception. It only varies the manner of conceiving, and makes a difference to the feeling or sentiment. Belief, therefore, in all matters of fact arises only from custom, and is an idea conceived in a peculiar *manner*.

[22] Our author proceeds to explain the manner or feeling, which renders belief different from a loose conception. He seems sensible, that 'tis impossible by words to describe this feeling, which every one must be conscious of in his own breast. He calls it sometimes a *stronger* conception, sometimes a more *lively*, a more *vivid*, a *firmer*, or a more *intense* conception. And indeed, whatever name we may give to this feeling, which constitutes belief, our author thinks it evident, that it has a more forcible effect on the mind than fiction and mere conception. This he proves by its influence on the passions and on the imagination; which are only moved by truth or what is taken for such. Poetry, with all its art, can never cause a passion, like one in real life. It fails in the original conception of its objects, which never *feel* in the same manner as those which command our belief and opinion.

[23] Our author presuming, that he had sufficiently proved, that the ideas we assent to are different to the feeling from the other ideas, and that this feeling is more firm and lively than our common conception, endeavours in the next place to explain the cause of this lively feeling by an analogy with other acts of the mind. His reasoning seems to be curious; but could scarce be rendered intelligible, or at least probable to the reader, without a long detail, which would exceed the compass I have prescribed to myself.

[24] I have likewise omitted many arguments, which he adduces to prove that belief consists merely in a peculiar feeling or sentiment. I shall only mention one. Our past experience is not always uniform. Sometimes one effect follows from a cause, sometimes another: In which case we always

believe, that that will exist which is most common. I see a billiard-ball moving towards another. I cannot distinguish whether it moves upon its axis, or was struck so as to skim along the table. In the first case, I know it will not stop after the shock. In the second it may stop. The first is most common, and therefore I lay my account with that effect. But I also conceive the other effect, and conceive it as possible, and as connected with the cause. Were not the one conception different in the feeling or sentiment from the other, there would be no difference betwixt them.

[25] We have confin'd ourselves in this whole reasoning to the relation of cause and effect, as discovered in the motions and operations of matter. But the same reasoning extends to the operations of the mind. Whether we consider the influence of the will in moving our body, or in governing our thought, it may safely be affirmed, that we could never foretel the effect, merely from the consideration of the cause, without experience. And even after we have experience of these effects, 'tis custom alone, not reason, which 656 determines us to make it the standard of our future judgments. When the cause is presented, the mind, from habit, immediately passes to the conception and belief of the usual effect. This belief is something different from the conception. It does not, however, join any new idea to it. It only makes it be felt differently, and renders it stronger and more lively.

[26] Having dispatcht this material point concerning the nature of the inference from cause and effect, our author returns upon his footsteps, and examines anew the idea of that relation. In the considering of motion communicated from one ball to another, we could find nothing but contiguity, priority in the cause, and constant conjunction. But, beside these circumstances, 'tis commonly suppos'd, that there is a necessary connexion betwixt the cause and effect, and that the cause possesses something, which we call a *power*, or *force*, or *energy*. The question is, what idea is annex'd to these terms? If all our ideas or thoughts be derived from our impressions, this power must either discover itself to our senses, or to our internal feeling. But so little does any *power* discover itself to the senses in the operations of matter, that the *Cartesians* have made no scruple to assert, that matter is utterly deprived of energy, and that all its operations are perform'd merely by the energy of the supreme Being. But the question still recurs, *What idea have we of energy or power even in the supreme Being?* All our idea of a Deity (according to those who deny innate ideas) is nothing but a composition of those ideas, which we acquire from reflecting on the operations of our own minds. Now our own minds afford us no more notion of energy than matter does. When we consider our will or volition a *priori*, abstracting from experience, we are never able to infer any effect from it. And when we take the assistance of experience, it only shows us objects contiguous, successive, 657 and constantly conjoined. Upon the whole, then, either we have no idea at

all of force and energy, and these words are altogether insignificant, or they can mean nothing but that determination of the thought, acquir'd by habit, to pass from the cause to its usual effect. But whoever would thoroughly understand this must consult the author himself. 'Tis sufficient, if I can make the learned world apprehend, that there is some difficulty in the case, and that whoever solves the difficulty must say some thing very new and extraordinary; as new as the difficulty itself.

[27] By all that has been said the reader will easily perceive, that the philosophy contain'd in this book is very sceptical, and tends to give us a notion of the imperfections and narrow limits of human understanding. Almost all reasoning is there reduced to experience; and the belief, which attends experience, is explained to be nothing but a peculiar sentiment, or lively conception produced by habit. Nor is this all. When we believe any thing of *external* existence, or suppose an object to exist a moment after it is no longer perceived, this belief is nothing but a sentiment of the same kind. Our author insists upon several other sceptical topics; and upon the whole concludes, that we assent to our faculties, and employ our reason only because we cannot help it. Philosophy wou'd render us entirely *Pyrrhonian*, were not nature too strong for it.

[28] I shall conclude the logics of this author with an account of two opinions, which seem to be peculiar to himself, as indeed are most of his opinions. He asserts, that the soul, as far as we can conceive it, is nothing but a system or train of different perceptions, those of heat and cold, love and anger, thoughts and sensations; all united together, but without any perfect simplicity or identity. *Des Cartes* maintained that thought was the essence of the mind; not this thought or that thought, but thought in general. This seems to be absolutely unintelligible, since every thing, that exists, is particular: And therefore it must be our several particular perceptions, that compose the mind. I say, *compose* the mind, not *belong* to it. The mind is not a substance, in which the perceptions inhere. That notion is as unintelligible as the *Cartesian*, that thought or perception in general is the essence of the mind. We have no idea of substance of any kind, since we have no idea but what is derived from some impression, and we have no impression of any substance either material or spiritual. We know nothing but particular qualities and perceptions. As our idea of any body, a peach, for instance, is only that of a particular taste, colour, figure, size, consistence, &c. So our idea of any mind is only that of particular perceptions, without the notion of any thing we call substance, either simple or compound.

[29] The second principle, which I proposed to take notice of, is with regard to Geometry. Having denied the infinite divisibility of extension, our author finds himself obliged to refute those mathematical arguments, which have been adduced for it; and these indeed are the only ones of any weight.

This he does by denying Geometry to be a science exact enough to admit of conclusions so subtile as those which regard infinite divisibility. His arguments may be thus explained. All Geometry is founded on the notions of equality and inequality, and therefore according as we have or have not an exact standard of those relations, the science itself will or will not admit of great exactness. Now there is an exact standard of equality, if we suppose that quantity is composed of indivisible points. Two lines are equal when the numbers of the points, that compose them, are equal, and when there is a point in one corresponding to a point in the other. But tho' this standard be exact, 'tis useless; since we can never compute the number of points in any line. It is besides founded on the supposition of finite divis- 659 ibility, and therefore can never afford any conclusion against it. If we reject this standard of equality, we have none that has any pretensions to exactness. I find two that are commonly made use of. Two lines above a yard, for instance, are said to be equal, when they contain any inferior quantity, as an inch, an equal number of times. But this runs in a circle. For the quantity we call an inch in the one is supposed to be *equal* to what we call an inch in the other: And the question still is, by what standard we proceed when we judge them to be equal; or, in other words, what we mean when we say they are equal. If we take still inferior quantities, we go on *in infinitum*. This therefore is no standard of equality. The greatest part of philosophers, when ask'd what they mean by equality, say, that the word admits of no definition, and that it is sufficient to place before us two equal bodies, such as two diameters of a circle, to make us understand that term. Now this is taking the *general appearance* of the objects for the standard of that proportion, and renders our imagination and senses the ultimate judges of it. But such a standard admits of no exactness, and can never afford any conclusion contrary to the imagination and senses. Whether this reasoning be just or not, must be left to the learned world to judge. 'Twere certainly to be wish'd, that some expedient were fallen upon to reconcile philosophy and common sense, which with regard to the question of infinite divisibility have wag'd most cruel wars with each other.

[30] We must now proceed to give some account of the second volume of this work, which treats of the PASSIONS. 'Tis of more easy comprehension than the first; but contains opinions, that are altogether as new and extraordinary. The author begins with *pride* and *humility*. He observes, that the objects which excite these passions, are very numerous, and seemingly very different from each other. Pride or self-esteem may arise from the qualities of the mind; wit, good-sense, learning, courage, integrity: from those of the 660 body; beauty, strength, agility, good mein, address in dancing, riding, fencing: from external advantages; country, family, children, relations, riches, houses, gardens, horses, dogs, cloaths. He afterwards proceeds to

find out that common circumstance, in which all these objects agree, and which causes them to operate on the passions. His theory likewise extends to love and hatred, and other affections. As these questions, tho' curious, could not be rendered intelligible without a long discourse, we shall here omit them.

[31] It may perhaps be more acceptable to the reader to be informed of what our author says concerning *free-will*. He has laid the foundation of his doctrine in what he said concerning cause and effect, as above explained. " 'Tis universally acknowledg'd, that the operations of external bodies are necessary, and that in the communication of their motion, in their attraction, and mutual cohesion, there are not the least traces of indifference or liberty." — "Whatever therefore is in this respect on the same footing with matter, must be acknowledg'd to be necessary. That we may know whether this be the case with the actions of the mind, we may examine matter, and consider on what the idea of a necessity in its operations is founded, and why we conclude one body or action to be the infallible cause of another.

[32] "It has been observ'd already, that in no single instance the ultimate connexion of any objects is discoverable, either by our senses or reason, and that we can never penetrate so far into the essence and construction of bodies, as to perceive the principle, on which their mutual influence is founded. 'Tis their constant union alone, with which we are acquainted; and 'tis from the constant union the necessity arises, when the mind is determined to pass from one object to its usual attendant, and infer the existence of one from that of the other. Here then are two particulars, which we are to regard as essential to necessity, *viz.* the constant *union* and the *inference* of the mind; and wherever we discover these we must acknowledge a necessity." Now nothing is more evident than the constant union of particular actions with particular motives. If all actions be not constantly united with their proper motives, this uncertainty is no more than what may be observed every day in the actions of matter, where by reason of the mixture and uncertainty of causes, the effect is often variable and uncertain. Thirty grains of opium will kill any man that is not accustomed to it; tho' thirty grains of rhubarb will not always purge him. In like manner the fear of death will always make a man go twenty paces out of his road; tho' it will not always make him do a bad action.

[33] And as there is often a constant conjunction of the actions of the will with their motives, so the inference from the one to the other is often as certain as any reasoning concerning bodies: and there is always an inference proportioned to the constancy of the conjunction. On this is founded our belief in witnesses, our credit in history, and indeed all kinds of moral evidence, and almost the whole conduct of life.

[34] Our author pretends, that this reasoning puts the whole controversy in a new light, by giving a new definition of necessity. And, indeed, the most

zealous advocates for free-will must allow this union and inference with regard to human actions. They will only deny, that this makes the whole of necessity. But then they must shew, that we have an idea of something else in the actions of matter; which, according to the foregoing reasoning, is impossible.

[35] Thro' this whole book, there are great pretensions to new discoveries in philosophy; but if any thing can intitle the author to so glorious a name as that of an *inventor*, 'tis the use he makes of the principle of the association of ideas, which enters into most of his philosophy. Our imagi- 662 nation has a great authority over our ideas; and there are no ideas that are different from each other, which it cannot separate, and join, and compose into all the varieties of fiction. But notwithstanding the empire of the imagination, there is a secret tie or union among particular ideas, which causes the mind to conjoin them more frequently together, and makes the one, upon its appearance, introduce the other. Hence arises what we call the *apropos* of discourse: hence the connection of writing: and hence that thread, or chain of thought, which a man naturally supports even in the loosest *reverie*. These principles of association are reduced to three, *viz.* *Resemblance*; a picture naturally makes us think of the man it was drawn for. *Contiguity*; when *St. Dennis* is mentioned, the idea of *Paris* naturally occurs. *Causation*; when we think of the son, we are apt to carry our attention to the father. 'Twill be easy to conceive of what vast consequence these principles must be in the science of human nature, if we consider, that so far as regards the mind, these are the only links that bind the parts of the universe together, or connect us with any person or object exterior to ourselves. For as it is by means of thought only that any thing operates upon our passions, and as these are the only ties of our thoughts, they are really *to us* the cement of the universe, and all the operations of the mind must, in a great measure, depend on them.

FINIS

APPENDIX II

'Of the Immortality of the Soul' (1755)

[*THIS essay was originally planned for publication in a projected 1755 collection called* Five Dissertations, *but Hume decided to withdraw it (together with another religiously 'dangerous' piece on suicide) prior to publication. The two essays were replaced with 'Of the Standard of Taste', and the collection appeared in 1757 under the name* Four Dissertations. *The suppressed essays were eventually published posthumously and anonymously in 1777, but this text—like the standard edition of Miller (1987)—follows instead the 1755 version, of which a proof-copy exists in the National Library of Scotland with twenty corrections in Hume's handwriting. The marginal page numbers refer to Miller's edition, to facilitate cross-reference.*

Had the topic of immortality not been so dangerous, it is likely that the Enquiry *would have included more explicit discussion of it, especially given Section XI's overt concern with 'a future state'. But quite apart from this, the philosophical style of the essay is exactly in the spirit of the* Enquiry, *and provides an excellent illustration of Hume's approach. Its first and last paragraphs also illustrate the sort of 'theological lying' so common at the time, through which atheistic writers preserved the formal decencies by giving an appearance of orthodoxy. The* Enquiry *itself contains other examples, at the end of Sections VIII and X, at the beginning of Section XI, and also at 12.32.*]

590

OF THE IMMORTALITY OF THE SOUL

BY the mere light of reason it seems difficult to prove the Immortality of the Soul. The arguments for it are commonly derived either from *metaphysical* topics, or *moral* or *physical*. But in reality, it is the gospel, and the gospel alone, that has brought life and immortality to light.

591   I. METAPHYSICAL topics are founded on the supposition that the soul is immaterial, and that it is impossible for thought to belong to a material substance.

BUT just metaphysics teach us, that the notion of substance is wholly confused and imperfect, and that we have no other idea of any substance than as an aggregate of particular qualities, inhering in an unknown something. Matter, therefore, and spirit are at bottom equally unknown; and we cannot determine what qualities may inhere in the one or in the other.

THEY likewise teach us, that nothing can be decided *a priori* concerning any cause or effect; and that experience being the only source of our judgments of this nature, we cannot know from any other principle, whether matter, by its structure or arrangement, may not be the cause of thought. Abstract reasonings cannot decide any question of fact or existence.

BUT admitting a spiritual substance to be dispersed throughout the universe, like the etherial fire of the *Stoics*, and to be the only inherent subject of thought; we have reason to conclude from *analogy*, that nature uses it after the same manner she does the other substance, matter. She employs it as a kind of paste or clay; modifies it into a variety of forms and existences; dissolves after a time each modification; and from its substance erects a new form. As the same material substance may successively compose the body of all animals, the same spiritual substance may compose their minds: Their consciousness, or that system of thought, which they formed during life, may be continually dissolved by death; and nothing 592 interest them in the new modification. The most positive asserters of the mortality of the soul, never denied the immortality of its substance. And that an immaterial substance, as well as a material, may lose its memory or consciousness appears, in part, from experience, if the soul be immaterial.

REASONING from the common course of nature, and without supposing any *new* interposition of the supreme cause, which ought always to be excluded from philosophy; what is incorruptible must also be ingenerable. The soul, therefore, if immortal, existed before our birth: And if the former state of existence no wise concerned us, neither will the latter.

ANIMALS undoubtedly feel, think, love, hate, will, and even reason, tho' in a more imperfect manner than man. Are their souls also immaterial and immortal?

II. LET us now consider the *moral* arguments, chiefly those arguments derived from the justice of God, which is supposed to be farther interested in the farther punishment of the vicious, and reward of the virtuous.

BUT these arguments are grounded on the supposition, that God has attributes beyond what he has exerted in this universe, with which alone we are acquainted. Whence do we infer the existence of these attributes?

IT IS very safe for us to affirm, that, whatever we know the deity to have actually done, is best; but it is very dangerous to affirm, that he must always do what to us seems best. In how many instances would this reasoning fail us with regard to the present world?

BUT if any purpose of nature be clear, we may affirm, that the whole scope and intention of man's creation, so far as we can judge by natural reason, is limited to the present life. With how weak a concern, from the original, inherent structure of the mind and passions, does he ever look farther? What comparison, either for steddiness or efficacy, between so floating an idea, and the most doubtful persuasion of any matter of fact, that occurs in common life.

THERE arise, indeed, in some minds, some unaccountable terrors with 593 regard to futurity: But these would quickly vanish, were they not artificially fostered by precept and education. And those, who foster them; what is their motive? Only to gain a livelihood, and to acquire power and riches in this world. Their very zeal and industry, therefore, are an argument against them.

WHAT cruelty, what iniquity, what injustice in nature, to confine thus all our concern, as well as all our knowledge, to the present life, if there be another scene still awaiting us, of infinitely greater consequence? Ought this barbarous deceit to be ascribed to a beneficent and wise being?

OBSERVE with what exact proportion the task to be performed and the performing powers are adjusted throughout all nature. If the reason of man gives him a great superiority above other animals, his necessities are proportionably multiplied upon him. His whole time, his whole capacity, activity, courage, passion, find sufficient employment, in fencing against the miseries of his present condition. And frequently, nay almost always, are too slender for the business assigned them.

A PAIR of shoes, perhaps, was never yet wrought to the highest degree of perfection, which that commodity is capable of attaining. Yet is it necessary, at least very useful, that there should be some politicians and moralists, even some geometers, historians, poets, and philosophers among mankind.

THE powers of men are no more superior to their wants, considered merely in this life, than those of foxes and hares are, compared to *their* wants and to *their* period of existence. The inference from parity of reason is therefore obvious.

ON the theory of the soul's mortality, the inferiority of women's capacity is easily accounted for: Their domestic life requires no higher faculties either of mind or body. This circumstance vanishes and becomes absolutely insignificant, on the religious theory: The one sex has an equal task to perform with the other: Their powers of reason and resolution ought also to have been equal, and both of them infinitely greater than at present.

594 As every effect implies a cause, and that another, till we reach the first cause of all, which is the *Deity*; every thing, that happens, is ordained by him; and nothing can be the object of his punishment or vengeance.

BY what rule are punishments and rewards distributed? What is the divine standard of merit and demerit? Shall we suppose, that human sentiments have place in the deity? However bold that hypothesis, we have no conception of any other sentiments.

ACCORDING to human sentiments, sense, courage, good manners, industry, prudence, genius, &c. are essential parts of personal merit. Shall we therefore erect an elysium for poets and heroes, like that of the antient mythology? Why confine all rewards to one species of virtue?

PUNISHMENT, without any proper end or purpose, is inconsistent with *our* ideas of goodness and justice, and no end can be served by it after the whole scene is closed.

PUNISHMENT, according to *our* conceptions, should bear some proportion to the offence. Why then eternal punishment for the temporary offences of so frail a creature as man? Can any one approve of *Alexander's* rage, who intended to exterminate a whole nation, because they had seized his favourite horse, *Bucephalus*?[1]

HEAVEN and hell suppose two distinct species of men, the good and the bad. But the greatest part of mankind float between vice and virtue.

WERE one to go round the world with an intention of giving a good supper to the righteous and a sound drubbing to the wicked, he would frequently be embarrassed in his choice, and would find, that the merits and the demerits of most men and women scarcely amount to the value of either.

TO suppose measures of approbation and blame, different from the human, confounds every thing. Whence do we learn, that there is such a thing as moral distinctions but from our own sentiments?

WHAT man, who has not met with personal provocation (or what good natur'd man who has) could inflict on crimes, from the sense of blame alone, even the common, legal, frivolous punishments? And does any thing steel the breast of judges and juries against the sentiments of humanity but reflections on necessity and public interest?

BY the Roman law, those who had been guilty of parricide and confessed their crime, were put into a sack, along with an ape, a dog, and a serpent; and thrown into the river: Death alone was the punishment of those, who denied their guilt, however fully proved. A criminal was tryed before *Augustus*, and condemned after full conviction: But the humane emperor, when he put the last interrogatory, gave it such a turn as to lead the wretch into a denial of his guilt. *You surely*, said the prince, *did not kill your father*[2]. This lenity suits our natural ideas of RIGHT, even towards the greatest of all criminals, and even tho' it prevents so inconsiderable a sufferance. Nay, even the most bigotted priest would naturally, without reflection, approve of it; provided the crime was not heresy or infidelity. For as these crimes hurt himself in his *temporal* interests and advantages; perhaps he may not be altogether so indulgent to them.

THE chief source of moral ideas is the reflection on the interest of human society. Ought these interests, so short, so frivolous, to be guarded by punishments, eternal and infinite? The damnation of one man is an infinitely greater evil in the universe, than the subversion of a thousand millions of kingdoms.

NATURE has rendered human infancy peculiarly frail and mortal; as it were on purpose to refute the notion of a probationary state. The half of mankind dye before they are rational creatures.

595

596

---

[1] Quint. Curtius, lib. vi. cap. 5.
[2] Sueton. August. cap. 3.

III. THE *physical* arguments from the analogy of nature are strong for the mortality of the soul; and these are really the only philosophical arguments, which ought to be admitted with regard to this question, or indeed any question of fact.

WHERE any two objects are so closely connected, that all alterations, which we have ever seen in the one, are attended with proportionable alterations in the other; we ought to conclude, by all rules of analogy, that, when there are still greater alterations produced in the former, and it is totally dissolved, there follows a total dissolution of the latter.

SLEEP, a very small effect on the body, is attended with a temporary extinction; at least, a great confusion in the soul.

THE weakness of the body and that of the mind in infancy are exactly proportioned; their vigor in manhood; their sympathetic disorder in sickness; their common gradual decay in old age. The step further seems unavoidable; their common dissolution in death.

THE last symptoms, which the mind discovers, are disorder, weakness, insensibility, stupidity, the forerunners of its annihilation. The farther progress of the same causes, encreasing the same effects, totally extinguish it.

JUDGING by the usual analogy of nature, no form can continue, when transferred to a condition of life very different from the original one, in which it was placed. Trees perish in the water; fishes in the air; animals in the earth. Even so small a difference as that of climate is often fatal. What reason then to imagine, that an immense alteration, such as is made on the soul by the dissolution of its body and all its organs of thought and sensation, can be effected without the dissolution of the whole?

EVERY thing is in common between soul and body. The organs of the one are all of them the organs of the other. The existence therefore of the one must be dependent on that of the other.

597   THE souls of animals are allowed to be mortal; and these bear so near a resemblance to the souls of men, that the analogy from one to the other forms a very strong argument. Their bodies are not more resembling; yet no one rejects the arguments drawn from comparative anatomy. The *Metempsychosis* is therefore the only system of this kind, that philosophy can so much as hearken to.

NOTHING in this world is perpetual. Every being, however seemingly firm, is in continual flux and change: The world itself gives symptoms of frailty and dissolution: How contrary to analogy, therefore, to imagine, that one single form, seemingly the frailest of any, and, from the slightest causes, subject to the greatest disorders, is immortal and indissoluble? What a daring theory is that! How lightly, not to say, how rashly entertained!

HOW to dispose of the infinite number of posthumous existences ought also to embarrass the religious theory. Every planet, in every solar system, we are at liberty to imagine peopled with intelligent, mortal beings: At least, we can fix on no other supposition. For these, then, a new universe must, every generation, be created, beyond the bounds of the present universe; or one must have been created at first so prodigiously wide as to admit of this continual influx of beings. Ought such bold suppositions to be received by any philosophy; and that merely on the pretence of a bare possibility?

WHEN it is asked, whether *Agamemnon, Thersites, Hannibal, Nero*, and every stupid clown, that ever existed in *Italy, Scythia, Bactria*, or *Guinea*, are now alive; can any man think, that a scrutiny of nature will furnish arguments strong enough to answer so strange a question in the affirmative? The want of arguments, without revelation, sufficiently establishes the negative.

Quanto facilius, says *Pliny*[3], *certiusque sibi quemque credere, ac specimen securitatis antigenitali sumere experimento*. Our insensibility, before the composition of the body, seems to natural reason a proof of a like state after its dissolution. 598

WERE our horror of annihilation an original passion, not the effect of our general love of happiness, it would rather prove the mortality of the soul. For as nature does nothing in vain, she would never give us a horror against an impossible event. She may give us a horror against an unavoidable event, provided our endeavours, as in the present case, may often remove it to some distance. Death is in the end unavoidable; yet the human species could not be preserved, had not nature inspired us with an aversion towards it.

ALL doctrines are to be suspected, which are favoured by our passions. And the hopes and fears which gave rise to this doctrine, are very obvious.

IT IS an infinite advantage in every controversy, to defend the negative. If the question be out of the common experienced course of nature, this circumstance is almost if not altogether decisive. By what arguments or analogies can we prove any state of existence, which no one ever saw, and which no wise resembles any that ever was seen? Who will repose such trust in any pretended philosophy, as to admit upon its testimony the reality of so marvellous a scene? Some new species of logic is requisite for that purpose; and some new faculties of the mind, which may enable us to comprehend that logic.

NOTHING could set in a fuller light the infinite obligations, which mankind have to divine revelation; since we find, that no other medium could ascertain this great and important truth.

[3] Lib. vii. cap. 55.

APPENDIX III

Excerpts from Parts I and II of the
Dialogues concerning Natural Religion (1779)

[*HUME'S* Dialogues *were published posthumously in 1779, having been revised shortly before his death in 1776, though most of the content—especially of the early sections—was probably completed by 1752, only four years after the publication of the first* Enquiry. *Parts I and II of the* Dialogues *contain a good deal of general material on the understanding of scepticism, with Philo, the character described by Hume as a 'careless sceptic', presenting a point of view strikingly similar to that expressed in* Enquiry *Section XII. In Part I, Philo provides important explanation of the motivation for this scepticism, which in some respects goes beyond anything in the* Enquiry. *Then Cleanthes, the 'experimental theist' and proponent of the Design Argument for God's existence, makes interesting criticisms, some of which are not clearly answered by Philo (nor indeed by Hume in other works). This raises the interesting possibility that Hume himself might have been grappling with potentially strong objections to aspects of his scepticism, notably concerning the basis of his recommendation, expressed at E 12.25, to restrict our enquiries to 'common life'. In Part II, Cleanthes presents his Design Argument, the logic of which Philo elucidates for the benefit of Demea (an orthodox believer), before delivering criticisms closely related to those in* Enquiry *Section XI.*

The text that follows is taken from the first edition of 1779, with marginal page numbers to facilitate reference to the standard edition by Norman Kemp Smith (Macmillan, 1947).]

PART I

. . .

131   . . . The vulgar, [remarked PHILO], who are unacquainted with science and profound enquiry, observing the endless disputes of the learned, have commonly a thorough contempt for Philosophy; and rivet themselves the faster, by that means, in the great points of Theology, which have been taught them. Those, who enter a little into study and enquiry, finding many appearances of evidence in doctrines the newest and most extraordinary, think nothing too difficult for human reason; and presumptuously breaking through all fences, profane the inmost sanctuaries of the temple. But . . . after we have abandoned ignorance, the surest remedy, there is still one expedient left to prevent this profane liberty. Let . . . us become

thoroughly sensible of the weakness, blindness, and narrow limits of human reason: Let us duly consider its uncertainty and endless contrarieties, even in subjects of common life and practice: Let the errors and deceits of our very senses be set before us; the insuperable difficulties, which attend first principles in all systems; the contradictions, which adhere to the very ideas of matter, cause and effect, extension, space, time, motion; and in a word, quantity of all kinds, the object of the only science, that can fairly pretend to any certainty or evidence. When these topics are displayed in their full light, as they are by some philosophers and almost all divines; who can retain such confidence in this frail faculty of reason as to pay any regard to its determinations in points so sublime, so abstruse, so remote from common life and experience? When the coherence of the parts of a stone, or even that com- 132 position of parts, which renders it extended; when these familiar objects, I say, are so inexplicable, and contain circumstances so repugnant and contradictory; with what assurance can we decide concerning the origin of worlds, or trace their history from eternity to eternity?

. . .

You propose then, PHILO, said CLEANTHES, to erect religious faith on philosophical scepticism; and you think, that if certainty or evidence be expelled from every other subject of enquiry, it will all retire to these theological doctrines, and there acquire a superior force and authority. Whether your scepticism be as absolute and sincere as you pretend, we shall learn by and by, when the company breaks up: We shall then see, whether you go out at the door or the window; and whether you really doubt, if your body has gravity, or can be injured by its fall; according to popular opinion, derived from our fallacious senses and more fallacious experience. . . .

In reality, PHILO, continued he, it seems certain, that though a man, in a flush of humour, after intense reflection on the many contradictions and imperfections of human reason, may entirely renounce all belief and opinion; it is impossible for him to persevere in this total scepticism, or make it appear in his conduct for a few hours. External objects press in upon him: Passions solicit him: His philosophical melancholy dissipates; and even the utmost violence upon his own temper will not be able, during any time, to preserve the poor appearance of scepticism. And for what reason impose on 133 himself such a violence? This is a point, in which it will be impossible for him ever to satisfy himself, consistently with his sceptical principles: So that upon the whole nothing could be more ridiculous than the principles of the ancient PYRRHONIANS; if in reality they endeavoured, as is pretended, to extend throughout, the same scepticism, which they had learned from the declamations of their schools, and which they ought to have confined to them.

In this view, there appears a great resemblance between the sects of the STOICS and PYRRHONIANS, though perpetual antagonists: and both of them seem founded on this erroneous maxim, That what a man can perform sometimes, and in some dispositions, he can perform always, and in every disposition. When the mind, by Stoical reflections, is elevated into a sublime enthusiasm of virtue, and strongly smit with any *Species* of honour or public good, the utmost bodily pain and sufferance will not prevail over such a high sense of duty; and 'tis possible, perhaps, by its means, even to smile and exult in the midst of tortures. If this sometimes may be the case in fact and reality, much more may a philosopher, in his school, or even in his closet, work himself up to such an enthusiasm, and support in imagination the acutest pain or most calamitous event, which he can possibly conceive. But how shall he support this enthusiasm itself? The bent of his mind relaxes, and cannot be recalled at pleasure: Avocations lead him astray: Misfortunes attack him unawares: And the *philosopher* sinks by degrees into the *plebian*.

I allow of your comparison between the STOICS and SCEPTICS, replied PHILO. But you may observe, at the same time, that though the mind cannot, in Stoicism, support the highest flights of philosophy, yet even when it sinks lower, it still retains somewhat of its former disposition; and the effects of the Stoic's reasoning will appear in his conduct in common life, and through the whole tenor of his actions. The ancient schools, particularly that of ZENO, produced examples of virtue and constancy, which seem astonishing to pres-

134 ent times . . . . In like manner, if a man has accustomed himself to sceptical considerations on the uncertainty and narrow limits of reason, he will not entirely forget them when he turns his reflection on other subjects; but in all his philosophical principles and reasoning, I dare not say, in his common conduct, he will be found different from those, who either never formed any opinions in the case, or have entertained sentiments more favourable to human reason.

To whatever length any one may push his speculative principles of scepticism, he must act, I own, and live, and converse like other men; and for this conduct he is not obliged to give any other reason, than the absolute necessity he lies under of so doing. If he ever carries his speculations farther than this necessity constrains him, and philosophises, either on natural or moral subjects, he is allured by a certain pleasure and satisfaction, which he finds in employing himself after that manner. He considers besides, that every one, even in common life, is constrained to have more or less of this philosophy; that from our earliest infancy we make continual advances in forming more general principles of conduct and reasoning; that the larger experience we acquire, and the stronger reason we are endued with, we always render our principles the more general and comprehensive; and that what we call *philosophy* is nothing but a more regular and methodical operation of the same kind. To philosophise on such subjects is nothing essentially different from reasoning on common life; and we may only expect greater stability, if not greater truth, from our philosophy, on account of its exacter and more scrupulous method of proceeding.

But when we look beyond human affairs and the properties of the surrounding bodies: When we carry our speculations into the two eternities, before and after the present state of things; into the creation and formation of the universe; the existence and properties of spirits; the powers and operations of one universal spirit, existing without beginning and without end; omnipotent, omniscient, immutable, infinite, and incomprehensible: We must be far removed from the smallest tendency to scepticism not to be apprehensive, that we have here got quite beyond the reach of our faculties. So long as we confine our speculations to trade, or morals, or politics, or criticism, we make appeals, every moment, to common sense and experience, which strengthen our philosophical conclusions, and remove (at least, in part) the suspicion, which we so justly entertain with regard to every reasoning, that is very subtle and refined. But in theological reasonings, we have not this advantage; while at the same time we are employed upon objects, which, we must be sensible, are too large for our grasp, and of all others, require most to be familiarised to our apprehension. We are like foreigners in a strange country, to whom every thing must seem suspicious, and who are in danger every moment of transgressing against the laws and customs of the people, with whom they live and converse. We know not how far we ought to trust our vulgar methods of reasoning in such a subject; since, even in common life and in that province, which is peculiarly appropriated to them, we cannot account for them, and are entirely guided by a kind of instinct or necessity in employing them.

All sceptics pretend, that, if reason be considered in an abstract view, it furnishes invincible arguments against itself, and that we could never retain any conviction or assurance, on any subject, were not the sceptical reasonings so refined and subtle, that they are not able to counterpoise the more solid and more natural arguments, derived from the senses and experience. But it is evident, whenever our arguments lose this advantage, and run wide of common life, that the most refined scepticism comes to be upon a footing with them, and is able to oppose and counterbalance them. The one has no more weight than the other. The mind must remain in suspense between them; and it is that very suspense or balance, which is the triumph of scepticism.

But I observe, says CLEANTHES, with regard to you, PHILO, and all speculative sceptics, that your doctrine and practice are as much at variance in the most abstruse points of theory as in the conduct of common life. Where-ever evidence discovers itself, you adhere to it, notwithstanding your pretended scepticism; and I can observe too some of your sect to be as decisive as those, who make greater professions of certainty and assurance.

In reality, would not a man be ridiculous, who pretended to reject NEWTON'S explication of the wonderful phenomenon of the rainbow, because that explication gives a minute anatomy of the rays of light; a subject, forsooth, too refined for human comprehension? And what would you say to one, who having nothing particular to object to the arguments of COPERNICUS and GALILAEO for the motion of the earth, should with-hold his assent, on that general principle, That these subjects were too magnificent and remote to be explained by the narrow and fallacious reason of mankind?

There is indeed a kind of brutish and ignorant scepticism, as you well observed, which gives the vulgar a general prejudice against what they do not easily understand, and makes them reject every principle, which requires elaborate reasoning to prove and establish it. This species of scepticism is fatal to knowledge, not to religion; since we find, that those who make greatest profession of it, give often their assent, not only to the great truths of Theism, and natural theology, but even to the most absurd tenets, which a traditional superstition has recommended to them. They firmly believe in witches; though they will not believe nor attend to the most simple proposition of EUCLID. But the refined and philosophical sceptics fall into an inconsistence of an opposite nature. They push their researches into the most abstruse corners of science; and their assent attends them in every step, proportioned to the evidence, which they meet with. They are even obliged to acknowledge, that the most abstruse and remote objects are those, which are best explained by philosophy. Light is in reality anatomized: The true system of the heavenly bodies is discovered and ascertained. But the
137 nourishment of bodies by food is still an inexplicable mystery: The cohesion of the parts of matter is still incomprehensible. These sceptics, therefore, are obliged, in every question, to consider each particular evidence apart, and proportion their assent to the precise degree of evidence, which occurs. This is their practice in all natural, mathematical, moral, and political science. And why not the same, I ask, in the theological and religious? Why must conclusions of this nature be alone rejected on the general presumption of the insufficiency of human reason, without any particular discussion of the evidence? Is not such an unequal conduct a plain proof of prejudice and passion?
. . .

In vain would the sceptic make a distinction between science and common life, or between one science and another. The arguments, employed in all, if just, are of a similar nature, and contain the same force and evidence. Or if there be any difference among them, the advantage lies entirely on
138 the side of theology and natural religion. Many principles of mechanics are founded on very abstruse reasoning; yet no man, who has any pretensions to science, even no speculative sceptic, pretends to entertain the least doubt with regard to them. The COPERNICAN system contains the most

surprising paradox, and the most contrary to our natural conceptions, to appearances, and to our very senses: yet even monks and inquisitors are now constrained to withdraw their opposition to it. And shall PHILO, a man of so liberal a genius, and extensive knowledge, entertain any general undistinguished scruples with regard to the religious hypothesis, which is founded on the simplest and most obvious arguments, and, unless it meets with artificial obstacles, has such easy access and admission into the mind of man? . . .

PART II

. . .

Not to lose any time in circumlocutions, said CLEANTHES, addressing 143 himself to DEMEA, . . . I shall briefly explain how I conceive this matter. Look round the world: contemplate the whole and every part of it: You will find it to be nothing but one great machine, subdivided into an infinite number of lesser machines, which again admit of subdivisions, to a degree beyond what human senses and faculties can trace and explain. All these various machines, and even their most minute parts, are adjusted to each other with an accuracy, which ravishes into admiration all men, who have ever contemplated them. The curious adapting of means to ends, throughout all nature, resembles exactly, though it much exceeds, the productions of human contrivance; of human design, thought, wisdom, and intelligence. Since therefore the effects resemble each other, we are led to infer, by all the rules of analogy, that the causes also resemble; and that the Author of Nature is somewhat similar to the mind of man; though possessed of much larger faculties, proportioned to the grandeur of the work, which he has executed. By this argument *a posteriori*, and by this argument alone, do we prove at once the existence of a Deity, and his similarity to human mind and intelligence.

I shall be so free, CLEANTHES, said DEMEA, as to tell you, that from the beginning I could not approve of your conclusion concerning the similarity of the Deity to men; still less can I approve of the mediums, by which you endeavour to establish it. What! No demonstration of the Being of a God! No abstract arguments! No proofs *a priori*! . . . Can we reach no farther in this subject than experience and probability? . . .

. . .

. . . what sticks most with you, I observe, [said PHILO to DEMEA] is the 145 representation which CLEANTHES has made of the argument *a posteriori* . . . Now, however much I may dissent, in other respects, from the dangerous principles of CLEANTHES, I must allow, that he has fairly represented that argument; and I shall endeavour so to state the matter to you, that you will entertain no farther scruples with regard to it.

Were a man to abstract from every thing which he knows or has seen, he would be altogether incapable, merely from his own ideas, to determine what kind of scene the universe must be, or to give the preference to one state or situation of things above another. For as nothing which he clearly conceives, could be esteemed impossible or implying a contradiction, every chimera of his fancy would be upon an equal footing; nor could he assign any just reason, why he adheres to one idea or system, and rejects the others, which are equally possible.

146   Again; after he opens his eyes, and contemplates the world, as it really is, it would be impossible for him, at first, to assign the cause of any one event; much less, of the whole of things or of the universe. He might set his Fancy a rambling; and she might bring him in an infinite variety of reports and representations. These would all be possible; but being all equally possible, he would never, of himself, give a satisfactory account for his preferring one of them to the rest. Experience alone can point out to him the true cause of any phenomenon.

Now according to this method of reasoning, DEMEA, it follows (and is, indeed, tacitly allowed by CLEANTHES himself) that order, arrangement, or the adjustment of final causes is not, of itself, any proof of design; but only so far as it has been experienced to proceed from that principle. For aught we can know *a priori*, matter may contain the source or spring of order originally, within itself, as well as mind does; and there is no more difficulty in conceiving, that the several elements, from an internal unknown cause, may fall into the most exquisite arrangement, than to conceive that their ideas, in the great, universal mind, from a like internal, unknown cause, fall into that arrangement. The equal possibility of both these suppositions is allowed. But by experience we find, (according to CLEANTHES) that there is a difference between them. Throw several pieces of steel together, without shape or form; they will never arrange themselves so as to compose a watch: Stone, and mortar, and wood, without an architect, never erect a house. But the ideas in a human mind, we see, by an unknown, inexplicable oeconomy, arrange themselves so as to form the plan of a watch or house. Experience, therefore, proves, that there is an original principle of order in mind, not in matter. From similar effects we infer similar causes. The adjustment of means to ends is alike in the universe, as in a machine of human contrivance. The causes, therefore, must be resembling.

. . .

147   But can you think, CLEANTHES, that your usual phlegm and philosophy have been preserved in so wide a step as you have taken, when you compared to the universe houses, ships, furniture, machines; and from their similarity in some circumstances inferred a similarity in their causes? Thought, design, intelligence, such as we discover in men and other animals, is no more than

one of the springs and principles of the universe, as well as heat or cold, attraction or repulsion, and a hundred others, which fall under daily observation. It is an active cause, by which some particular parts of nature, we find, produce alterations on other parts. But can a conclusion, with any propriety, be transferred from parts to the whole? Does not the great disproportion bar all comparison and inference? From observing the growth of a hair, can we learn any thing concerning the generation of a man? Would the manner of a leaf's blowing, even though perfectly known, afford us any instruction concerning the vegetation of a tree?

. . .

Admirable conclusion! Stone, wood, brick, iron, brass, have not, at this   149
time, in this minute globe of earth, an order or arrangement without human art and contrivance: therefore the universe could not originally attain its order and arrangement, without something similar to human art. But is a part of nature a rule for another part very wide of the former? Is it a rule for the whole? Is a very small part a rule for the universe? Is nature in one situation, a certain rule for nature in another situation, vastly different from the former?

. . . When two *species* of objects have always been observed to be con-joined together, I can *infer*, by custom, the existence of one, where-ever I *see* the existence of the other: and this I call an argument from experience. But how this argument can have place, where the objects, as in the present case, are single, individual, without parallel, or specific resemblance, may be difficult to explain. And will any man tell me with a serious countenance,   150
that an orderly universe must arise from some thought and art, like the human; because we have experience of it? To ascertain this reasoning, it were requisite, that we had experience of the origin of worlds; and it is not sufficient surely, that we have seen ships and cities arise from human art and contrivance.

. . . What I had to suggest, said CLEANTHES, is only that you would not abuse terms, or make use of popular expressions to subvert philosophical rea-sonings. You know, that the vulgar often distinguish reason from experience, even where the question relates only to matter of fact and existence; though it is found, where that *reason* is properly analysed, that it is nothing but a species of experience. To prove by experience the origin of the universe from mind is not more contrary to common speech than to prove the motion of the earth from the same principle. And a caviller might raise all the same objections to the COPERNICAN system, which you have urged against my reasonings. Have you other earths, might he say, which you have seen to move? Have . . . .

Yes! cried PHILO, interrupting him, we have other earths. Is not the moon another earth, which we see to turn round its centre? Is not Venus another earth, where we observe the same phenomenon? Are not the revolutions of the sun also a confirmation, from analogy, of the same theory? All the planets, are they not earths, which revolve about the sun? Are not the satellites moons, which move round Jupiter and Saturn, and along with these primary planets, round the sun? These analogies and resemblances, with others, which I have not mentioned, are the sole proofs of the COPERNICAN system: and to you it belongs to consider, whether you have any analogies of the same kind to support your theory.

In reality, CLEANTHES, continued he, the modern system of astronomy is now so much received by all enquirers, and has become so essential a part even of our earliest education, that we are not commonly very scrupulous in examining the reasons, upon which it is founded. . . . But if we peruse GALILAEO's famous Dialogues concerning the system of the world, we shall find, that that great genius, one of the sublimest that ever existed, first bent all his endeavours to prove, that there was no foundation for the distinction commonly made between elementary and celestial substances. The schools, proceeding from the illusions of sense, had carried this distinction very far; and had established the latter substances to be ingenerable, incorruptible, unalterable, impassable; and had assigned all the opposite qualities to the former. But GALILAEO, beginning with the moon, proved its similarity in every particular to the earth; its convex figure, its natural darkness when not illuminated, its density, its distinction into solid and liquid, the variations of its phases, the mutual illuminations of the earth and moon, their mutual eclipses, the inequalities of the lunar surface, &c. After many instances of this kind, with regard to all the planets, men plainly saw, that these bodies became proper objects of experience; and that the similarity of their nature enabled us to extend the same arguments and phenomena from one to the other.

In this cautious proceeding of the astronomers, you may read your own condemnation, CLEANTHES; or rather may see, that the subject in which you are engaged exceeds all human reason and enquiry. Can you pretend to show any such similarity between the fabric of a house, and the generation of a universe? Have you ever seen Nature in any such situation as resembles the first arrangement of the elements? Have worlds ever been formed under your eye? and have you had leisure to observe the whole progress of the phenomenon, from the first appearance of order to its final consummation? If you have, then cite your experience, and deliver your theory.

APPENDIX IV
Excerpts from Hume's Letters

[*THE excerpts reprinted here shed light on different aspects of the* Enquiry *and its background. Several concern the* Treatise of Human Nature, *Hume's first book which he published in 1739 (Books I and II) and 1740 (Book III), and his increasing dissatisfaction with that 'juvenile work'. As reported in 'My Own Life' (see Appendix V), this dissatisfaction led to his 'recasting' of the material to create the two* Enquiries *and the* Dissertation on the Passions, *with the first* Enquiry *inheriting what remained from Book I and the Book II sections on 'Liberty and Necessity'. Other excerpts concern the religious content of the* Enquiry, *especially the controversial Section X on miracles. Hume was of course fully aware that such sceptical arguments would provoke opposition, and it is interesting to see his changing attitude to this as reflected in these letters.*]

To Henry Home, from London, 2 December 1737

[*Hume writes this letter to his kinsman Henry Home (generally known by his later title of Lord Kames) about some deletions that he is making from his* Treatise of Human Nature *prior to publication. Hume says that he is removing parts— evidently dealing with religion—that might be offensive to Dr Joseph Butler (1692–1752), an Anglican bishop whose major philosophical work,* The Analogy of Religion, *had been published the previous year. Hume plans to give Butler a copy of the* Treatise *in the hope of a good opinion. The letter indicates that the eventual* Treatise *is, in a sense, incomplete, and that Hume's interest in his philosophy's religious implications was there from the start. The letter also demonstrates in particular that Hume had written some material on miracles over a year before the publication of the* Treatise, *which also tends to undermine the old view (expressed by Selby-Bigge in the introduction to his* Enquiry *edition) that the religious material was artificially and rather frivolously added to the* Enquiry *to spice it up, as a means of provoking public interest, rather than from any serious philosophical concern.*]

Having a frankt Letter I was resolv'd to make Use of it, & accordingly enclose some Reasonings concerning Miracles, which I once thought of publishing with the rest, but which I am afraid will give too much Offence even as the World is dispos'd at present. There is Something in the turn of Thought & a good deal in the Turn of Expression, which will not perhaps appear so proper for want of knowing the Context: But the Force of the Argument you'll be judge of as it stands. Tell me your Thoughts of it. Is not the Style too diffuse?

Tho as that was a popular Argument I have spread it out much more than the other Parts of the Work. I beg of you to show it to no Body . . . & let me know at your Leizure that you have receiv'd it, read it, & burnt it. . . .

Your Thoughts & mine agree with Respect to Dr Butler, & I wou'd be glad to be introduc'd to him. I am at present castrating my Work, that is, cutting off its noble Parts, that is, endeavouring it shall give as little Offence as possible; before which I cou'd not pretend to put it into the Drs hands. This is a Piece of Cowardice, for which I blame myself; tho I believe none of my Friends will blame me. But I was resolv'd not to be an Enthusiast, in Philosophy, while I was blaming other Enthusiasms. If ever I indulge any 'twill be when I tell that I am Dear Sir Yours.

DAVID HUME. (*NHL* 2)

To Henry Home, from Ninewells, 1 June 1739

[*Barely four months after the publication of Books I and II of the* Treatise, *and with disappointing news of sales, Hume is already expressing doubts about the wisdom of publication.*]

I am now out of Humour with myself; but doubt not in a little time to be only out of Humour with the World, like other unsuccessful Authors. After all, I am sensible of my Folly in entertaining any Discontent, much more Despair upon this Account; since I cou'd not expect any better from such abstract Reasoning, nor indeed did I promise myself much better. My Fondness for what I imagin'd new Discoveries made me overlook all common Rules of Prudence; & having enjoy'd the usual Satisfaction of Projectors, tis but just I shou'd meet with their Dissappointments. (*NHL* 5)

To Francis Hutcheson, from Ninewells, 16 March 1740

[*The following year, Hume's dissatisfaction with the* Treatise *is clear, as he longs for the opportunity to make corrections in a second edition (which in fact never occurred).*]

I wait with some Impatience for a second Edition principally on Account of Alterations I intend to make in my Performance. This is an Advantage, that we Authors possess since the Invention of Printing & renders the Nonum prematur in annum not so necessary to us as to the Antients. Without it I shoud have been guilty of a very great Temerity to publish at my Years so many Noveltys in so delicate a Part of Philosophy: And at any Rate I am afraid, that I must plead as my Excuse that very Circumstance of Youth, which may be urg'd against me. I assure you, that without running any of the heights of Scepticism, I am apt, in a cool hour, to suspect, in general, that most of my Reasonings will be more useful by furnishing Hints & exciting People's Curiosity than as containing any Principles that will augment the Stock of Knowledge that must pass to future Ages. (*HL* i. 38–9)

To James Oswald of Dunnikier, from Ninewells, 2 October 1747

[*Eight years after the publication of the* Treatise, *Hume is now relatively unconcerned about the implications of publishing an 'infidel' book, though he reveals that 'Harry' (i.e. Henry Home) has seen the manuscript of the* Philosophical Essays *(i.e. the first edition of the* Enquiry*) and disapproves. The 1748 letter to Henry Home himself makes similar points.*]

. . . I have some thoughts of . . . printing the Philosophical Essays I left in your hands. Our friend, Harry, is against this, as indiscreet. But in the first place, I think I am too deep engaged to think of a retreat. In the second place, I see not what bad consequences follow, in the present age, from the character of an infidel; especially if a man's conduct be in other respects irreproachable. What is your opinion? (*HL* i. 106)

To Henry Home, from London, 9 February 1748

I leave here two works going on, a new edition of my Essays . . .

The other work is the Philosophical Essays, which you dissuaded me from printing. I won't justify the prudence of this step, any other way than by expressing my indifference about all the consequences that may follow. . . . (*HL* i. 111)

To Gilbert Elliot of Minto, March or April 1751

[*Having published the* Philosophical Essays *(i.e. the first* Enquiry*), Hume advises a close philosophical friend that it is far superior to the* Treatise, *which he now clearly regrets publishing.*]

I believe the philosophical Essays contain every thing of Consequence relating to the Understanding, which you woud meet with in the Treatise; & I give you my Advice against reading the latter. By shortening & simplifying the Questions, I really render them much more complete. *Addo dum minuo.* The philosophical Principles are the same in both: But I was carry'd away by the Heat of Youth & Invention to publish too precipitately. So vast an Undertaking, plan'd before I was one and twenty, & compos'd before twenty five, must necessarily be very defective. I have repented my Haste a hundred, & a hundred times. (*HL* i. 158)

To John Stewart, February 1754

[*Stewart had taken Hume to be denying the Causal Maxim in* Treatise *1.3.3, and after correcting him on this point, Hume continues with some comments indicating that he no longer has any interest in a second edition of the* Treatise.]

Where a man of Sense mistakes my Meaning, I own I am angry: But it is only at myself: For having exprest my Meaning so ill as to have given Occasion to the Mistake.

That you may see I wou'd no way scruple of owning my Mistakes in Argument, I shall acknowledge (what is infinitely more material) a very great Mistake in Conduct, viz my publishing at all the Treatise of human Nature, a Book, which pretended to innovate in all the sublimest Parts of Philosophy, & which I compos'd before I was five & twenty. Above all, the positive Air, which prevails in that Book, & which may be imputed to the Ardor of Youth, so much displeases me, that I have not Patience to review it. But what Success the same Doctrines, better illustrated & exprest, may meet with, Ad huc sub judice lis est. (*HL* i. 187)

To the Abbé Le Blanc, from Edinburgh, 12 September 1754

[*Le Blanc had translated Hume's* Political Discourses, *and Hume writes to advise about the best editions of his other works, should Le Blanc also be interested in translating those. The second sentence confirms Hume's awareness that the first* Enquiry *is both 'bold' (i.e. religiously daring) and 'metaphysical'.*]

The Booksellers are reprinting in London the philosophical Essays; but the second Edition differs very little from this new one. I doubt these Essays are both too bold & too metaphysical for your Climate; tho' we have lately, in some French Writers, been entertain'd with Liberties, that are not much inferior. (*HL* i. 192)

To the Reverend Hugh Blair, probably in the autumn of 1761

[*Blair had been instrumental in sending Hume a manuscript of George Campbell's* Dissertation on Miracles, *which would be published in 1762. This letter gives Hume's comments in reply, which throw interesting light on the material of* Enquiry *Section X.*]

Sect. I. I would desire the author to consider, whether the medium by which we reason concerning human testimony be different from that which leads us to draw any inferences concerning other human actions; that is, our knowledge of human nature from experience? Or why is it different? I suppose we conclude an honest man will not lie to us, in the same manner as we conclude that he will not cheat us. As to the youthful propensity to believe, which is corrected by experience; it seems obvious, that children adopt blindfold all the opinions, principles, sentiments, and passions, of their elders, as well as credit their testimony; nor is this more strange, than that a hammer should make an impression on clay.

Sect. II. No man can have any other experience but his own. The experience of others becomes his only by the credit which he gives to their testimony; which proceeds from his own experience of human nature.

Sect. III. There is no contradiction in saying, that all the testimony which ever was really given for any miracle, or ever will be given, is a subject of derision; and yet forming a fiction or supposition of a testimony for a particular miracle, which might not only merit attention, but amount to a full proof of it. For instance, the absence of the sun during 48 hours; but reasonable men would only conclude from this fact, that the machine of the globe was disordered during the time.

Page 28. I find no difficulty to explain my meaning, and yet shall not probably do it in any future edition. The proof against a miracle, as it is founded on invariable experience, is of that *species* or *kind* of proof, which is full and certain when taken alone, because it implies no doubt, as is the case with all probabilities; but there are degrees of this species, and when a weaker proof is opposed to a stronger, it is overcome.

Page 29. There is very little more delicacy in telling a man he speaks nonsense by implication, than in saying so directly.

Sect. IV. Does a man of sense run after every silly tale of witches or hobgoblins or fairies, and canvass particularly the evidence? I never knew any one, that examined and deliberated about nonsense who did not believe it before the end of his inquiries.

Sect. V. I wonder the author does not perceive the reason why Mr John Knox and Mr Alexander Henderson did not work as many miracles as their brethren in other churches. Miracle-working was a Popish trick, and discarded with the other parts of that religion. Men must have new and opposite ways of establishing new and opposite follies. The same reason extends to Mahomet. The Greek priests, who were in the neighbourhood of Arabia, and many of them in it, were as great miracle-workers as the Romish; and Mahomet would have been laughed at for so stale and simple a device. To cast out devils, and cure the blind, where every one almost can do as much, is not the way to get any extraordinary ascendant over men. I never read of a miracle in my life, that was not meant to establish some new point of religion. There are no miracles wrought in Spain to prove the Gospel, but St Francis Xavier wrought a thousand well attested ones for that purpose in the Indies. The miracles in Spain, which are also fully and completely attested, are wrought to prove the efficacy of a particular crucifix or relict, which is always a new point, or, at least, not universally received.

Sect. VI. If a miracle proves a doctrine to be revealed from God, and consequently true, a miracle can never be wrought for a contrary doctrine. The facts are therefore as incompatible as the doctrines.

I could wish your friend had not denominated me an infidel writer, on account of ten or twelve pages which seem to him to have that tendency: while I have wrote so many volumes on history, literature, politics, trade, morals, which, in that particular at least, are entirely inoffensive. Is a man to be called a drunkard, because he has been seen fuddled once in his lifetime?

Having said so much to your friend, who is certainly a very ingenious man, tho a little too zealous for a philosopher; permit me also the freedom of saying a word to yourself. Whenever I have had the pleasure to be in your company, if the discourse turned upon any common subject of literature or reasoning, I always parted from you both entertained and instructed. But when the conversation was diverted by you from this channel towards the subject of your profession; tho I doubt not but your intentions were very friendly towards me, I own I never received the same satisfaction: I was apt to be tired, and you to be angry. I would therefore wish for the future, wherever my good fortune throws me in your way, that these topics should be forborne between us. I have, long since, done with all inquiries on such subjects, and am become incapable of instruction; tho I own no one is more capable of conveying it than yourself.

After having given you the liberty of communicating to your friend what part of this letter you think proper,

I remain, Sir,

Your most obedient humble servant,

DAVID HUME. (*HL* i. 349–51)

To the Reverend George Campbell, 7 June 1762

[*Evidently Hume's comments on Campbell's manuscript had some effect, particularly on the style of the published* Dissertation. *In this letter directly to the author, Hume expresses his appreciation, but also his general reluctance to enter into controversies with philosophical opponents (which, regrettably for his commentators, he retained throughout his life). He also makes interesting comments about the genesis of his famous argument against miracles.*]

Dear Sir,

It has so seldom happened that controversies in philosophy, much more in theology, have been carried on without producing a personal quarrel between the parties, that I must regard my present situation as somewhat extraordinary, who have reason to give you thanks for the civil and obliging manner in which you have conducted the dispute against me, on so interesting a subject as that of miracles. Any little symptoms of vehemence, of which I formerly used the freedom to complain, when you favoured me with a sight of the manuscript, are either removed or explained away, or atoned for by civilities, which are far beyond what I have any title to pretend to. It will be natural for you to imagine, that I will fall upon some shift to evade the force of your arguments, and to retain my former opinion in the point controverted between us; but it is impossible for me not to see the ingenuity of your performance, and the great learning which you have displayed against me.

I consider myself as very much honoured in being thought worthy of an answer by a person of so much merit; and as I find that the public does you justice with regard to the ingenuity and good composition of your piece, I hope you will have no reason to repent engaging with an antagonist, whom, perhaps in strictness, you might have ventured to neglect. I own to you, that I never felt so violent an inclination to defend myself as at present, when I am thus fairly challenged by you, and I think I could find something specious at least to urge in my defence; but as I had fixed a resolution, in the beginning of my life, always to leave the public to judge between my adversaries and me, without making any reply. I must adhere inviolably to this resolution, otherways my silence on any future occasion would be construed an inability to answer, and would be matter of triumph against me.

It may perhaps amuse you to learn the first hint, which suggested to me that argument which you have so strenuously attacked. I was walking in the cloisters of the Jesuits' College of La Flèche, a town in which I passed two years of my youth, and engaged in a conversation with a Jesuit of some parts and learning, who was relating to me, and urging some nonsensical miracle performed in their convent, when I was tempted to dispute against him; and as my head was full of the topics of my Treatise of Human Nature, which I was at that time composing, this argument immediately occurred to me, and I thought it very much gravelled my companion; but at last he observed to me, that it was impossible for that argument to have any solidity, because it operated equally against the Gospel as the Catholic miracles;—which observation I thought proper to admit as a sufficient answer. I believe you will allow, that the freedom at least of this reasoning makes it somewhat extraordinary to have been the produce of a convent of Jesuits, tho perhaps you may think the sophistry of it savours plainly of the place of its birth. (*HL* i. 360–1)

To William Strahan, from Edinburgh, 26 October 1775

[*Here Hume asks his printer to prefix his famous 'Advertisement', publicly renouncing the* Treatise, *to future editions of the volume containing the* Enquiry. *He also makes clear that he is still at work on corrections to what would become the 1777 edition. See the Note on the Text, pp. lix–lx, for quotations from two letters in which he later expresses great satisfaction with how that edition is turning out.*]

But we must not part, without my also saying something as an Author. I have not yet thrown up so much all Memory of that Character. There is a short Advertisement, which I wish I had prefix'd to the second Volume of the Essays and Treatises in the last Edition. I send you a Copy of it. Please to enquire at the Warehouse, if any considerable Number of that Edition remain on hands; and if there do, I beg the favour of you, that you woud throw off an equal Number of this Advertisement, and give out no more Copies without prefixing it to the second volume. It is a compleat Answer to Dr Reid and to that bigotted silly Fellow, Beattie.

I believe that I have formerly mention'd to you, that no new Editions shoud be made of any of my Writings, without mentioning it to me; I shall still have some Corrections to make. . . . (*HL* ii. 301).

APPENDIX V

'My Own Life'

[*WRITTEN in the year of his death, when Hume was aware of the seriousness of his terminal illness, this was sent to his printer William Strahan for inclusion in the forthcoming final edition of Hume's works, but in the event was published separately in 1777. This text is taken from that original publication, with a few small corrections made by comparison against Hume's handwritten manuscript in the National Library of Scotland.*]

THE LIFE OF DAVID HUME, ESQ. WRITTEN BY HIMSELF

MR. HUME, a few months before his death, wrote the following short account of his own Life; and, in a codicil to his will, desired that it might be prefixed to the next edition of his Works. That edition cannot be published for a considerable time. The Editor, in the mean while, in order to serve the purchasers of the former editions; and, at the same time, to gratify the impatience of the public curiosity; has thought proper to publish it separately, without altering even the title or superscription, which was written in Mr. Hume's own hand on the cover of the manuscript.

MY OWN LIFE

[1] IT is difficult for a man to speak long of himself without vanity; therefore, I shall be short. It may be thought an instance of vanity that I pretend at all to write my life; but this Narrative shall contain little more than the History of my Writings; as, indeed, almost all my life has been spent in literary pursuits and occupations. The first success of most of my writings was not such as to be an object of vanity.

[2] I was born the 26th of April 1711, old style, at Edinburgh. I was of a good family, both by father and mother: my father's family is a branch of the Earl of Home's, or Hume's; and my ancestors had been proprietors of the estate, which my brother possesses, for several generations. My mother was daughter of Sir David Falconer, President of the College of Justice: the title of Lord Halkerton came by succession to her brother.

[3] My family, however, was not rich, and being myself a younger brother, my patrimony, according to the mode of my country, was of course very slender. My father, who passed for a man of parts, died when I was an infant, leaving me, with an elder brother and a sister, under the care of our mother, a woman of singular merit, who, though young and handsome,

devoted herself entirely to the rearing and educating of her children. I passed through the ordinary course of education with success, and was seized very early with a passion for literature, which has been the ruling passion of my life, and the great source of my enjoyments. My studious disposition, my sobriety, and my industry, gave my family a notion that the law was a proper profession for me; but I found an unsurmountable aversion to every thing but the pursuits of philosophy and general learning; and while they fancied I was poring upon Voet and Vinnius, Cicero and Virgil were the authors which I was secretly devouring.

[4] My very slender fortune, however, being unsuitable to this plan of life, and my health being a little broken by my ardent application, I was tempted, or rather forced, to make a very feeble trial for entering into a more active scene of life. In 1734, I went to Bristol, with some recommendations to eminent merchants, but in a few months found that scene totally unsuitable to me. I went over to France, with a view of prosecuting my studies in a country retreat; and I there laid that plan of life, which I have steadily and successfully pursued. I resolved to make a very rigid frugality supply my deficiency of fortune, to maintain unimpaired my independency, and to regard every object as contemptible, except the improvement of my talents in literature.

[5] During my retreat in France, first at Reims, but chiefly at La Fleche, in Anjou, I composed my *Treatise of Human Nature*. After passing three years very agreeably in that country, I came over to London in 1737. In the end of 1738, I published my Treatise, and immediately went down to my mother and my brother, who lived at his country-house, and was employing himself very judiciously and successfully in the improvement of his fortune.

[6] Never literary attempt was more unfortunate than my Treatise of Human Nature. It fell *dead-born from the press*, without reaching such distinction, as even to excite a murmur among the zealots. But being naturally of a cheerful and sanguine temper, I very soon recovered the blow, and prosecuted with great ardour my studies in the country. In 1742, I printed at Edinburgh the first part of my Essays: the work was favourably received, and soon made me entirely forget my former disappointment. I continued with my mother and brother in the country, and in that time recovered the knowledge of the Greek language, which I had too much neglected in my early youth.

[7] In 1745, I received a letter from the Marquis of Annandale, inviting me to come and live with him in England; I found also, that the friends and family of that young nobleman were desirous of putting him under my care and direction, for the state of his mind and health required it. I lived with him a twelvemonth. My appointments during that time made a considerable

accession to my small fortune. I then received an invitation from General St. Clair to attend him as a secretary to his expedition, which was at first meant against Canada, but ended in an incursion on the coast of France. Next year, to wit, 1747, I received an invitation from the General to attend him in the same station in his military embassy to the courts of Vienna and Turin. I there wore the uniform of an officer, and was introduced at these courts as aid-de-camp to the general, along with Sir Harry Erskine and Captain Grant, now General Grant. These two years were almost the only interruptions which my studies have received during the course of my life: I passed them agreeably, and in good company; and my appointments, with my frugality, had made me reach a fortune, which I called independent, though most of my friends were inclined to smile when I said so; in short, I was now master of near a thousand pounds.

[8] I had always entertained a notion, that my want of success in publishing the Treatise of Human Nature, had proceeded more from the manner than the matter, and that I had been guilty of a very usual indiscretion, in going to the press too early. I, therefore, cast the first part of that work anew in the Enquiry concerning Human Understanding, which was published while I was at Turin. But this piece was at first but little more successful than the Treatise of Human Nature. On my return from Italy, I had the mortification to find all England in a ferment, on account of Dr. Middleton's Free Enquiry, while my performance was entirely overlooked and neglected. A new edition, which had been published at London of my Essays, moral and political, met not with a much better reception.

[9] Such is the force of natural temper, that these disappointments made little or no impression on me. I went down in 1749, and lived two years with my brother at his country-house, for my mother was now dead. I there composed the second part of my Essays, which I called Political Discourses, and also my Enquiry concerning the Principles of Morals, which is another part of my Treatise that I cast anew. Meanwhile, my bookseller, A. Millar, informed me, that my former publications (all but the unfortunate Treatise) were beginning to be the subject of conversation; that the sale of them was gradually increasing, and that new editions were demanded. Answers by Reverends, and Right Reverends, came out two or three in a year; and I found, by Dr. Warburton's railing, that the books were beginning to be esteemed in good company. However, I had fixed a resolution, which I inflexibly maintained, never to reply to any body; and not being very irascible in my temper, I have easily kept myself clear of all literary squabbles. These symptoms of a rising reputation gave me encouragement, as I was ever more disposed to see the favourable than unfavourable side of things; a turn of mind which it is more happy to possess, than to be born to an estate of ten thousand a year.

[10] In 1751, I removed from the country to the town, the true scene for a man of letters. In 1752, were published at Edinburgh, where I then lived, my Political Discourses, the only work of mine that was successful on the first publication. It was well received abroad and at home. In the same year was published at London, my Enquiry concerning the Principles of Morals; which, in my own opinion (who ought not to judge on that subject), is of all my writings, historical, philosophical, or literary, incomparably the best. It came unnoticed and unobserved into the world.

[11] In 1752, the Faculty of Advocates chose me their Librarian, an office from which I received little or no emolument, but which gave me the command of a large library. I then formed the plan of writing the History of England; but being frightened with the notion of continuing a narrative through a period of 1700 years, I commenced with the accession of the House of Stuart, an epoch when, I thought, the misrepresentations of faction began chiefly to take place. I was, I own, sanguine in my expectations of the success of this work. I thought that I was the only historian, that had at once neglected present power, interest, and authority, and the cry of popular prejudices; and as the subject was suited to every capacity, I expected proportional applause. But miserable was my disappointment: I was assailed by one cry of reproach, disapprobation, and even detestation; English, Scotch, and Irish, Whig and Tory, churchman and sectary, freethinker and religionist, patriot and courtier, united in this rage against the man, who had presumed to shed a generous tear for the fate of Charles I. and the Earl of Strafford; and after the first ebullitions of this fury were over, what was still more mortifying, the book seemed to sink into oblivion. Mr. Millar told me, that in a twelve-month he sold only forty-five copies of it. I scarcely, indeed, heard of one man in the three kingdoms, considerable for rank or letters, that could endure the book. I must only except the primate of England, Dr. Herring, and the primate of Ireland, Dr. Stone, which seem two odd exceptions. These dignified prelates separately sent me messages not to be discouraged.

[12] I was, however, I confess, discouraged; and had not the war been at that time breaking out between France and England, I had certainly retired to some provincial town of the former kingdom, have changed my name, and never more have returned to my native country. But as this scheme was not now practicable, and the subsequent volume was considerably advanced, I resolved to pick up courage and to persevere.

[13] In this interval, I published at London my Natural History of Religion, along with some other small pieces: its public entry was rather obscure, except only that Dr. Hurd wrote a pamphlet against it, with all the illiberal petulance, arrogance, and scurrility, which distinguish the Warburtonian school. This pamphlet gave me some consolation for the otherwise indifferent reception of my performance.

[14] In 1756, two years after the fall of the first volume, was published the second volume of my History, containing the period from the death of Charles I. till the Revolution. This performance happened to give less displeasure to the Whigs, and was better received. It not only rose itself, but helped to buoy up its unfortunate brother.

[15] But though I had been taught by experience, that the Whig party were in possession of bestowing all places, both in the state and in literature, I was so little inclined to yield to their senseless clamour, that in above a hundred alterations, which farther study, reading, or reflection engaged me to make in the reigns of the two first Stuarts, I have made all of them invariably to the Tory side. It is ridiculous to consider the English constitution before that period as a regular plan of liberty.

[16] In 1759, I published my History of the House of Tudor. The clamour against this performance was almost equal to that against the History of the two first Stuarts. The reign of Elizabeth was particularly obnoxious. But I was now callous against the impressions of public folly, and continued very peaceably and contentedly in my retreat at Edinburgh, to finish, in two volumes, the more early part of the English History, which I gave to the public in 1761, with tolerable, and but tolerable success.

[17] But, notwithstanding this variety of winds and seasons, to which my writings had been exposed, they had still been making such advances, that the copy-money given me by the booksellers, much exceeded any thing formerly known in England; I was become not only independent, but opulent. I retired to my native country of Scotland, determined never more to set my foot out of it; and retaining the satisfaction of never having preferred a request to one great man, or even making advances of friendship to any of them. As I was now turned of fifty, I thought of passing all the rest of my life in this philosophical manner, when I received, in 1763, an invitation from the Earl of Hertford, with whom I was not in the least acquainted, to attend him on his embassy to Paris, with a near prospect of being appointed secretary to the embassy; and, in the meanwhile, of performing the functions of that office. This offer, however inviting, I at first declined, both because I was reluctant to begin connexions with the great, and because I was afraid that the civilities and gay company of Paris, would prove disagreeable to a person of my age and humour: but on his lordship's repeating the invitation, I accepted of it. I have every reason, both of pleasure and interest, to think myself happy in my connexions with that nobleman, as well as afterwards with his brother, General Conway.

[18] Those who have not seen the strange effects of modes, will never imagine the reception I met with at Paris, from men and women of all ranks and stations. The more I recoiled from their excessive civilities, the more I was loaded with them. There is, however, a real satisfaction in living at Paris,

from the great number of sensible, knowing, and polite company with which that city abounds above all places in the universe. I thought once of settling there for life.

[19] I was appointed secretary to the embassy; and, in summer 1765, Lord Hertford left me, being appointed Lord Lieutenant of Ireland. I was *chargé d'affaires* till the arrival of the Duke of Richmond, towards the end of the year. In the beginning of 1766, I left Paris, and next summer went to Edinburgh, with the same view as formerly, of burying myself in a philosophical retreat. I returned to that place, not richer, but with much more money, and a much larger income, by means of Lord Hertford's friendship, than I left it; and I was desirous of trying what superfluity could produce, as I had formerly made an experiment of a competency. But, in 1767, I received from Mr. Conway an invitation to be Under-secretary; and this invitation, both the character of the person, and my connexions with Lord Hertford, prevented me from declining. I returned to Edinburgh in 1769, very opulent (for I possessed a revenue of 1000 pounds a year), healthy, and though somewhat stricken in years, with the prospect of enjoying long my ease, and of seeing the increase of my reputation.

[20] In spring 1775, I was struck with a disorder in my bowels, which at first gave me no alarm, but has since, as I apprehend it, become mortal and incurable. I now reckon upon a speedy dissolution. I have suffered very little pain from my disorder; and what is more strange, have, notwithstanding the great decline of my person, never suffered a moment's abatement of my spirits; insomuch, that were I to name the period of my life, which I should most choose to pass over again, I might be tempted to point to this later period. I possess the same ardour as ever in study, and the same gaiety in company. I consider, besides, that a man of sixty-five, by dying, cuts off only a few years of infirmities; and though I see many symptoms of my literary reputation's breaking out at last with additional lustre, I knew that I could have but few years to enjoy it. It is difficult to be more detached from life than I am at present.

[21] To conclude historically with my own character. I am, or rather was (for that is the style I must now use in speaking of myself, which emboldens me the more to speak my sentiments); I was, I say, a man of mild dispositions, of command of temper, of an open, social, and cheerful humour, capable of attachment, but little susceptible of enmity, and of great moderation in all my passions. Even my love of literary fame, my ruling passion, never soured my humour, notwithstanding my frequent disappointments. My company was not unacceptable to the young and careless, as well as to the studious and literary; and as I took a particular pleasure in the company of modest women, I had no reason to be displeased with the reception I met with from them. In a word, though most men any wise eminent, have found reason to complain

of calumny, I never was touched, or even attacked by her baleful tooth: and though I wantonly exposed myself to the rage of both civil and religious factions, they seemed to be disarmed in my behalf of their wonted fury. My friends never had occasion to vindicate any one circumstance of my character and conduct: not but that the zealots, we may well suppose, would have been glad to invent and propagate any story to my disadvantage, but they could never find any which they thought would wear the face of probability. I cannot say there is no vanity in making this funeral oration of myself, but I hope it is not a misplaced one; and this is a matter of fact which is easily cleared and ascertained.

April 18, 1776.

TEXTUAL VARIANTS

SECTION I

[Section I, paragraph 14 originally ended with this note, which appeared only in the 1748 and 1750 editions. Hume's footnotes are indicated with numbers rather than the original symbols.]

That Faculty, by which we discern Truth and Falshood, and that by which we perceive Vice and Virtue had long been confounded with each other, and all Morality was suppos'd to be built on eternal and immutable Relations, which to every intelligent Mind were equally invariable as any Proposition concerning Quantity or Number. But a[1] late Philosopher has taught us, by the most convincing Arguments, that Morality is nothing in the abstract Nature of Things, but is entirely relative to the Sentiment or mental Taste of each particular Being; in the same Manner as the Distinctions of sweet and bitter, hot and cold, arise from the particular Feeling of each Sense or Organ. Moral Perceptions therefore, ought not to be clas'd with the Operations of the Understanding, but with the Tastes or Sentiments.

It had been usual with Philosophers to divide all the Passions of the Mind into two Classes, the selfish and benevolent, which were suppos'd to stand in constant Opposition and Contrariety; nor was it thought that the latter could ever attain their proper Object but at the Expense of the former. Among the selfish Passions were rank'd Avarice, Ambition, Revenge: Among the benevolent, natural Affection, Friendship, Public spirit. Philosophers may now[2] perceive the Impropriety of this Division. It has been prov'd, beyond all Controversy, that even the Passions, commonly esteem'd selfish, carry the Mind beyond Self, directly to the Object; that tho' the Satisfaction of these Passions gives us Enjoyment, yet the Prospect of this Enjoyment is not the Cause of the Passion, but on the contrary the Passion is antecedent to the Enjoyment, and without the former, the latter could never possibly exist; that the Case is precisely the same with the Passions, denominated benevolent, and consequently that a Man is no more interested when he seeks his own Glory than when the Happiness of his Friend is the Object of his Wishes; nor is he any more disinterested when he sacrifices his Ease and Quiet to public Good than when he labours for the Gratification of Avarice and Ambition. Here therefore is a considerable

---

[1] Mr. *Hutcheson.**
[2] See *Butler's* Sermons.**

Adjustment in the Boundaries of the Passions, which had been confounded by the Negligence or Inaccuracy of former Philosophers. These
two Instances may suffice to show us the Nature and Importance of this
Species of Philosophy.

SECTION III

*[Section III originally continued significantly beyond its current ending, starting
with an added final sentence in paragraph 3. The additional material varied
between the editions from 1748 to 1772, but was deleted in the final 1777 edition.
The text below is taken from the 1772 edition, except that Hume's footnote referring to Aristotle is here given in translation only, and with a modern reference.]*

[. . . is compleat and entire.] Instead of entering into a detail of this kind,
which would lead into many useless subtilties, we shall consider some of
the effects of this connexion upon the passions and imagination; where we
may open a field of speculation more entertaining, and perhaps more
instructive, than the other.

[4] As a man is a reasonable being, and is continually in pursuit of happiness, which he hopes to attain by the gratification of some passion or
affection, he seldom acts or speaks or thinks without a purpose and intention.
He has still some object in view; and however improper the means may
sometimes be, which he chuses for the attainment of his end, he never
loses view of an end; nor will he so much as throw away his thoughts or
reflections, where he hopes not to reap some satisfaction from them.

[5] In all compositions of genius, therefore, it is requisite, that the
writer have some plan or object; and though he may be hurried from this
plan by the vehemence of thought, as in an ode, or drop it carelessly, as in
an epistle or essay, there must appear some aim or intention, in his first
setting out, if not in the composition of the whole work. A production
without a design would resemble more the ravings of a madman, than the
sober efforts of genius and learning.

[6] As this rule admits of no exception, it follows, that, in narrative
compositions, the events or actions, which the writer relates, must be
connected together, by some bond or tye: They must be related to each
other in the imagination, and form a kind of *Unity*, which may bring them
under one plan or view, and which may be the object or end of the writer
in his first undertaking.

[7] This connecting principle among the several events, which form the
subject of a poem or history, may be very different, according to the
different designs of the poet or historian. Ovid* has formed his plan upon
the connecting principle of resemblance. Every fabulous transformation,

produced by the miraculous power of the gods, falls within the compass of
his work. There needs but this one circumstance in any event to bring it
under his original plan or intention.

[8] An annalist or historian, who should undertake to write the history
of EUROPE during any century, would be influenced by the connexion of
contiguity in time and place. All events, which happen in that portion of
space and period of time, are comprehended in his design, though in other
respects different and unconnected. They have still a species of unity,
amidst all their diversity.

[9] But the most usual species of connexion among the different events,
which enter into any narrative composition, is that of cause and effect;
while the historian traces the series of actions according to their natural
order, remounts to their secret springs and principles, and delineates their
most remote consequences. He chuses for his subject a certain portion of
that great chain of events, which compose the history of mankind: Each
link in this chain he endeavours to touch in his narration: Sometimes
unavoidable ignorance renders all his attempts fruitless: Sometimes, he
supplies by conjecture, what is wanting in knowledge: And always, he is
sensible, that the more unbroken the chain is, which he presents to his
reader, the more perfect is his production. He sees, that the knowledge of
causes is not only the most satisfactory; this relation or connexion being
the strongest of all others; but also the most instructive; since it is by this
knowledge alone, we are enabled to controul events, and govern futurity.

[10] Here therefore we may attain some notion of that *Unity* of *Action*,
about which all critics, after ARISTOTLE,* have talked so much: Perhaps,
to little purpose, while they directed not their taste or sentiment by the
accuracy of philosophy. It appears, that, in all productions, as well as in the
epic and tragic, there is a certain unity required, and that, on no occasion,
can our thoughts be allowed to run at adventures, if we would produce a
work, which will give any lasting entertainment to mankind. It appears
also, that even a biographer, who should write the life of ACHILLES,*
would connect the events, by shewing their mutual dependence and relation, as much as a poet, who should make the anger of that hero, the subject
of his narration[5]. Not only in any limited portion of life, a man's actions
have a dependence on each other, but also during the whole period of his
duration, from the cradle to the grave; nor is it possible to strike off one
link, however minute, in this regular chain, without affecting the whole

---

[5] Contrary to ARISTOTLE, 'A plot is not unitary, as some suppose, in virtue of being
about one individual. For many, indeed countless, things happen to the individual from
which there is no single outcome. Likewise, many are the actions of an individual, out of
which no unitary action ensues.' *Poetics* 1451^a 15–19.

series of events, which follow. The unity of action, therefore, which is to
be found in biography or history, differs from that of epic poetry, not in
kind, but in degree. In epic poetry, the connexion among the events is
more close and sensible: The narration is not carried on through such a
length of time: And the actors hasten to some remarkable period, which
satisfies the curiosity of the reader. This conduct of the epic poet depends
on that particular situation of the *Imagination* and of the *Passions*, which is
supposed in that production. The imagination, both of writer and reader, is
more enlivened, and the passions more enflamed than in history, biography,
or any species of narration, which confine themselves to strict truth and
reality. Let us consider the effect of these two circumstances, an enlivened
imagination and enflamed passion; circumstances, which belong to poetry,
especially the epic kind, above any other species of composition: And let us
examine the reason, why they require a stricter and closer unity in the fable.

[11] First. All poetry, being a species of painting, brings us nearer to
the objects than any other species of narration, throws a stronger light
upon them, and delineates more distinctly those minute circumstances,
which, though to the historian they seem superfluous, serve mightily to
enliven the imagery, and gratify the fancy. If it be not necessary, as in the
Iliad,* to inform us each time the hero buckles his shoes, and ties his
garters, it will be requisite, perhaps, to enter into a greater detail than in
the HENRIADE;* where the events are run over with such rapidity, that we
scarcely have leisure to become acquainted with the scene or action. Were
a poet, therefore, to comprehend in his subject, any great compass of time
or series of events, and trace up the death of HECTOR* to its remote
causes, in the rape of HELEN, or the judgment of PARIS,* he must draw
out his poem to an immeasurable length, in order to fill this large canvas
with just painting and imagery. The reader's imagination, enflamed with
such a series of poetical descriptions, and his passions, agitated by a continual sympathy* with the actors, must flag long before the period of the
narration, and must sink into lassitude and disgust, from the repeated
violence of the same movements.

[12] Secondly. That an epic poet must not trace the causes to any great
distance, will farther appear, if we consider another reason, which is drawn
from a property of the passions still more remarkable and singular. It is
evident, that, in a just composition, all the affections, excited by the different
events, described and represented, add mutual force to each other; and that,
while the heroes are all engaged in one common scene, and each action
is strongly connected with the whole, the concern is continually awake,
and the passions make an easy transition from one object to another. The
strong connexion of the events, as it facilitates the passage of the thought
or imagination from one to another, facilitates also the transfusion of the

passions, and preserves the affections still in the same channel and direction. Our sympathy and concern for EVE, prepares the way for a like sympathy with ADAM:* The affection is preserved almost entire in the
transition; and the mind seizes immediately the new object as strongly
related to that which formerly engaged its attention. But were the poet to
make a total digression from his subject, and introduce a new actor, nowise
connected with the personages, the imagination, feeling a breach in the
transition, would enter coldly into the new scene; would kindle by slow
degrees; and in returning to the main subject of the poem, would pass, as
it were, upon foreign ground, and have its concern to excite anew, in order
to take part with the principal actors. The same inconvenience follows in
a less degree; where the poet traces his events to too great a distance, and
binds together actions, which, though not entirely disjoined, have not so
strong a connexion as is requisite to forward the transition of the passions.
Hence arises the artifice of the oblique narration, employed in the *Odyssey*
and *Aeneid*;* where the hero is introduced, at first, near the period of his
designs, and afterwards shows us, as it were in perspective, the more
distant events and causes. By this means, the reader's curiosity is immediately
excited: The events follow with rapidity, and in a very close connexion: And
the concern is preserved alive, and, by means of the near relation of the
objects, continually increases, from the beginning to the end of the narration.

[13] The same rule takes place in dramatic poetry; nor is it ever permit-
ted, in a regular composition, to introduce an actor, who has no connexion,
or but a small one, with the principal personages of the fable. The spectator's
concern must not be diverted by any scenes disjoined and separated from
the rest. This breaks the course of the passions, and prevents that communication of the several emotions, by which one scene adds force to another,
and transfuses the pity and terror, which it excites, upon each succeeding
scene, till the whole produces that rapidity of movement, which is peculiar
to the theatre. How must it extinguish this warmth of affection, to be
entertained, on a sudden, with a new action and new personages, no wise
related to the former; to find so sensible a breach or vacuity in the course
of the passions, by means of this breach in the connexion of ideas; and
instead of carrying the sympathy of one scene into the following, to be
obliged, every moment, to excite a new concern, and take part in a new
scene of action?

[14] To return to the comparison of history and epic poetry, we may
conclude, from the foregoing reasonings, that, as a certain unity is requisite
in all productions, it cannot be wanting in history more than in any other;
that, in history, the connexion among the several events, which unites them
into one body, is the relation of cause and effect, the same which takes
place in epic poetry; and that, in the latter composition, this connexion is

only required to be closer and more sensible, on account of the lively imagination and strong passions, which must be touched by the poet in his narration. The PELOPONNESIAN war is a proper subject for history, the siege of ATHENS for an epic poem, and the death of ALCIBIADES* for a tragedy.

[15] As the difference, therefore, between history and epic poetry consists only in the degrees of connexion, which bind together those several events, of which their subject is composed, it will be difficult, if not impossible, by words, to determine exactly the bounds, which separate them from each other. That is a matter of taste more than of reasoning; and perhaps, this unity may often be discovered in a subject, where, at first view, and from an abstract consideration, we should least expect to find it.

[16] It is evident, that HOMER, in the course of his narration, exceeds the first proposition of his subject; and that the anger of ACHILLES, which caused the death of HECTOR, is not the same with that which produced so many ills to the GREEKS. But the strong connexion between these two movements, the quick transition from one to another, the contrast[6] between the effects of concord and discord among the princes, and the natural curiosity which we have to see ACHILLES in action, after so long a repose; all these causes carry on the reader, and produce a sufficient unity in the subject.

[17] It may be objected to MILTON,* that he has traced up his causes to too great a distance, and that the rebellion of the angels produces the fall of man by a train of events, which is both very long and very casual. Not to mention, that the creation of the world, which he has related at length, is no more the cause of that catastrophe, than of the battle of PHARSALIA, or any other event, that has ever happened. But if we consider, on the other hand, that all these events, the rebellion of the angels, the creation of the world, and the fall of man, *resemble* each other, in being miraculous and out of the common course of nature; that they are supposed to be *contiguous* in time; and that being detached from all other events, and being the only original facts, which revelation discovers, they strike the eye at once, and naturally recall each other to the thought or imagination: If we consider all these circumstances, I say, we shall find, that these parts of the action have a sufficient unity to make them be comprehended in one fable or narration. To which we may add, that the rebellion of the angels and the fall of man have a peculiar resemblance, as being counterparts to each other, and presenting to the reader the same moral, of obedience to our Creator.

---

[6] Contrast or contrariety is a connexion among ideas, which may, perhaps, be considered as a mixture of causation and resemblance. Where two objects are contrary, the one destroys the other, i.e. is the cause of its annihilation, and the idea of the annihilation of an object implies the idea of its former existence. [This note was reworded in the 1777 edition, and moved to the third paragraph of the section.]

[18] These loose hints I have thrown together, in order to excite the curiosity of philosophers, and beget a suspicion at least, if not a full persuasion, that this subject is very copious, and that many operations of the human mind depend on the connexion or association of ideas, which is here explained. Particularly, the sympathy between the passions and imagination will, perhaps, appear remarkable; while we observe that the affections, excited by one object, pass easily to another object connected with it; but transfuse themselves with difficulty, or not at all, along different objects, which have no manner of connexion together. By introducing, into any composition, personages and actions, foreign to each other, an injudicious author loses that communication of emotions, by which alone he can interest the heart, and raise the passions to their proper height and period. The full explication of this principle and all its consequences would lead us into reasonings too profound and too copious for this enquiry. It is sufficient, at present, to have established this conclusion, that the three connecting principles of all ideas are the relations of *Resemblance*, *Contiguity*, and *Causation*.

EXPLANATORY NOTES

ADVERTISEMENT

ADVERTISEMENT: an announcement or notice. Hume sent this text to his printer William Strahan with a letter dated 26 October 1775 (see Appendix IV, p. 168) which indicates that the two writers he had mainly in mind were Thomas Reid and James Beattie: see under 'Scottish Common-Sense Philosophers' in the Glossarial Index of Major Philosophers and Philosophical Movements.

never acknowledged: Hume talks of the *Treatise* as 'never acknowledged' because he published it anonymously.

the following Pieces: the 'Advertisement', though now standardly attached to the *Enquiry concerning Human Understanding*, was originally intended for the second volume of Hume's *Essays and Treatises on Several Subjects* (1772 and 1777), which also contained *A Dissertation on the Passions*, the *Enquiry concerning the Principles of Morals*, and *The Natural History of Religion*.

SECTION I

1.1   *Moral philosophy*: 'moral' is here used in the common eighteenth-century sense, meaning related to the human sphere, rather than in the more usual modern sense of *ethics*. Hence Hume's equation of 'moral philosophy' with 'the science of human nature'.

1.1   *two different manners*: Hume goes on to distinguish two different styles of philosophy, the 'easy' and the 'abstruse'; see §8 of the Introduction, above.

1.2   *his understanding*: 'understanding' here is a noun rather than a verb, referring to a human faculty of the mind. In this sense, 'the understanding' is another name for the faculty of *reason*—whereby we discover truths—which was standardly distinguished from *the will*—whereby we form desires and intentions. See also explanatory notes to 2.1 and to the Textual Variant to 1.14 (p. 210).

1.3   *plebeian*: a common or ordinary person (deriving from the Roman social class distinction between *patricians*, who were from noble families, and *plebeians* or *plebs*).

1.4   *CICERO ... LOCKE*: Hume identifies Aristotle, Malebranche, and Locke as 'abstruse philosophers'; Cicero, La Bruyère, and Addison as more popular 'easy philosophers'. For *Aristotle, Malebranche, Locke*, and *Cicero*, see Glossarial Index for more information. *Jean de la Bruyère* (1645–96) was a French author, writing principally on moral issues. *Joseph Addison* (1672–1719) was an English essayist and politician, best known today for having founded *The Spectator* magazine (1711–12) with Richard Steele.

1.6   *Abstruse thought . . . communicated*: this description of the fate of 'abstruse philosophy' appears to be somewhat autobiographical. In the conclusion of Book I of his *Treatise of Human Nature*, Hume finds himself reduced by sceptical anxieties to 'the most deplorable condition imaginable' (*T* 1.4.7.8), while in 'My Own Life' he famously describes the *Treatise* as having fallen *'dead-born from the press'* (Appendix V, p. 170—an allusion to Pope's *Epilogue on the Satires*, Dialogue ii: 'All, all but truth, drops dead-born from the press').

1.6   *Be a philosopher . . . man*: the eloquence of this maxim can give the impression that Hume is voicing it himself. But it is *nature* that 'seems' to say this, and Hume will spend most of the remainder of Section I arguing the contrary case in favour of 'abstruse' philosophy, at least when it is practised properly.

1.8   *pictures*: an 'easy philosopher' is here thought of as like a painter, painting a picture of human life, to whom accurate knowledge of human nature can be serviceable (i.e. 'subservient') in the same way as knowledge of human anatomy is useful to a portrait painter.

1.8   *a VENUS or an HELEN*: Venus, the Roman goddess of love—also known by the Greek name Aphrodite—was judged by Paris, prince of Troy (an ancient city of Anatolia), to be the most beautiful of the goddesses. In return, Venus gave him the love of Helen of Sparta, wife of King Menelaus and the world's most beautiful woman. This was the origin of the Trojan War, in which the Greek forces led by Agamemnon of Mycenae, the brother of Menelaus, besieged Troy and ultimately destroyed it. After ten years of failure, the Greeks gained entrance to the city through the famous ruse of the Trojan Horse (devised by Odysseus or Ulysses), a wooden horse seemingly left as a peace offering on their departure, but within which Greek soldiers were hidden.

1.11   *popular superstitions*: here 'superstition' is used in a general sense to cover (irrational) religious beliefs. The word also has a more specific sense, associated with magic and ritualism; in this sense it was common for Roman Catholicism to be described by its enemies as 'superstition' (see §5 of the Introduction, above).

1.12   *too sensible an interest*: too strong a motive. 'Sensible' in this eighteenth-century usage does not mean 'showing good sense', but instead 'apparent to the senses or feeling'. People who exploit dubious metaphysics for personal gain (e.g. priests and charlatans) thus *feel* an interest in its perpetuation.

1.12   *catholic remedy*: general cure.

1.12   *careless*: carefree, unconcerned, not taking great care.

1.13   *mental geography*: systematic description of superficial behaviour of the mind, as opposed to discovery of the 'secret springs and principles'

(1.15)—the underlying causes—that are responsible for that behaviour. See §8 of the Introduction, above.

1.14 *the compass of human understanding*: the range of human rational enquiry (the phrase was used by John Locke in his *Essay*, IV. xxi. 1).

1.14 *intimately concerned*: in the first two editions of the *Enquiry* (1748 and 1750), a note appeared at this point, crediting Francis Hutcheson (1694–1746) and Joseph Butler (1692–1752) with important insights: see Textual Variants, above (pp. 177–8), and also p. 210.

1.15 *secret springs and principles*: the underlying causes of the behaviour of the human mind. Hume's comparison with astronomy in these two paragraphs indicates that 'mental geography' can be a very sophisticated activity, analogous to the work of Kepler in systematizing the motion of the planets. Discovery of 'secret springs and principles' is ascribed only to Newton's monumental synthesis, and applying this analogy back to Hume's work suggests that his own discoveries—such as the identification of custom as a central feature of human inference— will come under the heading of 'mental geography'. The *Enquiry* thus seems to show less ambition than the *Treatise*, which had suggested that the association of ideas is a fundamental force analogous to gravitation (1.1.4.6).

1.15 *Till a philosopher*: an allusion to Isaac Newton, see Glossarial Index.

SECTION II

2.0 *the ORIGIN of IDEAS*: Hume follows the pattern of Locke's *Essay* by starting his investigation into the human understanding with the question of where our ideas come from. Their answer to this is often thought to represent the key difference between 'rationalists' and 'empiricists' (see pp. 223–6), and as in the *Treatise* (1.1.1.4), Hume's *Copy Principle* (2.5) puts him in the empiricist camp with Locke, denying innate ideas (cf. 2.9 endnote [A]). In Book I of the *Treatise* Hume's discussion then continues forward with the same Lockean agenda, asking how we acquire our various ideas: of the memory and imagination, of relations, abstractions, space and time, causation, body, the self, etc. In the *Enquiry*, by contrast, Hume soon turns to the very different issue of how we acquire *information* about the world, focusing on the role of factual inference (Section IV). Only after establishing that this intimately involves the idea of causation, and hence necessary connexion, does he come back to considering the origin of that one specific idea (in Section VII), before returning again to epistemological questions for most of the rest of the *Enquiry*.

2.1 *perceptions of the mind*: Hume uses the term 'perceptions' for what Descartes and Locke had called 'ideas', and then draws his own distinction within the category of such perceptions, between 'ideas' and 'impressions'. See §9 of the Introduction, above.

2.1   *These faculties*: in addition to the very broad distinction between 'the understanding' (or 'reason') and 'the will' (see explanatory note to 1.2), Hume also sometimes refers to other faculties of the mind, notably *the senses* (sight, touch, etc.), *the memory*, *the imagination* (also called 'the fancy'), and *the passions* (i.e. feelings or sentiments). Talk of such faculties does not imply that they correspond to real divisions within the mind; indeed John Locke was emphatic that making such an assumption would be a mistake (*Essay*, II. xxi. 17–20). Hume's own usage of the terms is accordingly rather flexible, particularly in respect of reason (or 'the understanding') and its boundary with 'the imagination' (though he is most explicit about this in the *Treatise*, e.g. 1.3.9.19 n, 1.4.4.1, 1.4.7.7).

2.3   *force and vivacity*: it is unclear whether Hume intends to *define* the distinction between impressions and ideas in terms of 'force and vivacity', or whether this is simply an attempt to capture the difference between sensations or feelings and thoughts (cf. explanatory note to 5.12, and Introduction, p. xxxiii n. 17).

2.5   *all our ideas . . . more lively ones*: this is Hume's famous Copy Principle, by which he denies the existence of *innate ideas* (cf. 2.9 endnote [A]). See §9 of the Introduction, above.

2.7   *A LAPLANDER or NEGROE*: Lapland is an Arctic region of northern Scandinavia; a negro is someone with dark skin, typically of African origin. In Hume's day, very few people from these places would have experienced the taste of wine.

2.8   *one contradictory phaenomenon*: Hume now presents his puzzling example of the 'missing shade of blue', which seems to show that 'the simple ideas are not always . . . derived from the correspondent impressions'. He does not seem to be particularly disturbed by the apparent counter-example to his Copy Principle, perhaps for the reason suggested in the Introduction, p. xxxiv n.18.

2.9   *from what . . . derived?*: Hume now wields his Copy Principle as a method of clarifying obscure ideas, and explicitly links it with the issue of meaning: the meaning of a word being determined by the idea with which it is associated. He will use this principle in Section VII, to investigate the meaning of terms such as '*power, force, energy*, or *necessary connexion*' (7.3).

SECTION III

3.0   *ASSOCIATION of IDEAS*: John Locke (*Essay*, II. xxxiii. 4–7), like other philosophers, had criticized the association of ideas as irrational and even akin to madness, because it determines the train of our thoughts not by reason, but instead on the basis of chance, or of custom (i.e. our tendency to form habitual trains of thought in response to repeated experience). Hume aims to overturn this traditional view, by showing in Sections IV and V that all factual reasoning depends on custom, so that without it, we could never learn anything beyond the reach of our memory and senses.

3.3   *possible*[6]: note 5 in Beauchamp's numbering system relates to text omitted from the 1777 edition; please see Note on the Text, p. lviii, above. For the wording of note 6 in the 1772 edition, see p. 182.

3.3   *compleat and entire*: in all editions of the *Enquiry* prior to 1777, Section III continued with a discussion of the association of ideas in its application to literature: see Textual Variants, pp. 178–83.

SECTION IV

4.1   *Relations of Ideas, and Matters of Fact*: a distinction commonly known as *Hume's Fork*: see §10 of the Introduction, above.

4.1   *EUCLID*: Greek mathematician who flourished in Alexandria around 300 BC, and whose *Elements* provided the authoritative axiomatic treatment of geometry until the nineteenth century, when *non-Euclidean* geometries were discovered. Perhaps the most famous example of a proposition 'demonstrated by Euclid' is Pythagoras' Theorem, that in any right-angled triangle, the square of the hypotenuse (the side opposite the right angle) is equal to the sum of the squares of the other two sides—so for example a triangle whose sides are of lengths 3, 4, and 5 metres will be right-angled, since $3^2 + 4^2 = 5^2$ (cf. 12.27).

4.2   *The contrary . . . is still possible*: Hume here states what is widely known as his *Conceivability Principle*, that any proposition which is distinctly conceivable is logically possible, implying no contradiction. The Principle has already been anticipated at 2.4, and will occur again at 4.18.

4.6   *reasonings à priori*: reasonings are a priori if they do not rely on any empirical information, e.g. from observation or experience. However, Hume's interest here is on what, if anything, can be inferred from our observations. So he uses the term '*à priori*' in a slightly different way, to mean inference which does not rely on any *remembered* empirical information (as opposed to immediate observation). See §10 of the Introduction.

4.6   *ADAM*: according to Genesis, the first book of the Hebrew Bible, Adam was the first man created by God. Here Hume imagines a thought-experiment in which Adam, newly created with ideal human faculties but no experience to call on, would be quite unable to predict the behaviour of natural objects.

4.6   *discovers*: reveals. See the Glossary, below, for other words whose meaning is ambiguous or has changed since the eighteenth century.

4.7   *loadstone*: a lodestone is a magnetized stone containing iron, which if suspended from a string can act as a compass by aligning itself with the Earth's magnetic field.

4.8   *one Billiard-ball . . . upon impulse*: Hume borrows Malebranche's example
        of two colliding balls (*Search after Truth*, VI. ii. 3.10) to make the point
        that even the most familiar and apparently 'intelligible' causal interactions
        can only be known through experience. See §2 of the Introduction,
        above.

4.10   *may I not conceive*: it might seem that Hume is appealing to his
        Conceivability Principle (4.2) here, to establish only that other effects are
        logically possible. However, he is claiming much more: that a priori
        many different effects are *equally possible*, with no basis for choosing
        between them, so that the choice between them would be 'entirely
        arbitrary' (4.9).

4.12   *reduce the principles . . . observation*: Hume spells out what he sees as the
        only legitimate ambition of science, given that a priori intelligibility is
        not to be had. See §7 of the Introduction, above. It is in this unifying
        spirit that he will later sketch some hypotheses of his own in the science
        of mind, arguing that custom is analogous to the association of ideas (5.20)
        and that it can account for probabilistic inference (6.3). Later in the
        paragraph, the phrase 'springs and principles' recalls 1.15: see explanatory
        notes to 1.13 and 1.15.

4.13   *mixed mathematics*: what we would now call 'applied mathematics', the
        application of mathematics to the physical world.

4.13   *the moment or force . . . motion*: Hume here alludes to what is now known
        as *momentum*, the mass of a body multiplied by its velocity (i.e. its speed
        in a particular direction). One of the most fundamental laws of mechan-
        ics is the *conservation of momentum*, whereby the total momentum of a
        number of colliding bodies will be the same after the collision as it was
        before. It follows, as Hume remarks, that a small body, if accelerated to
        a great enough speed, can achieve sufficient momentum to displace a
        much larger body which is moving relatively slowly.

4.13   *the discovery . . . experience*: though demonstrative mathematical reason-
        ing is useful in physics, this does not mean that the behaviour of objects
        can be known a priori through mathematics, because the physical laws
        through which the mathematics is applied (e.g. the conservation of
        momentum) can be discovered only by experience.

4.14   *sifting humour*: probing frame of mind.

4.15   *pretend*: claim, or aspire, with no connotation of *pretence* in the modern
        sense.

4.16   *force or power . . . others*: the inertia of bodies was supposed to involve a
        force, the *vis inertiae* or inert power; see explanatory note to endnote [D].

4.16   n. 7 *See Sect. 7*: this note was added in the 1750 edition, and seems
        designed to obviate an objection made by Kames, that Hume was incon-
        sistent in referring to objects' powers in the previous three sentences,
        when Section VII will go on to deny that objects in themselves strictly
        have any powers. Hume here indicates that his language of 'powers'
        should not be taken to prejudge how that language is to be interpreted.

4.16 *a medium*: a middle term in an inference, connecting the premiss(es) with the conclusion. We have now reached the heart of Hume's famous sceptical argument concerning induction, outlined in §11 of the Introduction, above. Having shown that all factual arguments depend on a supposition of uniformity, he is now asking what basis there could be for such a supposition. It cannot be founded on what we perceive, nor is it known to be true by immediate intuition; hence Hume deduces that it could only be well founded if it is inferable by reasoning that involves at least one intermediate step—some *medium*. See explanatory note to 4.21.

4.18 *moral reasoning*: in the first two editions of the *Enquiry*, Hume refers here to 'moral or probable Reasonings'. The term is used by Hume to mean reasoning which is less than perfectly certain (delivering 'probability' or at best 'moral certainty'), and the word 'moral' carries no connotation of *ethical* relevance. See §10 of the Introduction, above.

4.18 *demonstrative arguments*: arguments that lead with total logical certainty from premiss(es) to conclusion, such as valid arguments in mathematics. See §10 of the Introduction, above.

4.19 *experimental conclusions*: things inferred on the basis of experience.

4.20 *I cannot imagine . . . reasoning*: Hume understandably overlooks *statistical inference*, commonplace since the development of mathematical statistics, in which the strength of a conclusion can be shown to depend (in appropriate circumstances) on the size of the statistical sample. However, it is doubtful whether such inference could provide a solution to Hume's so-called *Problem of Induction*, because statistical inference depends on the assumption that the observed sample is *representative* or randomly chosen, and this cannot be guaranteed when inferring from past to future.

4.21 *the interposing ideas*: an allusion to Locke's *Essay*, IV. xvii. 2, which spoke of 'intermediate *Ideas*' as forming a chain of inference from premiss to conclusion, constituting either a demonstrative or a probable argument depending on the strength of the links.

SECTION V

5.1 *EPICTETUS, and other Stoics*: see Glossarial Index.

5.1 *ACADEMIC or SCEPTICAL philosophy*: see Glossarial Index.

5.3 *into this world*: Hume briefly summarizes the sceptical argument of Section IV, starting with the Adam thought-experiment.

5.5 *CUSTOM or HABIT*: see §11 of the Introduction, above. As Hume goes on to explain, all he is doing here is giving a name to a causal principle of human nature that he has observed to be operative. We do in fact make factual inferences in response to repeated experience, though he has shown that all such inferences involve a step—namely the supposition of uniformity (5.2)—that cannot be founded on reason. Reason does not 'engage us' to make that step, but we evidently make it nonetheless, so it is apparently a basic fact about human nature that we function in this way. It is a form of habituation in response to repetition, hence 'habit' seems an appropriate name for this 'principle of human nature'. But Hume usually prefers the term *custom*, which Locke had used (see explanatory note to 3.0), though with highly negative connotations which Hume reverses.

5.6   *Custom, then, is the great guide of human life*: Hume pointedly echoes Bishop Joseph Butler's famous phrase in the introduction to his *Analogy of Religion* (1736), that 'Probability is the very guide of life'. He agrees with Butler on the importance of probable or factual reasoning, our only means of discovering anything about the world. However, such reasoning does not depend—as Locke and Butler had assumed—on any type of rational insight into why things must (or are likely to) behave uniformly. Instead it depends on *custom*, an instinctive principle of human nature that just leads us to assume that they will do so.

5.8   *What then . . . matter?*: the upshot of Hume's discussion is that all human belief about the world that goes beyond what is perceived or remembered is based on customary inference from something that we have perceived or remembered.

5.8   *It is an operation of the soul*: Hume emphasizes that custom is involuntary and instinctive, at its most basic level not subject to rational control. 'Soul' here is just another word for 'mind', with no religious connotation intended.

5.9   *the remaining . . . neglected*: see the Introduction, p. xl.

5.12   *Were we to . . . sentiment*: in *Treatise* 1.3.7.5, Hume had purported to give a definition of belief as 'A LIVELY IDEA RELATED TO OR ASSOCIATED WITH A PRESENT IMPRESSSION'. In the Appendix to the *Treatise*, as here, he acknowledged that the difference between imagining something and believing it cannot be characterized so crudely, as just a matter of *liveliness* (i.e. the same thing that is supposed to distinguish ideas from impressions, as at 2.3).

5.16   *shadow out*: represent or symbolize, by an imperfect image.

5.17 n. 9   *"Naturane nobis . . . disciplina"*: this passage, from Cicero's *De Finibus Bonorum et Malorum* (*On the Chief Good and Evil*), is translated thus by H. Rackham (Loeb, 1921): 'Why are we more affected, asked Piso, when we learn that the places we see were often frequented by famous men than we are when we hear a report of the same men's exploits or read a written account of them? Is it a natural endowment we have, or is it some sort of aberration? I feel the effect now, for example. For I am put in mind of Plato, who we are told was the first to practice disputation here; indeed the adjoining gardens not only bring him back to mind but seem to place the man himself before my eyes. Here is Speusippus, here Xenocrates, and here his follower Polemo: The bench we see over there was Polemo's. In the same way, even when looking at our own senate building—I mean the Hostilia, not the new building, which looks slighter to me since it was enlarged—I used to think of

Scipio, Cato, Laelius, and especially my grandfather. So great is the suggestive power of places, that it is no accident that they shape our memory training.'

5.20   *the belief . . . is always presupposed*: Hume is about to make the claim that the operation of custom is similar or analogous to the operation of the three principles of association (resemblance, contiguity, and causation—see 3.2–3). But he first points out a difference: custom leads to new beliefs, whereas the three principles operate to enliven thoughts about things that we already believe to exist.

5.21   *pre-established harmony*: a notion associated with the great German philosopher Gottfried Wilhelm Leibniz (1646–1716), who advocated a world-view having some resemblance to occasionalism (cf. §6 of the Introduction, above). Leibniz agreed with Malebranche in denying any actual causation between objects, but whereas Malebranche saw their apparent interaction as effected by God on each occasion, Leibniz attributed this instead to the self-contained behaviour of each object, acting quite independently but all choreographed in advance by God to act in a pre-established harmony. Hume's comment evinces some amusement at the parallel between Leibniz's highly theological theory and his own naturalistic view.

5.21   *final causes*: explanation of change by reference to purposes or goals. The term is associated with Aristotle, who attributed the motion of objects to their *striving* to reach their natural place in the cosmos (see §§1–2 of the Introduction, above). Again Hume's comment is not to be taken too seriously.

SECTION VI

6.0 n. 10   *demonstrations, proofs, and probabilities*: see §12 of the Introduction, above.

6.1   *no such thing . . . world*: Hume is a determinist: he believes that everything in the world operates according to uniform laws that could, in principle, enable prediction of what will happen from the complete current state of the world (see §§4 and 14 of the Introduction, above). But in this section he will argue that ignorance of underlying causes leaves us relying on probability just as if the relevant events (e.g. throws of dice) were genuinely random.

6.3   *an inexplicable . . . nature*: belief turns out to arise from probabilistic thinking in much the same way as it does from uniform custom. Hume is not claiming to give any precise explanation of this (something of a contrast to *Treatise*, 1.3.11–12), but will now suggest that it can 'perhaps, in some measure, be accounted for' given the similarity.

6.4   *rhubarb . . . purge . . . opium . . . soporific*: a purge promotes evacuation of the bowels; a soporific makes one sleepy (cf. p. xv of the Introduction).

6.4   *received . . . sensible . . . difficulty*: 'received systems' are those that are standard or widely accepted; 'sensible of' implies felt awareness.

SECTION VII

7.0 *Of the* IDEA . . . CONNEXION: in the first two editions of the *Enquiry* (1748 and 1750), the title of Section VII was '*Of the* IDEA *of* POWER *or necessary* CONNEXION'. Throughout the section, Hume treats 'power' and 'connexion' as virtual synonyms, as he had done also in the corresponding section of the *Treatise*, where he explains that 'the terms of *efficacy, agency, power, force, energy, necessity, connexion*, and *productive quality*, are all nearly synonimous' (*T* 1.3.14.4).

7.2 *EUCLID*: see explanatory note to 4.1.

7.2 *chimera and conceit*: both terms refer to something imagined and fanciful (in Greek mythology, a chimera is a monster with a lion's head, a goat's body, and a snake's tail).

7.4 *all our ideas. . . impressions*: Hume refers back to his Copy Principle of Section II: see explanatory notes to 2.5 and 2.9.

7.5 *let us search . . . derived*: for a description of Hume's extended argument in this section, see §13 of the Introduction, above.

7.6 *outward . . . inward impression*: Hume follows Locke (see p. xvii of the Introduction) in distinguishing between *sensation* (i.e. outward senses such as sight and touch) and *reflection* (i.e. inward sense—awareness of our own feelings).

7.8 n. 12 *Mr. LOCKE*: see Glossarial Index; the reference is to Locke's *Essay*, II. xxi.

7.8 n. 12 *simple idea*: Hume makes the assumption that the idea whose impression he seeks is simple (as apparent also at 7.4). This may be because he is focusing not on any very specific idea, but on the general notion of one thing following from another—the basic idea of *connexion* (see Introduction, p. xlii n. 24).

7.13 *palsy*: paralysis.

7.14 *animal spirits*: a supposed fluid providing the medium of communication within the nervous system.

7.21 n. 14 Θεος απο μηχανης: Greek phrase equivalent to the more familiar Latin *deus ex machina*, meaning 'god out of a machine'. It refers to the practice used by some classical playwrights, of resolving a plot (often rather implausibly) through the intervention of a god, lowered onto the stage by a mechanism.

7.21 *many philosophers*: Hume refers to Malebranche and other occasionalists. See Glossarial Index and §6 of the Introduction.

7.28 *this . . . necessary connexion*: for a discussion of this important but somewhat puzzling claim, see p. xliv of the Introduction.

7.29 *we may define a cause*: on Hume's famous two definitions, see pp. xlv–xlvi of the Introduction. In 'defining' a cause, Hume is acknowledging that the notion is a *legitimate* one, despite any impression to the contrary that his arguments might have given. *Treatise* 1.4.5.32 provides perhaps the most explicit statement of this: 'all objects, which are found to be constantly conjoin'd, are upon that account only to be regarded as causes and effects'.

SECTION VIII

8.2 *liberty and necessity*: see the Introduction, §14 for a discussion of Hume's treatment of this topic, and §4 for some background.

8.3 *doctrine . . . liberty*: the doctrine of necessity is the thesis of universal determinism, and the doctrine of liberty is the thesis that humans have genuine free will (as presumed to be required for moral responsibility). Both terms derive from Hobbes, see p. xxi of the Introduction.

8.4 *universally allowed*: agreed by everyone. No doubt an exaggeration, but adherents of the modern 'mechanical philosophy' (see pp. xiv, xxi) were agreed that matter acts in a way that is causally determined.

8.5 *Beyond . . . connexion*: here Hume appeals to his two 'definitions of cause' to illuminate the issue—see p. xlvii of the Introduction.

8.7 *ARISTOTLE, and HIPPOCRATES*: *Aristotle*'s theory of four elements is discussed in §1 of the Introduction, and see also p. 220. *Hippocrates of Cos* (*c*.460–377 BC), known as the 'father of medicine', was the source of the famous 'Hippocratic Oath' which is still widely affirmed by doctors today. He was a major influence on the Greek physician Galen (*c*. AD 129–216), whose theories dominated medieval medicine until the sixteenth century, in much the same way as Ptolemy's theories, derived mainly from Aristotle, dominated medieval astronomy.

8.7 *POLYBIUS and TACITUS*: *Polybius* (*c*.200–118 BC) was a Greek historian who lived much of his life in Rome, and whose *Histories* concern the rise of Rome to world supremacy. *Cornelius Tacitus* (*c*. AD 56–120) was a Roman historian known best for his *Annals* and *Histories*, covering the reign of Roman emperors from Tiberius (AD 14) onwards.

8.8 *QUINTUS CURTIUS . . . ALEXANDER*: *Alexander the Great* (356–323 BC) was a king of Macedonia who quickly conquered a vast empire encompassing Greece, Persia, and most of the known world as far as India, before dying of fever in Babylon at the age of 32. Although his military empire soon fell apart after his death, his conquests ushered in the Hellenistic period, in which Greek culture exerted a wide influence. *Quintus Curtius Rufus* was a Roman historian who wrote a *History of Alexander*, very popular in medieval times. He may be the same as a Curtius Rufus mentioned by Tacitus, who became proconsul of Africa and died around AD 53.

8.9 *specious colouring of a cause*: superficially plausible and artfully slanted presentation of a position (what might now be called 'spin').

8.13 *The vulgar . . . appearance*: this important paragraph, taken from the *Treatise* (1.3.12.5), introduces a discussion of scientific methodology which advocates the search for hidden causes of inconstant phenomena.

We should seek explanations in terms of uniform underlying causes rather than erratic superficial causes.

8.15 *A stupid ... carriage*: a dull man is uncharacteristically vivacious.

8.16 *Thus it appears ... nature*: Hume perhaps goes too far here, in apparently endorsing a strong form of psychological determinism. For example the obliging person of the previous paragraph, who has a toothache, is influenced behaviourally by *physical* happenings in his brain as well as motives.

8.18 *politics be a science*: one of Hume's aims in this section is to make the case that human thought and behaviour is fully amenable to scientific explanation, a natural rather than a mysterious phenomenon. The phrase is reminiscent of the title of one of his essays 'That Politics may be Reduced to a Science' (1741).

8.19 *interest*: influence.

8.19 *wheel*: an instrument of torture.

8.20 *Charing-Cross*: an area commonly regarded as the centre of London, and now most familiarly associated with Charing Cross railway station.

8.21 *what ... reason*: the Introduction, p. xlvii, explains what is going on in this and the next paragraph, where Hume appeals again to his two 'definitions of cause' to illuminate the issue of free will.

8.23 *a power ... will*: this equates free action with *intentional* action, and is therefore not to be equated with 'freedom' in any more everyday sense (e.g. freedom from unwanted rules, legal constraints, or coercive threats). It is therefore dubious to see Hume's notion of liberty here as equivalent to what in the *Treatise* he referred to as 'liberty of *spontaneity*, as it is call'd in the schools ... the most common sense of the word; and ... that species of liberty, which it concerns us to preserve' (2.3.2.1).

a prisoner ... chains: this example suggests that Hume's intended meaning of 'liberty' is excluded only by extreme physical constraint or compulsion, and is entirely compatible with coercive threats. If I give someone access to a bank vault because they threaten my family with a gun, then in this sense I do so freely, because I act *intentionally*—'according to the determinations of my will'—in unlocking the door. But Hume's approach can easily accommodate the common-sense idea that I am not blameworthy for doing so. If I am blameless for opening the vault, this is not because I did not act *freely*. Rather, it is because I did not do anything *wrong*. In that situation, faced with the alternatives of opening the vault or having my family murdered, opening the vault was not a blameworthy act.

8.25 *nothing exists ... existence*: Hume discussed this Causal Maxim in *Treatise*, 1.3.3 See also explanatory note to 6.1.

8.26 *consistent with morality*: in the final 1772 and 1777 editions of the *Enquiry*, 'morality' replaced 'Morality and Religion'. Hume apparently decided to give up the pretence that his discussion of religion later in the section is anything other than negative.

8.27 *Necessity . . . cause*: Hume again refers back to his two definitions of 7.29.

8.28 *All laws . . . mind*: here Hume begins to argue that determinism ('the doctrine of necessity'), so far from being incompatible with morality, is actually required by it. See pp. xlvii–xlviii of the Introduction.

8.32 *no indifference; no liberty*: 'indifference' means behaviour that is *not* causally determined: immediately prior to its occurrence, such behaviour could not be predicted even in principle (modern quantum physics seems to provide the most convincing examples). The opponent Hume is imagining here is advocating *libertarianism*, by insisting that *liberty*— i.e. free will—requires *indifference*. The libertarian maintains that we cannot be genuinely free, in the sense appropriate to moral responsibility, unless we are undetermined. Typically the compatibilist will reply, as Hume does, that undetermined behaviour is merely random and hence not morally accountable. (In *Treatise* 2.3.1–2 and *Abstract* 31 Hume's overall position was similar, but he confusingly used 'liberty' to mean indifference rather than free will of the morally relevant kind.)

8.32 *train*: the trail of gunpowder leading to a mine (i.e. a buried store of gunpowder), which is 'fired' (i.e. set alight) to explode the mine, usually to bring down a castle wall or other structure.

8.34 *the ancient Stoics*: see Glossarial Index.

8.34 *malignant humours*: a supposed disorder of the fluids (blood, bile, and phlegm) in the body, considered in medieval medicine to be the cause of disease.

8.35 *sentiment of approbation or blame*: Hume bases his own moral theory on such sentiments, and here sketches its application to the question of free will and moral responsibility. See p. xlviii of the Introduction.

8.36 *These are mysteries*: an appeal to mystery enables Hume to give the appearance of orthodoxy, while he points out the serious difficulties that the Problem of Evil poses for theism.

8.36 *To reconcile . . . prescience*: if what happens is not determined, then how can God possibly have foreknowledge of what will happen?

8.36 *to defend . . . sin*: if what happens, including human sin, is absolutely determined by laws ordained by God, then how can God be supposed to be perfectly good? See §4 of the Introduction, above for a brief discussion of some related issues.

SECTION IX

9.1 *ANALOGY*: Hume starts the section with a general point about analogical reasoning, which will be applied later in Section XI. See §15 of the Introduction, above. Here he suggests that customary and analogical inference are closely related because both are based on similarity.

9.2 *the hare in her doubles*: a hare chased by dogs will often double back on itself, sharply changing direction, so a dog which anticipates this can take advantage.

9.6   *the experimental . . . beasts*: our reasoning from experience is fundamentally based on a non-rational instinct, just like that of the animals. See
p. xl of the Introduction.

SECTION X

10.1   *Dr. TILLOTSON'S writings . . . real presence*: the *real presence* refers to
the Roman Catholic doctrine of transubstantiation, which claims that
bread and wine, when blessed in the ceremony of the Christian
Eucharist, are substantially changed into the body and blood of Christ
(see the Introduction, p. xx). *John Tillotson* (1630–94) was a Protestant
preacher, well known for his attacks on Roman Catholicism, who
ultimately became archbishop of Canterbury. He argued against
transubstantiation on the basis that our only evidence of its truth is
from the reported sense experience of the Disciples, but this must be
balanced against the clear evidence of the senses that transubstantiation
is false. Hume's argument against miracles is structurally parallel, in
first reducing the evidence of testimony to experience, and then arguing
that this experiential evidence in favour of testimony can never out-
weigh the strength of the experience against a miracle.

10.3   *moral evidence*: evidence that is less than certain, typically deriving from
experience of cause and effect—see explanatory note to 4.18.

10.4   *A wise . . . evidence*: Hume is applying his account of probability *norma-
tively*, as prescribing how we *ought* to reason. See §16 of the
Introduction for a discussion of the following extended argument.

10.4   *experiments*: observations from experience, not implying any special
scientific context.

10.6   *proof*: an extremely strong 'moral' (i.e. factual) argument, typically
based on totally uniform experience (e.g. the inference that fire is hot,
or snow cold). Hume introduced this notion in the footnote to the title
of Section VI. In this sense the notion of *proof* carries no implication of
being formal or mathematical, and is quite distinct from the notion of a
demonstrative argument (cf. 4.18 and §12 of the Introduction, above).

10.9   *CATO*: Cato the Younger (95–46 BC), a Roman politician and Stoic (see
Glossarial Index), renowned for his truthfulness according to Plutarch.

10.10 *The INDIAN prince*: Hume appears to borrow the story of the Indian
prince from §3 of the introduction to Joseph Butler's *Analogy of Religion*
(1736), which mentions a 'prince who had always lived in a warm climate'. Butler attributes the story to Locke's *Essay*, IV. xv. 5, though in
fact Locke's example is of the King of Siam.

10.12 *violation of . . . nature*: Hume assumes that the theist will understand a
miracle as being an event that is contrary to nature's normal ways of
working, brought about by the intervention of some invisible spirit (see
10.12 endnote [K]).

10.13 *deducting the inferior*: Hume's most explicit account of how such 'deduction' would operate is at *Treatise* 1.3.11.9–12. Applied to a simple case of probabilistic assessment based on equally likely alternatives or on past frequencies, this seems to imply that he takes the force of such evidence to be measurable as the balance of positive over negative instances, divided by the total number of instances. Such a measure is coherent, but would yield a probabilistic scale from 1 to −1 instead of the now conventional 1 to 0.

10.17 *an enthusiast*: 'enthusiasm' refers to charismatic religious faith, often combined with a firm conviction that God has personally revealed Himself to the believer. See §5 of the Introduction, above.

10.18 *a TULLY or a DEMOSTHENES*: '*Tully*' is another name for Cicero (i.e. Marcus Tullius Cicero, see p. 221). *Demosthenes* (384–322 BC) was a celebrated Athenian orator, whose recorded speeches, together with Cicero's, are discussed in Hume's essay 'Of Eloquence' (1742).

10.18 *Capuchin*: friar of the order of St Francis, famed as very effective preachers.

10.21 *wonderful historians*: historians who report numerous wonders or miracles.

10.22 *ALEXANDER . . . PAPHLAGONIA . . . LUCIAN*: Around AD 160, *Alexander of Abonouteichos* in Paphlagonia (a region of northern Asia Minor) devised a trick to make it appear as though Asclepius, the god of healing in the form of a snake with a human head, was being born from a goose egg. *Lucian of Samosata* (c. AD 120–80+), a Greek rhetorician and satirist known best for his amusing dialogues, wrote an exposé entitled *Alexander, or the False Prophet*.

10.22 *MARCUS AURELIUS*: Marcus Aurelius Antoninus (AD 121–80) became Roman emperor in succession to his adoptive father, Antoninus Pius, who had adopted him as heir on the insistence of the previous emperor Hadrian. Famed for his wisdom and virtue, his *Meditations* is one of the classics of Stoic philosophy (see Glossarial Index).

10.23 *his impostures*: the editions of the *Enquiry* until 1768 included a note, as follows: 'It may here, perhaps, be objected, that I proceed rashly, and form my Notions of *Alexander* merely from the Account, given of him by *Lucian*, a profess'd Enemy. It were indeed to be wish'd, that some of the Accounts publish'd by his Followers and Accomplices had remain'd. The Opposition and Contrast between the Character and Conduct of the same Man, as drawn by a Friend or an Enemy is as strong, even in common Life, much more in these religious Matters, as that betwixt any two Men in the World, betwixt *Alexander* and St. *Paul*, for Instance. See a Letter to *Gilbert West* Esq; on the Conversion and Apostleship of St. *Paul*.'

10.24 *MAHOMET*: founder and principal Prophet of the Islamic religion, also known as Muhammad or Mohammed (c. AD 570–632).

10.24 TITUS LIVIUS, PLUTARCH, TACITUS: Titus Livius (*c*.59 BC–AD 17), more commonly known as Livy, wrote a celebrated history of Rome from its foundation until 9 BC. *Plutarch* (*c*. AD 46–119+) was a Greek historian, best known for his *Lives* of famous Greeks and Romans. *Tacitus*: see explanatory note to 8.7.

10.25 VESPASIAN: (AD 9–79) the first Roman emperor of the Flavian family, followed by his sons Titus (AD 39–81) and Domitian (AD 51–96).

10.25 n. 24 SUETONIUS: (*c*. AD 69–122+) Roman historian, wrote *Lives of the Twelve Caesars*, covering Julius Caesar to Domitian.

10.25 DEMETRIUS: (336–283 BC) son of Antigonus, a former general of Alexander the Great, who attempted to reunite his empire (cf. explanatory note to 8.8). He became king of Macedonia in 294, but was driven out in 288. Like Alexander, he seems to have encouraged conquered peoples to view him as a god.

10.26 *Cardinal DE RETZ*: (1613–79) archbishop of Paris, whose *Mémoires* describe his travels through Spain, including the reported miracle described by Hume.

10.26 *vouched by . . . the church*: attested or endorsed by the approved Roman Catholic criteria or *canons* for assessing the authenticity of a miracle.

10.27 *Abbé PARIS, the famous JANSENIST*: François de Paris (1690–1727), famed for his saintliness, founded a small religious community in the Saint-Marceau quarter of Paris. He died young, weakened by rigorous fasting and 'mortification' (e.g. self-torture by wearing a hair shirt with bristling iron wires, and a spiked metal belt). While the body was on display, parts of his nails, hair, and clothes were taken as relics, and an elderly woman who kissed his feet was supposedly cured of a paralysed arm. The celebrity of this miracle brought crowds of sick people to his tomb, with the results that Hume describes. Abbé Paris supported the theology of Cornelius Jansen (1585–1638), Bishop of Ypres, whose posthumous book *Augustinus* (1640) emphasized divine grace and strict predestination (see the Introduction, p. xxii), along with rigorous moral austerity. In France, the rise of the Jansenists provoked intense dispute with the Jesuits (see explanatory note below), whom they accused of moral laxity and Pelagianism (the heresy that man can earn salvation through good works). The controversy was sufficiently fierce to provoke three papal decrees against Jansenism, in 1643, 1653, and 1713. The last of these, *Unigenitus*, was issued by Pope Clement XI under pressure from the French king Louis XIV, keen to insist on theological unity to promote the unity of the state. Hume's focus on Jansenism may be motivated by the thought that both Protestants and orthodox Roman Catholics would be opposed to it, so the vast majority of his readers can be expected to favour a sceptical attitude towards the Jansenist miracles.

10.27 *Jesuits*: members of the Society of Jesus founded by Ignatius Loyola (1491–1556), a Roman Catholic order committed to serving the Pope and noted for its intellectual orientation and for its commitment to education and missionary work. The Jesuits set up many colleges including the one at La Flèche where Descartes studied, and near which Hume stayed when composing the *Treatise* (see pp. lxiii, 170). Jesuits were often accused by their enemies—notably the Jansenists—of devious reasoning to circumvent the rigours of Christian morality (particularly to placate wealthy donors)—hence the adjective 'Jesuitical'.

10.28 *PHILIPPI or PHARSALIA . . . CAESAREAN and POMPEIAN*: at the battle of Pharsalia (or Pharsalus) in Greece (48 BC), Julius Caesar defeated Pompey to end the Wars of the First Triumvirate and leave Caesar in sole charge of Rome (cf. explanatory note to 12.28). At the battle of Philippi in Macedonia (42 BC), Mark Antony and Octavian (later the Emperor Augustus) defeated Brutus and Cassius (Caesar's murderers) to end the Wars of the Second Triumvirate.

10.28 *HERODOTUS*: (*c*.484–425 BC) Greek writer sometimes known as 'The Father of History', though widely criticized for a tendency towards fabrication. His *Histories* cover the growth of the Persian Empire and Xerxes' attempt to conquer Greece, which ended in defeat at Salamis (480 BC) and Plataea (479 BC).

10.28 *MARIANA, BEDE*: *Juan de Mariana* (1536–1624), a Spanish Jesuit, published in 1592 a history of Spain reporting several miracles. *Saint Bede* (or The Venerable Bede, *c*.672–735), a Benedictine monk living in Northumbria, wrote 'The Life and Miracles of St Cuthbert', which is replete with reported miracles. However his celebrated *Ecclesiastical History of the English People*, in virtue of which he has been called 'The Father of English History', is somewhat less fanciful, and volume i of Hume's own *History of England* uses it extensively as a source.

10.30 *avidum genus auricularum*: a Latin phrase meaning 'a race with eager little ears'. It is an abbreviated version of a remark of Lucretius (*De Rerum Natura*, 4.594, see p. 222), 'humanum genus est avidum nimis auricularum', which in context suggests that humans are eager to relate stories that attract listeners.

10.35 *has ever amounted to*: in the first two editions of the *Enquiry* (1748 and 1750), this was stated more strongly: 'no testimony for any kind of miracle can ever possibly amount to a probability'.

10.37 *Queen ELIZABETH*: Elizabeth I was a popular queen of England from 1558 to 1603, bringing order and relative toleration to a country that had been divided by bitter religious controversy under her half-siblings Edward VI (a zealous Protestant) and Mary (an equally zealous Roman Catholic).

10.39 *Lord BACON*: see Glossarial Index.

10.39 *LIVY*: see explanatory note to 10.24.

10.40 *Pentateuch*: the first five books of the Hebrew Bible, namely Genesis, Exodus, Leviticus, Numbers, and Deuteronomy.

10.41 *And whoever . . . to it*: Hume's ironical ending is a conventional piece of 'theological lying', preserving the decencies by formally acknowledging theism. See p. xxiii of the Introduction.

SECTION XI

11.0   *Of a* PARTICULAR PROVIDENCE . . . STATE: in the first edition of 1748, this section was entitled '*Of the* PRACTICAL CONSEQUENCES *of* NATURAL RELIGION', which Hume perhaps came to think was too pointed, since the conclusion of the section is that 'natural religion'—the attempt to establish religious conclusions by appeal to the nature of the world—has no practical consequences whatever. The changed title focuses on the notion of God's *particular* providence towards individuals (as opposed to His *general* providence in establishing beneficial laws of nature), and Christians' hope for a 'future state', that is, an afterlife in heaven. It is striking, in view of the latter, that Hume omits the powerful arguments against immortality that he put in his suppressed essay on the topic (see Appendix II, above).

11.1   *he advanced . . . approve*: Hume here distances himself from his most religiously dangerous views, by putting them in the mouth of a sceptical friend. See §4 of the Introduction, above.

11.2   PROTAGORAS . . . SOCRATES: *Protagoras* (*c*.485–410 BC) was the first of the ancient Greek Sophists, most famous for his advocacy of relativism (i.e. denial of objective truth) as recorded in Plato's dialogue *Theaetetus*. He was banished from Athens for heretically questioning the existence of the Greek gods. *Socrates* (469–399 BC), Plato's teacher and reputedly one of the greatest philosophers of antiquity, was convicted of impiety and corrupting the youth of Athens through his teaching. His punishment was to commit suicide by drinking hemlock, as famously recorded in Plato's *Phaedo*.

11.2   EPICURUS . . . EPICUREANS: see Glossarial Index. The footnoted reference is to Lucian (cf. explanatory note to 10.22).

11.2   *the wisest of . . . emperors*: an allusion to Marcus Aurelius (cf. explanatory note to 10.22). The footnoted reference is to Lucian and to Dio Cassius Cocceianus (*c*.150–235), who wrote a history of Rome in eighty books, extending from the foundation of the city to 229.

11.4   *a wise magistrate*: this discussion, presumably written in the 1745–8 period, has a strong autobiographical resonance. In 1745, Hume's application for the Chair of Moral Philosophy at Edinburgh was vetoed by the Town Council under pressure from the Church. Hume's sceptical friend now argues that a wise magistrate should tolerate irreligious speculation, since such speculation does not really have its alleged 'pernicious consequences', being instead 'entirely indifferent to the peace of society and security of government'.

11.7 *fill all . . . white beans*: in ancient Greece, beans were commonly used for voting, with white beans signifying agreement and black beans disagreement.

11.11 *argument drawn . . . to causes*: see §17 of the Introduction, above.

11.13 *ZEUXIS*: a celebrated Greek painter of the late fifth century BC.

11.14 *JUPITER*: the supreme god of the Romans, based on the Greek god Zeus (though the Roman name would have been more familiar in the eighteenth century). By portraying the speech as made by Epicurus to the Athenians, Hume is able to avoid any direct reference to the God of Christianity, and thus reduces the overt impression of impiety.

11.17 *ill appearances of nature*: Hume introduces a brief discussion of the Problem of Evil, dealt with at far greater length in his *Dialogues*, Parts X and XI.

11.21 *this life . . . porch*: 'the porch view', whose irrationality Hume quickly demonstrates.

11.23 *the field . . . senate . . . school . . . closet*: 'the field' alludes to battle, 'the senate' to government, 'the school' to education, and 'the closet' to private study.

11.27 *who discovers himself*: who reveals himself.

11.27 *my apology for EPICURUS*: my defence on behalf of Epicurus.

11.29 *enthusiasm*: see explanatory note to 10.17.

SECTION XII

12.1 *Atheists*: in the *Enquiry* Hume never overtly expresses support for atheism, though a hint might be detectable here in his association of atheism with scepticism (cf. also 5.1). By far the best evidence for Hume's atheism is the general tendency of his arguments, especially in Sections VIII, X, and XI of the *Enquiry*; 'Of the Immortality of the Soul'; *The Natural History of Religion*; and the *Dialogues concerning Natural Religion*. For a brief review of this evidence, see chapter 1, §3 in my *Reading Hume on Human Understanding* (OUP, 2002).

12.3 *scepticism, antecedent*: see §18 of the Introduction, above for an outline of Hume's discussion of the varieties of scepticism.

12.3 *DES CARTES*: see Glossarial Index.

12.3 *diffident*: mistrustful, lacking confidence.

12.4 *education or rash opinion*: the word 'education' often, in Hume, carries connotations of indoctrination.

12.6 *the evidence of sense*: 'scepticism with regard to the senses' is covered in far greater detail in *Treatise* 1.4.2, but with a very different focus. The *Enquiry*'s argument is summarized in the Introduction above, pp. liii–liv.

12.10 *cavils*: quibbling arguments.

12.13 *a very unexpected circuit*: Descartes famously appealed to God's non-deceitfulness in order to establish the ultimate reliability of our faculties if used properly.

12.15 *another sceptical topic*: this argument broadly follows that of *Treatise* 1.4.4, 'Of the modern philosophy'.

12.15 *merely secondary*: Locke's distinction between primary and secondary qualities, against which Hume here deploys an argument of Berkeley's, is discussed in §3 of the Introduction, above. For Locke and Berkeley see also Glossarial Index.

12.15 *Abstraction*: Locke appealed to the notion of abstraction to explain the origin of general ideas, see the Introduction, p. xvii.

12.15 *Isoceles nor Scalenum*: an isosceles triangle is one that has two sides the same length, while a scalene triangle's sides are all of different lengths. Berkeley (*Principles of Human Knowledge*, Introduction §13) famously took advantage of Locke's confused description of the abstract idea of a triangle (in *Essay*, IV. vii. 9) to ridicule his notion of abstraction.

12.16 *no sceptic . . . against it*: the last sentence of this paragraph was added only in the final 1777 edition of the *Enquiry*, and its interpretation is unclear. Hume appears to be dismissive of the notion of 'a certain unknown, inexplicable *something*, as the cause of our perceptions', but rather than reject the notion as incoherent, he seems to suggest that it is sufficiently thin to be harmless. No dubious metaphysics (e.g. claiming to know the powers or inherent limits of matter) can possibly be based on something so meagre.

12.21 *Pyrrhonism*: see Glossarial Index.

12.22 *more profound researches*: Hume now summarizes his own argument from Section IV, 'Sceptical doubts concerning the operations of the understanding', incorporating also the lesson from Section VII (cf. 4.16 n.7). He highlights the sceptical worry that the instinct of custom, 'like other instincts, may be fallacious and deceitful'. For an overview of Hume's strategy at this point in Section XII, see the Introduction, p. lv.

12.23 *COPERNICAN or PTOLEMAIC*: see §1 of the Introduction, above.

12.23 *STOIC or EPICUREAN*: see Glossarial Index.

12.24 *result of this PYRRHONISM*: since the *arguments* for Pyrrhonism are supposed to be irrefutable, Hume seems to be suggesting that it results in mitigated scepticism by a natural causal route rather than rational reflection. If we reflect on the Pyrrhonian arguments, then we will naturally find ourselves drawn towards mitigated scepticism even when common life renders the Pyrrhonian arguments impossible to believe.

12.25 *limitation of our enquiries*: see the extract from the *Dialogues* (Appendix III, above) for Cleanthes' doubts about the cogency of this recommendation.

12.25 *methodized and corrected*: see pp. lv–lvi of the Introduction for a sketch of how this approach to science might work.

12.27 *As the component . . . similar*: Hume's reason for restricting demonstration to mathematics is that only mathematical ideas have sufficiently precise and intricate relations with each other to make demonstration fruitful.

12.27 *the square of the hypothenuse*: this result is known as Pythagoras' Theorem; see explanatory note to 4.1.

12.28 *CAESAR*: Julius Caesar (100–44 BC) became dictator of Rome by defeating his rivals in the first Triumvirate, and hence ended the Republic. His murder by Brutus and Cassius, intended to restore the Republic, led to a second civil war in which Octavian triumphed to become the first Roman emperor, under the name Augustus (cf. explanatory note to 10.28). Hume refers to Caesar's famous book *The Gallic War* in various places, and takes his existence as a paradigm example of a fact securely established by moral evidence (e.g. *Treatise* 1.3.4.2, 1.3.13.4, 2.3.1.15).

12.28 *the angel GABRIEL*: best known from the New Testament book of Luke (1: 26–38), where as God's messenger he informs Mary about the forthcoming birth of Jesus. In making reference to Gabriel, Hume is clearly hinting at a more significant application of his principle, namely that the non-existence of God Himself is 'perfectly conceivable, and implies no contradiction'. Hence any attempt to prove the existence of God a priori (e.g. by Anselm's or Descartes's so-called Ontological Argument) must be doomed to failure.

12.29 *It is only experience*: Hume here repeats his result about our knowledge of causation from 4.11. In the context of the previous sentence, he also seems to be hinting at a corollary, that any causal argument for God's existence must be founded entirely on causal principles established by experience. This cripples any attempt to argue beyond what is manifest in experience, as already demonstrated in Section XI, and hence any form of the so-called Cosmological Argument.

12.32 *But its best . . . revelation*: this pious sentence seems to be disingenuous, another instance of 'theological lying' (see p. 146). Hume suggests that 'Divinity . . . has a foundation in *reason*, so far as it is supported by experience', but Sections X and XI have argued—based on Hume's theory of experiential reasoning—that the specific doctrines of Christianity cannot be backed up by miraculous endorsement, while natural theology establishes nothing. So divinity is *not* 'supported by experience' at all. Note also the fate of books of divinity at 12.34.

12.33 *Morals . . . sentiment*: 'criticism' means *artistic* criticism or aesthetic judgement. Hume grounds both morality and aesthetics on sentiment rather than reason—see the Introduction, p. xlviii.

12.34 *Commit it then to the flames*: Burning had long been a common fate of atheistic books. Perhaps Hume is suggesting here that the wrong books have been destroyed, bearing in mind that Section XII started with a comment on atheism.

HUME'S ENDNOTES

A　　*LOCKE*: John Locke (see Glossarial Index) devoted Book I of his famous *Essay* to an attack on 'Innate Notions', and is clearly the main philosopher Hume has in mind amongst 'those, who denied innate ideas'.

　　　　the schoolmen: see Glossarial Index.

B　　*TIBERIUS . . . NERO*: Roman emperors (reigning AD 14–37 and 54–68 respectively) famed for their immorality and abuse of power.

D　　*vis inertiae*: the supposed 'force of inertia' that makes a body resistant to change, and hence gives it a tendency to remain in a uniform state of rest or motion until acted upon by an active force.

　　　　we only mark these facts: Hume seems to be extending his generally instrumentalist interpretation of causation (see Introduction, pp. xix, xxviii) to the sorts of quantitative powers and forces found in physics. In the *Treatise*, by contrast, he confined his attention to relations between types of specific events rather than variable interactions mediated by mathematical relationships. (This change might explain the contrast between T 1.3.15 and E 9.5 endnote [H].)

　　　　Sir ISAAC NEWTON . . . second causes: see pp. xix–xx and §6 of the Introduction. Hume seems in this endnote to be distinguishing between Newton and his followers, presumably so as to refuse them the great authority of his name. 'Second causes' are causes in nature, as opposed to God's own power, but some of those influenced by Newton embraced occasionalism, denying that anything but God has genuine efficacy (see also pp. 226, 228).

　　　　DES CARTES . . . MALEBRANCHE . . . LOCKE: see Glossarial Index.

　　　　CLARKE, and CUDWORTH: *Samuel Clarke* (1675–1729) was an English theologian and philosopher, best known at the time for his Boyle Lectures in defence of Christianity, and today for his correspondence with Leibniz (cf. explanatory note to 5.21), in which he defended a Newtonian view of space and time. Clarke's popular Cosmological Argument for God's existence is thought likely to be the model for the similar argument advanced by Demea, and refuted by Cleanthes, in Part IX of Hume's *Dialogues concerning Natural Religion*. *Ralph Cudworth* (1617–88) was leader of the Cambridge Platonists, in its day an influential group of whom Henry More (1614–87) was also a prominent member. Attracted by Descartes's dualism and also his 'mechanical philosophy', Cudworth adopted a combination of mechanistic atomism and Platonic metaphysics which he believed to have originated with Moses (and been transmitted to the Greeks by Pythagoras). The principal target of his arguments was Hobbes, against whom he sought both to refute determinism as applied to human action and to establish the eternal truth of morality as depending on Platonic ideas (rather than the Hobbesian state). His daughter Damaris, as Lady Masham, was a close friend of Locke and corresponded with Leibniz.

E   *The dispute*: Hume here alludes to the *vis viva* controversy, in which Leibniz maintained that the force of a body in motion should be measured as its mass multiplied by the square of its velocity. The Newtonians, such as Samuel Clarke, instead preferred to use momentum (i.e. mass multiplied by velocity, cf. explanatory note to 4.13). As seen from a modern perspective, both views reflected a partial truth, on the one hand the law of conservation of momentum, and on the other the law of conservation of energy (in which the *kinetic energy* of a moving body is proportional to Leibniz's *vis viva*). Conservation of momentum governs all collisions and gravitational interactions, but is of little use in ascertaining the flight of projectiles (since changes in the Earth's momentum are unmeasurable). Conservation of kinetic energy applies only to 'fully elastic' collisions in which energy is not dissipated as heat, but is of much greater use for calculating motion under gravity.

mensuration: measurement.

As to the frequent: this note was absent in the 1748 edition of the *Enquiry*, and in the 1750 edition its final paragraph was much shorter: 'A *Cause* is different from a *Sign*; as it implies Precedency and Contiguity in Time and Place, as well as Constant Conjunction. A Sign is nothing but a correlative Effect from the same Cause.'

H   *We shall here*: this discussion is the closest that remains, in the *Enquiry*, to *Treatise* 1.3.15, 'Rules by which to judge of causes and effects'. See explanatory note to endnote [D].

L   *Mons. MONTGERON*: Louis-Basile Carré de Montgeron (1686–1754), himself a Jansenist (cf. explanatory note to 10.27), wrote *La Vérité des miracles*, giving medical details of the alleged miraculous cures. He delivered a copy of the book to Louis XV, King of France, at the Palace of Versailles, at the same time warning against the Pope and the Jesuits' political power. For this he was later arrested under authority of the lieutenant of police René Hérault (1691–1740), who attempted to suppress the Jansenist supporters of Abbé Paris.

Recueil des Miracles de l'Abbé PARIS: book written anonymously and presented by twenty-three priests to the archbishop of Paris on 13 August 1731. The *Recueil* was meanwhile published but the archbishop did not respond, prompting twenty-two priests to send another formal request for investigation on 4 October 1731.

cardinal NOAILLES: Cardinal Louis Antoine Noailles (1651–1729) tried to prevent the condemnation of Jansenism, ultimately failing when pressure from the French government led in 1713 to the papal decree *Unigenitus*. This decree prompted a major controversy, with many books and pamphlets on each side. Noailles's successor, Archbishop Vintimille of Aix, supported the Pope and assisted Hérault in pursuing Jansenists.

MOLINIST . . . Madamoiselle le FRANC: Molinism, the theological system of the Spanish Jesuit Luis de Molina (1535–1600), was strongly supported by the French Jesuits in opposition to the predestinarian Jansenists (cf. §4 of the Introduction, above). It claims that human choice is entirely free and undetermined, but that nevertheless God knows in advance what any possible person *would* do in any possible circumstances. This counterfactual 'middle knowledge' enables Him to arrange things providentially by deciding which possibilities to actualize, without infringing the freedom of those individuals He decides to create. *Anne Le Franc* was supposedly cured of blindness and paralysis after offering prayers to Abbé Paris.

THIBAUT... DE SYLVA: the reported healing of Marguerite Thibault was attested by Montgeron and the *Recueil*, and investigated by the physician Jean-Baptiste Silva (1682–1742) on Hérault's instructions.

the resource of the JEWS: Jews had dismissed the miracles of Jesus and his apostles as witchcraft.

JERICHO... St. PAUL: the biblical book of Joshua (6: 1–20) reports that the walls of the besieged city of Jericho collapsed in response to the sounding of ram's horn trumpets, on divine instructions. The Israelites under Joshua then slaughtered virtually everyone in the city (and even the animals), in accordance with the extreme genocidal policy prescribed by God in Deuteronomy (7: 2, 20: 16–17). According to the Acts of the Apostles (16: 25–6), an earthquake shook the prison where St Paul and his companion Silas were held, opening all the doors and unfastening the chains.

Duc de CHATILLON: Paul Sigismond de Montmorency (1663–1731), mentioned in the published *Recueil*.

PORT-ROYAL: the Abbey of Port-Royal near Paris became during the 1630s a centre for Jansenism through the influence of Jean Duvergier de Hauranne, the main proponent of French Jansenism. Its teaching and textbooks became renowned, in particular *Logic or The Art of Thinking* (1662) by Antoine Arnauld (1612–94) and Pierre Nicole (1625–95), widely known as the *Port-Royal Logic*, which presented a Cartesian approach to Aristotelian logic. With the final suppression of Jansenism by the French King Louis XIV and the Pope, the community of Port-Royal was forcibly dispersed in 1709. Shortly afterwards, the buildings were destroyed and even the corpses in the cemetary dug up to be thrown into a nearby common grave.

PASCAL: Blaise Pascal (1623–62), a notable mathematician and theologian, was a frequent visitor to Port-Royal, where from 1651 his sister Jacqueline was a nun. He is now most famed for 'Pascal's Wager', his notorious suggestion that belief in God is justifiable on pragmatic grounds, even if the evidence is very poor, by weighing up the prospective posthumous benefits of belief (i.e. heaven), and costs of unbelief (i.e. hell).

RACINE: Jean Racine (1639–99), educated at Port-Royal, was one of the most celebrated seventeenth-century French dramatists (along with

Molière and Corneille). His *Abrégé de l'histoire de Port-Royal* reports this 'miracle of the holy thorn', by which Pascal's niece Marguerite Périer was cured of an ulcerated eye through the application of a thorn (supposedly from the crown of thorns worn by Jesus).

bishop of TOURNAY: Gilbert de Choiseul du Plessis-Praslin (1613–89), whose advocacy of the miracle of the holy thorn is reported by Racine.

queen-regent of FRANCE: Anne of Austria (1601–66), widow of King Louis XIII and regent during the infancy of her son Louis XIV, sent her personal physician, M. Félix, to investigate the alleged miracle. He returned convinced, but she refrained from any public statement so as to avoid theological controversy.

N   *Dr.* BERKLEY . . . BAYLE: for *Berkeley*, see Glossarial Index. *Pierre Bayle* (1647–1706) was a French Protestant author, best known for his *Dictionnaire historique et critique* (1697). Bayle's *Dictionary* is particularly notable for its collection of sceptical arguments, which Hume acknowledged using as a source for his *Treatise of Human Nature*. However Bayle, unlike Hume, was a fideist, undermining reason only to make room for faith. As such, he may be the model, or at least a partial model, for the character of Philo in Hume's *Dialogues concerning Natural Religion* (1779), who appears to advocate fideism towards the end of the work.

O   *mathematical points*: indivisible points without any extension.

  supposed infinitely divisible: in the first two editions of the *Enquiry* (1748 and 1750), the following three sentences were inserted here: 'In general, we may pronounce, that the Ideas of *greater*, *less*, or *equal*, which are the chief Objects of Geometry, are far from being so exact or determinate as to be the Foundation of such extraordinary Inferences. Ask a Mathematician what he means, when he pronounces two Quantities to be equal, and he must say, that the Idea of *Equality* is one of those, which cannot be defin'd, and that 'tis sufficient to place two equal Quantities before any one, in order to suggest it. Now this is an Appeal to the general Appearance of Objects to the Imagination or Senses, and consequently can never afford Conclusions so directly contrary to these Faculties.'

P   *particular . . . term*: a sketch of Hume's theory of abstraction from *Treatise* 1.1.7.

  ridicule . . . ignorant: Hume has a specific motive for wanting to 'avoid absurdities and contradictions', because these sorts of paradoxes were standardly used to promote religion by showing the weakness of mere human reason (thus supposedly making room for faith).

Q   *Ex nihilo, nihil fit*: most commonly rendered as 'nothing comes from nothing', hence anything that exists must have a cause of its existence. Hume famously discussed this causal maxim in *Treatise* 1.3.3, concluding that it could not be proved intuitively or demonstratively, though he evinced (both there and in other sources) a belief in the maxim as based on experience.

TEXTUAL VARIANTS

Section I (note to 1.14)

n. 1 *Mr. Hutcheson*: Francis Hutcheson (1694–1746), Professor of Moral Philosophy at Glasgow University, who influentially attributed moral judgements to a 'moral sense' analogous to our perception of secondary qualities such as colours and tastes. He was keen to insist, against Hobbes, that humans do not always act selfishly, but have natural feelings of benevolence. Hence beneficial actions bring pleasure and approval, which is the source of the moral sense. Hutcheson applied a similar theory to aesthetics, and it seems likely that his approach influenced the young Hume in at least these fields. Norman Kemp Smith—the most notable Hume scholar of the early twentieth century—speculated that the influence went even deeper, and that Hutcheson might have inspired the central thrust of Hume's philosophy, that even in epistemology we must rely on feeling rather than rational perception. Section I of Hutcheson's *Illustrations upon the Moral Sense* (1728) mentions 'the common Division of the Faculties of the Soul'. According to this taxonomy, Reason and Will are primary, with the Senses subordinate to Reason and the Passions to the Will. Reason's role is to present 'the natures and relations of things, antecedently to any Act of Will or Desire', which corresponds well to Hume's description of it in this note as 'That Faculty, by which we discern Truth and Falshood' (cf. *Treatise* 3.1.1.9).

n. 2 *See Butler's Sermons*: Joseph Butler (1692–1752), theologian and Anglican bishop, best known for *The Analogy of Religion* (1736), of which Hume thought highly despite his disagreements. Hume was anxious to win Butler's good opinion, and for this reason removed his most contentious religious claims from the *Treatise* (see pp. 161–2). The note to Butler alludes to the argument stressed in his Sermon XI on Romans 13: 9, 'Upon the Love of our Neighbour', though Hume's interpretation of 'interested' puts it somewhat paradoxically. The central point is that in acting selfishly one acts to satisfy some desire— perhaps for food, riches, personal success, companionship, another's well-being, or whatever—and that selfish action therefore presupposes some desire *other than* pure self-interest. Therefore it is impossible to reduce all desires to self-interest; indeed, self-interest depends upon having *other* more basic desires. These more basic desires can perfectly well be benevolent as well as self-directed; indeed both Butler and Hume are emphatic that humans are naturally inclined towards fellow feeling with others, and hence concern for their well-being.

Section III

3.7 *OVID*: a Roman poet whose most famous work is *Metamorphoses*, recounting legends about bodily transformations of various types.

3.10 *ARISTOTLE*: see Glossarial Index.

3.10 *ACHILLES*: Greek hero involved in the Trojan war, who pulled out of fighting for some time over a dispute with Agamemnon. See explanatory note to 1.8.

3.11 *the Iliad*: an ancient Greek epic poem attributed to Homer, describing the events of the Trojan war surrounding Achilles' withdrawal from battle and his subsequent return.

3.11 *the HENRIADE*: an epic poem about Henry of Navarre, written by Voltaire (François Marie Arouet, 1694–1778).

3.11 *HECTOR*: elder brother of Paris (see explanatory note to 1.8), killed by Achilles.

3.11 *HELEN . . . PARIS*: see explanatory note to 1.8.

3.11 *sympathy*: Hume uses the word 'sympathy' in its original sense, meaning not *compassion* but rather *fellow feeling* (so 'empathy' is a closer modern equivalent). He sees sympathy as a fundamental process of human nature that tends to make us share in the perceived concerns of those we observe or think about, and he builds his naturalistic, broadly utilitarian moral theory on this basis (see for example Sections V and IX of his *Enquiry concerning the Principles of Morals*).

3.12 *EVE . . . ADAM*: Adam and Eve were the first man and woman, created by God in the Garden of Eden, according to the biblical book of Genesis. They were cast out of Eden for the sin of eating fruit from a forbidden tree, Eve having been tempted by a serpent to do so.

3.12 *Odyssey and Aeneid*: the *Odyssey*, attributed to Homer, tells the story of Odysseus' return from the Trojan war (see explanatory note to 1.8); the *Aeneid* of Virgil tells how the Trojan prince Aeneas' travels after the war eventually led to the founding of Rome.

3.14 *PELOPONNESIAN war . . . ALCIBIADES*: the Peloponnesian war was fought between Athens and Sparta, 431–404 BC. Athens eventually surrendered after being besieged into starvation. Alcibiades (*c.*450–404 BC) was a prominent Athenian statesman, orator and general, murdered while the Spartans were in control of Athens.

3.17 *MILTON*: John Milton (1608–74), English poet and author of *Paradise Lost*, elaborating on the biblical story of creation.

GLOSSARY

[*MANY of Hume's words are now relatively unfamiliar, and some have changed in meaning. A fair number also vary in meaning between different occurrences in his text; in such cases, only those senses that are less familiar have been included here (e.g. under 'affect', the occurrences of 'affected' in the Advertisement and at 10.25 are listed, but not those at 5.2 and 5.18 which use the word in its modern everyday sense). For the sake of brevity, subtle nuances of meaning are ignored, and cognate words (e.g. 'actuate', 'actuated', 'actuates') treated as one; in the case of verbs, the gloss is then usually prefixed by 'to' (e.g. 'to motivate or cause activity of'). References to the text are by section and paragraph number, or, in the case of Hume's endnotes, endnote letter and paragraph number; passim (i.e. scattered) indicates a word used in too many places for individual listing to be appropriate.*

Readers who experience difficulty with Hume's language in the Enquiry *might find it helpful to consult the 'translation' into modern English by Jonathan Bennett, available from the website www.earlymoderntexts.com. Reading this in parallel with the original can ease both appreciation and understanding of Hume's elegant prose, and largely remove the need for repeated reference to a glossary or dictionary.*]

&c. etc. (*passim*)

à priori knowable without experience (see Introduction §10; 4.6, 4.7, 4.9, 4.10, 4.11, 4.13, 4.18, 10.8, 12.29, B.1, C.1, E.2, I.1, Q.1)

abate to diminish (12.24)

abound to be abundant or plentiful (10.20, 10.24, 11.17)

abstruse deep and hard to understand (1.3, 1.3, 1.6, 1.12, 1.12, 1.12, 1.17, 4.23, 7.2, 9.5)

abundance of many (5.1)

abundantly plentifully (5.16)

academic of academic scepticism; (see Glossarial Index; 5.1, 10.29, 12.0, 12.24)

accession addition (1.10)

acquiesce to raise no objection (11.10)

actuate to motivate or cause activity of (1.3, 1.15, 2.2, 5.22, 7.8, 7.11, 7.13, 8.4, 8.34, 12.21)

admonish to urge or warn (1.6, 11.18)

adulterate spurious or corrupt (1.12)

adventures, at at random (3.1, 10.17)

affect to give the appearance of (Advertisement, 1.14, 7.22, 10.25)

affections feelings or emotions (1.1, 1.3, 1.3, 2.2, 5.1, 6.3, 8.31, 8.34, 10.18)

afford to provide (1.12, 1.16, 2.5, 4.16, 4.17, 5.12, 6.2, 8.11, 8.23, 10.4, 11.2, 11.12, 11.13, 12.18, C.1)

agree to to conform to (7.28, 10.12)

alchimy alchemy (10.39)

allow to agree (*passim*)

alluring attractive or attracting (1.1, 11.29)

altercation dispute (10.32)

annex to to attach to (2.9, 5.10, 5.11, E.2)

antecedent prior (7.4, 11.20, 12.3)

appellation name (2.3, 10.12)

application diligence (1.5, 1.15)

apprehend to understand (1.8, 1.13, 7.1, 7.4, 7.30, 11.3)

apprehensive fearful (9.3, B.4)

apprized of knowledgeable of (7.24)

approbation approval (1.2, 1.15, 8.31, 8.35, 8.35)

artifice devious trick (Advertisement, 10.37, 11.24)

artificer craftsman (8.12, 8.17)

asseverations solemn declarations (10.7)

atchieve to achieve (1.12, 1.15)

atheism disbelief in God (see p. 203; 10.25, 12.1, L.12, N.1)

attend to accompany (*passim*)

attest to bear witness to (10.8, 10.15, 10.25, 10.27)

auditor listener (5.17 n. 9, 10.17)

aught anything (4.16, 11.17, 11.28, Q.1)

ax axe (8.19)

bane ruin (4.3)

bar barrier (7.2)

barely merely (1.13, 8.21)

batteries guns (Advertisement)

beget to produce or give rise to (4.9, 5.14, 6.1, 6.2, 6.3, 6.4, 10.4, 10.19, 12.2)

bent inclination (1.6)

bereave to rob (12.16)

beseech to ask earnestly (4.9, 7.25)

biass bias (1.6, 5.1)

big with full of; pregnant with (12.18)

bondage slavery (10.40)

bottom, at basically (8.27, B.3)

byasses biases (H.10)

calumny malicious slander (11.2)

canvass to discuss (8.1, 8.2, 10.17)

caprice whimsical fancy (1.4, 8.15)

careless carefree, unconcerned (1.12)

catholic universally applicable (1.12)

cavils quibbling arguments (12.10)

celestial heavenly (11.16)

chace to chase (9.2, 1.11)

check to restrain (12.24)

chimerical fanciful (see p. 194; 1.14)

chuse to choose (5.15, 8.19, 8.23)

chymistry chemistry (12.31)

circumscribed confined (7.12, 7.18)

cloaths clothes (5.18)

cognizance observation (4.16)

commodities useful things (8.17)

compass range (1.14, 1.15, 5.13, 7.2)

compleat complete (3.3, 3.3, 4.22, 8.17, F.1)

complexion temperament (F.1)

compounded complex (2.6, 3.1)

comprehend to understand (1.5, 1.14, 7.21, 7.25, 7.26, 11.6, D.1, H.2, H.4)

comprehend to include (3.1, 6.3, 8.17, 8.25, 8.34, 11.25, 11.26, 11.30)

comprehension understanding (1.5, 1.14, 1.16, 4.16, 4.22, 7.11, 7.14, 7.17, 8.14, 8.25, 10.34)

conceit imagination (7.2, 11.21)

concession thing admitted or allowed (7.22, 10.14, 11.11)

concourse coming together (11.10)

condition social status (10.19)

confound to defeat (10.40, 12.23, L.5)

confounded confused (2.9, 12.18)

confutation refutation (7.23)

consistence consistency, texture (4.16, 4.21)

controul to control (8.35, 12.25, 12.29)

correspondent corresponding (2.7, 2.8, 2.8, 5.22, 7.4)

cotemporary contemporary, of the same time (10.25, 10.26, A.1)

couched expressed (4.21)

counterpoise (-ize) to counterbalance (10.8, 12.24)

craft trickery (1.11)

criticism artistic (e.g. literary) criticism (1.2, 8.18, 12.33)

custom source of habitual inference (see pp. 191–2; *passim*)

deceitful misleading or deceptive (1.12, 12.3, 12.22)

deduct to subtract (10.4, 10.13)

deliberate carefully considered (1.13)

delicacy sensitivity and propriety (1.5)

delicate perceptive and precise (1.8, 11.30)

delineate to portray (draw or describe) (1.8, 1.13, 1.14)

deluge flood (10.40)

demonstrate (etc.) to infer deductively (see p. xxxvii; 4.1, 4.2, 4.18, 4.21, 6.0 n. 10, 12.18, 12.27, 12.28, F.1)

denominate to call or name (2.3, 7.21, 7.8, 9.5, 9.6, 12.15, I.1, K.1)

deportment demeanour and manners (11.20)

desart desert (4.4)

despoiled deprived (10.25)

destroy to neutralise or eliminate (1.12, 3.3 n. 6, 4.3, 5.2, 10.1, 10.6, 10.7, 10.8, 10.12, 10.13, 10.16, 10.24, 12.9, 12.17, 12.21, 12.22)

devotions prayers, worship (10.26)

diffident lacking confidence (7.28, 12.3, 12.18, 12.24)

diffuse to spread or propagate (1.5, 1.9)

dint means (7.7)

disabuse to undeceive or free from error (11.28)

disclaim to renounce or give up (12.14)

discover to reveal (4.6, 4.12, 5.8, 5.17, 5.22, 7.8, 7.21, 8.14, 8.15, 8.19, 8.21, 10.5, 11.27)

disinterestedness lack of bias (8.9)

disquisitions investigations (7.2, 7.3, 9.6, 11.9, 11.10, 12.30)

dissipate to disperse or cause to disappear (1.3)

divested stripped (8.8)

divines priests or theologians (12.2, L.12)

durst dared (L.8)

dye die (as in a game of dice) (6.2, 6.3)

eat ate (4.16)

edict authoritative order (L.9)

effaced erased or wiped away (11.24, 11.25)

effected brought about (5.21, 7.10, 7.15)

ellipsis ellipse, oval (7.1)

elude to escape from (4.12)

encrease to increase (4.13, 6.2, 10.11, 10.17, 12.18)

endued clothed or endowed (4.16)

engage to induce (4.19, 4.23, 5.2, 5.4, 8.17, 9.5, 10.10)

engage to attract and hold (1.1, 8.35, 10.22)

engage in to take part in (8.18)

engaging attractive (1.4, 1.8)

enjoin to command (10.25)

enow enough (8.36, 10.21)

entertain to consider or maintain (1.14, 2.9, 7.30, 8.12, 8.18, 8.21, 8.25, 9.1, 10.7, 12.1, 12.8, 12.21, 12.24)

entertain(ment) amuse(ment) (1.1, 1.5, 1.6, 5.9, 8.2)

enthusiasm ardent zeal (see p. 199; 10.17, 11.29, L.5)

enumerate to specify or itemize (3.2, 3.3, 4.17, 4.22, 7.4)

ere before (7.14, 7.24)

esteem to judge (1.10, 1.13, 1.14, 4.10, 4.12, 7.27, 8.28, 10.12, 10.33, B.4, K.1)

exalt to praise (1.8)

excite to stimulate or provoke (*passim*)

exigence urgent need (1.5)

expedient resource (4.14)

experiment observation from experience (*passim*)

experimental from experience (4.19, 4.20, 4.21, 8.17, 9.1, 9.6, 12.34)

explication explanation (4.12, 4.14, 4.16 n. 7, 4.19, 5.9, 5.12, 8.17, 8.25, 9.5, E.1)

exploded discredited (8.8, 10.23, 10.25, 10.31)

expressly directly, explicitly (10.24)

extension spatial extent (see p. xiv; *passim*)

extirpate to destroy, root out (5.1, 10.20)

fabric constitution (1.8, 4.4, 7.22)

fabulous legendary (10.40)

facility ease (4.2, 7.2)

faculties abilities (see p. 188; *passim*)

false counterfeit (1.12, 10.22, F.1)

fancied imagined (7.24)

fancy imagination (see p. 188; 4.8, 5.11, 5.16, 7.21, 10.18, O.1)

faster firmer (5.12)

feign to imagine, invent (5.10)

fiat decree (7.20)

fine subtle, refined (1.9, 1.13, 1.14, 7.1, 10.34)

fly to flee (1.11)

forbear to refrain from (3.3)

forborne refrained from (8.26)

foretel to foretell, prophesy (7.27, 7.28, 10.41)

fortuitous random (11.10)

foster to encourage (5.1)

frame construction (8.35, 10.20)

furnish to provide (5.10, 8.7, 11.27)

gaoler jailer (8.19)

generation procreation (7.21)

genius spirit or aptitude (1.5, 1.9, 10.25, 10.26, L.12)

governour governor (11.20)

graces divine favours (L.9)

graver more serious or solemn (12.2)

gross flagrant, glaring (10.22, 10.23, 10.25, 11.20)

gross solid or earthy (7.4, 7.11, 7.25, 10.18)

hands, on all by everyone (4.16, 8.2, 10.1)

harangue speech (11.7, 11.24)

haughtiness pride (12.24)

head topic (12.21)

heads headings (1.13)

hid hidden (8.13)

hither here (11.9)

humane tending to civilize (1.8)

husbandman farmer (8.9)

hypothenuse hypotenuse: longest side of a right-angled triangle (4.1, 12.27)

idea a thought (see p. xxxiii; *passim*)

illiberal narrow-minded (1.5)

illustrious renowned (1.1)

imagination, the faculty of imagination (see p. 188; *passim*)

imbibed absorbed (12.4)

impediment obstruction (8.13)

impel to force or push (5.5, D.1)

impertinent impudent, brazen (10.2)

imports is important (7.29)

impression a sensation or feeling (see p. xxxiii; *passim*)

imprudent ill-advised (5.1, B.1)

impulse impact (4.8, 4.10, 4.12, 5.5, 5.11, 6.4, 7.6, 7.21, 7.25, 7.28)

imputation allegation (10.25)

inculcated persistently urged (12.3)

incumbent a duty (2.6, 4.16, 8.21)

incur to bring on oneself (B.4)

indifference chance, absence of necessity (8.32, 8.36, F.1)

indifferent impartial, neutral (11.9)

indolence laziness (1.12, 5.1)

infinitum, in to infinity (5.7, 12.18)

inforces enforces (5.12)

infringement violation (11.28)

ingenuous frank (A.3)

insensible too small or gradual to be perceived (2.8, 5.14)

insinuated introduced subtly (D.1)

intangling entangling (1.11)

intercourse interactions (8.17, 12.9)

interest benefit, stake (1.9, 1.12, 8.35, 10.7, 11.3, 11.9, 11.27, 11.29)

interposition intervention (K.1)

interred buried (10.37)

inundation flood (11.24)

invent to make up or devise (4.9, 4.10, 4.11, 12.18)

invested authorized (L.6)

inveterate obstinate, bitter (2.7, 11.3)

inviolable unbreakable (4.13, 10.20)

irresolution hesitation (N.1)

isoceles isosceles (12.15)

issue conclusion (8.22, 10.32, 11.23)

jealousy resentment, suspicion (11.2, 11.4, 11.5)

judicature administration of justice (10.32)

juncture state of affairs (5.11)

justest most just or deserved (1.4, 1.11)

justness reasonableness (11.10, B.5)

landskip landscape (2.1)

latitude breadth, scope (11.11, 11.17)

laudable praiseworthy (8.33)

lend to grant (10.29, 10.38)

letters, men of learned authors (L.12)

letters, polite refined literature (1.5, 1.8)

liberal generous (10.14)

libertine freethinking (about religion) (5.1, 10.26)

licence excessive freedom (11.12, 11.26, 11.27)

lights perspectives (7.28, 7.29, 7.30, 8.16, 1.1, 1.2, 5.18, 7.2, 7.4, 10.24, 12.18, 12.18)

magnanimous noble (5.1)

magnifies praises (10.29)

mart marketplace (10.23)

mediate indirect (8.35, 8.36)

medium middle term or state (4.16, 4.21, 11.22, 12.27)

members parts of the body (7.13, 7.14, 7.21, 11.25)

mensuration measurement (E.1)

methodized reduced to order (12.25)

mitigated moderated (12.24, 12.25)

modern in contrast to ancient (see p. 225; 1.9, 4.3, 12.15, D.1, N.1)

moment force, momentum (4.13)

moral of human nature (see p. 185; *passim*)

moral reasoning factual reasoning (see p. xxxvii; 4.18, 7.2, 10.3, 12.21, 12.29, 12.30)

mortified deadened, subdued (5.1)

mount to ascend or climb (8.9, 8.22, 11.14, 11.16, 11.25)

mummeries ridiculous ceremonies (5.16)

muscovy principality of Moscow, or Russia (I.1)

narration narrative, story (8.8)

natural philosophy natural science (see pp. 226–8; *passim*)

nay and more than that, even (3.1, 4.23, 4.23, 10.22)

negligences slips, careless mistakes (Advertisement)

nice precise, requiring care (2.2, 11.30, H.8)

nisus effort, endeavour (C.1, E.2)

nowise in no way (4.16, 4.20)

nursery nest, place of rearing young (9.6)

obloquy abuse (5.1)

obviate get round, dispose of (8.32, 12.10)

oeconomy economy: organized system (1.15, 8.1, 8.14, 8.34, 9.6)

office role (7.13, 7.15, L.6)

office, good beneficial act (10.23)

omnipotent all-powerful (7.21)

open clear (1.3, 6.4)

opulent wealthy (8.20)

ought aught, anything (12.29)

outmost utmost, most extreme (12.27)

overmatch more than a match (4.13)

own to admit (7.17, 8.2, 8.21, 8.22, 10.36, 11.16, 11.17, 11.30, A.3)

palpable evident (10.25, 12.19, L.10)

palsy paralysis (7.13)

panegyric eulogy, a speech giving praise (11.27)

partakes has a portion of a quality (10.8)

partizans devotees of a party or cause (5.1)

parts capacities (1.13)

peculiar distinctive (1.1, 5.10, 5.12, 8.11)

peevish irritable (8.15)

penetration insight, discernment (1.11, 1.13, 4.17, 7.27, 8.21, 10.25, L.6)

perception impression or idea
(see p. xxxiii; *passim*)

perplexes bewilders, confuses (12.24)

pertinacious stubborn (11.3)

phaenomenon phenomenon,
something perceived (*passim*)

philosophic philosophical (5.1, 9.5)

philosophy pursuit of knowledge or
wisdom; relevant texts or principles
(*passim*)

physic medicine (12.31)

polemical aggressively disputatious
(Advertisement)

polite cultivated, refined (1.5, 1.8,
8.18, 11.6)

politician political theorist (1.15, 8.7)

pompous magnificent (5.7)

positive definite (1.13, 4.22, 8.34, I.1)

posterity future generations (1.2, 1.4)

pray please, I urge you to (11.8)

precarious insecure (4.4)

precedent previous (2.6, A.2)

precipitately rashly and hastily
(12.24)

prefatory preliminary, as a
preface (L.2)

prepossession prejudice (12.7)

prerogative right, privilege (12.3)

prescience foreknowledge (8.36)

prescribed laid down (8.4)

presently soon (11.9)

preservative defence (12.3)

pretence pretext, excuse (4.23, 5.1,
8.18, 8.26, 10.38, 11.24)

pretend to claim (or aspire) (*passim*)

pretended claimed (1.6, 4.12, 8.9,
8.21, 8.25, 8.27, 10.24, 10.37,
10.40, 12.10, 12.18, 12.27, C.1)

pretenders claimants (1.13)

pretension claim (1.15, 4.14, 5.1,
7.10, 10.17)

pretexts outward displays (8.9)

principle fundamental proposition or
causal agency (*passim*)

probable reasoning factual reasoning
(see pp. xxxvii, xli; 4.19, 6.0 n. 10)

prodigious enormous, magnificent
(12.18, L.12)

prodigy strange marvel (7.21, 8.8,
10.2, 10.14, 10.16, 10.20, 10.21,
10.24, 10.26, 10.39, 10.40, I.1)

profane non-religious, or
blasphemous (5.1, 10.2, 10.25)

promptitude speed (H.9)

proportionable proportionate (6.2)

prosecute to pursue (1.15, 2.6,
4.3, P.1)

prospect view of things (1.10)

prudent careful, judicious (7.2, B.5)

purposes intends (1.4)

quickening enlivening (5.16)

racking pain intense pain, as of
torture (8.34)

ratiocination sequential reasoning
(4.23, 12.17)

reap to obtain as a result of action
(1.10, 10.37)

reared built (L.12)

recal to recall or remember (5.19, 7.1)

receive to accept (1.11, 8.25, 10.17,
10.30, 10.36, 10.40, 12.18)

received generally accepted (6.4, 8.27,
10.20, B.3)

reckons relies (8.17)

rectilineal involving straight
lines (12.18)

rectitude moral propriety (8.34)

redound contribute (8.29)

refute to show to be false (2.6, 4.21,
8.26, 10.1, 10.22, 10.27, 11.24, 12.1,
12.5, 12.21, L.12)

relater narrator, reporter (10.26)

reliques relics, revered mementoes
(5.18)

relish taste (1.5, 1.6, 2.7, 4.20)

remit to slacken or interrupt (1.11)

renounce to give up (5.1, 10.17)

renown celebrity, fame (1.4)

repining fretting (5.5)

repose to place (e.g. trust in
something) (10.5, 12.7, B.4)

reproach disgrace or censure (1.2, 5.1)

requisite required, necessary (*passim*)

resource resort, expedient (7.4, L.8)

reveries abstracted musings (3.1, 5.11)

run over to review in quick succession (3.3, 12.34)

sacerdotal priestly (11.2)

sagacity wisdom (1.12, 7.27, 8.15, 9.2)

sage wise (or wise person) (5.1, 10.22)

sanction ratification (10.20)

sanguine confident (1.12)

savours tastes or smells (11.27)

scalenum scalene (triangle with unequal sides) (7.1, 12.15)

scarce scarcely, hardly (8.17)

sceptic one who doubts or questions (see pp. 220–1; *passim*)

scepticism doubt or questioning (see pp. 220–1; *passim*)

schoolmen, schools Aristotelian philosophers (see p. 220; 8.27, 12.21, 12.34, A.3, F.1)

science systematic body of knowledge (*passim*)

scope purpose (10.24, 12.17)

scruple to hesitate or doubt (4.16, 7.27, 8.19, 10.29, 12.23, 12.25, B.3)

scrutinous close and critical (11.10)

season proper time (10.33)

secret concealed (*passim*)

senates parliaments (B.4)

sensible apparent to the senses or feeling (*passim*)

sentiment inner feeling or emotion (*passim*)

sentiments judgements or opinions (*passim*)

sepulchre tomb (10.27)

shadow out to represent or symbolize (5.16)

shew to show (*passim*)

shock collision (7.28, 7.30, 8.4)

signal conspicuous (10.37)

similitude similarity (8.5)

singly alone (8.8)

soever to any possible extent (1.8)

solicitations persistent appeals (10.2)

solidity reliability, firmness (see also p. xvi; 1.14, 5.20, 10.25)

sooths supports (10.30)

sophism, sophistry deceitful argument (8.2, 11.20, 11.25, 12.27, 12.34)

soul mind (5.8, 7.9, 7.11, 7.17, 7.21, 8.22)

sovereign supremely effective (12.3)

specious superficially plausible (8.9, 8.34, 10.38)

springs underlying motives or causes (1.15, 4.12, 8.7, 8.13, F.1)

standish inkstand (8.20)

station social status (8.9)

statuary sculptor of statues (11.13)

stigmatize to defame (5.1)

stoutest most resolute (1.11)

subservient serviceable, of use (1.8, 1.9)

subsist to continue existing (12.21)

substract to subtract (10.35)

subtile subtle (1.4, 10.24)

subtility, subtilty subtlety (1.9, H.7)

subvert to overturn or undermine (1.12)

suffers undergoes (12.9)

sufficiency competence (4.14)

suitable appropriate (1.6, 8.34, 8.35, 8.36, 10.13, 11.3, 11.14, 11.16)

suitably comfortably (7.29)

supine lethargic (5.1)

surprize surprise (8.14, 8.17, 10.16, 10.26, 10.37)

susceptible capable of having (2.7, 8.31)

suspence suspense, uncertainty (12.18)

suspends delays (12.24)

syllogistical like syllogism, Aristotelian logic (12.27)

synonimous synonymous, meaning the same (7.17, 8.25, G.1)

tacitly without being stated (8.27, 11.27)

tangent straight line touching a curve (12.18)

taste faculty of aesthetic discernment (1.1, 1.5, 1.7, 1.8, 11.13, 12.33)

tautology saying the same thing twice (4.21)

temerity rashness (7.15, 7.27, 8.36)

temper temperament (5.1, 8.7, 8.30, 12.24, F.1)

thence from that source (5.7, 8.11, 8.11, 8.21, 8.36, 12.21, B.1)

thenceforth from that time forward (8.22)

timorous cautious (12.4)

tincture trace, infusion (4.7, 12.24)

toothake toothache (8.15)

tract track, route (3.1)

transgression violation, contravention (K.1)

transposing interchanging (2.5)

treasure up to store in memory (8.9, 9.2)

trite commonplace, overused (12.6)

topic theme of argument (1.12, 8.16, 8.26, 8.32, 8.34, 11.6, 11.10, 11.30, 12.6, 12.14, 12.15, 12.21, 12.22, 12.25)

try to test (8.22, 11.6, F.1)

turpitude depravity (8.32, 8.33, 8.36)

tye tie, bond (4.10, 7.26)

tyger tiger (4.7)

types symbols (5.16, 5.18)

uncontestable indisputable (L.12)

uncontrouled uncontrolled (5.1)

undeceive to free from deception or error (8.22, 10.33)

understanding, the faculty of reason (see p. 185; *passim*)

undertaking task undertaken or entered upon (1.8, 10.40, 11.20)

undeterminate indeterminate, imprecise (12.27)

undisputably indisputably (L.4)

undistinguishable impossible to distinguish (2.1)

undistinguished indiscriminate (12.24)

unexceptionable free from objection (12.18)

unpremeditately without thinking in advance (8.30)

upbraided reproached, criticized (5.16)

utility usefulness (7.29)

vain, in uselessly (1.8, 1.12, 4.2, 4.11, 4.12, 4.21, 7.26, 10.37, 11.23)

vehemence passion (1.3, 10.19)

velleïty slight inclination, insufficient for action (F.1)

verisimilitude appearance of truth (7.24)

villany villainy, wickedness (10.5)

violence force (8.31, 12.24)

violent forceful, passionate (10.7)

vivacity liveliness (see p. 188; 2.1, 2.3, 5.17, 5.20)

viz that is to say, namely (F.1)

votaries devoted followers (10.22)

vouched attested, confirmed (10.26)

vouchsafe to condescend (4.20)

vulgar common, unsophisticated (people) (7.21, 8.13, 9.5, 10.18, 10.21, 10.34, 11.3, B.4, C.1)

warrant evidence (10.24)

waxen made of wax (11.27)

whence from what source (5.9, 7.25, 8.4, 8.16, 8.32, 8.35, 10.36, 11.21, M.1)

wherein in what, or in which (5.10, 11.19, L.2)

whimsical capricious, fanciful (12.23, Q.1)

whit, not a not at all (7.26, 10.38)

wit, to that is to say, namely (2.7, 4.1, 7.30, 12.33)

withal moreover (10.25)

wonted usual (8.14)

writ written (L.1)

wrought worked, performed (10.24, 10.27, 10.27, L.8, L.12)

ye you (11.9)

GLOSSARIAL INDEX OF MAJOR PHILOSOPHERS AND PHILOSOPHICAL MOVEMENTS

[*HUME'S thought in the* Enquiry *draws on knowledge of a wide range of classical and modern thinkers, whose views are often closely interrelated and therefore most easily assimilated in combination. The summaries below are intended to facilitate this, while also providing an aide-memoire and an organized catalogue of Hume's references to other philosophers within the text of the* Enquiry.]

Aristotle and the Medieval 'Schools'

Aristotle (384–322 BC) is widely considered the greatest philosopher of antiquity, making seminal contributions in the philosophy of logic and language, metaphysics, aesthetics, ethics, and politics, as well as developing influential theories of physics, psychology, and biology. A pupil of Plato in the *Academy* (see below), he went on to be tutor to Alexander the Great of Macedonia, and in 355 BC founded his own school near Athens, at the *Lyceum*. For discussion of his theory of the world, and its long influence, see §1 of the Introduction, above. By medieval times the pagan schools of philosophy had been suppressed, and Aristotelianism, incorporated into a Christian framework, was so dominant that it was often referred to as simply the philosophy of 'the schools', with Aristotle himself known as 'the Philosopher'. Nevertheless the Philosopher's own works were not always taken as uniquely authoritative, and some of the most influential elements of the medieval synthesis were later developments of Aristotelianism, such as Ptolemy's system of the heavens and Galen's medicine.

Aristotle is mentioned twice in the main text of the *Enquiry*, an example of an 'abstract reasoner' whose 'fame is utterly decayed' (1.4) and whose theory of the elements is antiquated (8.7). Aristotle's theory of literary criticism also gets a mention in the long deleted passage from Section III (3.10 variant). The medieval 'schools' are mentioned twice in Section VIII (8.22 endnote [F], 8.27), and 'schoolmen' at 2.9 endnote [A]. Most famously, at the end of the *Enquiry*, Aristotelian 'school metaphysics' typifies the sort of philosophy that is to be committed to the flames (12.34).

Pyrrhonian and Academic Scepticism

Pyrrho of Elis (*c*.365–270 BC) was the best-known sceptic of antiquity, who supposedly had to be accompanied by friends for his own safety, since he saw no reason for believing that carts, precipices, or wild animals would do him harm. He wrote nothing himself, and the works of his followers— like those of most ancient philosophers other than Plato and Aristotle— were suppressed during the early Christian era. Their arguments were preserved chiefly through the compendious *Outlines of Pyrrhonism* by Sextus Empiricus (a Greek of the third century AD), which was rediscovered in the sixteenth century and had a major influence in casting doubt on the medieval consensus. Descartes's pivotal use of sceptical arguments to dismiss anything that cannot be perceived 'clearly and distinctly' to be true (including the established philosophy of the medieval schools) can probably be traced to the rediscovery of Sextus.

Plato (427–347 BC) was one of the pre-eminent philosophers of antiquity, particularly influential through his founding of the *Academy* at Athens, and also in later years because Neoplatonism proved amenable to incorporation within Christianity (most notably through Augustine of Hippo, AD 354–430). In the centuries after Plato, under Arcesilaus (*c*.315–242 BC), Carneades (*c*.213–129 BC), and others, his Academy became synonymous with sceptical thought, although 'Academic scepticism' was generally less radical than that of the Pyrrhonians, accepting that some things are more *probable* than others, even if all are uncertain. These ideas were preserved into the modern era principally through the writings of Marcus Tullius Cicero, a Roman who briefly studied at the Academy and was also influenced by Stoicism (see below).

It is debatable how far Hume's characterization of Pyrrhonian scepticism is faithful to its historical sources. He draws a contrast between 'excessive' Pyrrhonian scepticism (12.21, 12.23–5), which he understands as involving a denial of all belief, and 'mitigated' Academic scepticism (5.1, 12.0, 12.24), which is far less extreme. As he expounds it, Academic scepticism involves only a denial of dogmatic *certainty*, while allowing for rational discrimination between beliefs that are more, or less, *probable*. He also connects this with a second type of 'mitigated scepticism' (12.25–6), which advocates a limitation of our enquiries to 'such subjects as are best adapted to the narrow capacity of human understanding'. Hume most explicitly identifies himself as an Academic sceptic in Part iii of Section XII, though he also expresses sympathy with sceptical views at a number of other places (e.g. 4.0, 5.1, 7.28). However, he clearly dissociates himself from extreme scepticism, both of the Pyrrhonian (12.21, 12.23) and Cartesian (12.3) varieties, dismissing them as unsustainable and self-defeating.

Epicurus and Epicureanism

Epicurus (341–271 BC) was a materialist and atomist, accounting for our situation in the universe as due to the ever-changing configuration of atoms in the infinite void. Man lives and dies as part of this nature, with no supernatural obligations and nothing to hope for or fear after death. Morally, this recognition of our true situation can give us peace of mind, enabling us to live in moderation, valuing friendship and avoiding hurt to ourselves and others. Epicurus' writings were understandably considered dangerously atheistical, and accordingly most of them were destroyed during the early Christian era. Our best source for Epicureanism is the long poem *De Rerum Natura* (*On the Nature of Things*), written by the Roman Lucretius (*c*.94–55 BC), which fortunately survived in a single manuscript (and is briefly quoted by Hume at 10.30). In the early modern period Epicurus was considered the archetypal atheist, so when Hume's 'sceptical friend' in *Enquiry*, Section XI chooses Epicurus as his model (11.2, 11.4–7, 11.24, 11.27, 11.30), the implication is clear. The only mention of Epicureanism elsewhere in the *Enquiry* is very brief, in an apparently approving allusion to its moral principles (12.23).

Stoicism

Stoicism, a movement originating with Zeno of Citium (334–262 BC), was named after the 'painted Stoa' (covered walk) in Athens where he taught. Stoicism is mentioned several times in the *Enquiry* (5.1, 8.34, 12.23), as are three of the most notable Stoics of the Roman period, the freed slave Epictetus (*c*.55–135 AD, mentioned at 5.1), the orator Marcus Tullius Cicero (106–43 BC, at 1.4, 5.17 n. 9, 10.18) and the 'wisest of all the Roman emperors', Marcus Aurelius (AD 121–80, at 10.22, 11.2). Morally, Stoicism has some resemblance to Epicureanism (cf. 12.23), emphasizing moderation, control of the passions, and self-discipline. Unlike Epicureanism, however, it bases this on a rational ideal, seeing the world as providentially ordered by God's reason. Hume evinces a clear dislike both of such providentialism (cf. 8.34) and of the Stoic approach to morality (5.1), which he sees as being founded on refined rational selfishness rather than the generous human passion of sympathy or fellow feeling for others. However 'Christian Stoicism', which became prominent amongst the moderate clergy and others in eighteenth-century Scotland, differed from ancient Stoicism in precisely this respect. Thinkers such as Francis Hutcheson (1694–1746), Hugh Blair, and William Robertson, all well known to Hume, sought to reconcile Christian belief with a broadly secular ethical outlook. But Hutcheson especially followed Lord Shaftesbury (1671–1713) in basing his moral theory on 'sentiment' rather than pure reason, significantly influencing Hume and in turn Adam Smith (1723–90), an admirer and close friend of Hume now best known as an economist.

Descartes, Malebranche, and Occasionalism

René Descartes (1596–1650) is often called 'the father of modern philosophy', because he was so influential in the downfall of Aristotelianism. He used sceptical arguments to clear the ground (see above), but his own philosophy was rationalistic, aiming to build a solid edifice of knowledge on pure reason. His famous *cogito*, 'I think, therefore I am' is used to establish, by example, the unique reliability of rational 'clear and distinct' perception, and also that the mind's *essence* is thinking. He aims to evade scepticism by proving God's existence from his own (supposedly innate) idea of a perfect being together with causal principles which he claims to perceive clearly and distinctly (e.g. that any idea must have a cause that is at least as perfect and real). Having established the existence of a perfect—and therefore non-deceiving—creator, he then concludes that human faculties must be essentially trustworthy if used appropriately, and this vindicates the project of investigating the world scientifically, relying on our natural senses and innate judgement rather than tradition.

Descartes had strong interests in *natural* philosophy (i.e. science); for example he was the first to give a full explanation of the rainbow, and founded analytic geometry—the reduction of geometrical problems to algebra—through his invention of what are still called 'Cartesian coordinates'. He also formed the hypothesis of the circulation of the blood in opposition to Galen's traditional view (independently of William Harvey who published his more famous account in 1632), and concluded that the Earth orbits the Sun, echoing Copernicus (1543) and Galileo (1610). For an account of Descartes's very influential physical theory, based on the notion that the essence of matter is *extension*, see §2 of the Introduction, above.

Descartes is explicitly mentioned twice in the *Enquiry*, together with the Cartesian movement named after him (7.25 endnote [D], 12.3). The most prominent Cartesian of the later seventeenth century, Nicolas Malebranche (1638–1715), is also mentioned twice by name (1.4, 7.25 endnote [D]), and his 'occasionalist' theory is criticized at length at 7.21–5. For a brief account of this theory and his arguments for it, see §6 of the Introduction. Some of Hume's own arguments in Section VII of the *Enquiry*, for the conclusion that causal necessity is unperceivable, are reminiscent of Malebranche.

Thomas Hobbes

Thomas Hobbes (1588–1679), the first great philosopher to write in the English language, had a considerable—though unacknowledged—influence on Hume. Still today important as a political philosopher, he expressed the ambition to give a genuinely scientific account of man, based on theories of the material world, the passions, and natural law. There are hints of a similar structure in Hume's *Treatise*, and very clear Hobbesian echoes in Section VIII of the *Enquiry* (see §4 of the Introduction, above), where Hume presents a compatibilist position serving a fundamentally similar agenda: the legitimation of a deterministic science of man.

Though often thought of as empiricist in outlook (for example, he denies innate principles), Hobbes is in many respects rather close to Descartes, with considerable emphasis on the role of logical demonstration—as opposed to experiment—in science. He also follows Descartes in viewing the physical world as a plenum (see §2 of the Introduction). But he conspicuously differs in his *materialism*, denying the intelligibility of Descartes's immaterial mental substance, and viewing all minds—both human and divine—as material things. This provoked widespread accusations of 'atheist' and 'Epicurean', with 'Hobbist' becoming a comparable term of abuse in the seventeenth century. Hence Hume's reluctance to make reference to Hobbes's views, except when he has something critical to say (e.g. *Treatise* 1.3.3.4 n, *Moral Enquiry* 3.15 n), as when summing Hobbes up in the *History of England* (vi. 153):

Hobbes's politics are fitted only to promote tyranny, and his ethics to encourage licentiousness. Though an enemy to religion, he partakes nothing of the spirit of scepticism; but is as positive and dogmatical as if human reason, and his reason in particular, could attain a thorough conviction in these subjects. Clearness and propriety of style are the chief excellencies of Hobbes's writings.

Bacon and Gassendi: Precursors of Modern Empiricism

Francis Bacon (1561–1626) was a prominent lawyer and politician under Queen Elizabeth I and James I of England, rising to the position of Lord Chancellor. He also wrote on history, science, and scientific method, the latter works being strongly critical of Aristotelianism and its emphasis on logical deduction from first principles. Bacon instead advocated an inductive, empirical approach based largely on 'eliminative' methods (i.e. identifying the correct hypothesis by experimentally ruling out alternatives). He is mentioned approvingly by Hume in the introduction to the *Treatise*, described as 'the father of experimental physicks' in the second paragraph of the *Abstract*, and quoted in the *Enquiry* at 10.39. This last paragraph is of particular interest for its implication that the sceptical attitude which Hume shows towards miracles is not to be confined either to religious contexts or to allegedly unique events, but is also to be extended to 'every thing that is to be found in the writers of natural magic or alchimy', and hence presumably what we would now call 'New Age' or allegedly paranormal phenomena.

Pierre Gassendi (1592–1655) was a French philosopher and scientist, best known today for his authorship of a set of *Objections* to Descartes's *Meditations*, but in his time arguably the first modern empiricist. Influenced both by Epicurus and scepticism, he attacked Aristotle, denied innate ideas, emphasized sense experience as the source of all ideas and knowledge, and displayed a Lockean agnosticism about the essences of things. He also anticipated Hume's views about the reason of animals, though whether Hume ever read him is doubtful. His most significant legacy was in reviving Epicurean atomism, though with important modifications (e.g. unlike Epicurus he viewed space as isotropic, with no intrinsic 'up' or 'down'). Whether directly or indirectly, this was to influence Boyle, Locke, and Newton, and thus the development of modern science, as explained in §3 of the Introduction, above.

Locke and the 'Modern' or 'New' Philosophy

John Locke (1632–1704), widely considered the greatest ever English philosopher (Hume, of course, being Scottish), was also arguably the most important single influence on Hume. Though now most noted as an epistemologist, he also wrote major works on the theory of politics, property, education, and religion, becoming a standard-bearer for liberalism and tolerant moderation. In the early eighteenth century he was possibly the most famous intellectual in the western world, and his influence persisted throughout that century, as evident for example in the American Declaration of Independence of 1776 (which echoes his words and phrasing). Not surprisingly, Locke is mentioned several times in the pages of the *Enquiry* (1.4, 2.9 endnote [A], 6.0 n. 10, 7.8 n. 12, 7.25 endnote [D]).

For discussion of Locke's epistemological views, see §3 and §6 of the Introduction, above. His approach has some significant similarities with that of Descartes, notably in mounting a vigorous attack on Aristotelian positions, and in adopting a distinction between primary and secondary qualities together with a representative theory of perception. This combination of positions was common to most of the 'modern' philosophers of the period (contrasting with the 'ancient' Aristotelians). Hume's references to 'the modern philosophy' (e.g. *Treatise* 1.4.4), 'modern enquirers' (*E* 12.15), and 'the new philosophy' (*E* 7.25 endnote [D]) should be interpreted accordingly, though his emphasis on *solidity* as a primary quality clearly indicates that he has Locke's formulation specifically in mind. Locke's epistemology contrasts most sharply with that of Descartes in its relatively rigorous *empiricism*, basing our ideas and understanding of the world on experience and probability rather than the alleged innate certainties of pure reason.

Berkeley and 'Modern Metaphysicians'

George Berkeley (1685–1753), Anglican bishop of Cloyne in Ireland from 1734, is commonly thought of as the second of the three classical 'British Empiricists', lined up with Locke and Hume against the three 'Continental Rationalists' Descartes, Spinoza, and Leibniz. But this is a crude oversimplification, both brought about by (and in its turn promoting) the neglect of philosophers and trends that fit uneasily into that simplistic structure. It is true that Berkeley's arguments react mainly to

Locke, and also that Hume adopts some of these (most notably against the primary/secondary quality distinction at *E* 12.15 endnote [N]). However, in overall metaphysical orientation, Berkeley's *immaterialism* has far more in common with the *occasionalism* of the Cartesian Malebranche (see above, and §6 of the Introduction). Hume probably has both immaterialists and occasionalists in mind when he talks of 'modern metaphysicians' at 7.25 endnote [D], and perhaps in particular Andrew Baxter (1686–1750), a Scottish occasionalist who lived near Hume for some time, corresponded with Hume's kinsman Henry Home (see below), and expressed strong views about the inertness of matter and its theological implications.

The Scottish Common-Sense Philosophers

The philosophers in the 'common-sense' tradition produced their main works after—and in reaction to—Hume. However Kames, Reid, and Beattie all flourished in Hume's lifetime, and all are mentioned in the letter extracts included in this volume (see Appendix IV, above).

Henry Home (1696–1782) was related to Hume, came from nearby in the Scottish Borders, and played the role of a mentor when Hume went to study in Edinburgh. In 1752 he was appointed as a judge and took the title Lord Kames. Though best-known for his aesthetics (in which he takes a sentimentalist position), his *Essays on the Principles of Morality and Natural Religion* (1751) are of most relevance to the *Enquiry*. Here Kames argues for an anti-sceptical providential naturalism in which our natural intuitions and senses have been implanted by God as reliable guides, and are therefore to be taken as epistemologically authoritative.

Thomas Reid (1710–96), a friend of Kames who shared his providential naturalism and consequent respect for 'common-sense', was the most important critic of Hume during his lifetime. *An Inquiry into the Human Mind on the Principles of Common Sense*, published in 1764, systematically attacks the 'theory of ideas' so widely taken for granted by early modern philosophers, arguing that Hume's ridiculously extreme scepticism is its logical result and thereby demonstrates its falsity. Reid directs all his fire at Hume's *Treatise*, in which the theory of ideas plays a far larger role than in the *Enquiry* and the scepticism is far more corrosive. James Beattie (1705–1803) likewise mainly attacked the *Treatise* in his abusive *Essay on the Nature and Immutability of Truth* of 1770, and it is possible that this partly provoked Hume's public disavowal of the *Treatise* through his 'Advertisement' (see the letter to Strahan, 26 October 1775, in Appendix IV).

Natural Philosophers (i.e. Scientists)

Nicolaus Copernicus (1473–1543) was a Polish astronomer and mathematician who devised the first modern formulation of a *heliocentric* theory of the solar system (i.e. with the Sun at the centre, and Earth orbiting). His book *On the Revolutions of the Celestial Spheres* was published in the year of his death, with an introduction presenting the theory more as a means of calculating the apparent motions of the heavens (as an aid to devising an accurate calendar) than as a claim to astronomical truth. Copernicus was not the first to put forward a heliocentric theory: Aristarchus of Samos (*c*.310–230 BC) proposed one, though this work was lost, like most other pagan texts, during the early Christian era.

Galileo Galilei (1564–1642) was an Italian physicist and astronomer whose observations provided the first decisive evidence for the heliocentric theory, notably the phases of Venus which proved that Venus is sometimes on the opposite side of the Sun from the Earth. Galileo also did important work in dynamics, helping to establish the principle of *inertia*. See §§1–2 of the Introduction for more on all this, and §4 on his famous condemnation by the Roman Catholic Inquisition. Hume greatly admired Galileo, and mentions him in the extracts from the *Dialogues* in this volume (see Appendix III).

Tycho Brahe (1546–1601) was a Danish astronomer and nobleman who built an observatory on the island of Hven and made the most accurate astronomical measurements then available. In 1572 he observed a supernova in the constellation Cassiopeia, indicating that the heavens are not unchanging as Aristotle had taught. However, unconvinced that the Earth moves, he proposed an alternative theory of the solar system in which the Sun orbits the Earth, while the planets orbit the Sun.

Johannes Kepler (1571–1630) was a German astronomer and mathematician who became assistant to Brahe and inherited his observations. Using these, he established that the planets move not in circles (as both Copernicus and Galileo had assumed), but in *ellipses*, and he devised three mathematical laws of planetary motion—based on a heliocentric model— that provided the first genuinely accurate method of predicting astronomical phenomena.

Robert Boyle (1627–91) was an Irish natural philosopher, arguably the first modern chemist, and famous for *Boyle's Law* which relates the pressure to the volume of an enclosed quantity of gas at constant temperature. His impact on Locke is described in §3 of the Introduction, while Hume's *History of England* (vi. 541) provides a useful summary:

there flourished during this period a Boyle and a Newton; men who trod, with cautious, and therefore the more secure steps, the only road, which leads to true philosophy.

Boyle improved the pneumatic engine invented by Otto Guericke, and was thereby enabled to make several new and curious experiments on the air as well as on other bodies: His chemistry is much admired by those who are acquainted with that art: His hydrostatics contain a greater mixture of reasoning and invention with experiment than any other of his works; but his reasoning is still remote from that boldness and temerity, which had led astray so many philosophers. Boyle was a great partizan of the mechanical philosophy; a theory, which, by discovering some of the secrets of nature, and allowing us to imagine the rest, is so agreeable to the natural vanity and curiosity of men. He died in 1691, aged 65.

Isaac Newton (1643–1727), perhaps the most celebrated scientist in history, was an English mathematician and physicist. He invented the calculus (but delayed publication, provoking a bitter priority battle with the German philosopher Leibniz), and used it to give the first comprehensive account of terrestrial and astronomical motion, as explained in §3 of the Introduction, above. Hume's *History of England* (vi. 542) gives a glowing summary, highlighting the significant irony that Newton's physics, while establishing accurate laws describing phenomena, at the same time seemed to make nature less 'intelligible' because gravity could not be explained *mechanically*:

In Newton this island may boast of having produced the greatest and rarest genius that ever arose for the ornament and instruction of the species. Cautious in admitting no principles but such as were founded on experiment; but resolute to adopt every such principle, however new or unusual: From modesty, ignorant of his superiority above the rest of mankind; and thence, less careful to accommodate his reasonings to common apprehensions: More anxious to merit than acquire fame: He was from these causes long unknown to the world; but his reputation at last broke out with a lustre, which scarcely any writer, during his own lifetime, had ever before attained. While Newton seemed to draw off the veil from some of the mysteries of nature, he shewed at the same time the imperfections of the mechanical philosophy; and thereby restored her ultimate secrets to that obscurity, in which they ever did and ever will remain. He died in 1727, aged 85.

Newton is mentioned in the important endnote [D] to *E* 7.25, which aims to dissociate him from some of his 'Newtonian' followers who— as explained in §6 of the Introduction—tended towards *occasionalism* with a theological agenda.

HUME'S INDEX

Abstraction, what, *Note* [P] (131).

Alexander the Imposter of Lucian, his Artifice, 10.22 (86).

Animals, their Reason, 9.1 (76), &c.

Atheism, whether possible, 12.1 (109).

BACON, quoted, 10.39 (93).

BELIEF, what, 5.11 (35), &c.

Berkeley, Dr. a real Sceptic, *Note* [N] (130).

Cartes, Des, quoted, *Note* [D] (124).

CAUSE and EFFECT its Ideas, whence, 4.4 (19), 4.5 (19), &c. Its Definition, 7.29 (56), *Note* [G] (125).

Causation, a Reason of Association, 3.2 (23); 5.16 (37), &c.

Chance, what, 6.3 (41).

Christian Religion founded in Faith, not in Reason, 10.40 (94).

CICERO quoted, 5.17 n. 9 (38).

CONJUNCTION frequent, constant, the only circumstance from which we know Cause and Effect, 7.21 (51), 7.27 (54), 7.30 (56), &c.

CONNEXION necessary, our Idea of it, 7.1 (44), &c.

Contiguity, a Reason of Association, 3.2 (16), 5.14 (36).

---

[1] Another entry of this type, mischievously suggesting that most religious people are really sceptics, is the reference (not included here) from 'SCEPTICISM, Religious' to a passage in the *Natural History of Religion* where Hume alleges that 'the conviction of the religionists, in all ages, is more affected than real'.

CUSTOM or Habit the Source of
experimental Reasoning, 5.5 (32).
————— The great Guide of Life, 5.6 (32).

Elizabeth, Queen, whether her
Resurrection could be proved,
10.37 (92).
Energy, its Idea, 7.3 (45), 7.5 (46).
Epicurus, his Apology, 11.9 (98), &c.
Evidence, natural and moral, of the same
Kind, 8.17 (65).
EXPERIENCE, Source of all our
Reasoning with Regard to Fact,
4.7 (20), &c.
————— why we reason from Experience,
4.16 (24, 25), 8.13 (63).
————— Often the same with what we call
Reason, Note [B] (121).

Fact, Matters of, one Object of Reason,
4.2 (18), 4.4 (19).

Ice, Reports of it not credible to an
Indian, 10.10 (82).
Ideas, their Association, 3.1 (16),
3.2 (16), &c., 5.14 (36).
————— their Origin, 2.1 (12), &c.
Immortality of the Soul, on what
founded, 11.21 (103).
Impressions, what, 2.3 (12).
Indians justly incredulous with regard to
Ice, 10.10 (82).

Jansenists, their Genius, Note [L]
(128, 129).

LIBERTY and NECESSITY, a dispute of
words, 8.2 (58).
LOCKE, Mr. quoted, 6.0 n. 10 (41),
7.8 n. 12 (47), Note [A] (121),
Note [D] (124).
LUCIAN quoted, 10.22 (86), 11.2 (96).
LUCRETIUS quoted, 10.30 (91).

Malebranche, quoted, Note [D] (124).
Mathematics, their Foundation,
Note [P] (131). their Advantages,
7.1 (44).
Metaphysics, what, 1.7 (6), 1.8 (6).

MIRACLES, on what their Evidence is
founded, 10.1 (79), &c.
————— defined, 10.12 (83). one
mentioned by De Retz, 10.26 (89).
Molinists, their Genius, Note [L] (128).

NECESSITY, its definition,
8.5 (60), 8.27 (70).
Nisus, or strong Endeavour, not the
Origin of the Idea of Power, Note [C]
(123).

Paris, L'Abbé de, his Miracles,
Note [L] (128).
Pascal quoted, Note [L] (129).
Philosophy, the two Kinds of it, the
obvious and abstruse, 1.1 (3).
POWER, what its Idea, 7.5 (46),
Note [E] (124).
Probability, what, 6.2 (41), 10.4 (80).
Proof, what, 6.0 n. 10 (41), 10.4 (80).
Providence, particular, on what founded,
11.21 (103).

RACINE, quoted, Note [L] (129).
Relations of Ideas, one Object of Reason,
4.1 (18).
Resemblance, a Source of Association,
3.2 (16), 5.15 (37).
RETZ, Cardinal de, quoted, 10.26 (89).

SCEPTICISM, 4.1 (18), 5.1 (30), excessive,
12.2 (109), &c. moderate, 12.4 (109).
with regard to the Senses, 12.6 (110).
with regard to Reason, 12.17 (113).
Sciences, their Division, 12.27 (119).
Stoics, their idea of Providence, 8.33 (73).
SUETONIUS quoted, 10.25 n. 24 (88).

TACITUS quoted, 10.25 (88).
Tillotson, his Argument against the real
Presence, 10.1 (79).

Vespasian, his Miracle, 10.25 (88).
Vis inertiae, Note [D] (123).

Wonder, the Passion of, inclines us to
believe Miracles, 10.16 (84).

INDEX OF MAJOR THEMES, CONCEPTS, AND EXAMPLES

[*This index can be used to locate the sections and most important paragraphs where major topics (and some particularly notable examples) are discussed in the* Enquiry *itself, in the corresponding editorial notes (pp. 185–211), and in the relevant sections of the Introduction (pp. xxx–lvi). Other parts of the volume referring to specific paragraphs of the* Enquiry *can then easily be identified using the Index of References to Hume's Works. The Index of Names Mentioned in the* Enquiry *can be used in a similar manner, to track down discussions and examples associated with specific individuals. See also the Glossary.*

References are to section and paragraph numbers, except that 6.0, for example, indicates a reference to the title of Section VI.]

abstraction 12.20 endnote [P]
abstruse philosophy Section I
analogy, reasoning from 4.7, 4.12, 9.1, 10.10, 11.26, 11.30
animals, reason of Section IX
association of ideas Section III, 5.14–20

belief, irresistibility of 5.2, 5.8, 5.20–22, 12.7, 12.21–23; *see also* custom, analogous to association of ideas
belief, nature of 5.10–13
billiard balls 4.8–10, 5.11, 7.6, 7.21, 7.29, 7.30

cause, definitions of 7.29, 8.25; *see also* necessity, definitions of
Copy Principle 2.5–9, 7.4–5, 7.26, 7.30
custom Section V Part i, 5.21, 7.28–30, 9.4–6, 12.22
custom, analogous to association of ideas 5.20–21

demonstration 4.1, 4.18, 6.0 n. 10, 12.18, 12.27–28
Design Argument for God's existence Section XI
determinism 6.1, 8.4, 8.6, 8.16, 8.21, 8.25, 8.27, 8.32; *see also* necessity, definitions of

easy philosophy Section I
Evil, Problem of 8.32–3, 8.35–6
existence, proof of 12.28–29

free will *see* liberty

God, idea of 2.6, 7.25

Hume's Fork 4.1–2, 12.27–29, 12.34

ideas and impressions 2.1–3; *see also* association of ideas; God, idea of; impressions of reflection; innate ideas; necessary connexion, idea of; origin of ideas; power, idea of; relations of ideas
immortality Section XI
impressions of reflection 2.2–3, 7.6, 7.9–20
impressions of sensation 2.1, 2.3, 2.7, 7.5–8; *see also* scepticism, concerning the senses
induction Section IV; *see also* analogy, reasoning from; custom, analogous to association of ideas; scepticism, concerning induction
infinite divisibility 12.18–20
innate ideas 2.9 endnote [A]
intuition 4.1

liberty, doctrine of Section VIII
liberty, meaning of 8.23

matter of fact, reasoning concerning, *see* analogy, reasoning from; induction
matters of fact 4.2, 12.28–34
mental geography 1.13–14
metaphysics, *see* abstruse philosophy

miracles Section X
miracles, general maxim concerning 10.13
missing shade of blue 2.8
moral responsibility 8.28–31, 8.34–5

necessary connexion, idea of Section VII
necessity, definitions of 8.5, 8.27;
    see also cause, definitions of
necessity, doctrine of Section VIII;
    see also determinism

occasionalism 7.21–5
origin of ideas Section II; *see also* Copy
    Principle

philosophers 4.12, 7.21, 8.13–15, 9.5
    endnote [H], 10.4; *see also* vulgar, the
power, idea of 4.16 n. 7, 7.8 n. 12, 7.15
    endnote [C], 7.29 endnote [E];
    see also necessary connexion, idea of
probability Sections VI, X; *see also*
    analogy, reasoning from; induction
proofs 6.0, 10.4–12, 10.38
proportionality, when inferring causes
    11.12–14

relations of ideas 4.1, 4.18, 12.27

scepticism Sections IV, XII
scepticism, antecedent 12.3–4
scepticism, Cartesian 12.3
scepticism, concerning induction
    Section IV, 12.22
scepticism, concerning reason
    Section XII Part ii
scepticism, concerning the senses
    12.6–16
scepticism, consequent 12.5 ff.
scepticism, mitigated 12.4,
    Section XII Part iii
senses *see* scepticism concerning the
    senses
springs and principles (hidden) 1.15,
    4.12, 8.13, 8.22 endnote [F]
superstition 1.11–1.12, 1.17, 5.1,
    5.16–18, 11.3; *see also* miracles

testimony Section X

vulgar, the 7.21, 8.13, 9.5, 10.21,
    10.33–34; *see also* philosophers

INDEX OF NAMES MENTIONED IN
THE *ENQUIRY*

[References are to section and paragraph numbers, except that 3.0, for example, indicates a reference to the title of Section III.]

Academic sceptics 5.1, 12.0
Adam 4.6
Addison, Joseph 1.4
Alexander the Great 8.8, 10.25
Alexander of Paphlagonia 10.22, 10.23
Alexandria 10.25
Arabians 10.24
Aristotle 1.4, 8.7
Arnauld, Antoine endnote [L]12
Arragon 10.26
Athenians 10.18, 11.7, 11.9,
    11.16, 11.23
Athens 10.23, 11.2, 11.6

Bacon, Francis 10.39
Bayle, Pierre endnote [N]1
Bede, Saint 10.28
Berkeley, George endnote [N]1
Bruyère, Jean de la 1.4

Caesar, Julius 10.28, 12.28
Capuchins 10.18
Cartesians 12.3, endnote [D]1
Cato the Younger 5.17 n. 9, 10.9,
    10.9 n. 21
Charing Cross 8.2
Chatillon, Duc de endnote [L]10
China 10.24
Christians 10.1, 10.40, 10.41
Cicero (Tully) 1.4, 5.17 n. 9, 10.18
Clarke, Samuel endnote [D]1
Copernicans 12.23
Cudworth, Ralph endnote [D]1

Demetrius 10.25
Demosthenes 10.18
Descartes, René 12.3, endnote [D]1
Dio Cassius Cocceianus 11.2 n. 30

Elizabeth I, Queen 10.37
England, English 8.7, 10.37, endnote [D]1
Epictetus 5.1

Epicurus, Epicureans 11.2, 11.4, 11.5,
    11.6, 11.7, 11.24, 11.27, 11.30, 12.23
Euclid 4.1, 7.2
Europe 6.4, endnote [L]12

Flavian family 10.25
France 4.4, 10.27, endnote [L]6, [L]10,
    [L]11, [L]12
French 8.7, endnote [L]2

Gabriel, angel 12.28
God (or Creator, Deity) 2.6, 7.21, 7.22,
    8.32, 8.33, 8.34, 8.36, 10.40, 11.26,
    11.28, 11.30, 12.1, 12.32, endnotes
    [D]1, [K]1, [L]2, [L]9
Greeks 8.7, 10.22, 10.24

Helen 1.8
Hérault, René endnote [L]6
Herodotus 10.28
Hippocrates 8.7

Indians 10.10, endnote [I]1

Jansenists 10.27, endnote [L]2, [L]4,
    [L]5, [L]9
Jericho endnote [L]9
Jesuits 10.27, endnote [L]12
Jesus ('our Saviour') 10.1,
    endnote [L]2
Jews endnote [L]8
Jupiter 11.14, 11.17

Laelius 5.17 n. 9
Laplanders 2.7
Le Franc, Anne endnote [L]5
Livy (Titus Livius) 10.24, 10.39
Locke, John 1.4, 6.0 n. 10, 7.8 n. 12,
    endnotes [A]1, [A]3, [D]1
Lucian 10.22, 10.23, 11.2 n. 28,
    11.2 n. 29
Lucretius Carus, Titus 10.30 n. 26

Mahomet 10.24
Malebranche, Nicolas 1.4, endnote [D]1
Marcus Aurelius Antoninus 10.22
Mariana, Juan de 10.28
Molinists endnote [L]5, [L]8
Montgeron, Louis Basile Carré de
  endnote [L]1
Muscovy endnote [I]1

Nero endnote [B]4
Newton, Isaac endnote [D]1
Nicole, Pierre endnote [L]12
Noailles, Cardinal endnote [L]3

Paphlagonia 10.22, 10.23
Paris, Abbé 10.27, endnote [L]1, [L]2,
  [L]3, [L]4, [L]5, [L]11
Pascal, Blaise endnote [L]12
Paul, Saint endnote [L]9
Pentateuch 10.4
Pharsalia, Battle of 10.28
Philippi, Battle of 10.28
Plato 5.17 n. 9
Plutarch 10.24, 10.28, 10.9 n. 21
Polemo 5.17 n. 9
Polybius 8.7
Pompey 10.28
Port Royal, Abbey of endnote [L]12
Protagoras 11.2
Ptolemaics 12.23
Pyrrhonism 12.21, 12.23, 12.24, 12.25

Quintus Curtius Rufus 8.8

Racine, Jean endnote [L]12
Retz, Cardinal de 10.26
Roman Catholics 5.16, 10.24
Romans 8.7, 10.18, 10.23, 11.2
Rome 10.9, 10.22, 10.24

Saragossa 10.26
Scipio 5.17 n. 9
Serapis 10.25
Siam 10.24
Socrates 11.2
Spain 10.26
Speusippus 5.17 n. 9
Stoics 5.1, 8.34, 12.23
Suetonius 10.25 n. 24
Sumatra endnote [I]1
Sylva, Jean-Baptiste (de) endnote [L]7

Tacitus, Cornelius 8.7, 10.24, 10.25
Thibaut, Marguerite endnote [L]7
Tiberius endnote [B]4
Tillotson, John 10.1
Tournay, Bishop of endnote [L]12
Tully, *see* Cicero
Turkey 10.24

Venus 1.8
Vespasian 10.25, 10.25 n. 24

Xenocrates 5.17 n. 9

Zeuxis 11.13

INDEX OF REFERENCES TO
HUME'S WORKS

[Listed below are most of the references to Hume's works that occur in the volume, except for those listed in the Glossary. In the case of the first Enquiry, *only editorial references to specific paragraphs are included here. For other works, all references are included.]*

A Treatise of Human Nature

General references: i, x-xi, xxiii, lxiii,
   133, 161–4, 167, 170, 171, 185, 186,
   187, 192, 201, 206, 209, 210, 223,
   224, 226
Specific references:
Book I Part i (*Of ideas; their origin,
   composition, abstraction, connexion, &c.*):
   1.1.1.2 xxxiii
   1.1.1.4 187
   1.1.1.7 xxxiv
   1.1.4.6 187
   1.1.6.1 xxxv
   1.1.7 liv, 209
Book I Part ii (*Of the ideas of space and
   time*):
   1.2.6.2–5 xxxv
Book I Part iii (*Of knowledge and
   probability*):
   1.3.3 163, 196, 209
   1.3.3.4 224
   1.3.4.2 205
   1.3.6.3 xliv
   1.3.7.5 192
   1.3.9.19 188
   1.3.11–12 193

1.3.11.9–12 199
1.3.12.5 195
1.3.13.4 205
1.3.14.31 xlv
1.3.14.4 194
1.3.15 206, 207
Book I Part iv (*Of the sceptical and other
   systems of philosophy*):
   1.4.2 202
   1.4.4 204, 225
   1.4.4.1 188
   1.4.4.12–14 xxxv
   1.4.5.3–4 xxxv
   1.4.5.32 xlvi, 194
   1.4.7.7 188
   1.4.7.8 186
Book II Part iii (*Of the will and direct
   passions*):
   2.3.1–2 197
   2.3.1.15 205
   2.3.2.1 196
Book III Part i (*Of virtue and vice in
   general*):
   3.1.1.9 210

An Enquiry concerning Human Understanding

[Here references are to section and paragraph numbers, except that 3.0, for example, indicates a reference to the title of Section III.]

Section I (*Of the Different Species of
   Philosophy*):
   1.2 185, 188
   1.3 185, 209
   1.3–6 xxxi
   1.4 185, 220, 222, 223, 225
   1.6 186
   1.7 xxxi

1.8 186, 211
1.11 186
1.11–12 xxxi
1.12 186
1.13 186, 190
1.13–14 xxxii
1.14 xl, 177, 185, 187, 210
1.15 xxxii, xl, 187, 190

Section II (*Of the Origin of Ideas*):
2.1 xxxiii, 185, 187, 188
2.3 188, 192
2.4 189
2.5 xxxiii, xxxiv, 187, 188, 194
2.6 xxxiv
2.7 xxxiv, 188
2.8 xxxiii, xxxiv, 188
2.9 xxxv, 188, 194
2.9[A] xxxii, 187, 188, 206, 220, 225

Section III (*Of the Association of Ideas*):
3.0 192
3.2–3 193
3.3 lviii, 182, 189
3.7 211
3.10 190, 211, 220
3.11 211
3.12 211
3.14 211
3.15 224
3.17 211

Section IV (*Sceptical Doubts concerning the Operations of the Understanding*):
4.0 221
4.1 xxxvi, 189, 194, 205
4.2 xxxvi, 189, 190
4.3 xxxvii
4.4 lvi
4.6 189
4.6–11 xxxviii
4.6–13 lvi
4.7 189
4.8 190
4.9 190
4.10 190
4.11 205
4.12 xxx, xl, xli, xlvii, 190
4.12–13 lv
4.13 190, 207
4.14 190
4.15 190
4.16 xxxviii, xxxix, 190, 191
4.18 xxxvii, 189, 191, 198
4.19 xxxviii, xxxix, 191
4.20 191
4.21 xxxviii, xxxix, 191
4.23 xxxix

Section V (*Sceptical Solution of these Doubts*):
5.1 191, 221, 222
5.2 xxxix, 191

5.3 191
5.5 191
5.5[B] 206
5.6 xl, 192
5.8 xl, 192
5.9 x, xl, 192
5.12 188, 192
5.16 192
5.17 lx, 192, 222
5.20 xxxv, xl, 190, 193
5.21 193, 206

Section VI (*Of Probability*):
6.0 xli, 193, 198, 225
6.1 193, 196
6.2–4 lv
6.3 190, 193
6.4 193

Section VII (*Of the Idea of Necessary Connexion*):
7.0 194
7.2 194
7.3 xlii, 188
7.4 xxxv, xlii, xlv, 194
7.5 194
7.6 194
7.6–8 lvi
7.7 xlii
7.8 lx, 194, 225
7.9 xliii
7.9–20 lvi
7.10–15 xliii
7.13 194
7.14 194
7.16–20 xliii
7.21 xliii, 194
7.21–5 xxvi, 223
7.24–5 xliii
7.25[D] xx, lv, 190, 206, 207, 223, 225, 226, 228
7.28 xliv, liii, 194, 221
7.29 xlvi, 194, 197
7.29[E] xiv, lv, 207

Section VIII (*Of Liberty and Necessity*):
8.2 195
8.3 195
8.4 195
8.5 xlvii, liii, 195
8.7 195, 200, 220
8.8 195, 200
8.9 195
8.13 xlvii, 195

8.13–15 lv
8.15 196
8.16 196
8.18 196
8.19 196
8.20 196
8.21 xlvii, 196
8.22[F] xlv, 220
8.23 xlvi, 196
8.25 xliv, 196
8.26 196
8.27 xlvii, 197, 220
8.28 197
8.28–30 xlvii
8.32 197
8.34 197, 222
8.34–5 xlviii
8.35 xlviii, 197
8.36 197

Section IX (*Of the Reason of Animals*):
9.1 lv
9.2 197
9.5[H] 206, 207
9.6 198

Section X (*Of Miracles*):
10.1 198
10.3 198
10.3–4 xlix
10.3–7 lv
10.4 xlix, 198
10.6 198
10.7 xlix
10.9 198
10.10 198
10.12 198
10.12[K] 198
10.13 l, 199
10.15 l
10.16–19 li
10.17 199
10.18 199, 222
10.20–3 li
10.21 199
10.22 199, 202, 222
10.23 199
10.24 199, 200, 201
10.25 200
10.25–7 li
10.26 200
10.27 200, 207
10.27[L] 207–9

10.28 201, 205
10.30 201, 222
10.35 li, 201
10.37 li, 201
10.38 li
10.39 201, 224
10.40 201
10.41 202

Section XI (*Of a Particular Providence and of a Future State*):
11.1 202
11.2 202, 222
11.4 202
11.4–7 222
11.7 202
11.11 202
11.12–16 lv
11.13 202
11.14 202
11.16 lii
11.17 202
11.21 202
11.23 202
11.24 222
11.24–6 lv
11.25–7 liii
11.26–30 liii
11.27 202, 222
11.29 202
11.30 222

Section XII (*Of the Academical or Sceptical Philosophy*):
12.0 221
12.3 202, 221, 223
12.3–4 liii
12.4 202
12.6 202
12.8 liii
12.9 liii
12.10 202
12.13 lvi, 204
12.15 xxxv, liii, 204, 225
12.15[N] 209
12.16 liv, 204
12.18[O] 209
12.20[P] xxviii, xxxv, liv, 209
12.21 liv, 204, 221
12.22 liv, 204
12.23 204, 221, 222
12.23–5 221
12.24 lv, 204, 221

12.25 xliii, lv, 152, 204
12.25–6 221
12.27 lvi, 205
12.28 201, 205
12.28–9 lvi

12.29 lvi, 205
12.29[Q] lix, 209–10
12.32 146, 205
12.33 205
12.34 lvi, 205, 220

Other Works

Abstract of the Treatise x, lxiii, 133–45, 197, 224

Dialogues concerning Natural Religion xxiv, lii, lv–lvi, lix, lxii, lxv, 152–60, 202, 204, 206, 209, 227
Dissertation on the Passions lvii, lxiv, 161, 185

Enquiry concerning the Principles of Morals xlviii, lx, lxiv, 161, 171, 172, 185, 211
Essays, Moral, Political and Literary i, lxii, lxiii, 163, 170, 171; 'Of Eloquence' 199; 'Of Suicide' 146; 'Of Superstition and Enthusiasm' xxiii; 'Of the Immortality of the Soul' xiv, xlix, lii, 146–51, 202; 'Of the Standard of Taste' 146; 'That Politics may be Reduced to a Science' 196

Essays and Treatises on Several Subjects lvii, 167–8, 185

Four Dissertations 146

History of England, The lix–lx, lxiv, 172, 173, 201, 224, 227, 228

Letter from a Gentleman to His Friend in Edinburgh xxxviii, xxxix, lxiv

'My Own Life' lix, 161, 169–75

Natural History of Religion lvii, lxii, lxiv, 172, 202

Philosophical Essays concerning Human Understanding (original title of the first *Enquiry*) lvii, lxiv, 163
Political Discourses (second set of *Essays*) 164, 171